Constructive Methods in
Computing Science

NATO ASI Series

Advanced Science Institutes Series

A series presenting the results of activities sponsored by the NATO Science Committee, which aims at the dissemination of advanced scientific and technological knowledge, with a view to strengthening links between scientific communities.

The Series is published by an international board of publishers in conjunction with the NATO Scientific Affairs Division

A	Life Sciences	Plenum Publishing Corporation
B	Physics	London and New York
C	Mathematical and Physical Sciences	Kluwer Academic Publishers Dordrecht, Boston and London
D	Behavioural and Social Sciences	
E	Applied Sciences	
F	Computer and Systems Sciences	Springer-Verlag Berlin Heidelberg New York
G	Ecological Sciences	London Paris Tokyo Hong Kong
H	Cell Biology	

Series F: Computer and Systems Sciences Vol. 55

Constructive Methods in Computing Science

International Summer School directed by
F.L. Bauer, M. Broy, E.W. Dijkstra, C.A.R. Hoare

Edited by
Manfred Broy
Universität Passau
Fakultät für Mathematik und Informatik
Postfach 2540, D-8390 Passau, FRG

Springer-Verlag Berlin Heidelberg New York
London Paris Tokyo Hong Kong
Published in cooperation with NATO Scientific Affairs Division

Proceedings of the NATO Advanced Study Institute on Constructive Methods
in Computing Science held at Marktoberdorf, Federal Republic of Germany,
July 24 – August 5, 1988.

ISBN 3-540-51369-8 Springer-Verlag Berlin Heidelberg New York
ISBN 0-387-51369-8 Springer-Verlag New York Berlin Heidelberg

Library of Congress Cataloging-in-Publication Data. NATO Advanced Study Institute on Constructive Methods
in Computing Science (1988 : Marktoberdorf, Germany). Constructive methods in computing science : international summer school directed by F.L. Bauer ... [et al.] / edited by Manfred Broy. p. cm.—(NATO ASI series.
Series F. Computer and systems sciences : vol. 55) "Proceedings of the NATO Advanced Study Institute on
Constructive Methods in Computing Science held at Marktoberdorf, Federal Republic of Germany,
July 24 – August 5, 1988"—CIP verso t.p.
ISBN 0-387-51369-8 (U.S.)
1. Electronic data processing—Congresses. I. Broy, M., 1949– . II. Title. III. Series: NATO ASI series. Series F,
Computer and systems sciences : vol. 55. QA75.5.N383 1988 004—dc20 89-19650.

This work is subject to copyright. All rights are reserved, whether the whole or part of the material is
concerned, specifically the rights of translation, reprinting, re-use of illustrations, recitation, broadcasting,
reproduction on microfilms or in other ways, and storage in data banks. Duplication of this publication or
parts thereof is only permitted under the provisions of the German Copyright Law of September 9, 1965, in
its version of June 24, 1985, and a copyright fee must always be paid. Violations fall under the prosecution
act of the German Copyright Law.

© Springer-Verlag Berlin Heidelberg 1989
Printed in Germany

Printing: Druckhaus Beltz, Hemsbach; Binding: J. Schäffer GmbH & Co. KG, Grünstadt
2145/3140-543210 – Printed on acid-free-paper

Preface

Computing Science is a science of constructive methods. The solution of a problem has to be described formally by constructive techniques, if it is to be evaluated on a computer. Thus constructive methods are of major interest for a computing scientist. The Marktoberdorf Advanced Study Institute 1988 presented a comprehensive survey of the recent research in constructive methods in Computing Science.
Some approaches to a methodological framework and to supporting tools for specification, development and verification of software systems were discussed in detail. Also the relevance of the foundations of logic for questions of program construction was subject of the lectures. Further topics were new programming paradigms and formalisms which have proven to be useful for a constructive approach to software development. In this context especially the following main issues were stressed:

- Specification formalisms for requirements engineering, formal modelling, and the validation of requirement specifications;
- calculi for the constructive design of software that is correct by construction;
- verification calculi for software systems and their integration in the program construction process;
- programming support systems and programming environments;
- special purpose constructive methods for the design of concurrent systems.

The construction, specification, design, and verification especially of distributed and communicating systems was discussed in a number of complementary lectures.
Examples for those approaches were given on several levels such as semaphores, nondeterministic state transition systems with fairness assumptions, decomposition of specifications for concurrent systems in liveness and safety properties and functional specifications of distributed systems.
Construction methods in programming that were presented range from type theory, the theory of evidence, theorem provers for proving properties of functional programs to category theory as an abstract and general concept for the description of programming paradigms.

The summer school provided an excellent overview over the field, included lively discussions and finally showed a number of stimulating questions to the participants and lecturers.

Also this time, like several times before, the Marktoberdorf Summer School turned out to be a highlight in scientific discussions, for the exchange of ideas and for establishing professional as well as personal relationships.

The outstanding scientific quality was completed by the excellent organisation and the perfect environment that was provided by the members of organisational staff. It is a pleasure for me to thank all the people who helped to make the Summer School a success again. In particular my thanks go to Rainer Weber who did a nice job in helping me to edit this volume and to Bernhard Möller who provided the theory of rabbits as a

> **T**heoretical
> **I**nvestigation of the
> **B**ringing in and
> **B**ringing out of
> **A**rguments in
> **R**easoning

together with the illustrations as printed in this volume.

Passau, May 1989   Manfred Broy

Table of Contents

J. Misra
      A Visionary Decision (After-dinner Speech) 1

Part I Constructive Logic and Type Theory

R.C. Backhouse
      Constructive Type Theory - An Introduction 9

R.L. Constable
      Assigning Meaning to Proofs: A Semantic Basis for Problem
      Solving Environments 63

R.S. Boyer, J.S. Moore
      The Addition of Bounded Quantification and Partial Functions to a
      Computational Logic and Its Theorem Prover 95

Part II Design Calculi

R.S. Bird
      Lectures on Constructive Functional Programming 151

E.W. Dijkstra
      On a Problem Transmitted by Doug McIlroy 219

E.W. Dijkstra
      A Computing Scientist's Approach to a Once-deep Theorem
      of Sylvester's 223

E.W. Dijkstra
      The Derivation of a Proof by J.C.S.P. van der Woude 233

C.A.R. Hoare
      Notes on an Approach to Category Theory for Computer Scientists .. 245

Part III Specification, Construction, and Verification Calculi for Distributed Systems

M. Broy
    Towards a Design Methodology for Distributed Systems 311

B.W. Lampson
    Specifying Distributed Systems 367

J. Misra
    A Foundation of Parallel Programming 397

A.J. Martin, J.L.A. van de Snepscheut
    Design of Synchronization Algorithms..................................... 447

A VISIONARY DECISION*

Jayadev Misra
Department of Computer Sciences,
University of Texas at Austin,
Austin, Texas 78712
U.S.A.

Ladies and Gentlemen:

I am pleased to be here and honored to be addressing you. I thank the organizers for giving me this opportunity to talk to you. I will go home with many pleasant memories: the excellent organization; the mountain trip and the Bavarian songs; this great farewell dinner; the hospitality of Profs. Bauer and Broy; lecturers, students, and Willem Paul de Roever; the city of Marktoberdorf, and its pubs, in particular. But I also leave with some sadness; we the lecturers have neglected a vital part of your education here: sales.

The act of selling involves two parties: a seller and a buyer. In this summer school you have seen ten smooth-talking salesmen peddling their theories and formal systems. My speech today is to the participants on how to resist these sales efforts; how to become what Americans call "informed buyers"; how to fight a new idea every inch of the way. In America, for over a century, we have successfully resisted the sales efforts of this English chap: Charles Darwin.

But first a major theoretical result. It had long been conjectured that there is a limit point at which any new idea is immediately rejected. This result has now been proven constructively; the limit point is known as the de Roever point.

I have done some historical research on successful resistance of sales efforts. I have been assisted in this work by an able research assistant. If you have been missing him in the lectures, or wondering about that suspicious trip to the Deutsche Museum on Sunday, now you know the answer. A hand for Prof. Bauer, who has unearthed a rare document.

This is a transcript of a conversation that took place in ancient Rome; the date is around 100 A.D. In this corner, we have a smooth talking Hindu salesman pushing the Hindu-Arabic numeral system. His motive is clear; he wants to get a foot-hold in Rome and then take over

---

*This is a slightly revised version of an after-dinner speech given on August 3, 1988, at the International Summer School in Marktoberdorf, Germany. I am grateful to Richard Bird for pointing out that one of the weaknesses of the Hindu-Arabic numerals is the presence of a symbol for zero.

the rest of the continent by dumping low-cost mathematics which are produced using cheap foreign labor. Fortunately for the western civilization, in the other corner we have the informed Roman buyer who knows that Roman numerals are superior. I will now read out the document (I will use the abbreviation Hindu System for Hindu-Arabic System).

Hindu: Sir, I have brought some samples of our amazing new product, Hindu number system. You can do the four arithmetic operations in sublinear space and time. You just let the symbols do the work.

Roman: We have slaves to do our work. (pause) I have assembled a distinguished group of experts in the science of computation who are well aware of the superiority of the Roman System. Let us hear from them.

Dijkstra: I have been most impressed by the elegance and simplicity of calculations in the Roman System: Simple concatenation for addition and pairing for subtraction. They have avoided needless complexities such as multiplication and division. The Hindu System forces me to carry around many large tables in one small head.

Hoare: One can clearly see the large number of algebraic identities in the Roman System. Associativity of concatenation immediately tells us that addition is associative. Hindu System offers a poor basis for such deductions.

Backhouse: I was using the Hindu System. Since the position of each symbol in a number determines its value, I had to carry around too much context. That is why I switched to Roman numerals, and I have never been happier.

Bird: The Roman System allows you to abstract away from the actual numbers and study the operations, concatenation, for instance. The Hindu System is operational; it gives you an imperative procedure for addition and hence forces you down to the level of numbers.

Broy: The Hindu System forces you to add in a deterministic fashion. The Roman System is clearly superior because it avoids overspecification.

Constable: The Roman System is object-oriented. A model for a Roman number is immediate—a flock of sheep, for instance. The meaning function maps each vertical bar in the number to a sheep, and consistency of the whole system is immediately obvious.

Lampson: The Roman System maintains the relationship with reality all through a computation. When you have counted three bars you have counted three sheep, for instance. In the Hindu System what do the figures represent halfway through an addition; what is the physical meaning of a carry? It is a symbolic jungle without any intuitive appeal. Then they have the most unnatural way of working—from right to left. Their system is too complex for average people.

Moore: The Roman System is most attractive from a theorem-proving viewpoint. It is faster to prove than to compute.

van de Snepscheut: I see rich possibilities for symbol manipulation in the Roman System. By inventing new symbols such as 'v' and 'x' they can replace groups of other symbols. The Hindu System offers no such symbol manipulation possibilities because it lacks the flexibility of admitting new digits. Also, using a symbol to represent nothing—they call it a zero—is a poor design decision.

Hindu: Let us talk about multiplication. Consider the following arithmetic problem dealing with consumptions of christians by lions. Suppose that a lion can consume two christians every hour. How do you compute the number of christians that must be supplied to keep three lions happy for two hours?

Roman: That is simple. I will run a live simulation. (pause) You have seen that we can conceptualize, animate and communicate. We are now transferring this technology to the city of Carthage. We are planning to destroy them shortly, though.

Hindu: (Aside) Your number system will destroy them first. (Pause) Let me make a last effort. How can you divide in your notation?

Roman: People in the real world don't divide.

History does not record the name of this informed Roman buyer, but thanks to him and the group of experts, Europe enjoyed the beauty and elegance of the Roman System for the next twelve centuries.

Part I

Constructive Logic and Type Theory

Constructive logic and type theory are in the centre of a theoretical, logical foundation of program design calculi. Proving by constructive techniques, designing algorithms and deriving programs are activities of one nature. The corresponding theory forms the basis for verification and construction support systems.

R.C. Backhouse

R.L. Constable

J.S. Moore

Whereas many lecturers concentrated on rabbit introduction only, Roland Backhouse also showed rules for rabbit elimination. In categorical terms, this corresponds to the notion of a pushback. It arises as the dual of the pullout by reversing the arrow.

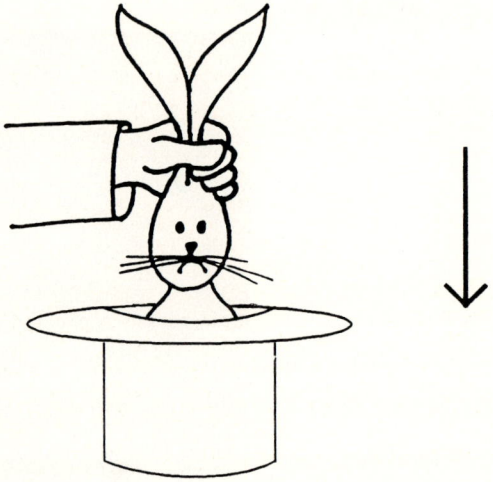

Constructive Type Theory—An Introduction*

Roland C. Backhouse
Rijksuniversiteit Groningen

Abstract

This paper explains the notion of propositions as types within the context of Per Martin-Löf's theory of types. The relationship between constructive and classical logic is also discussed. In addition mention is made of the connection between the natural-deduction-style reasoning used here and the theory of preorders discussed by Hoare elsewhere in this volume.

---

*The material in these notes is adapted from an excerpt of the forthcoming book entitled "Constructive Type Theory" and is reproduced here with the permission of its publishers, Prentice/Hall International, Inc.

1 Introduction

These notes explore in some depth one particular aspect of constructive type theory, namely the notion of propositions-as-types. Other aspects of the theory, some of which were discussed in the summer school, are expanded by the author (and coauthors) elsewhere [1,3,4]. Reference should also be made to the companion contribution of R. Constable in this volume.

The notion of propositions-as-types is sometimes refered to as the Curry-Howard principle, giving credit for its discovery to H.B. Curry[9] and Howard[14]. It is a principle that is central to a number of formulations of constructive logic; as a consequence a sound understanding of the principle seems to be somewhat essential.

Our discussion of the principle is based around the formal theory of types developed by Per Martin-Löf [17]. The reason for choosing this particular formalisation of constructive mathematics rather than any other is that it is the most elegant such system known to the author. (This is a view that seems to be shared by many other computing scientists since Martin-Löf's theory has attracted quite a considerable amount of attention in recent years.) These notes can therefore also be regarded as an introduction to the constructive logic which is an integral part of Martin-Löf's theory.

The mode of presentation consists almost entirely of a large number of examples. No attempt is made to explain the philosophical background to the theory. To understand the examples properly it is necessary that the reader is familiar with the lambda notation for naming functions (the account by Stoy[20] or similar accounts be be found in any book on functional programming are more than adequate for our purposes), with basic tautologies of the (classical) propositional calculus and with the cartesian product, disjoint sum and function space type constructors that are ubiquitous in all modern functional programming languages.

Some attempt has been made to relate the material here to the lectures of C.A.R. Hoare on category theory. To this end a section has been added that demonstrates how certain proofs within the formal system discussed here can be translated into proofs within the theory of preorders expounded by Hoare. A major reason for wishing to do so was to be able to take the opportunity of highlighting particular aspects of the (natural deduction) style of proof derivation that we have used.

2 Propositions as Types

2.1 Preliminaries

The principle of propositions-as-types can be summarised by the statement that a proposition is identified with the set (or "type") of its proofs. Such a statement is very difficult (if not impossible) to grasp without having first seen several examples. In order to present such examples in a completely formal way this first section introduces a number of apparently ad hoc rules, for which we ask the reader's forbearance.

The primitive types in Martin-Löf's theory include the set of natural numbers, denoted $\mathbb{N}$, and enumerated types like $\{nil\}$ and $\{red, yellow, blue\}$. Formally, we have the rule

$$\mathbb{N} \ type \qquad (1)$$

which is read as "$\mathbb{N}$ (the set of natural numbers) is a type". The statement $\mathbb{N}$ *type* is called a *judgement*. (There are four judgement forms but only two are considered until section 2.)

The objects of $\mathbb{N}$ are of course 0, 1, 2 etc. For the purposes of this discussion we only need the fact that 0 is an object of $\mathbb{N}$, which is written formally as the judgement

$$0 \in \mathbb{N} \qquad (2)$$

(and read "0 is an object of $\mathbb{N}$"). Similarly we have the judgements

$$nil \in \{nil\} \qquad (3)$$

and

$$red \in \{red, yellow, blue\} \qquad (4)$$

The judgement form "$p \in P$" is central to Martin-Löf's theory and can be read as "p is an object of P" or "p has type P". (As mentioned earlier, we also interpret it in other ways.)

The primitive types are objects of a universe of types denoted by U_1. (As the notation suggests there is, in fact, a hierarchy of universes U_1, U_2, ... but this is something we do not consider.) The universe, U_1, is itself a type so we have the judgements

$$U_1 \; type \tag{5}$$

and (for example)

$$\mathbb{N} \in U_1 \tag{6}$$

Already, by introducing U_1 at this stage, we have diverged from Martin-Löf's preferred order of presentation of his theory. Indeed, in the theory a judgement of the form $P \; type$ has a rather precise meaning to do with knowing how to form objects of P, and with knowing when two objects of P are equal. For the purposes of this paper we must be content with a rather shallow understanding of the judgement $P \; type$ as meaning simply that P is a well-formed formula, or P is a syntactically-correct type expression.

Our first example of an inference rule is the following.

$$\frac{P \in U_1}{P \; type} \quad U_1\text{-elimination}$$

The rule states that if P is an object of U_1 then P is a type. Using it we can infer (0) from (5) as follows:

1    $\mathbb{N} \in U_1$

    $\{1, U_1 - elim.\}$

2    $\mathbb{N} \; type$

The two steps 1 and 2 form a *proof-derivation*. The numbering of steps and the explanations enclosed within braces are not part of the derivation but appear only as aids to the reader.

Terminology. Objects of U_1 are generally referred to as the *small types*. Thus $\mathbb{N}$ is a small type. We shall adopt this terminology from now on.

2.2 Assumptions and Scope

An important aspect of the theory is the ability to make hypothetical judgements, that is judgements that depend on certain assumptions. An assumption is introduced using the following rule of inference.

$$
\frac{P\ type}{\begin{array}{l}\|[\ x \in P \\ \triangleright\ x \in P \\ ]\|\end{array}} \quad \text{Assumption}
$$

In the inference part of this rule the symbol x denotes a variable and can be any identifier, sign or mark that does not occur free in P. (It should however be readily distinguishable from other syntactic marks in the language.) The brackets $\|[$ and $]\|$ delimit the *scope* of the assumption and are pronounced "scopen" and "sclose", respectively.

The two occurrences of P stand for arbitrary expressions. In a valid use of the rule they must be replaced by *definitionally equal* expressions. For the moment you may read "definitionally equal" as identical but it has a broader meaning. (For example we shall shortly introduce a number of abbreviations; an expression and its abbreviation are then said to be definitionally equal.)

We verbalise the rule as the statement that if P is a type it is permissible to introduce a new *context* (delimited by the scope brackets) in which it is assumed that x is an object of P.

Assumptions look like variable declarations in conventional programming languages (particularly if one uses **begin** and **end** instead of $\|[$ and $]\|$), and there is no harm in adopting this view. Indeed, a vital (meta-) rule of the formal system is that *any use of a variable must be within the scope of a declaration of the variable.*

Example 1

$$|[\ A \in U_1$$
$$\triangleright\ A\ type$$
$$]|$$

In a context in which A is assumed to be a small type (an object of U_1), A is a type.

Derivation

1   U_1 *type*
        {1, assumption}
2      $|[\ \ A \in U_1$
       $\triangleright$ {2, U_1-elim.}
3   A *type*
     $]|$

Step 1 is a statement of the primitive rule that U_1 is a type. This enables the use of the assumption rule, in step 2, to introduce a context in which A is assumed to be a small type. Note that step 2 simultaneously introduces the sclose bracket at the end of the derivation. Note also that judgement 2 is not repeated after the "$\triangleright$" symbol although formally this should be the case — to do so is, we feel, over-pedantic.

(End of example)

NB. The use of scope brackets in these notes is the most radical departure from Martin-Löf's system. The difference is one of presentation, and not of semantics, but it is a difference that I regard as very important. For illustrations of Martin-Löf's style of proof derivation see [5] and [18]. Petersson [19] has implemented this style as a replacement for PPLambda in the Edinburgh LCF system [12]. For an alternative, top-down, style of proof derivation see the NuPRL system [7].

2.3 Type Formation Rules

In this section we present a number of type-formation rules — rules for making judgements of the form P *type*. We also take the opportunity to introduce informally the notion of propositions as types. In presenting the rules — here and elsewhere — we use P, Q, R to denote type expressions, p, q, r, s to denote object expressions and w, x, y, z to denote variables.

2.3.1 Implication

$$\frac{\begin{array}{l} P \text{ type} \\ \|[\quad x \in P \\ \triangleright \quad Q \text{ type} \\ ]\| \end{array}}{P \Rightarrow Q \text{ type}} \Rightarrow\text{-formation}$$

The $\Rightarrow$-formation rule has two premises. The first premise is that P is a type. The second premise is that in a context in which it is assumed that x is an object of P it is possible to prove that Q is a type. If these two premises are satisfied then it is possible to infer that $P \Rightarrow Q$ is a type. (Note that the conclusion is read as $(P \Rightarrow Q)$ is a type, not $P \Rightarrow (Q$ is a type). Viewed as a unary operator, the keyword *type* has lowest precedence.)

The rule is said to *discharge* the assumption, $x \in P$, in the second premise, and x is not in scope in the conclusion. As a consequence, the expression Q cannot contain any free occurrences of x since, otherwise, the scope rule would be violated.

The complicated second premise permits the use of *conditional* or *nonstrict* implication in type expressions. For example, the expression $(\forall n \in \mathbb{N})(0 \neq n \Rightarrow 0 \text{ div } n = 0)$[1] is a valid type expression even though $0 \text{ div } n$ is undefined when $0 = n$. For our present purposes, however, the $\Rightarrow$-formation rule is unnecessarily complicated and we shall assume the following, simpler, formation rule.

$$\frac{P \text{ type} \qquad Q \text{ type}}{P \Rightarrow Q \text{ type}} \text{(simplified)}\Rightarrow\text{-formation}$$

Example 2

---

[1] The conventional notation for universal quantification has been used here. The notation actually used in these notes is somewhat different.

$$\begin{aligned}&\|[\quad A \in U_1 \\ &\triangleright\quad A \Rightarrow A\ type \\ &\]|\end{aligned}$$

In a context in which A is a small type, $A \Rightarrow A$ is a type.

Derivation

1	$U_1\ type$	
2	$\|[\quad A \in U_1$	
	$\triangleright\qquad \{2, U_1\text{-elim.}\}$	
3	$\quad A\ type$	
	$\qquad \{3,3, \Rightarrow\text{-form.}\}$	
4	$\quad A \Rightarrow A\ type$	
	$\]|$	

(End of example)

In constructive mathematics, a proof of $A \Rightarrow B$ is a method of proving B given a proof of A. Thus $A \Rightarrow B$ is identified with the type $A \to B$ of (total) functions from the type A into the type B. Assuming that A is a small type, an elementary example would be the proposition $A \Rightarrow A$. (We use the words proposition and type interchangeably here and elsewhere.) A proof of $A \Rightarrow A$ is a method of constructing a proof of A given a proof of A. Such a method would be the identity function on A, $\lambda([x]x)$, since this is a function that, given an object of A, returns the same object of A.

Example 3

$$\begin{aligned}&\|[\quad A \in U_1 \\ &\triangleright\quad \|[\quad B \in U_1 \\ &\qquad \triangleright\quad A \Rightarrow (B \Rightarrow A)\ type \\ &\qquad \]| \\ &\]|\end{aligned}$$

In a context in which A and B are both small types, $A \Rightarrow (B \Rightarrow A)$ is a type.

Derivation

1	$U_1\ type$	
2	$\|[\quad A \in U_1$	
	$\triangleright\qquad \{2, U_1\text{-elim.}\}$	
3	$\quad A\ type$	
4	$\quad \|[\quad B \in U_1$	

```
5          ▷     {4, U₁-elim.}
                 B type
                      {5,3, ⇒-form.}
6                B ⇒ A type
                      {3,6, ⇒-form.}
7                A ⇒ (B ⇒ A) type
           ]|
   ]|
```

(End of example)

The proposition $A \Rightarrow (B \Rightarrow A)$ provides a second, slightly more complicated, example of the constructive interpretation of implication. Assuming that A and B are small types, a proof of $A \Rightarrow (B \Rightarrow A)$ is a method that, given a proof of A, constructs a proof of $B \Rightarrow A$. Now, a proof of $B \Rightarrow A$ is a method that from a proof of B constructs a proof of A. Thus, given that x is a proof of A, the constant function $\lambda([y]x)$ is a proof of $B \Rightarrow A$. Hence the function $\lambda([x]\lambda([y]x))$ is a proof of $A \Rightarrow (B \Rightarrow A)$. (The function $\lambda([x]\lambda([y]x))$ is known as the K-combinator (see, for example, [20,21]).)

2.3.2 Conjunction

P *type*

$|[\ x \in P$

▷ Q *type*

$]|$

$P \wedge Q$ *type* $\qquad$ ∧-formation

Apart from the change of symbol from $\Rightarrow$ to $\wedge$ there is no difference in the formation rules for implication and conjunction. The complicated second premise permits the use of a conditional or non-strict conjunction (sometimes denoted **cand** in programming languages). As before, we shall assume a simpler formation rule as follows:

P *type*

Q *type*

$P \wedge Q$ *type* $\qquad$ (simplified) ∧-formation

Example 4

$$\begin{aligned}&\| \quad A \in U_1 \\ &\triangleright \quad \| \quad B \in U_1 \\ &\qquad \triangleright \quad A \wedge B \Rightarrow A \; type \\ &\qquad \;\;\;]| \\ &\;\;]| \end{aligned}$$

In a context in which A and B are small types, $A \wedge B \Rightarrow A$ is a type.

Derivation

1	U_1 $type$	
2	$\|[\quad A \in U_1$	
	$\triangleright \qquad \{2, U_1\text{-elim.}\}$	
3	A $type$	
4	$\|[\quad B \in U_1$	
	$\triangleright \qquad \{4, U_1\text{-elim.}\}$	
5	B $type$	
	$\qquad \{3, 5, \wedge\text{-form.}\}$	
6	$A \wedge B$ $type$	
	$\qquad \{6, 3, \Rightarrow\text{-form.}\}$	
7	$A \wedge B \Rightarrow A$ $type$	
	$\qquad]|$	
	$\;]|$	

(End of example)

The proposition $A \wedge B \Rightarrow A$ is true in classical mathematics and in constructive mathematics. The constructive proof goes as follows: Assume that A and B are small types. We have to exhibit a method that given a pair $\langle x, y \rangle$, where x is an object of A and y is an object of B, constructs an object of A. Such a method is clearly the projection function $fst_{A,B}$ that projects an object of $A \wedge B$ onto its first component.

Another example of a constructive proof involving conjunction is the proof of the proposition $A \wedge B \Rightarrow B \wedge A$. Such a proof is a function that with argument an ordered pair $\langle x, y \rangle$ of objects x, y in A, B, respectively, reverses their order to construct the pair $\langle y, x \rangle$.

2.3.3 Disjunction

$$\frac{P \ type \qquad Q \ type}{P \vee Q \ type} \quad \vee\text{-formation}$$

A constructive proof of $P \vee Q$ consists of either a proof of P or a proof of Q together with information indicating which of the two has been proved. Thus $P \vee Q$ is identified with the disjoint sum of the types P and Q. That is, objects of $P \vee Q$ take one of the two forms $\mathbf{inl}(x)$ or $\mathbf{inr}(y)$, where x is an object of P, y is an object of Q, and the reserved words **inl** (inject left) and **inr** (inject right) indicate which operand has been proved.

As elementary examples of provable propositions involving disjunction we take $A \Rightarrow A \vee A$, $A \Rightarrow A \vee B$ and $A \vee B \Rightarrow B \vee A$, where A and B are assumed to be small types. There are two possible proofs of $A \Rightarrow A \vee A$. The first, $\lambda([x]\mathbf{inl}(x))$, maps an argument x of type A into the left operand of $A \vee A$, and the second, $\lambda([x]\mathbf{inr}(x))$, maps an argument x of type A into the right operand of $A \vee A$. In a proof of $A \Rightarrow A \vee B$ there is no choice but to map an object x of A into the left operand of $A \vee B$. Thus the proof takes the form $\lambda([x]\mathbf{inl}(x))$. A proof of $A \vee B \Rightarrow B \vee A$ must map an argument w, say, of type $A \vee B$ into $B \vee A$. This is achieved by examining w to discover whether it takes the form $\mathbf{inl}(x)$ or whether it takes the form $\mathbf{inr}(y)$. In the former case w is mapped into $\mathbf{inr}(x)$, in the latter case w is mapped into $\mathbf{inl}(y)$. Thus, in the notation introduced later, a proof of $A \vee B \Rightarrow B \vee A$ is $\lambda([w]\mathbf{when}(w, [x]\mathbf{inr}(x), [y]\mathbf{inl}(y)))$.

Note that the $\vee$-formation rule does not permit the use of conditional disjunction. The reason is that the conventional meaning of A **cor** B assumes the law of the excluded middle — A **cor** B is true if A is true, or, A is false and B is true. It is of course feasible in type theory to define A **cor** B for Boolean types A, but this is not a primitive notion.

Exercise 5 *Prove the following*

|[$A \in U_1$
▷ |[$B \in U_1$
  ▷ $A \vee B \Rightarrow B \vee A$ *type*
  ]|
]|
(End of Exercise)

2.3.4 Universal Quantification

$$\frac{\begin{array}{c} P \text{ type} \\ |[\ x \in P \\ \triangleright\ Q(x)\ type \\ ]| \end{array}}{\forall(P, [x]Q(x))\ type} \quad \forall\text{-formation}$$

The ∀-formation rule also has two premises, but now the complication in the second premise is of unavoidable importance. The first premise states simply that P is a type. The second premise is that, in a context in which it is assumed that x has type P, it is the case that $Q(x)$ is a type. The conclusion is that $\forall(P, [x]Q(x))$ (pronounced "for all P x it is the case that $Q(x)$") is a type.

Typically $Q(x)$ will be an expression containing free occurrences of the variable x. Such occurrences become bound in the expression $\forall(P, [x]Q(x))$. Note that the introduction of an abstraction accompanies the discharge of an assumption. (Compare the ∀-formation rule with the ⇒-formation rule. In the former the variable x becomes bound by ∀, and it is therefore legitimate — and usual — for $Q(x)$ to contain free occurrences of x; in the latter there is no binder for x and hence, to comply with scope rules, Q must *not* contain free occurrences of x.)

We prefer the notation $\forall(P, [x]Q(x))$ to the more conventional $(\forall x \in P)Q(x)$ because it makes clear the scope of the binding of the variable x. An expression of the form $[x]R$ is called an *abstraction*. $Q(x)$ is called a *family of types dependent on x*.

In order to prove constructively the proposition $\forall(P, [x]Q(x))$ it is necessary to provide a method that, given an object p of type P, constructs an object of $Q(p)$. (The notation $Q(p)$ denotes the result obtained by replacing all free occurrences of x in $Q(x)$ by p.) Thus proofs of $\forall(P,[x]Q(x))$ are functions (as for implication), their domain being P and their range, $Q(p)$, being dependent on the argument p supplied to the function. The fact that the range depends on the argument is what distinguishes universal quantification from implication.

Example 6

$$\forall(U_1, [A]A \Rightarrow A) \ type$$

Derivation

```
1       U₁ type
            {Example 2}
2       ‖[  A ∈ U₁
3        ▷  A ⇒ A type
        ]‖
            {1,2,3, ∀-form.}
4       ∀(U₁, [A]A ⇒ A) type
```

(End of example)

According to the semantics of $\forall$ and $\Rightarrow$, a proof of $\forall(U_1, [A]A \Rightarrow A)$ is a function that takes a small type A as argument and returns a function mapping A into A. Such a function is the *type-parametric* identity function $\lambda([A]\lambda([x]x))$. This function maps a small type A into the identity function on A. Another example of a type-parametric function is the K-combinator $\lambda([A]\lambda([B]\lambda([x]\lambda([y]x))))$ which proves the proposition $\forall(U_1, [A]\forall(U_1, [B]A \Rightarrow (B \Rightarrow A)))$ — it is a function that takes two types A and B as arguments and returns a proof of $A \Rightarrow (B \Rightarrow A)$, which we recall from section 2.4.1 is the function $\lambda([x]\lambda([y]x))$.

2.3.5 Existential Quantification

$$
\begin{array}{l}
P \ type \\
\|[\quad x \in P \\
\triangleright \quad Q(x) \ type \\
\|] \\
\hline
\exists(P, [x]Q(x)) \ type
\end{array} \quad \exists\text{-formation}
$$

The ∃-formation rule is identical to the ∀-formation rule in that ∃ binds free occurrences of x in the expression $Q(x)$. (The notation we use for existential quantification takes the same form as that for universal quantification rather than the conventional $(\exists x \in P)Q(x)$.)

Example 7 $\exists(U_1, [A]A) \ type$

Derivation
1. $U_1 \ type$
2. $\|[\quad A \in U_1$
    $\triangleright \qquad \{2, U_1\text{-elim.}\}$
3. $\qquad A \ type$
    $\|]$
    $\qquad \{1,2,3, \exists\text{-form.}\}$
4. $\exists(U_1, [A]A) \ type$

(End of example)

A constructive proof of $\exists(P, [x]Q(x))$ consists of exhibiting an object p of P together with a proof of $Q(p)$. Thus proofs of $\exists(P, [x]Q(x))$ are pairs $\langle p, q \rangle$ where p is a proof of P and q is a proof of $Q(p)$.

The type $\exists(P, [x]Q(x))$ is called a *dependent* type because the second component, q, in a pair $\langle p, q \rangle$ in the type depends on the first component, p (and thus distinguishes it from $P \wedge Q$). This is illustrated by our example. There are many objects of the type $\exists(U_1, [A]A)$. Each consists of a pair $\langle A, a \rangle$ where A is a small type and a is an object of that type. (Thus the proposition is interpreted as the statement "there is a small type that is provable", or "there is a small type that is non-empty".) For example, $\langle \mathbb{N}, 0 \rangle$ is an object of $\exists(U_1, [A]A)$ since $\mathbb{N}$ is a small type (an object of U_1) and 0 is an object of $\mathbb{N}$. Two further examples are $\langle \{red, yellow, blue\}, red \rangle$ and $\langle \mathbb{N} \Rightarrow \mathbb{N}, \lambda([x]x) \rangle$.

Objects of the type $\exists(U_1, [A]A)$ are the simplest possible examples of *algebras* (one or more sets together with a number of operations defined on the sets) since they each consist of a set A together with a single constant of A. A slightly more complicated algebra is specified by the type $\exists(U_1, [A]A \wedge A \Rightarrow A)$. An object of this type consists of a small type A together with a single binary operation defined on A.

2.3.6 Negation

Negation is not a primitive concept of type theory. It is defined via the *empty type*. The empty type, denoted $\emptyset$, is the type containing no elements. Its formation rule is very simple.

$$\frac{}{\emptyset \; type} \quad \emptyset\text{-formation}$$

Moreover, $\emptyset$ is a small type.

$$\frac{}{\emptyset \in U_1} \quad U_1\text{-introduction}$$

The negation $\neg P$ is defined to be $P \Rightarrow \emptyset$.

$$\neg P \equiv P \Rightarrow \emptyset$$

($\equiv$ stands for definitionally equal to.) This means that a proof of $\neg P$ is a method for constructing an object of the empty type from an object of P. Since it would be absurd to construct an object of the empty type this is equivalent to saying that it is absurd to construct a proof of P.

The proposition $\neg \forall (U_1, [A]A)$ provides an example of a provable negation. It states that not every small type is provable, or not every small type is non-empty. The basis for its proof is very ordinary — we exhibit a counter-example, namely the empty type $\emptyset$. Formally, we have to construct a function that maps an argument f, say, of type $\forall (U_1, [A]A)$ into $\emptyset$. Now f is itself a function mapping objects, A, of U_1 into objects of A. So, for any small type A, the application of f to A, denoted $f.A$, has type A. In particular, $f.\emptyset$ has type $\emptyset$. Thus the proof object we require is $\lambda([f]f.\emptyset)$.

2.3.7 Families of Types

An important concept in the theory — that has already been illustrated in several ways — is that of a *family of types*. For example, $A \Rightarrow A$ is a family of types that includes the particular instances $\emptyset \Rightarrow \emptyset$ and $\mathbb{N} \Rightarrow \mathbb{N}$. Generally we say that R is a family of types indexed by $x \in P$ if the judgement R *type* can be made in a context in which x is assumed to be an object of P.

The rich type-definition mechanism is reflected in the construction of such families of types. Further examples (with hopefully obvious meanings) are

> **case** x **is**
> > $male \rightarrow \{Bill, Joe\}$
> > $female \rightarrow \{Mary, Jane\}$

indexed by $x \in \{male, female\}$, and

> **when** x **is**
> > $\mathbf{inl}(a) \rightarrow C$
> > $\mathbf{inr}(b) \rightarrow \{error\}$

indexed by $x \in A \vee B$.

The first example has two instances (a) $\{Bill, Joe\}$ and (b) $\{Mary, Jane\}$. The second example also has two instances (a) C and (b) $\{error\}$. Such dependent type structures have obvious programming applications: we might use the first type structure to specify a database in which the names of males and females are taken from different sets; the second example might be used to specify a function that returns a value of type C when its argument is of one type and returns error when its argument is of another type (eg. the function **div**).

The notion of a family of types is central to many of the inference rules in the theory but to give it full justice would go beyond the modest aims of this paper.

2.4 Introduction and Elimination Rules

For some time now, computing scientists have recognised the need for program structure to reflect data structure. In the words of C.A.R. Hoare [13]

> "There are certain close analogies between the methods for structuring data and the methods for structuring a program which processes that data. Thus, a Cartesian product corresponds to a compound statement, which assigns values to its components. Similarly, a discriminated union corresponds to a conditional or case construction, selecting an appropriate processing method for each alternative ..."

This has had an important influence on program design methodologies, a notable example being Jackson's program design method [15].

In Martin-Löf's theory the "analogy" between data structure and program structure is made explicit. With each type constructor is associated zero or more so-called *introduction rules* together with a single *elimination rule*. The introduction rules show how to construct the primitive objects of the type; they thus define the data structure. The elimination rule shows how to manipulate or "destruct" objects of the type.

In Martin-Löf's terminology, the introduction rules define *canonical* objects and the elimination rules define *non-canonical* objects. The canonical objects of a type are the primitive objects of the type in the sense that they may be viewed as programs that have themselves as value. The non-canonical objects are not primitive; for each non-canonical object a computation rule is supplied that shows how to evaluate the object.

The terminology "introduction" and "elimination" rule is borrowed from Gentzen's account of natural deduction [10]. Indeed, the form of Martin-Löf's rules for the propositional connectives follows closely the form of Gentzen's rules. Martin-Löf's contribution has been to add proof objects which summarise the steps used to establish a proposition and which can be given computational meaning. Some familiarity with proofs in Gentzen's system may therefore be helpful to the reader.

In this section we exhibit the introduction and elimination rules for the propositional connectives, and use them to establish a number of familiar tautologies of the (classical) propositional calculus. Verbal descriptions accompanying the examples interpret them both in a logical sense and in a computational sense.

Throughout the remainder of this paper we assume that A, B and C are small types. Formally, we write

$\|[\quad A, B, C \in U_1$
$\triangleright$

The sclose terminating the scope of these assumptions will be found immediately before the concluding section. The notation $\|[\ A, B \in U_1\ \triangleright\ ]\|$ is just an ad hoc abbreviation for $\|[\ A \in U_1\ \triangleright\ \|[\ B \in U_1\ \triangleright\ ]\|\ ]\|$.

2.4.1 Implication

Our first rule is the introduction rule for implication.

⟨premises of ⇒-formation⟩

$\|[\quad x \in P$
$\triangleright\quad q(x) \in Q$
$]\|$

$$\frac{\qquad\qquad\qquad\qquad\qquad}{\lambda([x]q(x)) \in P \Rightarrow Q} \text{⇒-introduction}$$

In a logical sense the rule may be read as "if assuming that x is a proof of P it is possible to construct a proof of Q then $\lambda([x]q(x))$ is a proof of $P \Rightarrow Q$". In a computational sense the rule is read differently. "If in a context in which x is an object of type P the object $q(x)$ has type Q then the function $\lambda([x]q(x))$ is an object of type $P \Rightarrow Q$".

In general, $q(x)$ will be an expression containing zero or more free occurrences of x. Such occurrences of x become bound in the expression $\lambda([x]q(x))$. As we remarked earlier, binding of variables is always associated with the discharge of assumptions.

Note Martin-Löf omits several premises in his presentation of the inference rules and this has led to several misunderstandings and errors. In particular, in a rule with inference of the form $p \in P$ he omits premises of the form P *type*. Other authors have tried to remedy this by specifying a minimal set of additional premises. I prefer the more systematic approach of simply prefacing each rule with a reminder of the missing premises. Thus, it can be argued that the premises of $\Rightarrow$-formation are all superfluous in the above rule; however, such premises are essential to the correct application of later rules.

Example 8 $\quad \lambda([x]x) \in A \Rightarrow A$

This is a continuation of example 2. We now show formally how to derive the judgement that the identity function is a proof of the proposition $A \Rightarrow A$.

Derivation

```
            {assumption}
1      |[   x ∈ A
2       ▷   x ∈ A
       ]|
            {1,2, Example 2, ⇒-intro.}
3      λ([x]x) ∈ A ⇒ A
```

Note that 1 and 2 make implicit use of the assumption at the beginning of this section that $A \in U_1$. Example 2 is quoted in the explanation of step 3 because it includes the required premises of the form P *type*.

(End of example)

Example 9 $\quad \lambda([x]\lambda([y]x)) \in A \Rightarrow (B \Rightarrow A)$

Derivation

```
1      |[   x ∈ A
2       ▷  |[   y ∈ B
             ▷      {1}
3                x ∈ A
            ]|
                 {Example 3, 2,3, ⇒-intro.}
4           λ([y]x) ∈ B ⇒ A
       ]|
            {Example 3, 1,4, ⇒-intro.}
5      λ([x]λ([y]x)) ∈ A ⇒ (B ⇒ A)
```

(End of example)

The ⇒-elimination rule is easily recognisable as the rule of modus ponens.

$$\begin{array}{l} \langle \text{premises of} \Rightarrow\text{-formation} \rangle \\ p \in P \\ r \in P \Rightarrow Q \\ \hline r.p \in Q \end{array} \quad \Rightarrow\text{-elimination}$$

In a logical sense the rule states that if p is a proof of P and r is a proof of $P \Rightarrow Q$ then $r.p$ is a proof of Q. In a computational sense it states that if p has type P and r is a function from P to Q then $r.p$, the result of applying r to p, has type Q.

The notation we are using for λ-expressions and function application is unconventional but emphasises much more clearly the scope of bound variables. Specifically, the bound variable in a λ-expression is indicated by enclosing it in brackets immediately after the opening parenthesis. Its scope then extends to the matching closing parenthesis. Function application is denoted by a dot and is assumed to associate to the left. Corresponding to the latter convention we have the convention that implication associates to the right. Thus $P \Rightarrow Q \Rightarrow R$ is read as $P \Rightarrow (Q \Rightarrow R)$. Occasionally, but not always, we use this convention to reduce the number of parentheses. However, we prefer to retain the parentheses when it makes the import of the examples and exercises clearer.

Example 10

$$\lambda([f]\lambda([g]\lambda([x]g.(f.x)))) \in (A \Rightarrow B) \Rightarrow (B \Rightarrow C) \Rightarrow (A \Rightarrow C)$$

The example asserts that implication is transitive. I.e., given a proof f of $A \Rightarrow B$, and given a proof g of $B \Rightarrow C$, the object $\lambda([x]g.(f.x))$ is a proof of $A \Rightarrow C$.

In the following derivation we omit judgements such as $A \Rightarrow B$ type, $B \Rightarrow C$ type. Strictly, these are necessary to the use of the assumption rule and the ⇒-introduction rule but their inclusion would obscure the main details.

Derivation

```
1      ||  f ∈ A ⇒ B
2    ▷    ||  g ∈ B ⇒ C
3         ▷  ||  x ∈ A
```

4	▷	$\{1,3 \Rightarrow\text{-elim.}\}$
		$f.x \in B$
5		$\{2,4, \Rightarrow\text{-elim.}\}$
		$g.(f.x) \in C$
	]|	
		$\{3,5,\Rightarrow\text{-intro.}\}$
6		$\lambda([x]g.(f.x)) \in A \Rightarrow C$
	]|	
		$\{2,6, \Rightarrow\text{-intro.}\}$
7		$\lambda([g]\lambda([x]g.(f.x))) \in (B \Rightarrow C) \Rightarrow (A \Rightarrow C)$
	]|	
		$\{1,7, \Rightarrow\text{-intro.}\}$
8		$\lambda([f]\lambda([g]\lambda([x]g.(f.x)))) \in (A \Rightarrow B) \Rightarrow (B \Rightarrow C) \Rightarrow (A \Rightarrow C)$

(End of example)

Exercise 11 *Verify the following.*

(a) $\lambda([f]\lambda([g]\lambda([x]f.x.(g.x))))$
$\in (A \Rightarrow (B \Rightarrow C)) \Rightarrow ((A \Rightarrow B) \Rightarrow (A \Rightarrow C))$

(b) $\lambda([f]\lambda([x]\lambda([y]f.(\lambda([z]y)).x)))$
$\in ((A \Rightarrow B) \Rightarrow (A \Rightarrow C)) \Rightarrow (A \Rightarrow (B \Rightarrow C))$

(End of Exercise)

(Equivalence is defined as the conjunction of two implications. Exercise 11 is therefore a proof that implication distributes over implication. I.e.

$$(A \Rightarrow (B \Rightarrow C)) \iff ((A \Rightarrow B) \Rightarrow (A \Rightarrow C)). \ )$$

Exercise 12   *Prove, and construct proof objects for, the propositions:*

(a) $(A \Rightarrow B \Rightarrow C) \Rightarrow (B \Rightarrow A \Rightarrow C)$

(b) $(B \Rightarrow C) \Rightarrow (A \Rightarrow B) \Rightarrow (A \Rightarrow C)$

(c) $(((A \Rightarrow B) \Rightarrow B) \Rightarrow B) \Rightarrow (A \Rightarrow B)$

(d) $A \Rightarrow ((A \Rightarrow B) \Rightarrow B)$

(End of Exercise)

Note Example 9, exercise 11(a) and exercises 12(a) and (b) are motivated by the K, S, B and C combinators [21]. See later for more general forms of S and K. Exercises (c) and (d) are discussed again in section 2.4.6.

2.4.2 Conjunction

The semantics of conjunction in constructive mathematics identifies $P \wedge Q$ with the Cartesian product $P \times Q$. That is, a proof of $P \wedge Q$ is an ordered pair $\langle p, q \rangle$ where p is a proof of P and q is a proof of Q. The introduction rule is therefore very straightforward.

$$\frac{\langle\text{premises of } \wedge\text{-formation}\rangle \\ p \in P \\ q \in Q}{\langle p, q \rangle \in P \wedge Q} \quad \wedge\text{-introduction}$$

Example 13 $\quad \lambda([x]\langle x, x \rangle) \in A \Rightarrow A \wedge A$

A proof of $A \wedge A$ can be constructed from a proof of A simply by repeating the proof object. (Note that conjunction takes precedence over implication in the expression $A \Rightarrow A \wedge A$.)

Derivation

```
1      |[   x ∈ A
        ▷        {1,1, ∧-intro}
2               ⟨x, x⟩ ∈ A ∧ A
       ]|
                {1,2, ⇒-intro}
3      λ([x]⟨x, x⟩) ∈ A ⇒ A ∧ A
```

(End of example)

Example 14 *(Currying)*

$$\lambda([f]\lambda([x]\lambda([y]f.\langle x, y \rangle))) \in (A \wedge B \Rightarrow C) \Rightarrow (A \Rightarrow B \Rightarrow C)$$

This is one of my favourite examples of the principle of propositions-as-types. In a logical sense the example is very familiar to all English speakers since it is legitimate to say either "if A *and* if B then C" or "if A *then* if B then C". In a computational sense it also expresses a very familiar rule, namely that any function f of a pair of arguments $\langle x, y \rangle$ can be "curried" (after Haskel B. Curry), i.e. converted into a function that maps the single argument x into a function that maps the second argument y into the result of applying f to the pair $\langle x, y \rangle$.

Derivation

1. $\ \ \ \|[\ \ f \in A \wedge B \Rightarrow C$
2. $\ \ \ \ \ \triangleright\ \ \|[\ \ x \in A$
3. $\ \ \ \ \ \ \ \ \ \ \ \triangleright\ \ \|[\ \ y \in B$
   $\ \ \ \ \ \ \ \ \ \ \ \ \ \ \ \ \ \ \triangleright\ \ \ \{2,3, \wedge\text{-intro.}\}$
4. $\ \langle x, y \rangle \in A \wedge B$
   $\ \{1,4, \Rightarrow\text{-elim.}\}$
5. $\ f.\langle x, y \rangle \in C$
   $\ \ \ \ \ \ \ \ \ \ \ \ \ \ \ \ \ ]|$
   $\ \ \ \ \ \ \ \ \ \ \ \ \ \ \ \ \ \ \{3,5, \Rightarrow\text{-intro.}\}$
6. $\ \ \ \ \ \ \ \ \ \ \ \ \ \ \ \ \ \lambda([y]f.\langle x, y \rangle) \in B \Rightarrow C$
   $\ \ \ \ \ \ \ \ \ ]|$
   $\ \ \ \ \ \ \ \ \ \ \ \ \{2,6, \Rightarrow\text{-intro.}\}$
7. $\ \ \ \ \ \ \ \ \ \ \ \lambda([x]\lambda([y]f.\langle x, y \rangle)) \in A \Rightarrow B \Rightarrow C$
   $\ \ \ \ \ ]|$
   $\ \ \ \ \ \ \ \ \{1,7, \Rightarrow\text{-intro.}\}$
8. $\ \ \ \ \ \ \ \lambda([f]\lambda([x]\lambda([y]f.\langle x, y \rangle))) \in (A \wedge B \Rightarrow C) \Rightarrow (A \Rightarrow B \Rightarrow C)$

(End of example)

Many of the propositions we prove have implication as the principal connective. Correspondingly, derivations often end with at least one application of the $\Rightarrow$-introduction rule. We hope that by now the reader is familiar with this rule and we shall omit it, except in a few places. We shall also compact several consecutive assumptions into one. As illustration the following is an abbreviation of the last derivation.

Abbreviated derivation

1    $|[\quad f \in A \wedge B \Rightarrow C; x \in A; y \in B$

     ▷ $\{1, \wedge\text{-intro.}\}$

2        $\langle x, y \rangle \in A \wedge B$

         $\{1, 2, \Rightarrow\text{-elim.}\}$

3        $f.\langle x, y \rangle \in C$

    $]|$

End of abbreviated derivation

The latter derivation may be summarised as the statement that in a context in which f has type $A \wedge B \Rightarrow C$, x has type A and y has type B, it is the case that $f.\langle x, y \rangle$ has type C. This is semantically equivalent to the statement that $\lambda([f]\lambda([x]\lambda([y]f.\langle x, y \rangle)))$ has type $(A \wedge B \Rightarrow C) \Rightarrow (A \Rightarrow B \Rightarrow C)$.

In Gentzen's system there are two elimination rules for conjunction. The first states that it is possible to infer A from $A \wedge B$, the second states that it is possible to infer B from $A \wedge B$. Martin-Löf has combined these two rules into one, which takes the following form:

⟨premises of ∧-formation⟩

$|[\;\; w \in P \wedge Q$

▷ $R(w)\ type$

$]|$

$r \in P \wedge Q$

$|[\;\; x \in P; y \in Q$

▷ $s(x, y) \in R(\langle x, y \rangle)$

$]|$

──────────────────────── ∧-elimination

$\mathbf{split}(r, [x, y]s(x, y)) \in R(r)$

The first premise states that $R(w)$ is a type in a context in which w is an object of $P \wedge Q$. Typically, therefore, $R(w)$ is a family of types, one for each such object. More precisely $R(w)$ is a type expression containing an arbitrary number of occurrences of the dummy variable w such that $R(r)$ is a type whenever r is an object of $P \wedge Q$. Given this premise, the rule is used to prove $R(r)$ as follows. First, establish that r has type

$P \wedge Q$. Second, assume that x and y are individual objects of P and Q, respectively, and construct an object $s(x,y)$ of type $R(\langle x,y \rangle)$. Then the exhibited **split** construct is a proof of $R(r)$. Computationally the **split** construct has the effect of splitting a pair, r, into its components, the value of the expression $s(x,y)$ is then computed with the components being bound to the variables x and y occurring free in the expression.

The $\wedge$-elimination rule is one of those that, as yet, we can only illustrate in a limited way. Thus, although the rule permits the type R to depend on the object r, none of the examples in this section illustrate such a dependence.

Example 15 $\lambda([w]\mathbf{split}(w,[x,y]x)) \in A \wedge B \Rightarrow A$

The function, fst, which projects a pair onto its first component is the function that splits its argument w into the pair $\langle x,y \rangle$ and returns x.

Derivation
```
1        |[  w ∈ A ∧ B
2         ▷  |[  x ∈ A; y ∈ B
              ▷     {2}
3                x ∈ A
              ]|
                 {1,2,3, ∧-elim.}
4             split(w,[x,y]x) ∈ A
         ]|
```

The function, snd, which projects a pair onto its second component is obtained similarly.

(End of example)

Example 16   *(Uncurrying)*

$\lambda([f]\lambda([w]\mathbf{split}(w,[x,y]f.x.y))) \in (A \Rightarrow B \Rightarrow C) \Rightarrow (A \wedge B \Rightarrow C)$

Derivation
```
1        |[  f ∈ A ⇒ B ⇒ C
2         ▷  |[  w ∈ A ∧ B
3              ▷  |[  x ∈ A; y ∈ B
                   ▷     {1,3, ⇒-elim.}
4                     f.x ∈ B ⇒ C
                         {4,3, ⇒-elim.}
```

```
5                    f.x.y ∈ C
                  ]|
                     {2,3,5, ∧-elim.}
6                 split(w, [x, y]f.x.y) ∈ C
               ]|
            ]|
```

(End of example)

Exercise 17   *Verify the following:*

(a) $\lambda([w]\mathbf{split}(w, [x, y]\langle y, x\rangle))$

$\in A \wedge B \Rightarrow B \wedge A$

(b) $\lambda([f]\langle \lambda([x]\mathbf{fst}.(f.x)), \lambda([x]\mathbf{snd}.(f.x))\rangle)$

$\in (A \Rightarrow B \wedge C) \Rightarrow (A \Rightarrow B) \wedge (A \Rightarrow C)$

(c) $\lambda([w]\mathbf{split}(w, [f, g]\lambda([x]\langle f.x, g.x\rangle)))$

$\in (A \Rightarrow B) \wedge (A \Rightarrow C) \Rightarrow (A \Rightarrow B \wedge C)$

(End of Exercise)

Exercise 18   *Parts (b) and (c) of the last exercise can be interpreted as the claim that implication distributes over conjunction; part (a) establishes that conjunction is symmetric. Establish as many other algebraic properties of conjunction and implication as you can.*

(End of Exercise)

2.4.3 Disjunction

A proof of $P \vee Q$ is a proof of P or a proof of Q together with information as to which has been proved. Thus, $P \vee Q$ is identified with the disjoint sum of P and Q and has two introduction rules.

⟨premises of ∨-formation⟩   ⟨premises of ∨-formation⟩

$p \in P$ $q \in Q$

———————————   ———————————   ∨-introduction

$\mathbf{inl}(p) \in P \vee Q$ $\mathbf{inr}(q) \in P \vee Q$

The constants **inl** and **inr** are called *injection functions* and stand for inject left and inject right, respectively.

Example 19 $\quad \lambda([x]\mathbf{inl}(x)) \in A \Rightarrow A \vee A$

There are two functions of type $A \Rightarrow A \vee A$ depending on whether the argument x is injected into the first or second operand of $A \vee A$. Our derivation takes the first option.

Derivation

```
1     |[   x ∈ A
         ▷    {1, ∨-intro.}
2          inl(x) ∈ A ∨ A
      ]|
```

(End of example)

Example 20 $\quad \lambda([f]\lambda([x]f.(\mathbf{inl}(x)))) \in (A \vee B \Rightarrow C) \Rightarrow (A \Rightarrow C)$

Given a function mapping elements of the disjoint union $A \vee B$ into C it is possible to construct a function mapping A into C. Alternatively, if either A or B implies C then A implies C.

Derivation

```
1     |[   f ∈ A ∨ B ⇒ C
2       ▷  |[   x ∈ A
              ▷    {2, ∨-intro.}
3                inl(x) ∈ A ∨ B
                   {1,3, ⇒-elim.}
4                f.(inl(x)) ∈ C
           ]|
      ]|
```

(End of example)

Exercise 21 $\quad$ *Verify the following :*

$$\lambda([f]f.(\mathbf{inr}(\lambda([x]f.(\mathbf{inl}(x)))))) \in ((A \vee (A \Rightarrow B)) \Rightarrow B) \Rightarrow B$$

(End of Exercise)

Example 20 and exercise 21 are motivated by properties of negation that are considered later in section 2.4.6.

The ∨-elimination rule corresponds to case analysis as in the following argument. Suppose it has been established that just two cases P and Q need to be considered and suppose it is possible to prove R both in the case P and in the case Q. Then R is true in general.

⟨premises of ∨-formation⟩

‖ $w \in P \vee Q$
▷ $R(w)$ type
‖

$r \in P \vee Q$

‖ $x \in P$
▷ $s(x) \in R(\mathbf{inl}(x))$
‖

‖ $y \in Q$
▷ $t(y) \in R(\mathbf{inr}(y))$
‖

───────────────────────────── ∨-elimination
$\mathbf{when}(r, [x]s(x), [y]t(y)) \in R(r)$

The ∨-elimination rule is used to prove a proposition R by a case analysis on P or Q. Although we are unable to illustrate the full generality of the rule at this stage, the first premise indicates that, typically, R is a family of types indexed by the (dummy) variable w of type $P \vee Q$. We prove R at r ("$R(r)$" in the inference) by showing that R is provable at $\mathbf{inl}(x)$ whenever x is an object of P and at $\mathbf{inr}(y)$ whenever y is an object of Q (cf. the last two premises).

Note that the rule discharges two assumptions. Thus within the **when** statement the variable x is bound in $s(x)$ and the variable y is bound in $t(y)$.

A **when** statement is similar to an **if** statement in conventional languages. Computationally the rule states that if $s(x)$ constructs an object of $R(\mathbf{inl}(x))$ when supplied with an argument x of type P and if $t(y)$ constructs an object of $R(\mathbf{inr}(y))$ when supplied with an argument y of type Q then it is always possible to construct an object of $R(r)$ from an object r of $P \vee Q$. To do so, examine the form of r and if it is $\mathbf{inl}(p)$ bind x to p and apply $s(x)$, if it is $\mathbf{inr}(q)$ bind y to q and apply $t(y)$.

Example 22

$$\lambda([d]\mathbf{when}(d,[x]x,[x]x)) \in A \vee A \Rightarrow A$$

An object x of A that is injected into the disjoint sum $A \vee A$ must either be injected into the left or into the right operand. The exhibited function performs the reverse process.

Derivation

```
1      |[  w ∈ A ∨ A
2       ▷  |[  x ∈ A
3           ▷  x ∈ A
               ]|
               {1,2,3,2,3, ∨-elim.}
4          when(w,[x]x,[x]x) ∈ A
       ]|
```

(End of example)

Example 23

$$\lambda([w]\mathbf{when}(w,[f]\lambda([x]f.(\mathit{fst}.x)),[g]\lambda([x]g.(\mathit{snd}.x))))$$
$$\in ((A \Rightarrow C) \vee (B \Rightarrow C)) \Rightarrow ((A \wedge B) \Rightarrow C)$$

Derivation

```
1      |[  w ∈ (A ⇒ C) ∨ (B ⇒ C)
2       ▷  |[  f ∈ A ⇒ C
3           ▷  |[  x ∈ A ∧ B
                ▷   {3, Example 15}
4                  fst.x ∈ A
                    {2,4, ⇒-elim.}
5                  f.(fst.x) ∈ C
                ]|
                {3,5, ⇒-intro.}
6               λ([x]f.(fst.x)) ∈ A ∧ B ⇒ C
           ]|
7          |[  g ∈ B ⇒ C
            ▷   {similarly}
8               λ([x]g.(snd.x)) ∈ A ∧ B ⇒ C
           ]|
           {1,2,6,7,8, ∨-elim.}
```

9    $\mathbf{when}(w, [f]\lambda([x]f.(\mathrm{fst}.x)), [g]\lambda([x]g.(\mathrm{snd}.x))) \in A \wedge B \Rightarrow C$
]|

(End of example)

Exercise 24   *Prove the following:*

(a) $A \vee B \Rightarrow B \vee A$

(b) $A \vee (B \vee C) \Rightarrow (A \vee B) \vee C$

(c) $A \vee (B \wedge C) \Rightarrow ((A \vee B) \wedge (A \vee C))$

(d) $A \vee (B \Rightarrow C) \Rightarrow ((A \vee B) \Rightarrow (A \vee C))$

(e) $((A \Rightarrow B) \vee (A \Rightarrow C)) \Rightarrow (A \Rightarrow (B \vee C))$

(f) $((A \Rightarrow C) \wedge (B \Rightarrow C)) \Rightarrow ((A \vee B) \Rightarrow C)$

(End of Exercise)

Exercise 25   *Conjecture some more algebraic properties of $\wedge$, $\vee$ and $\Rightarrow$ and try to prove them.*

(End of Exercise)

2.4.4   Universal Quantification

We recall from our informal account of the semantics of universal quantification that, like an implication, the type $\forall(P, [x]Q(x))$ is identified with a function type but that the type of the range, $Q(x)$, may depend on the argument, x. In Martin-Löf's terminology, $Q(x)$ is a family of types, one for each object, x, in A. That is, typically $Q(x)$ will be a type expression containing zero or more free occurrences of x. (Of course such free occurrences become bound in the expression $\forall(P, [x]Q(x))$.)

We can infer $\forall(P, [x]Q(x))$ if it is always possible to establish Q in a context in which it is assumed that x has type P. This is the $\forall$-introduction rule.

⟨premises of $\forall$-formation⟩

$$
\begin{array}{l}
|[\quad x \in P \\
\triangleright\quad q(x) \in Q(x) \\
]|
\end{array}
$$
───────────────────── $\forall$-introduction

$$\lambda([x]q(x)) \in \forall(P, [x]Q(x))$$

Two binders are introduced when the assumption $x \in P$ is discharged. The lambda, λ, binds the first x in $q(x)$, and, as already mentioned, the universal quantification binds the second x in $Q(x)$.

Example 26 $\lambda([A]\lambda([x]x)) \in \forall(U_1, [A]A \Rightarrow A)$

$A \Rightarrow A$ is a family of types, one for each small type A. The function $\lambda([A]\lambda([x]x))$ is the type-parametric identity function.

Derivation

1     $|[\quad A \in U_1$
       $\triangleright\quad$ {Example 8}
2        $\lambda([x]x) \in A \Rightarrow A$
    $]|$
       {Example 6, 1,2, $\forall$-intro.}
3     $\lambda([A]\lambda([x]x)) \in \forall(U_1, [A]A \Rightarrow A)$

(End of example)

Many examples similar to example 26 can now be quoted simply by discharging the assumptions $A, B, C \in U_1$ introduced at the beginning of this section. We give just a few.

Example 27

(a) $\lambda([A]\lambda([B]\lambda([x]\mathbf{inl}(x)))) \in \forall(U_1, [A]\forall(U_1, [B]A \Rightarrow A \vee B))$

(b) $\lambda([A]\lambda([B]\lambda([w]\mathbf{split}(w, [x,y]x)))) \in \forall(U_1, [A]\forall(U_1, [B]A \wedge B \Rightarrow A))$

(c) $\lambda([A]\lambda([B]\lambda([C]\lambda([f]\lambda([x]f.(\mathbf{inl}(x))))))))$

$\in \forall(U_1, [A]\forall(U_1, [B]\forall(U_1, [C](A \vee B \Rightarrow C) \Rightarrow A \Rightarrow C)))$

(End of example)

The ∀-elimination rule is almost identical to the ⇒-elimination rule.

⟨premises of ∀-formation⟩

$r \in \forall(P, [x]Q(x))$

$p \in P$

_____ ∀-elimination

$r.p \in Q(p)$

If r is a function that given an arbitrary argument x of type P constructs a proof of Q and if p has type P then $r.p$ (the result of applying r to p) has type (or proves) $Q(p)$.

Several examples of the properties of universal quantification may be obtained by a straightforward generalisation of properties of implication. For instance:

Example 28

‖ $F, G \in A \Rightarrow U_1$
▷ $\lambda([f]\lambda([g]\lambda([z]f.z.(g.z))))$
    $\in \forall(A, [x]F.x \Rightarrow G.x) \Rightarrow \forall(A, [y]F.y) \Rightarrow \forall(A, [z]G.z)$
‖

This example generalises exercise 11(a). (To obtain the latter replace occurrences of "$F.x$" and "$F.y$" by "B", "$G.x$" and "$G.z$" by "C", and "$\forall(A, [x]\ldots)$", "$\forall(A, [y]\ldots)$", "$\forall(A, [z]\ldots)$" by "$A \Rightarrow \ldots$".) The assumption $F, G \in A \Rightarrow U_1$ may be read as F and G are properties of elements of A.

We begin by establishing that a number of type expressions are well-formed. Note that judgements 6 and 5 are prerequisites for the assumptions 7 and 8, respectively.

Derivation

```
1       ‖  F, G ∈ A ⇒ U₁
2       ▷  ‖  y ∈ A
           ▷     {1,2, ⇒-elim.}
3              F.y ∈ U₁
                 {3, U₁-elim.}
```

```
4                   F.y type
                ]|
                    {A type, 2,4, ∀-form.}
5                   ∀(A, [y]F.y) type
                    {exercise}
6                   ∀(A, [x]F.x ⇒ G.x) type
7               ‖[  f ∈ ∀(A, [x]F.x ⇒ G.x)
8                ▷ ‖[  g ∈ ∀(A, [y]F.y)
9                    ▷ ‖[  z ∈ A
                         ▷   {8,9, ∀-elim.}
10                           g.z ∈ F.z
                             {7,10, ∀-elim.}
11                           f.z ∈ F.z ⇒ G.z
                             {11,10, ⇒-elim.}
12                           f.z.(g.z) ∈ G.z
                         ]|
                     ]|
                 ]|
             ]|
```

In this example we have been careful to use distinct bound variables so as to illustrate the process of substitution in ∀-elimination. (See steps 10 and 11.) We shall not be so careful in the future.

(End of example)

A second example will illustrate further the process of generalising implication to universal quantifications. Note particularly in this example the importance of well-formedness of type expressions.

Example 29

```
‖[  F ∈ A ∨ B ⇒ U₁
 ▷  λ([f]λ([x]f.(inl(x)))) ∈ ∀(A ∨ B, [w]F.w) ⇒ ∀(A, [x]F.(inl(x)))
]|
```

In a context in which F is a family of small types, one element of the family for each object of $A \vee B$, the function $\lambda([f]\lambda([x]f.(\textbf{inl}(x))))$ is a proof of $\forall(A \vee B, [w]F.w) \Rightarrow \forall(A, [x]F.(\textbf{inl}(x)))$. This result generalises the proof of the proposition $(A \vee B \Rightarrow C) \Rightarrow A \Rightarrow C$ in example 20. The well-formedness of the type expressions is a non-trivial part of the derivation and so we begin by establishing a number of judgements of the form

P type. Note that judgement 5 is a prerequisite to assumption 10, and judgement 9 is a prerequisite to the use of ∀-introduction in step 4.

Derivation

```
1       ‖[  F ∈ A ∨ B ⇒ U₁
2        ▷  ‖[  w ∈ A ∨ B
              ▷     {1,2, ⇒-elim.}
3                F.w ∈ U₁
                    {3, U₁-elim.}
4                F.w type
              ]‖
                    {A ∨ B type, 2,4, ∀-form.}
5            ∀(A ∨ B, [w]F.w) type
6            ‖[  x ∈ A
              ▷     {6, ∨-intro.}
7                inl(x) ∈ A ∨ B
                    {1,7, ⇒-elim., U₁-elim.}
8                F.(inl(x)) type
              ]‖
                    {A type, 6,8, ∀-form.}
9            ∀(A, [x]F.(inl(x))) type
10           ‖[  f ∈ ∀(A ∨ B, [w]F.w)
11            ▷  ‖[  x ∈ A
                  ▷     {11, ∨-intro.}
12                   inl(x) ∈ A ∨ B
                        {10,12, ∀-elim.}
13                   f.(inl(x)) ∈ F.(inl(x))
                  ]‖
                        {9,11,13, ∀-intro.}
14               λ([x]f.(inl(x))) ∈ ∀(A, [x]F.(inl(x)))
              ]‖
                    {10,14, ⇒-intro.}
15           λ([f]λ([x]f.(inl(x)))) ∈ ∀(A ∨ B, [w]F.w) ⇒ ∀(A, [x]F.(inl(x)))
        ]‖
```

(End of example)

From now on we shall omit the verification of the first set of premises (those relating to the formation rule), except in some cases where it is non-trivial or is especially relevant.

Exercise 30 Construct proof objects for the following.

(a) *(cf. example 14)*

$$\begin{aligned}
\|[\ & H \in A \wedge B \Rightarrow U_1 \\
\triangleright \ & \forall(A \wedge B, [w]H.w) \Rightarrow \forall(A, [x]\forall(B, [y]H.\langle x, y\rangle)) \\
]\| &
\end{aligned}$$

(b) *(cf. example 16)*

$$\begin{aligned}
\|[\ & H \in A \wedge B \Rightarrow U_1 \\
\triangleright \ & \forall(A, [x]\forall(B, [y]H.\langle x, y\rangle)) \Rightarrow \forall(A \wedge B, [w]H.w) \\
]\| &
\end{aligned}$$

(End of Exercise)

2.4.5 Existential Quantification

In the same way that universal quantification generalises implication, existential quantification generalises conjunction. To prove $\exists(P, [x]Q(x))$ it is necessary to exhibit an object p of P and an object q of $Q(p)$. Thus the proof object is a pair $\langle p, q \rangle$ where now the type of the second component may depend on the first.

$$\begin{array}{l}
\langle \text{premises of } \exists\text{-formation} \rangle \\
p \in P \\
q \in Q(p) \\
\hline
\langle p, q \rangle \in \exists(P, [x]Q(x))
\end{array} \quad \exists\text{-introduction}$$

Example 31 $\langle \mathbb{N}, 0 \rangle \in \exists(U_1, [A]A)$

This example illustrates the dependence of the second component on the first. (The inspiration for it came from [6].)

Derivation
1       $\mathbb{N} \in U_1$
2       $0 \in \mathbb{N}$
        $\{1, 2, \exists\text{-intro}\}$

3          $\langle \mathbb{N}, 0 \rangle \in \exists(U_1, [A]A)$

(End of example)

Example 32

|[$F \in A \Rightarrow U_1$
▷ $\lambda([f]\lambda([x]\lambda([y]f.\langle x, y \rangle))) \in (\exists(A, [x]F.x) \Rightarrow C) \Rightarrow \forall(A, [x]F.x \Rightarrow C)$
]|

This generalisation of example 14 is obtained by substituting "$\exists(A, [x]F.x)$" for "$A \wedge B$" and "$\forall(A, [x]F.x \Rightarrow C)$" for "$A \Rightarrow (B \Rightarrow C)$".

Derivation

1 |[$F \in A \Rightarrow U_1$
2   ▷ |[$f \in \exists(A, [x]F.x) \Rightarrow C$
3   ▷ |[$x \in A$
4   ▷ |[$y \in F.x$
                   ▷   {3,4, ∃-intro.}
5                        $\langle x, y \rangle \in \exists(A, [x]F.x)$
                            {2,5, ⇒-elim.}
6                        $f.\langle x, y \rangle \in C$
                  ]|
             ]|
       ]|
]|

Following the convention introduced earlier with regard to the omission of steps involving the use of ⇒-elimination, we also omit final steps in a derivation that involve the use of ∀-introduction.

(End of example)

Exercise 33   *Fill in all the details in the last derivation. (I.e. include proofs of judgements of the form P type.)*

(End of exercise)

The following exercise is a further generalisation of example 14.

Exercise 34   *Prove the following :*

|[$F \in A \Rightarrow U_1$; $G \in \exists(A, [x]F.x) \Rightarrow U_1$
▷ $\lambda([f]\lambda([x]\lambda([y]f.\langle x, y\rangle)))$
  $\in \forall(\exists(A, [x]F.x), [w]G.w) \Rightarrow \forall(A, [x]\forall(F.x, [y]G.\langle x, y\rangle))$
]|
(End of exercise)

The elimination rule for existential quantification enables one to assume that a proof r of $\exists(P, [x]Q(x))$ can be split into two components.

⟨premises of ∃-formation⟩

|[$w \in \exists(P, [x]Q(x))$
▷ $R(w)$ type
]|

$r \in \exists(P, [x]Q(x))$

|[$y \in P$; $z \in Q(y)$
▷ $s(y, z) \in R(\langle y, z\rangle)$
]|
———————————————— ∃-elimination
$\mathbf{split}(r, [y, z]s(y, z)) \in R(r)$

The first premise states that $R(w)$ is a type in a context in which w is a proof of $\exists(P, [x]Q(x))$. Typically, therefore, $R(w)$ is a family of types, one for each object, w, in the existential quantification. Given this premise, one proves $R(r)$ by first establishing that r proves $\exists(P, [x]Q(x))$ and, second, establishing $R(\langle y, z\rangle)$ whenever y is an object of P and z is an object of $Q(y)$.

Example 35

|[$F \in A \vee B \Rightarrow U_1$
▷ $\exists(A \vee B, [x]F.x) \Rightarrow \exists(A, [a]F.(\mathbf{inl}(a))) \vee \exists(B, [b]F.(\mathbf{inr}(b)))$
]|

Derivation

{*conc* abbreviates $\exists(A, [a]F.(\text{inl}(a))) \vee \exists(B, [b]F.(\text{inr}(b)))$}

1    $|[\ \ p \in \exists(A \vee B, [x]F.x)$
2    $\triangleright\ \ |[\ \ x \in A \vee B; f \in F.x$
3         $\triangleright\ \ |[\ \ a \in A$
4              $\triangleright\ \ |[\ \ g \in F.(\text{inl}(a))$
                 $\triangleright$ {3,4, $\exists$-intro,$\vee$-intro}
5                   $\text{inl}(\langle a, g \rangle) \in conc$
           $]|$
               {4,5, $\Rightarrow$-intro}
6              $\lambda([g]\text{inl}(\langle a, g \rangle)) \in F.(\text{inl}(a)) \Rightarrow conc$
       $]|$
           {similarly}
7         $|[\ \ \ \ \{b \in B\}$
8         $\triangleright\ \ \lambda([g]\text{inr}(\langle b, g \rangle)) \in F.(\text{inr}(b)) \Rightarrow conc$
       $]|$
           {2,3,6,7,8, $\vee$-elimination}
9         $\text{when}(x, [a]\lambda([g]\text{inl}(\langle a, g \rangle)), [b]\lambda([g]\text{inr}(\langle b, g \rangle))) \in F.x \Rightarrow conc$
           {9,2, $\Rightarrow$-elimination}
10         $\text{when}(x, [a]\lambda([g]\text{inl}(\langle a, g \rangle)), [b]\lambda([g]\text{inr}(\langle b, g \rangle))).f \in conc$
   $]|$
       {1,2,10 $\exists$-elimination}
11    $\text{split}(p, [x, f]\text{when}(x, [a]\lambda([g]\text{inl}(\langle a, g \rangle)), [b]\lambda([g]\text{inr}(\langle b, g \rangle))).f) \in conc$
$]|$

The above proof was suggested by Erik Saaman. It is an excellent illustration of the use of a family of types in an elimination rule. (Note particularly step 9; the family of types used here is $F.w \Rightarrow conc$ indexed by $w \in A \vee B$.) Nevertheless I still find the derivation unsatisfactory since the final proof object contains a, to my mind, spurious λ-abstraction and function application. This example has therefore acted as a catalyst for a number of proposed changes to Martin-Löf's rules. For further discussion see [2]. *(End of example)*

Exercise 36   *Assuming that F and G have type $A \Rightarrow U_1$, construct proof objects for the following.*

(a) $\exists(A, [x]F.x \Rightarrow C) \Rightarrow \forall(A, [x]F.x) \Rightarrow C$

(b) $\exists(A, [x]F.x) \vee \exists(A, [x]G.x) \iff \exists(A, [x]F.x \vee G.x)$

(c) $\forall(A, [x]F.x \Rightarrow G.x) \Rightarrow \exists(A, [x]F.x) \Rightarrow \exists(A, [x]G.x)$

Assuming that F has type $A \vee B \Rightarrow U_1$, construct a proof object for the following.

(d) $\exists(A, [x]F.(\mathbf{inl}(x))) \vee \exists(B, [y]F.(\mathbf{inr}(y))) \Rightarrow \exists(A \vee B, [w]F.w)$

Assuming that F has type $A \wedge B \Rightarrow U_1$ and G has type $A \Rightarrow U_1$, construct proof objects for the following.

(e) $\exists(A \wedge B, [p]F.p) \Rightarrow \exists(A, [a]\exists(B, [b]F.\langle a, b\rangle))$

(End of Exercise)

2.4.6 Negation

As mentioned earlier, negation is not a primitive of type theory. Instead $\neg A$ is modelled by $A \Rightarrow \emptyset$, where $\emptyset$ is the empty type. I.e. a proof that A is not true is interpreted as a method of constructing an object of the empty type given an object of A.

Several properties of negation arise immediately from earlier examples by substituting $\emptyset$ for one of the type variables A, B or C. Specifically, the substitution rule we use is the following.

$$p \in P$$

$$\begin{array}{l} [\![\ x \in P \\ \triangleright \ r(x) \in R(x) \\ ]\!] \end{array}$$

_____   Substitution

$$r(p) \in R(p)$$

Example 37 $\lambda([x]x) \in \neg\emptyset$

The identity function maps the empty type to itself. Equally, the identity function is a method of proving that $\emptyset$ is not true.

Derivation

```
              {U₁-intro.}
1        ∅ ∈ U₁
              {Example 8}
2        [[    A ∈ U₁
```

3   ▷ $\lambda([x]x) \in A \Rightarrow A$
      ]|
          $\{1,2,3, A := \emptyset\}$
4         $\lambda([x]x) \in \emptyset \Rightarrow \emptyset$

Notes

(a) There is of course a more direct derivation obtained by replacing A by $\emptyset$ in the derivation (rather than the result of example 8).

(b) An assignment statement is used to indicate a substitution. My apologies to ardent functional programmers but, after all, the semantics of assignment is substitution.

(End of example)

Some examples of familiar properties of negation are as follows. In each case the property is established by substituting $\emptyset$ for the type variable C in the relevant example or exercise.

Example 38

(a) $\lambda([w]\mathbf{when}(w, [f]\lambda([x]f.(fst.x)), [g]\lambda([x]g.(snd.x))))$
$\in (\neg A \vee \neg B) \Rightarrow \neg(A \wedge B)$

(c.f. Example 23)

(b) $\lambda([f]\lambda([x]\lambda([y]f.\langle x, y\rangle))) \in \neg\exists(A, [x]F.x) \Rightarrow \forall(A, [x]\neg(F.x))$

(c.f. Example 32)

(c) $\lambda([f]\lambda([w]\mathbf{split}(w, [x,y]f.x.y))) \in \forall(A, [x]\neg F.x) \Rightarrow \neg\exists(A, [x]F.x)$

(c.f. Exercise 36(a))

(d) $\lambda([w]\mathbf{split}(w, [x, g]\lambda([f]g.(f.x)))) \in \exists(A, [x]\neg F.x) \Rightarrow \neg\forall(A, [x]F.x)$

(c.f. Exercise 36(b))

Examples (b), (c) and (d) are valid judgements in a context in which F has type $A \Rightarrow U_1$.

(End of example)

Note that examples 38(b), (c) and (d) establish "three-quarters" of DeMorgan's laws for universal and existential quantification, viz. "$\neg\exists \iff \forall\neg$" and "$\exists\neg \Rightarrow \neg\forall$". The final "quarter", "$\neg\forall \Rightarrow \exists\neg$", is not generally true in constructive mathematics. Similarly, it is straightforward to establish that

$$\neg(A \vee B) \Rightarrow \neg A \wedge \neg B$$

which, together with example 38(a), forms "three-quarters" of DeMorgan's laws for conjunction and disjunction. Again, the final "quarter"

$$\neg(A \wedge B) \Rightarrow \neg A \vee \neg B$$

is not generally true.

Exercise 39   *Construct proof objects for the following.*

(a) $\neg A \wedge \neg B \Rightarrow \neg(A \vee B)$

(b) $(B \Rightarrow A) \Rightarrow (\neg A \Rightarrow \neg B)$

(c) $\neg\neg\neg A \Rightarrow \neg A$

(d) $\neg(A \vee B) \Rightarrow \neg A \wedge \neg B$

(e) $\neg(A \wedge \neg A)$

(f) $A \Rightarrow \neg\neg A$

(g) $\neg(A \Rightarrow B) \Rightarrow \neg B$

(h) $(\neg\neg(A \Rightarrow B) \wedge \neg B) \Rightarrow \neg A$

Make use of exercise 24(f) in the proof of (a), example 10 in the proof of (b) and exercise 12(c) in the proof of (c). Note that (f) is a curried version of (e).

(End of Exercise)

The empty type, ∅, is an instance of an enumerated type. It is peculiar in that it has no introduction rules. It does, however, have an elimination rule, namely that it is possible to construct an object of any type from an object of the empty type.

$$
\begin{array}{l}
|[\ w \in \emptyset \\
\quad \triangleright\ R(w)\ type \\
]| \\
\\
\dfrac{q \in \emptyset}{z(q) \in R(q)} \qquad \emptyset\text{-elimination}
\end{array}
$$

(For uniformity with the enumerated-type elimination rules discussed later we should write "**case**(q)" instead of $z(q)$. The absence of cases in the expression looks odd and so we prefer the abbreviated form.)

A first example of a tautology that relies on the ∅-elimination rule is the following.

Example 40 $\neg\neg(\neg\neg A \Rightarrow A)$

Derivation

1 $\quad |[\ \ f \in \neg(\neg\neg A \Rightarrow A)$
2 $\quad \triangleright\ \ |[\ \ g \in \neg\neg A$
3 $\qquad \triangleright\ \ |[\ \ x \in A$
    $\qquad\qquad \triangleright\ \ \{\text{example 9}\}$
4 $\qquad\qquad \lambda([y]x) \in \neg\neg A \Rightarrow A$
    $\qquad\qquad \{1,4,\Rightarrow\text{-elim}\}$
5 $\qquad\qquad f.\lambda([y]x) \in \emptyset$
    $\qquad\quad]|$
    $\qquad\qquad \{3,5,\Rightarrow\text{-intro.}\}$
6 $\qquad\quad \lambda([x]f.\lambda([y]x)) \in \neg A$
    $\qquad\qquad \{2,6,\Rightarrow\text{-elim.}\}$
7 $\qquad\quad g.\lambda([x]f.\lambda([y]x)) \in \emptyset$
    $\qquad\qquad \{7,\emptyset\text{-elim.}\}$
8 $\qquad\quad z(g.\lambda([x]f.\lambda([y]x))) \in A$
    $\qquad]|$
    $\qquad\qquad \{2,8,\Rightarrow\text{-intro}\}$
9 $\qquad \lambda([g]z(g.\lambda([x]f.\lambda([y]x)))) \in \neg\neg A \Rightarrow A$
    $\qquad\qquad \{1,9,\Rightarrow\text{-elim}\}$
10 $\qquad f.\lambda([g]z(g.\lambda([x]f.\lambda([y]x)))) \in \emptyset$
    $\ ]|$

(End of example)

Exercise 41   *Prove the following.*

(a) $\neg(A \Rightarrow B) \Rightarrow \neg\neg A$

(b) $A \vee B \Rightarrow \neg A \Rightarrow B$

(End of Exercise)

In presentations of the classical propositional calculus it is common to see a list of tautologies describing the algebraic properties of the connectives. It is usual also to provide one or two examples of propositional forms that are not tautologies, a single counterexample being sufficient to refute each. For example, $A \Rightarrow A$ is a tautology and $A \Rightarrow B$ is not. A counterexample for the latter is $A = \mathbf{true}$, $B = \mathbf{false}$.

In these notes, a *tautology* is a family of types $P(A, B, C, \ldots)$, dependent on the type variables $A, B, C, \ldots$ assumed to be objects of U_1, such that

$$\forall(U_1, [A]\forall(U_1, [B]\forall(U_1, [C]\ldots P(A, B, C, \ldots))))$$

is provable. Given such a family of types P there are now three possibilities:

(a) P can be proved to be a tautology.

(b) A counterexample refuting the universal validity of P can be exhibited.

(c) Neither of (a) or (b) is the case.

Example 42 $\exists(U_1, [A]\neg A)$

A is not a tautology.

Derivation

1     $\emptyset \in U_1$
       {example 37}
2     $\lambda([x]x) \in \neg\emptyset$
       {1,2, $\exists$-intro}
3     $\langle\emptyset, \lambda([x]x)\rangle \in \exists(U_1, [A]\neg A)$

(End of example)

Example 43 $\exists(U_1,[A]\exists(U_1,[B]\neg(A \Rightarrow B)))$

Here we use $\emptyset$ to represent **false** and $\mathbb{N}$ to represent **true**. (Any non-empty type will do in place of $\mathbb{N}$.)

Derivation

1. $\mathbb{N} \in U_1$
2. $\emptyset \in U_1$
3. $\Vert \quad f \in \mathbb{N} \Rightarrow \emptyset$
4. $\quad \triangleright \quad 0 \in \mathbb{N}$
    $\{3,4, \Rightarrow\text{-elim}\}$
5. $\quad\quad f.0 \in \emptyset$
    $\Vert$
    $\{3,5, \Rightarrow\text{-intro}\}$
6. $\lambda([f]f.0) \in \neg(\mathbb{N} \Rightarrow \emptyset)$
    $\{1,2,6, \exists\text{-intro}\}$
7. $\langle \mathbb{N}, \langle \emptyset, \lambda([f]f.0)\rangle\rangle \in \exists(U_1,[A]\exists(U_1,[B]\neg(A \Rightarrow B)))$

(End of example)

Exercise 44   *Construct counterexamples to the following propositions:*

(a) $A \vee \neg B \Rightarrow \neg(A \vee B)$

(b) $(A \Rightarrow (B \Rightarrow C)) \Rightarrow ((A \Rightarrow B) \Rightarrow C)$

(c) $((A \wedge B) \Rightarrow (A \wedge C)) \Rightarrow A \wedge (B \Rightarrow C)$

(End of Exercise)

The law of the excluded middle is an example of a propositional form that can neither be proved to be a tautology, not can it be refuted by a counterexample. Specifically, by substituting $\emptyset$ for B in exercise 21 we obtain the tautology

$$\neg\neg(A \vee \neg A).$$

Quantifying over A we obtain

$$\forall(U_1,[A]\neg\neg(A \vee \neg A))$$

and applying the result that "$\forall\neg \Rightarrow \neg\exists$" we obtain

$$\neg\exists(U_1,[A]\neg(A \vee \neg A)).$$

We interpret the last proposition as the statement that it is impossible to exhibit a type, A, for which the law of the excluded middle does not hold. (The last two steps can be proved formally within the theory. We have not done so because the mechanism for applying "$\forall\neg \Rightarrow \neg\exists$" has not yet been discussed. As an exercise the reader may like to prove $\neg\exists(U_1, [A]\neg(A \vee \neg A))$ directly. Refer to exercise 21 for hints.)

The form $\neg\neg P$ is of interest because it asserts that P cannot be refuted. There are many propositions P that cannot be derived constructively but cannot be refuted. Indeed it is a theorem attributed by Kleene[16] to Glivenko[11] that if P is any tautology of the classical propositional calculus then the proposition $\neg\neg P$ is always constructively valid. Another example is the following.

Example 45 $\neg\neg((A \Rightarrow B) \vee (B \Rightarrow A))$

A classical proof of $(A \Rightarrow B) \vee (B \Rightarrow A)$ when translated into type theory would take the following form. Consider three cases, A non-empty, B non-empty, and both A and B empty. In the first case choose an arbitrary element x, say, of A. Then the constant function $\lambda([y]x)$ is a proof of $B \Rightarrow A$ and so $\mathbf{inr}(\lambda([y]x))$ is a proof of $(A \Rightarrow B)\vee(B \Rightarrow A)$. Similarly, $\mathbf{inl}(\lambda([x]y))$ is a proof of $(A \Rightarrow B)\vee(B \Rightarrow A)$, where y is an arbitrary element of B. Finally, if A and B are both empty the identity function proves $A \Rightarrow B$ (or $B \Rightarrow A$).

This proof is not valid in type theory because it relies on the law of the excluded middle — that it is decidable whether A and/or B is nonempty. The statement that it is impossible to refute $(A \Rightarrow B) \vee (B \Rightarrow A)$ is therefore the best we can hope for.

Derivation

1 |[$f \in \neg((A \Rightarrow B) \vee (B \Rightarrow A))$
2 ▷ |[$x \in A$
3 ▷ $\lambda([y]x) \in B \Rightarrow A$
   {3, ∨-intro.}
4 $\mathbf{inr}(\lambda([y]x)) \in (A \Rightarrow B) \vee (B \Rightarrow A)$
   {1,4, ⇒-elim.}
5 $f.(\mathbf{inr}(\lambda([y]x))) \in \emptyset$
   {5, ∅-elim}
6 $z(f.(\mathbf{inr}(\lambda([y]x)))) \in B$
   ]|
   {2,6, ⇒-intro}
7 $\lambda([x]z(f.(\mathbf{inr}(\lambda([x]y))))) \in A \Rightarrow B$

8   {7, ∨-intro}
        $\text{inl}(\lambda([x]z(f.(\text{inr}(\lambda([x]y)))))) \in (A \Rightarrow B) \vee (B \Rightarrow A)$
        {1,8, ⇒-elim}
9       $f.(\text{inl}(\lambda([x]z(f.(\text{inr}(\lambda([x]y))))))) \in \emptyset$
   ]|

(End of example)

Exercise 46

(Hard) Prove :

$$\neg\neg((A \Rightarrow B \vee C) \Rightarrow ((A \Rightarrow B) \vee (A \Rightarrow C)))$$

(Easy) Explain why the classical tautology

$$(A \Rightarrow B \vee C) \Rightarrow ((A \Rightarrow B) \vee (A \Rightarrow C))$$

is not constructively true.

(End of Exercise)

To conclude this discussion some comments on "indirect proof" in classical mathematics may be of value. Indirect proof (as I understand it, anyway) takes one of two forms. The first form is that to prove that a proposition A is true one proves that $\neg A$ is false. In other words one proves $\neg\neg A$ which, in constructive mathematics is not the same as A. Another form of indirect proof is used to establish a proposition like $A \Rightarrow B$. The strategy is to assume $\neg B$ and use it to establish $\neg A$. This is based on the classical tautology $(\neg B \Rightarrow \neg A) \Rightarrow A \Rightarrow B$. However, this is also not a valid argument form in constructive mathematics. Indeed, it *is* a tautology of constructive mathematics that

$$(\neg B \Rightarrow \neg A) \Rightarrow A \Rightarrow \neg\neg B$$

(this is easy to prove) and, also,

$$\neg\neg[(\neg B \Rightarrow \neg A) \Rightarrow A \Rightarrow B]$$

(this is a little harder to prove).

Thus a proof that $\neg B$ implies $\neg A$ establishes that in a context in which A is true B cannot be refuted. Moreover the classical basis for such a proof of $A \Rightarrow B$ can itself not be refuted in constructive mathematics, but it is not constructively valid because a proof of $\neg B \Rightarrow \neg A$ does not provide a method of constructing an element of B given an element of A.

Exercise 47 *(See [8], section 3.3)*

Make the following definitions (where P and Q are small types)

$$[P] \equiv \neg\neg P$$
$$P?Q \equiv \neg P \Rightarrow [Q]$$

([P] is interpreted as the classical truth of P, and ? is interpreted as classical disjunction.)

Prove the following :

(a) $A?\neg A$

(b) $[A]?[B] \Rightarrow A?B$

(c) $[A?B] \Rightarrow A?B$

(d) $A?\emptyset \Longleftrightarrow [A]$

(End of Exercise)

The following sclose is the one promised at the beginning of the paper. It terminates the scope of the assumptions $A, B, C \in U_1$.

]|

3 A Comparison

The style of proof derivation we have been using is a form of so-called "natural deduction". Its essential characteristic is the explicit delimitation of the scope of assumptions.

In order to emphasise the benefits of the derivation style this section repeats the derivation in example 40 but this time using the laws for preorders given by Hoare elsewhere in this volume. By comparing the two derivations it is possible to be much more explicit in our comments.

We begin by repeating the derivation of example 40 but this time omitting the proof objects. (In fact the proof object constructed in example 40 has no computational content and can be formally replaced by the identity function.)

Derivation

```
1        |[   ¬(¬¬A ⇒ A)
2          ▷   |[  ¬¬A
3                ▷  |[  A
                      ▷    {example 9}
4                        ¬¬A ⇒ A
                           {1,4, ⇒-elim}
5                        ∅
                    ]|
                      {3,5, ⇒-intro.}
6                  ¬A
                    {2,6, ⇒-elim.}
7                  ∅
                    {7, ∅-elim.}
8                  A
                ]|
                  {2,8, ⇒-intro}
9              ¬¬A ⇒ A
                  {1,9, ⇒-elim}
10            ∅
          ]|
```

(End of derivation)

To repeat the above derivation within the theory of preorders we need to provide a definition of $\neg p$ and we need to say what it is to "prove" q. Specifically, we define $\neg p$ to be $p \Rightarrow \bot$ (where $\Rightarrow$ is the relative pseudocomplement and $\bot$ is the bottom element of the preorder). "Proving" q is interpreted as establishing $\top \leq q$.

The properties required in our derivation are given below together with names that we use for reference in the derivation. The motivation for some of the names will become clear later. Note that we have switched to lower case letters to emphasise the fact that we are now working completely within the preorder calculus. The symbol "$\Leftrightarrow$" denotes the equivalence relation. (The symbol "$\equiv$" has not been used because Hoare uses it for other purposes.) Similarly "$\Rightarrow$" denotes implication.

(assumption)	$z \wedge x \leq x$		
(adjoint)	$x \wedge y \leq z$	$\Leftrightarrow$	$x \leq y \Rightarrow z$
(K-rule)	$z \leq x$	$\Rightarrow$	$z \leq y \Rightarrow x$
($\Rightarrow$-elim.)	$\neg x \leq x$	$\Rightarrow$	$\neg x \leq \bot$
($\Rightarrow$-elim.)	$z \wedge \neg x \leq x$	$\Rightarrow$	$z \wedge \neg x \leq \bot$
(absurdity)	$z \leq \bot$	$\Rightarrow$	$z \leq x$

Two rules have been dubbed "$\Rightarrow$-elim". This is because the first is in fact a special instance of the second if we make use of the fact that $\top \wedge x \equiv x$ (NB. Hoare's definition of "$\equiv$" is being used here) and $\equiv$ has the substitutivity property. (Thus, for example, $\neg x \leq x \Leftrightarrow \top \wedge \neg x \leq x$.) Another use we make of this same fact is to observe that proving $\neg p$ is equivalent, by the adjoint rule, to proving $p \leq \bot$. Formally,

$\qquad\qquad\qquad \neg p$
$\Leftrightarrow \qquad\qquad$ {definition}
$\qquad\qquad\qquad \top \leq p \Rightarrow \bot$
$\Leftrightarrow \qquad\qquad$ {adjoint}
$\qquad\qquad\qquad \top \wedge p \leq \bot$
$\Leftrightarrow \qquad\qquad$ {$p \equiv \top \wedge p$, substitutivity}
$\qquad\qquad\qquad p \leq \bot$

Of the above rules only the adjoint rule and the K-rule are stated explicitly by Hoare. All the rules can, however, be derived from the adjoint rule above and the following axioms — all of which are stated by Hoare. We leave this as an exercise for the reader.

$x \leq x$			(reflexivity)
$x \leq y \wedge z$	$\Leftrightarrow$	$x \leq y$ and $x \leq z$	($\wedge$-intro)
$\bot \leq x$			($\emptyset$-elim)
$x \leq \top$			

We are now ready to proceed to a derivation of $\neg\neg(\neg\neg A \Rightarrow A)$. In fact, following the remarks made earlier, we establish $\neg(\neg\neg A \Rightarrow A) \leq \bot$. To streamline the derivation we introduce the abbreviation C for $\neg(\neg\neg A \Rightarrow A)$.

		true
1	$\Leftrightarrow$	{assumption}
		$C \wedge \neg\neg A \wedge A \leq A$
	$\Rightarrow$	{K-rule}
2		$C \wedge \neg\neg A \wedge A \leq \neg\neg A \Rightarrow A$
	$\Rightarrow$	{defn. of C, $\Rightarrow$-elim}
3		$C \wedge \neg\neg A \wedge A \leq \bot$
	$\Leftrightarrow$	{adjoint}
4		$C \wedge \neg\neg A \leq \neg A$
	$\Rightarrow$	{$\Rightarrow$-elim}
5		$C \wedge \neg\neg A \leq \bot$
	$\Rightarrow$	{absurdity}
6		$C \wedge \neg\neg A \leq A$
	$\Leftrightarrow$	{adjoint}
7		$C \leq \neg\neg A \Rightarrow A$
	$\Rightarrow$	{defn. of C, $\Rightarrow$-elim}
8		$C \leq \bot$

Let us now return to the type theory derivation. Apart from the first three steps which introduce the assumptions $\neg(\neg\neg A \Rightarrow A)$ (i.e. C) and $\neg\neg A$ that derivation has exactly 8 steps. Each step can be compared directly with the same step in the preorder derivation. Note that the right hand side of the inequality in the preorder derivation is the judgement in the type theory derivation, and the left hand side is the context for that judgement. What we have illustrated by way of this example is thus Hoare's claim that from the axioms of a preorder one can prove all theorems of the intuitionistic propositional calculus.

The point of this exercise was to draw the reader's attention to the different styles of derivation. In assessing a style of calculation what one should observe is which properties are used invisibly or almost invisibly — because, if the style is well-chosen, these are the properties that are considered most important. In equational reasoning, for example, symmetry and transitivity of equality are used almost invisibly — certainly, explicit mention of these properties is rarely made. As a second example, elsewhere in this volume Bird makes extensive use of the associativity of function composition but that use is almost invisible and never explicitly referenced.

In the natural deduction style of reasoning used here it is the use of context that is made "almost invisible". The rule of assumption in type theory resembles more the reflexivity axiom of a preorder rather than the (preorder) assumption rule given above; the context "z" has to be stated explicitly in the rule $z \wedge x \leq x$. The same remark can be made for the K-rule, the $\Rightarrow$-elim rule and the absurdity rule. In the preorder derivation the context has to be repeated explicitly at each step. Note, however, that in going from 2 to 3 implicit use has been made of the symmetry and associativity of $\wedge$ (in fact in both derivations).

References

[1] R.C. Backhouse. Constructive type theory — a perspective from computing science. Presented at the Institute on Formal Development of Programs and Proofs, Austin, Texas, 26–30 October, 1987. To appear.

[2] R.C. Backhouse. Overcoming the mismatch between programs and proofs. In P. Dybjer, B. Nordström, K. Petersson, and J.M. Smith, editors, *Proceedings of the Workshop in Programming Logic*, pages 116–122, Marstrand, June 1987.

[3] R.C. Backhouse, P. Chisholm, and G. Malcolm. Do-it-yourself type theory, part 1. *EATCS Bulletin*, 34, February 1988.

[4] R.C. Backhouse, P. Chisholm, and G. Malcolm. Do-it-yourself type theory, part 2. *EATCS Bulletin*, 35, June 1988.

[5] M.J. Beeson. *Foundations of Constructive Mathematics*. Springer-Verlag, Berlin, 1985.

[6] R.M. Burstall and B. Lampson. A kernel language for abstract data types and modules. In G. Kahn, D.B. MacQueen, and G. Plotkin, editors, *Semantics of Data Types*, pages 1–50, Springer-Verlag Lecture Notes in Computer Science, 1984. volume 173.

[7] R.L. Constable, et al. *Implementing Mathematics in the Nuprl Proof Development System*. Prentice-Hall, 1986.

[8] T. Coquand and G. Huet. Constructions: a higher order proof system for mechanizing mathematics. In *Proceedings of EUROCAL 85*, Linz, Austria, April 1985.

[9] H.B. Curry and R. Feys. *Combinatory Logic*. Volume 1, North-Holland, 1958.

[10] G. Gentzen. Investigations into logical deduction. In M.E. Szabo, editor, *The Collected Papers of Gerhard Gentzen*, pages 68–213, North-Holland, Amsterdam, 1969.

[11] V. Glivenko. Sur quelques points de la logique de m. brouwer. *Bulletins de la classe des sciences*, 15:183–188, 1929.

[12] M.J. Gordon, R. Milner, and C.P. Wadsworth. *Edinburgh LCF*. Springer-Varlag, 1979.

[13] C.A.R. Hoare. Notes on data structuring. In O.-J. Dahl, E.W. Dijkstra, and C.A.R. Hoare, editors, *Structured Programming*, Academic Press, 1972.

[14] W.A. Howard. The formulas-as-types notion of construction. In J.P. Seldin and J.R. Hindley, editors, *To H.B. Curry: Essays on Combinatory Logic, Lambda Calculus, and Formalism*, pages 479–490, Academic Press, 1980.

[15] M.A. Jackson. *Principles of Program Design*. Academic Press, 1975.

[16] S.C. Kleene. *Introduction to Metamathematics*. North-Holland, Amsterdam, 1952.

[17] P. Martin-Löf. Constructive mathematics and computer programming. In C.A.R. Hoare and J.C. Shepherdson, editors, *Mathematical Logic and Computer Programming*, pages 167–184, Prentice-Hall, 1984.

[18] P. Martin-Löf. *Intuitionistic Type Theory*. Bibliopolis, 1984. Notes by Giovanni Sambin of a series of lectures given in Padova.

[19] K. Petersson. *A Programming System for Type Theory*. Technical Report LPM 9, Department of Computer Science, University of Göteborg/Chalmers, 1984.

[20] J. Stoy. *Denotational Semantics*. The MIT Press, Cambridge, Mass, 1977.

[21] D. Turner. A new implementation technique for applicative languages. *Software-Practice and Experience*, 9:31–49, 1979.

Robert Constable presented some really foundational material. In particular, the concept of the magic hat, that is really the subject of all our discussion, can be described as

magic (🎩) = 🎩🐰 ∨ 🎩

expressing the law of the excluded middle: "rabbit or no rabbit". To do the rabbit count he introduced the formal system HA of Hare Arithmetic. Also, he presented the constructive hierarchy: rabbits, large rabbits, very large rabbits, etc.:

🐰 🐰 🐰 ...

Assigning Meaning to Proofs: a semantic basis for problem solving environments

Robert L. Constable*

Cornell University

Ithaca, NY 14853

Abstract

According to Tarski's semantics, the denotation of a sentence in the classical predicate calculus with respect to a model is its truth value in that model. In this paper we associate with every sentence a set comprising evidence for it and show that a statement is true in a model exactly when there is evidence for it. According to this semantics, the denotation of a sentence is this set of evidence.

Proofs are regarded as expressions which denote evidence. Assigning this meaning to proofs gives them the same status as other algebraic expressions, such as polynomials. There are laws governing equality and simplification of proofs which can be used to explain the notion of constructive validity. A proof is called *constructive* when the evidence it denotes can be *computed* from it. A sentence is constructively valid when it has a constructive proof. These proofs turn out to be practical ways to present algorithms as has been demonstrated by an implementation of them in the Nuprl proof development system.

---

*This research was supported in part by NSF grants MCS-81-04018 and (joint Cornell-Edinburgh) MCS-83-03336.

1 Introduction

If I correctly stated the winning lottery number before it has been publicly announced, many people will be more interested in my evidence for the assertion than in its truth. Even for routine utterances we are interested in the evidence. "How do you know?" we ask. In formal logic the "truth" of a sentence can be defined following Tarski [Tar44] who put the matter this way for the case of a universal statement: $\forall x.B(x)$ is true in a model **m** if the model assigns to B some propositional function $\mathbf{m}(B)$ which has value true for every element of the *universe of discourse D* of the model. That definition ignores evidence. We want to give a precise definition of evidence and relate it to truth as defined by Tarski.

In mathematics there is a persistent interest in evidence even though the official definition of truth does not refer to it. So if I claim that there is a regular 17-gon, then you may wish to see one. The ancient Greeks would require that I *construct* one or in some way actually exhibit it. As another interesting example, suppose that I claim that there are two irrational numbers, say x and y, such that x^y is rational. I might prove that they exist this way. Consider $\sqrt{2}^{\sqrt{2}}$, it is either rational or irrational. If it is rational, take $x = \sqrt{2}$, $y = \sqrt{2}$. If it is irrational, take $x = \sqrt{2}^{\sqrt{2}}$ and $y = \sqrt{2}$. Then $x^y = (\sqrt{2}^{\sqrt{2}})^{\sqrt{2}} = \sqrt{2}^2 = 2$. So in either case there are the desired x, y. But notice that the evidence for existence here is *indirect*. I have not actually exhibited x by this method, even though you might be convinced that the statement is *true* in Tarski's sense. A constructive proof of this statement would actually exhibit x and y, say for example $x = \sqrt{2}$ and $y = 2 \cdot \log_2 3$ are irrational plus the computation $2^{(2 \cdot \log_2 3)/2} = 3$.

We begin to understand how the concept of evidence is defined if we examine its use in ordinary discourse. Existence statements like those above are especially significant. Evidence for **there is an x such that B holds**, symbolized $\exists x.B(x)$, consists of an element a and evidence for B holding on a. Consider now evidence for a universal statement such as *for every natural number x there is a pair of prime numbers, $p, p+2$ greater than x*. Given 0, the evidence could be 2, 3 and given 2 it could be 5, 7, etc. But what is evidence for the universal statement? It should include in some way these instances, so it could be a function f which given a number n produces $f(n)$ as evidence for the assertion, e.g. $f(n)$ could be a pair $p, p+2$ and proof that p is greater than n.

Consider next evidence for a conjunction such as **n is odd and n is perfect**. We would expect to have evidence for both statements, say a pair containing (or comprising) a factorization of n as $2m+1$ and a summation of all of the factors in n.[1] Evidence for a disjuntion such as A or B will be either evidence for A or evidence for B. We also imagine that we could tell which case the evidence applied to.

Consider this implication: if there is a polynomial time algorithm to decide whether an arbitrary boolean expression is satisfiable, then there is an algorithm to determine whether a finite graph has a clique of any given size. This is a typical statement in modern computational complexity theory. The truth value of the antecedent is not known, yet the implication is true. It is true because we have a method to transform any (hypothetical) algorithm for satisfiability into one for clique. It is this method which bears witness for the implication. A more mundane example is this. When I say "if there is a 6 in the array A, then there is a 6 in the array B obtained from A by replacing each odd value and only odd values by 5;" you can recognize this as a true implication because you know a method of taking evidence for "6 is in A", say an index i and the value $A[i] = 6$, to evidence that "6 is in B," the same index i and $B[i] = 6$ will suffice for instance.

What is evidence for a negation such as "4 is not prime." First, notice that I mean "it is not the case that 4 is prime" rather than taking "not prime" as a separate predicate meaning 4 is composite. So in general we are looking at a uniform negation, $\neg A$. This is sometimes equivalent to

---

[1] A perfect number is one which is equal to the sum of its proper factors, e.g. $6 = 3 + 2 + 1$.

some positive statement, such as "4 is composite." But if we do not know anything about A other than that it is a proposition, then we cannot hope to reformulate it positively; so we ask whether we can say anything about negation uniformly in A. Intuitively it seems sensible to say that evidence for $\neg\ A$ is evidence that there is no evidence for A. So the question then is "how do we show that sets are empty?" We cannot do this by producing an element.

One way to show that a set, say described by term A, is empty is to show it as a subset of the canonical empty set, say ϕ, i.e. $A \subseteq \phi$. This amounts to showing an implication, if $x \epsilon A$ then $x \epsilon \phi$. One formula whose evidence set is clearly empty is *false*; that is the definition of the formula *false*, one with no proofs. So one way of proving $\neg F$ uniformly is to prove $F \Rightarrow false$. This is not the only way, but it is sufficient. We might for example prove that $F = G$ and $\neg G$ holds. But also, if we know $\neg F$, then we know that the evidence set for F is empty, so it is a subset of ϕ and so $(F \Rightarrow false)$. Thus we can take $F \Rightarrow false$ as the *definition* of a general negation; we adopt this definiton.

These explanations may not be definitive, but they provide a good starting point. In the next section we define a particular specimen of formal logic and give a precise definition of both truth and evidence. Then in section 3 we examine proofs and show how they encode evidence.

This interpretaion of evidence is not new, its origins go back at least to L.E.J. Brouwer who discovered in the early 1900's that to treat mathematics in a constructive or computational way, one must also treat logic in such a manner. He showed that this could be done by basing logic on the judgement that a sentence is *known to be true from evidence* rather than on the judgement that it is true. At this point in the discussion, we are not concerned with computable evidence exclusively, but with an abstract notion of evidence. In some sense we are extending Brouwer's ideas to classical logics as well. Later we will make connection to constructive logic via the so-called *propositions-as-types* principle due to Curry, Howard, and de Bruijn (for references see [CAB+86,deB80]). This **principle can be seen as formalizing the notion of evidence in *type theory*, see also [ML84], [CAB+86].**

2 The Logic

Syntax

We present a standard kind of predicate calculus. The formulas of our logic are built using the binary propositional connectives $\&, |, \neg, \Rightarrow$ (and, or, not, implies) and the quantifiers $\forall x, \exists x$ (*all and some*) where x ranges over the class of objects called *individual variables*. There must be at least one *propositional function constant*, there may be several but only a finite number of them (for simplicity), say $P_1, P_2, \ldots, P_k$. There may also be ordinary *function constants*, say $f_1, f_2, \ldots, f_m$. With each propositional or ordinary function constant we specify the number of arguments it takes; this is called its *arity*. The arity can be zero. The language will have *terms*, these include (individual) variables written $x_1, x_2, \ldots, \ldots$ If there are ordinary function constants, then the terms include expressions of the form $f_i(t_1, \ldots, t_n)$ where the t_j $j = 1, \ldots, n$ are terms and the f_i has arity n. If the arity of f_i is zero, then f_i is also an individual constant.

A *formula* of the logic is defined as follows:

(i) *false* is a formula (it is a *propositional constant*)

(ii) if P_i is a propositional function of arity n, and $t_1, \ldots, t_n$ are terms, then $P_i(t_1, \ldots, t_n)$ is a formula

(iii) if *A and B* are formulas, then so are

  $(A \& B)$

  $(A \mid B)$

  $(A \Rightarrow B)$

(iv) if B is a formula, then so are

$(\exists x.B)$ and $(\forall x.B)$.

A particular instance of this language that is quite familiar arises by taking 0 and 1 as individual constants (arity zero ordinary functions), taking $+$ and $*$ as ordinary function constants, (writing $+(1,2)$ for $1+2$) and $=$ and $<$ as propositional functions of arity 2 so that $=(x,y)$ and $<(x+(x,1))$ stand for $x = y$ and $x < (x+1)$. In the remaining examples we will write these familiar functions in their usual infix manner taking them as abbreviations for the "official" form. Formulas in (i) and (ii) are atomic. Those in (iii) are *compound* with principle operator &, |, or $\Rightarrow$ (in that order). Those in (iv) are quantified formulas, and their principle operators, are $\forall x$ or $\exists x$.

The quantifiers $\forall x$, $\exists x$ are called *binding operators* because they bind occurrences of the variable x in the formulas to which they are applied. In $\forall x.B$ and in $\exists x.B$, the formula part B is called the *scope* of the quantifier. Any occurrence of x in B is bound. It is bound by the quantifier of smallest scope that causes it to be bound.

A variable occurrence in a formula F which is not bound is said to be *free*. If x is a free variable of F, and t is a term, we write $F(t/x)$ to denote the formula that results by substituting t for all free occurrences of x and renaming bound variables of F as necessary to prevent *capture of* free variables of t. Thus if *t contains a free variable y* and x occurs in the scope of a subformula whose quantifier binds y, say $\exists y.C$, then the quantifier is rewritten with a new variable, say $\exists y'.C$ because otherwise y would be captured by $\exists y.A$. For example, in the formula $\exists y.x < y$ the variable x is free. If we substitute the term $(y+1)$ for x we do not obtain $\exists y.(y+1) < y$ but instead $\exists y'.(y+1) < y'$. See [Kle52,ML82,ML84] for a thorough discussion of these points.

A formula with no free variables is called *closed*. A closed formula is called a sentence.

If for convenience we want to avoid writing all of the parentheses, then we adopt the convention that all the binary operators are right associative with the precedence &, |, ⇒ and then quantifiers. Thus $\forall x.B(x) \& C \Rightarrow \exists y.P(x,y) \mid B(y)$ abbreviates $(\forall x.((B(x) \& C) \Rightarrow (\exists y.(P(x,y) \mid B(y))))))$.

Semantics of Truth

The meaning of a formula is given with respect to a model which consists of a set D, called the *domain* of discourse, and a function **m** called *interpretation* which maps each ordinary function constant f of arity n to a function from D^n into D denoted $\mathbf{m}(f)$ and maps each propositional function constant P of arity n to a function from D^n into $\{T, F\}$ denoted $\mathbf{m}(P)$.

To give the meaning of formulas with free variables x_i we need the idea of a *state* which is a mapping of variables to values, that is $s(x_i)$ belongs to D. When we want to alter a state at a variable x_i we write $s[x_i := a]$ which denotes $s(y)$ if $y \neq x_i$ and denotes a if $y = x_i$. We define the relation that formula F is true in model **m** and state s, written

$$\mathbf{m} \models_s F.$$

Preliminary to this concept we need to define the meaning of a term in state s, written $\mathbf{m}(t)(s)$. The meaning of constants is given by **m**, so $\mathbf{m}(c_i)(s) = \mathbf{m}(c_i)$. The meaning of variables is given s, so $\mathbf{m}(x_i)(s) = s(x_i)$. The meaning of $f(t_1, \ldots, t_n)$ is $\mathbf{m}(f(t_1, \ldots, t_n))(s) = \mathbf{m}(f)(\mathbf{m}(t_1)(s), \ldots, \mathbf{m}(t_n)(s))$.

Truth Conditions

1. $\mathbf{m} \models_s P(t_1, \ldots, t_n)$

   $iff\ \mathbf{m}(P)(s)(n(t_1)(s), \ldots, n(t_n)(s)) = T$

   for P a propositional function constant of arity n.

2. $\mathbf{m} \models_s (A \& B)$

   $iff\ \mathbf{m} \models_s A\ and\ \mathbf{m} \models_s B$

3. $\mathbf{m} \models_s (A \mid B)$

   $iff\ \mathbf{m} \models_s A\ or\ \mathbf{m} \models_s B$

4. $\mathbf{m} \models_s (A \Rightarrow B)$

   $iff\ \mathbf{m} \models_s A\ implies\ \mathbf{m} \models_s B$

5. $\mathbf{m} \models_s \forall x.B$

   $iff\ \mathbf{m} \models_{s'} B\ for\ all\ s' = s[x := a]$ with a in D

6. $\mathbf{m} \models_s \exists x.B$

   $iff\ \mathbf{m} \models_{s'} B\ for\ some\ s' = s[x := a]$ for a in D

Semantics of Evidence

The following set constructors are needed in the semantics of evidence. Given sets A and B, let $A \times B$ denote their cartesian product, let $A + B$ denote their disjoint union, and let $A \to B$ denote all the functions from A to B. Given $B(x)$ a family of sets indexed by A, let

$$\Pi_{x \in A} B(x)$$

denote the set of functions f from A into,

$$\bigcup_{x \in A} B(x)$$

such that $f(a)$ belongs to $B(a)$. We also take

$$\sum_{x \in A} B(x)$$

to be the disjoint union of the family of sets. It can be defined as $\{<a,b> | a \in A, b \in B(a)\}$.

Now we define $\mathbf{m}[A](s)$, the evidence for formula A in model $\mathbf{m}$ and state s

1. $\mathbf{m}[false](s) = $ the empty set

2. $\mathbf{m}[P(t_1,\ldots,t_n)](s) = \{T\}$ if $\mathbf{m} \models_s P(x_1,\ldots,x_n)$
   empty otherwise   for P a propositional function constant.

3. $\mathbf{m}[A \& B](s) = \mathbf{m}[A](s) \times \mathbf{m}[B](s)$

4. $\mathbf{m}[A \mid B](s) = \mathbf{m}[A](s) + \mathbf{m}[B](s)$

5. $\mathbf{m}[A \Rightarrow B](s) = \mathbf{m}[A](s) \to \mathbf{m}[B](s)$

6. $\mathbf{m}[\forall x.B](s) = \Pi_{y \in D} \mathbf{m}[B](s[x := y])$

7. $\mathbf{m}[\exists x.B] = \{<a,b> | a \in D \& b \in \mathbf{m}[B](s[x := a])\} = \sum_{y \in D} \mathbf{m}[B](s[x := y])$

So we have defined inductively on the structure of a formula A a collection of objects that constitute the evidence for A in a particular model $\mathbf{m}$. In the base case, 1, the definition relies on the semantics of truth. Here is an example of evidence: $< 6, T >$ belongs to $\mathbf{m}[\exists y.5 < y](s)$. We need to know that $5 < 6$ is true so that T belongs to $\mathbf{m}[5 < 6](s)$. Truth and evidence are related in this simple way.

Theorem 1 *For every sentence B, model $\mathbf{m}$ and state s*

$$\mathbf{m} \models_s B \ iff \ there \ is \ b \ \epsilon \ \mathbf{m}[B](s).$$

proof

The proof is accomplished by induction on the structure of B showing both directions of the biconditional at each step. The easiest direction at each step is showing that if $b\epsilon \mathbf{m}[B](s)$, then $\mathbf{m} \models_s B$. We do these steps first, but the induction assumption at each step is the statement of the theorem for subformulas of B. To determine the subterms we proceed by case analysis on the outer operator of B. (We drop the state when it is not needed.)

1. If B is atomic, then the result is immediate.

    (1) B is $B_1 \& B_2$

    Then $b \ \epsilon \ \mathbf{m}[B_1 \& B_2]$ so b is a pair, say, $< b_1, b_2 >$ and $b_1 \epsilon \ \mathbf{m}[B_1]$ and $b_2 \epsilon \ \mathbf{m}[B_2]$. By induction then, $\mathbf{m} \models B_1$ and $\mathbf{m} = B_2$ so $\mathbf{m} \models B_1 \& B_2$.

    (2) B is $B_1 \mid B_2$

    Given $b \ \epsilon \ \mathbf{m}[B_1 \mid B_2] = \mathbf{m}[B_1] + [B_2]$, it must be in one disjunct or the other. That disjunct will be true by the induction hypothesis, so the whole disjunction is true.

    (3) B is $B_1 \Rightarrow B_2$

    Given $f \epsilon \ \mathbf{m}[B_1 \Rightarrow B_2]$, we consider two cases. Either $\mathbf{m}[B_1]$ is empty or there is some $b_1 \epsilon \ \mathbf{m}[B_1]$. In the later case $f(b_1) \epsilon \ \mathbf{m}[B_2]$ so B_2 is true and so is $B_1 \Rightarrow B_2$. If $\mathbf{m}[B_1]$ is empty, then by the hypothesis B_1 is false. So $B_1 \Rightarrow B_2$ is true.

(4) B is $\forall x.B_1$

Given
$$f\epsilon \prod_{v\epsilon D} m(B_1)(s[x := v])$$

then for any $a\epsilon D$, $f(a)\epsilon\ m(B_1)(s[x := a])$. So B_1 is true for all elements of D. Thus $\forall x.B$ is true.

(5) B is $\exists x.B_1$

Given c in $\{< a, b >|\ a\ \epsilon D \& b\ \epsilon\ m[B_1](s[x := a])\}$ we have that B_1 is true on a. So B is true.

2. Now we must show that if B is true in model m and state s, then there is evidence for $m[B](s)$. Again we proceed by induction on the structure of B. Clearly B cannot be false, and the result is immediate for other atomic B.

(1) B is $B_1 \& B_2$

Both B_1 and B_2 must be true if B is. So by the induction hypothesis there are $b_1\epsilon\ m[B_1], b_2\epsilon\ m[B_2]$. By definition $< b_1, b_2 > \epsilon\ m[B_1 \& B_2]$.

(2) B is $B_1\ |\ B_2$

Either B_1 or B_2 is true. In either case, by induction there is an element of $m[B_1]$ or of $m[B_2]$.

(3) B is $B_1 \Rightarrow B_2$

B_2 is either true or false. If it is true, then by the induction hypothesis there is $b_2\epsilon\ m[B_2]$. So the constant function returning this value is evidence for $B_1 \Rightarrow B_2$. If B_2 is false, then B_1 must also be false. This means by the induction hypothesis that $m[B_1]$ is empty. But then the identity function is evidence for $B_1 \Rightarrow B_2$.

(4) B is $\forall x.B_1$

Since this is true, we know that for every element a of D,

$$\mathbf{m} \models B_1 \; for \; s[s' = a].$$

By the axiom of choice there is a function f such that $f(a)\epsilon \; \mathbf{m}[B_1](s[x := a])$.

(5) B is $\exists x.B_1$

For B to be true, there must be some a in D on which B_1 is true. By the induction hypothesis, there is a $b_1 \epsilon \; \mathbf{m}[B_1](s[x := a])$. Then $< a, b_1 >$ is evidence for B_1.

qed.

3 Proofs

We now want to show that proofs are notations for evidence. They are expressions which denote objects and thus have direct mathematical meaning. The explanation of proofs comes in three parts. We define first their simple algebraic structure. Then we discuss the conditions needed to guarantee that they are meaningful expressions and to determine what they prove. The statement of these conditions corresponds most closely to what we think of as "proof rules." The format suggests also rules for determining type correctness of expressions. Finally we give the meaning of proof expressions with respect to a model. The method here is similar to that for giving meaning to algebraic expressions or to programs. We can in fact use rewrite rules to define most of the constructors.

The Syntax of Proof Expressions

Let $a, b, c, d, e, f, g, p, l$ range over proof expressions and let m, v, w, x, y denote variables (we will use x, y to denote ordinary variables over D and m, v, w, z to denote variables over proof expressions). Let A, B, C, G, L, R denote formulas. Then the following are proof expressions: variables z, w and

$andin(L:l;\ R:r)$ $andel(P:p;\ u:L,\ v:R.G:g)$

$somein(D:w;\ B:b)$ $somel(P:p;\ x:D, v:B.G:g)$

$impin(z:A.B:b)$ $impel(F:f;\ A:a;\ u:B.G:g)$

$allin(x:D.B:b)$ $allel(F:f;\ D:a;\ x:D,\ u:B.G:g)$

$orinl(L:l)$ $orel(T:d;\ u:L.G:g_1;\ v:R.G:g_2)$

$orinr(R:r)$

$absurd(u)$

$seq(S:s;\ u:S.G:g)$

$magic(F)$

In $andel(P:p\ ;\ l:L, v:R.G:g)$ the variables u, v are *binding occurrences* whose scope is $G:g$ so that all occurrences of u and v in G or g are *bound*. In $somel(P:p\ ;\ x:D, v:B.G:g)$ x, v are binding occurrences whose scope is $G:g$; so an occurrence of x in G is bound by $x:D$. In $impin(z:A.B:b)$ and $allin(x:D.B:b)$, z and x are binding occurrences whose scope is $B:b$. In $impel(F:f\ ;A:a\ ;\ u:B.G:g)$ and $allel(F:f\ D:a\ x:D,\ u:B.G:g)$, x, u are binding occurrences whose scope is $G:g$. In $orel(T:d;\ u:L.G:g1;\ v:R.G:g2)$ u is a binding occurrence whose scope is $G:g_1$ and v is one whose scope is $G:g_2$. In $seq(S:s;\ u:s.G:g)$ u is a binding occurrence whose scope is $G:g$.

To preserve the pattern of the notation we introduce a name for the domain of discourse D. For simplicity we take D to be the name of itself; this should cause no confusion since we could take a name like "domain" for D in the proof expressions and agree that the meaning of "domain" is D.

Correctness Restrictions

We impose certain restrictions on the parts of these expressions when we say what it means for a proof expression a to prove a formula A. For example in $impel(F : f, A : a; u : B.G : g)$ the expression F must be an implication, say $A \Rightarrow B$, and f must denote a proof F and a proof of A. The result is a proof expression for G. The constructor name, $impel$, is mnemonic for *implication elimination*, which is a rule usually written in logic books as shown below (and sometimes called *modus ponens* in the special case when G is B.

$$\frac{A, \quad A \Rightarrow B}{B}$$

In the implication introduction form, $impin(z : A.B : b)$, it must be that z denotes an assumption of a formula A and b a proof expression for B, and the $impin(z : A.B : b)$ is a proof expression for $A \Rightarrow B$. The expression b may use assumption z. One might think of z as a label for the assumption. In an informal proof we might see these elements in this relationship:

> show $A \Rightarrow B$
>
> assume $z : A$
>
> show B
>
> $\vdots$
>
> B
>
> qed

The proof of B from assumption z actually shows how to build a proof expression b which may refer to the label z. For example here is an informal proof $A \Rightarrow A$.

>   show $A \Rightarrow A$
>
>   assume $z : A$
>
> A by assumption z
>
>   qed.

The proof expression built by this derivation is $impin(z : A.A : z)$.

It is interesting to note that the part of a derivation that is sometimes called the *justification* [BC85,CO78] corresponds closely to the proof expression. For example, suppose we look at this fragment of a proof

> $A : a$
>
> $\vdots$
>
> $B : b$
>
> $A\&B$ by *and introduction* from a, b.

The rule name, *and introduction*, is used in conjunction with labels (or expressions themselves) to justify this line of the proof.

Generally in a proof expression, the operator names, such as *andin*, *andel* etc., correspond to the names of inference rules. Subexpressions of the form $z : A$ correspond to *labeled assumptions*, and subexpressions of the form $B : b$ correspond to subproofs of B by b. Thus we can read the following informal proof as the counterpart of the proof expression $impin(z : A.(B \Rightarrow A) : impin(u : B.A : z))$

>   show $A \Rightarrow (B \Rightarrow A)$ by
>
>   > assumption z that A holds
>   >
>   > show $(B \Rightarrow A)$ by
>   >
>   > > assumption u that B holds
>   > >
>   > > show A by assumption z.

In short, variables occur to the left of the colon and indicate an assumption of the formula while proof expressions appear to the right of the colon and indicate why the formula is true in the context of all of the assumptions in whose scope the formula lies.

The correctness conditions on proof expressions are given by rules that are thought of as *proof rules*. Thus the rule for *and introduction* is written

$$\frac{A \quad B}{A \& B}$$

The formulas above the line are the hypotheses, those below the line are conclusions. If we include the proof expressions as justifications, we would get a rule of the form

$$\frac{A \; by \; a \quad B \; by \; b}{A \& B \; by \; andin(A:a; B:b)}$$

This last rule shows the pattern that we will adopt. But one additional feature is needed to keep track of the variables. A proof expression such as $impin(z:A.B:y)$ has a free variable y in it. This represents some undischarged assumption. There are no such variables in a completed proof. But at some points in building a proof expression, there will be free variables and we must keep track of them. We must know what formula or what type the variable refers to so that the type conditions and correctness conditions can be checked. Thus it is usual in presenting a proof to have a mechanism for indicating the assumptions and variable bindings known at any point. This is done by keeping an environment with every rule and showing how the rules change the environment.

Environments will be represented as lists of variable bindings $x_1 : A_1, \ldots, x_n : A_n$. The A_i are either the domain D or formulas. The type bindings arise from *all introduction* while the formula bindings arise from *implication introductions*.

The use of environments may be familiar from certain logic texts. For example, they appear explicitly in Gentzen's sequent calculus [Kle52]. They are carefully defined in refinement logics [BC85]. In programming logics like PL/CV [CO78] they appear as they do in block structured programming languages. Some textbooks on natural deduction introduce the analogue of a block at least for propositional arguments.

The format we adopt for rules is to take as basic units the triple consisting of: a proof expression, the formula it proves and the environment for the variables, written together as

$$\text{from } H \text{ infer } A \text{ by } a$$

where a is a proof expression, A is a formula and H is a list of bindings, $x_1 : A_1, \ldots, x_n : A_n$. We sometimes isolate a specific binding by writing the environment as $H, x : A, H'$ where H, H' are the surrounding context. We call these basic units *sequents*, following Gentzen. Let $S_1, S_2, \ldots$ denote them.

A rule has the form of a production as is customary in logic:

$$\frac{S_1, \ldots, S_n}{S}$$

The S_i are the hypothesis; S is the conclusion. Here are the rules. These define the relationship *a is a proof expression for A* inductively.

Rules

1. $\dfrac{\text{from } H \text{ infer } L \text{ by } l \quad \text{from } H \text{ infer } R \text{ by } r}{\text{from } H \text{ infer } L\&R \text{ by } andin(L{:}l;\ R{:}r)}$

2. $\dfrac{\text{from } H \text{ infer } P \text{ by } p \quad \text{from } H,\ x{:}\ L,\ y{:}R \text{ infer } G \text{ by } g}{\text{from } H \text{ infer } G \text{ by } andel(P{:}p;\ x{:}L,\ y{:}R.G{:}g)}$

3. $\dfrac{\text{from } H \text{ infer } B[w/x] \text{ by } b \quad \text{for } w \text{ a term}}{\text{from } H \text{ infer } \exists x.B \text{ by } somin(D{:}w; B{:}b)}$

4. $\dfrac{\text{from } H \text{ infer } P \text{ by } p \quad \text{from } H,\ x{:}D,\ y{:}B \text{ infer } G \text{ by } g}{\text{from } H \text{ infer } G \text{ by } somel(P{:}p;\ x{:}D, y{:}B.G{:}g)}$

5. $\dfrac{\text{from } H,\ x{:}A \text{ infer } B \text{ by } b}{\text{from } H \text{ infer } A{\Rightarrow}B \text{ by } impin(x{:}A; B{:}b)}$

6. $\dfrac{\text{from } H \text{ infer } A{\Rightarrow}B \text{ by } f \quad \text{from } H \text{ infer} A \text{ by } a \quad \text{from } H, y{:}B \text{ infer } G \text{ by } g}{\text{from } H \text{ infer } G \text{ by } impel(A{\Rightarrow}B{:}f;\ A{:}a; y{:}B.G{:}g)}$

7. $\dfrac{\text{from } H,\ x{:}D \text{ infer } B \text{ by } b}{\text{from } H \text{ infer } \forall x.B \text{ by } allin(x{:}D.B{:}b)}$

8. $\dfrac{\text{from } H \text{ infer } \forall x.B \text{ by } f \quad \text{from } H, x{:}D, u{:}B \text{ infer } G \text{ by } g \quad \text{for } a \text{ a term}}{\text{from } H \text{ infer } G \text{ by } allel(\forall x.B{:}f;\ D{:}a;\ x{:}D, u{:}B.G{:}g)}$

9. $\dfrac{\text{from } H \text{ infer } L \text{ by } l}{\text{from } H \text{ infer } L|R \text{ by } orinl(L{:}l)}$

10. $\dfrac{\text{from } H \text{ infer } R \text{ by } r}{\text{from } H \text{ infer } L|R \text{ by } orinr(R{:}r)}$

11. $\dfrac{\text{from } H \text{ infer } L|R \text{ by } d \quad \text{from } H, u{:}L \text{ infer } G \text{ by } g_1 \quad \text{from } H,\ v{:}R \text{ infer} G \text{ by } g_2)}{\text{from } H \text{ infer } G \text{ by } orel(L|R{:}d;\ u{:}L.G{:}g_1;\ v{:}R.G{:}g_2)}$

12. $\text{from } H, x{:}false \text{ infer } G \text{ by } absurd(x)$

13. $\text{from } H \text{ infer } P \mid \neg P \text{ by } magic(P)$

14. $\dfrac{\text{from } H \text{ infer } S \text{ by } s \quad \text{from } H, u{:}S \text{ infer } G \text{ by } g}{\text{from } H \text{ infer } G \text{ by } seq(S{:}s;\ u{:}S.G{:}g)}$

A proof expression is built inductively using the constructors starting from the axiom *and* observing the correctness restrictions. These restrictions can be thought of as type restrictions on the formation of proof expressions. We give an example.

$\neg \forall x. \neg B(x) \Rightarrow \exists x. B(x)$:

$impin(h : \neg \forall x. \neg B(x).$

$\quad \exists x.B(x) : seq(\exists x.B(x) \mid \neg \exists x.B(x) : magic(\exists x.B(x)));$

$\quad\quad d1 : \exists x.B(x) \mid \neg \exists x.B(x).$

$\quad\quad \exists x.B(x) : orel(\exists x.B(x) \mid \neg \exists x.B(x) : d1 \;;$

$\quad\quad\quad u : \exists x.B(x).\ \exists x.B(x) : u \;;$

$\quad\quad\quad v : \neg \exists x.B(x).$

$\quad\quad\quad\quad \exists x.B(x) : seq(false :$

$\quad\quad\quad\quad\quad impel(\forall x. \neg B(x) \Rightarrow false : h \;;$

$\quad\quad\quad\quad\quad\quad \forall x. \neg B(x) : allin(x : D; \neg B(x) :$

$\quad\quad\quad\quad\quad\quad\quad seq(B(x) \mid \neg B(x) : magic(B(x)));$

$\quad\quad\quad\quad\quad\quad\quad d2 : B(x) \mid \neg B(x). \neg B(x) :$

$\quad\quad\quad\quad\quad\quad\quad orel(B(x) \mid \neg B(x) : d2;$

$\quad\quad\quad\quad\quad\quad\quad\quad z : B(x). \neg B(x) :$

$\quad\quad\quad\quad\quad\quad\quad\quad\quad impel(\exists x.B(x) \Rightarrow false : v$

$\quad\quad\quad\quad\quad\quad\quad\quad\quad\quad \exists x.B(x) : somin(D : x; B(x) : z);$

$\quad\quad\quad\quad\quad\quad\quad\quad\quad u : false. \neg B(x) : absurd(u))$

$\quad\quad\quad\quad\quad\quad\quad\quad w : \neg B(x).\ \neg B(x) : w)$

$\quad\quad\quad\quad\quad u : false.false : u)$

$\quad\quad\quad\quad v : false\ .\ \exists x.B(x) : absurd(v))\ ))$

the proof expression without the subformulas displayed is:

$inpin(h.$

$\quad seq(magic(\exists x.B(x)));$

$\quad\quad d1.orel(d1;$

$\quad\quad\quad u.u;$

$\quad\quad\quad v.seq(impel(h;$

$\quad\quad\quad\quad allin(x.seq(magic(B(x)));$

$\quad\quad\quad\quad\quad d2.orel(d2;$

$\quad\quad\quad\quad\quad\quad z.impel(v;$

$\quad\quad\quad\quad\quad\quad\quad somin(x,z);$

$\quad\quad\quad\quad\quad\quad\quad u.absurd(u));$

$\quad\quad\quad\quad\quad\quad w.w));$

$\quad\quad\quad u.u);$

$\quad\quad\quad\quad v.absurd(v))$ $))$

Semantics of Proof Expressions

We now assign meaning to proof expressions with respect to some model. The definition is given inductively on the structure of the expression and is only given for proof expressions which are correct, i.e. only for expresisons a for which we know that there is a formula A such that a proves A. We will not know that the definition makes sense until Theorem 2 is proved.

In the course of the definition we must apply the meaning function over a model $\mathbf{m}$ to a function body. To explain this we extend the definition of a state to account for variables ranging over formulas. We want to say that $s(z)\epsilon\ \mathbf{m}[A](s')$. But now A may depend on other variables over D whose meaning is given by a state, say s'.

We observe that the variables occurring in a proof expression a and in a formula A which it proves can be listed in order of dependency. For simplicity, assume that all variables, both free and bound, are uniquely and uniformliy named, say $x_1, x_2, x_3, \ldots,$. Let A_i be the type or formula over which x_i ranges. Then these can be listed in order, for simplicity $A_1, A_2, \ldots$ such that there are no free variables in A_1, only x_1 is free in A_2, only x_1, x_2 are free in A_3, etc. Let us call this a *cascade of variables* and write it as $x_1 : A_1, x_2 : A_1(x_1), \ldots, x_n : A_n(x_1, \ldots, x_{n-1})$. Now a state s will map x_i into $\mathbf{m}[A_i(x_i, \ldots, x_1)](s)$ and the appearence of s in the definition of $s(x_i)$ will be sensible. For the remainder of this section we assume that we are dealing with such a state. Now give the meaning of a proof expression with respect to a model and a state.

1. $\mathbf{m}(andin(L : l; R : r))(s) = < \mathbf{m}(L : l)(s), \mathbf{m}(R : r)(s) >$

2. $\mathbf{m}(andel(P : p; u : L, v : R.G : g))(s) =$
   $\mathbf{m}(g)(s[u := 1of\ (\mathbf{m})(p)(s)), v := 2of\ (\mathbf{m}(p)(s))])$

3. $\mathbf{m}(somin(D : w; B : b))(s) =$
   $< \mathbf{m}(w)(s), \mathbf{m}(b)(s) >$

4. $\mathbf{m}(somel(P : somin(D : w; B : b); x : D, y : B.G : g))(s) =$
   $\mathbf{m}(g)(s[x := 1of\ (\mathbf{m}(p)(s)), y := 2of\ (\mathbf{m}(p)(s))])$

5. $\mathbf{m}(impin(z : A; B : b))(s) = \lambda x : \mathbf{m}(A)(s).\mathbf{m}(b)(s[z := x])$

6. $\mathbf{m}(impel(F : f; A : a; u : B.G : g))(s) =$
   $\mathbf{m}(g)(s[u := (\mathbf{m}(f)(s))(\mathbf{m}(a)(s))])$

7. $\mathbf{m}(allin(z : D; B : b))(s) = \lambda x : D.\mathbf{m}(b)(s[z := x])$

8. $\mathbf{m}(allel(F : f; D : a; x : D, u : B.G : g))(s) =$
   $\mathbf{m}(g)(s[u := (\mathbf{m}(f)(s))(\mathbf{m}(a)(s))])$

9. $\mathbf{m}(orinl(L : l))(s) = inl(\mathbf{m}(l)(s))$

10. $\mathbf{m}(orinr(R:r))(s) = inr(\mathbf{m}(r)(s))$

11. $\mathbf{m}(orel(T:t; u:L.G:g_1; v:R.G.g_2))(s) =$

    $\mathbf{m}(g_1)(s[u := l])$ *if* $\mathbf{m}(t)(s)$ *is* $inl(l)$

    $\mathbf{m}(g_2)(s[v := r])$ *if* $\mathbf{m}(t)(s)$ *is* $inr(r)$

12. $\mathbf{m}(absurd(u))(s) = $ any $(s(u))$ when any maps the empty set into any set

13. $\mathbf{m}(magic(P))(s) = $ an element of $\mathbf{m}(P)(s) + \mathbf{m}(\neg P)(s)$

14. $\mathbf{m}(seq(T:t; u:T.G:g))(s) =$

    $\mathbf{m}(g)(s[u := \mathbf{m}(t)(s)])$

The operations inl, inr are injections of a set into its disjunct in a disjoint union, i.e.

$$inl : L \to (L+R)$$
$$inr : R \to (L+R)$$

We know by correctness that $orinl$ applies only if l is a proof expression for L and $orinl(l)$ is one for $L|R$. Similarly for $orinr$. So the mappings make sense in clauses 9 and 10.

In $orel(T_1, d : ; u.T_2.G : g_1 ; v : T_3.G : g_2)$ we know that d must be a proof expression for a disjunction, so T_1 is $A|B$. Thus $\mathbf{m}(d)(s)$ will be a member of $\mathbf{m}[A|B](a)$ as we show. Thus $\mathbf{m}(d)(s)$ is either $inl(a)$ or $inr(b)$ for a in $\mathbf{m}[A](s)$ and b in $\mathbf{m}[B](s)$.

The analysis of $somel(P:p ; x:D, y:B.G:g)$ is just as for $andel$. We know that $\mathbf{m}(p)(s)$ is a pair consisting of an element of D and evidence that the element is a witness for an existential quantifier. In case of $magic(A)$, we must use the axiom of choice to pick out an element of the inhabited type. We conclude this section with a theorem that shows that the meaning of a proof expression is well-defined when the proof expression proves a formula.

Theorem 2 *If a is a proof expression for formula A, and if $x_1 : A_1, x_2 : A_1(x_1), \ldots, x_n : A_1(x_1, \ldots, x_{n-1})$ is a cascaded enumeration of the free variables of a and A with their bindings, and if $\mathbf{m}$ is any model and s any state assigning $s(x_i)$ to $\mathbf{m}[A_i(x_i, \ldots, x_{i-1})](s)$, then $\mathbf{m}(a) \in \mathbf{m}[A](s)$.*

proof

The proof is by induction on the structure of the proof expression a. In the base case, a is some variable x_i or $magic(C)$ for a formula C. If a is a variable, then by hypotheses $\mathbf{m}(a)(s) = s(a) = s(x_i) \in \mathbf{m}[A_i(x_1, \ldots, x_{i-1})](s)$. If a is $magic(C)$, then A is $C|\neg C$ and $\mathbf{m}(a)(s) \in \mathbf{m}[C](s) + \mathbf{m}[\neg C](s)$.

Now consider the induction case. We assume that the result holds for any subexpression b of a, in any state s' assigning proper values to all free variables of b as required by the antecedent of the induction hypothesis.

$$induction\ hypothesis : assume\ \mathbf{m}(b)(s') \in \mathbf{m}[B](s)$$

where B is the formula proved by b for b a subexpression of a.

We proceed by cases on the outer structure of a (see the syntax of proof expressions).

1. a is $andin(L : l; R : r)$

    Then A must be the conjunction $L\&R$ because otherwise a would not be a proof expression for A. By the induction hypothesis the subexpressions of a satisfy the theorem, so $\mathbf{m}(l)(s) \in \mathbf{m}[L](s)$ and $\mathbf{m}(r)(s) \in \mathbf{m}[R](s)$. But then the result holds by the definition that $\mathbf{m}(andin(L : l; R : r))(s) = <\mathbf{m}(l)(s), \mathbf{m}(r)(s)> \in \mathbf{m}[L\&R](s)$.

2. a is $andel(P : p; u : L, v : R.G : g)$

    Then A is G according to the typing rules. Moreover, P must be the conjunction $L\&R$,

L and R must be formulas, p must be a proof expression for $L\&R$, and g is a proof expression for G in which variables u, v can occur. We also know by the typing rules that $u : L, v : R$ are hypotheses in typing g. Now consider any state s' which extends s and assigns $s'(u)$ to $\mathbf{m}(L)(s)$ and $s'(v)$ to $\mathbf{m}(R)(s)$. For this state and for g, the induction hypothesis holds, so that $\mathbf{m}(g)(s') \epsilon \ \mathbf{m}(G)(s')$. By definition, $\mathbf{m}(andel(P : p; u : L, v : R.Gg))(s) = \mathbf{m}(g)(s[u := 1of\ (\mathbf{m}(p)(s)), v := 2of\ (\mathbf{m}(p)(s))])$, and $s[u := 1of\ (\mathbf{m}(p)(s)), v := 2of\ (\mathbf{m}(p)(s))]$ is a state satisfying the condition on s' since $\mathbf{m}(p)(s) \epsilon \ \mathbf{m}[L\&R](s)$ is true by the induction hypothesis.

3. a is $somin(D : w; B : b)$

    Then according to the typing rules, A must be $\exists x.B$, w must be a term and b is a proof expression for $B[w/x]$. By the induction hypothesis, $\mathbf{m}(b)(s) \epsilon \ \mathbf{m}[B[x/x]](s)$, so by definition the meaning of a belongs to the right set.

4. a is $somel(P; p, x : D, y : B.G : g)$

    Then by the typing rules, P must be the existential statement $\exists x.B(x)$ and g is a proof expression for G using x a variable over D and y a variable over B. By the induction hypothesis, the meaning of p is a pair, say $< \mathbf{m}(w)(s), b >$ with $\mathbf{m}(w)(s)$ in D and b in $\mathbf{m}[B[w/x]](s)$. Just as in 2 we conclude $\mathbf{m}(a)(s) \epsilon \ \mathbf{m}[A](s)$.

5. a is $impin(z : P; B : b)$

    Then A is $P \Rightarrow B$ and b is a proof expression for B which can use the variable z assumed to range over $\mathbf{m}[P](s)$. This means that by the induction hypothesis, $\mathbf{m}(b)(s[z := l])$ is in $\mathbf{m}[B](s)$ for all l in $\mathbf{m}[P](s)$. Thus $\lambda x : \mathbf{m}[P](s).\mathbf{m}(b)(s[z := x])$ is a function from $\mathbf{m}[P](s)$ into $\mathbf{m}[B](s)$ as required to prove this case.

6. a is $impel(F : f; P : p; u : B.G : g)$

    By the typing rules, F must be the implication $P \Rightarrow B$, f is a proof expression for it, and the induction hypothesis, $\mathbf{m}(f)(s) \epsilon \ \mathbf{m}[F](s)$. Also, $\mathbf{m}(p)(s) \epsilon \ \mathbf{m}(P)(s)$ and for all states s' extending s and assigning u a value in $\mathbf{m}[B](s)$, $\mathbf{m}(g)(s') \in \mathbf{m}[G](s)$. Let b denote $(\mathbf{m}(f)(s))(\mathbf{m}(p)(s))$, since b belongs to $\mathbf{m}(B)(s)$, then $\mathbf{m}(g)(s[u := b]) \in \mathbf{m}[G](s)$; so the result holds.

7. a is $allin(z : D; B : b)$

    This case is like 5.

8. a is $allel(F : f; P : p; x : D, y : B.G : g)$

    This case is like 6.

9. a is $orinl(L : l)$

    Then A must be $L \mid R$ and l is a proof expression for L. So by the induction hypothesis $\mathbf{m}(l)(s) \in \mathbf{m}(L)(s)$. Thus $inl(\mathbf{m}(l)(s))$ belongs to $\mathbf{m}[A](s)$ as required.

10. a is $orin(R : r)$

    This case is like 9.

11. a is $orel(T : t; u : L.G : g_1; v : R.G : g_2)$

    By the typing rules, T must be $L \mid R$, and by the induction hypothesis $\mathbf{m}(t)(s) \in \mathbf{m}(T)(s)$. Thus t is either $inl(l)$ or $inr(r)$. Also by the typing rules we know that g_1 and g_2 are proof expressions for G under variable bindings for u and v so by induction hypothesis we know that $\mathbf{m}(g_1)(s[u := l]) \in \mathbf{m}(G)(s)$ and $\mathbf{m}(g_2)(s[v := r]) \in \mathbf{m}(G)(s)$. This is what is needed to show $\mathbf{m}(a)(s) \in \mathbf{m}[A](s)$.

12. a is $absurd(u)$

    By the typing rules, A is proved from the hypothesis $u : false$. That is, A is proved under the assumption that there is something in the empty set, $s(u) \in \phi$. But there is a trivial map from the empty set to any set, call it any, so $any(s(u))$ belongs to any set, in particular to $\mathbf{m}[\![A]\!](s)$.

13. a is $magic(P)$

    Then A must be $P \mid \neg P$ and by definition $\mathbf{m}(magic(P))(s) \in \mathbf{m}[\![P]\!](s) + \mathbf{m}[\![\neg P]\!](s)$ which is $\mathbf{m}[\![A]\!](s)$.

14. a is $seq(T:t; u:T.G:g)$

By the induction hypothesis $\mathbf{m}(t)(s)\epsilon\mathbf{m}[\![T]\!](s)$ and $\mathbf{m}(g)(s')\epsilon\ \mathbf{m}(G)(s)$ for any s' where $s'(u)\epsilon\ \mathbf{m}[\![T]\!](s$ thus $\mathbf{m}(g)(s[u := \mathbf{m}(t)(s)])$ since $s[u := \mathbf{m}(t)(s)]$ satisfies the condition for s'.

qed.

Computational Semantics and Constructive Logic

With the exception of $magic(A)$, all proof expressions are given meaning in terms of recursively defined equations. For example, $m(andin(L:l;\ R:r))(s) =< m(L:l)(s),\ m(R:r)(s) >$.

If the law of excluded middle, $P \mid \neg P$, is removed from the predicate logic, then we know that in some sense the underlying theory of evidence is *computable*. If we add expressions and rules which can be explained in terms of computable evidence, then the entire theory can be explained this way.

Predicate logics without the law of excluded middle or its equivalents are in some sense *constructive*, sometimes they are called *Intuitionistic logics* after Brouwer [Bro23]. Arithmetic based on this logic and the Peano axioms is called *Heyting arithmetic* after the Intuitionist A. Heyting [Hey66]. These topics are treated thoroughly in Kleene [Kle52], Dummett [Dum77] and Troelstra [Tro73]. Analysis built on such a logic extended to higher order is sometimes called *constructive analysis* see Bishop [Bis67]. These topics are discussed in Troelstra [Tro73] and Bridges [BB85].

Programming

The PRL programming systems built at Cornell in the early 1980's [BC85,ML84] are based on the idea that formal constructive logic, because of its conputational semantics, provides a new kind of very high level programming language. This idea was first explored in Constable [Con71] and

Bishop [Bis70]. It was later developed by Bates and put into practice by Bates and Constable [BC85]. The semantics of evidence discussed here is quite close to the actual implementation ideas in Nuprl [ML82].

Acknowledgements

I want to thank Ryan Stansifer and Todd Knoblock for helpful comments and Elizabeth Maxwell for preparing the manuscript.

References

[Acz78] Peter Aczel. The type theoretic interpretation of constructive set theory. In *Logic Colloquium '77*, pages 55–66. Amsterdam:North-Holland, 1978.

[BB85] Errett Bishop and Douglas Bridges. *Constructive Analysis.* NY:Springer-Verlag, 1985.

[BC85] Joseph L. Bates and Robert L. Constable. Proofs as programs. *ACM Trans. Program. Lang. and Syst.*, 7(1):53–71, 1985.

[Bis67] E. Bishop. *Foundations of Constructive Analysis.* McGraw-Hill, New York, 1967.

[Bis70] E. Bishop. Mathematics as a numerical language. In *Intuitionism and Proof Theory.*, pages 53–71. NY:North-Holland, 1970.

[Bro23] L.E.J. Brouwer. On the significance of the principle of excluded middle in mathematics. In *J. fur die Reine und Angewandte Math*, volume 154, pages 1–2, 1923.

[CAB+86] Robert L. Constable, S. Allen, H. Bromely, W. Cleveland, and et al. *Implementing Mathematics with the Nuprl Development System.* NJ:Prentice-Hall, 1986.

[CO78]   Robert L. Constable and Michael J. O'Donnell. *A Programming Logic*. Mass:Winthrop, 1978.

[Con71]   Robert L. Constable. Constructive mathematics and automatic program writers. In *Proc. IFP Congr.*, pages 229–33, Ljubljana, 1971.

[deB80]   N.G. deBruijn. A survey of the project automath. *Essays in Combinatory Logic, Lambda Calculus, and Formalism*, pages 589–606, 1980.

[Dum77]   M. Dummet. *Elements of Intuitionism, Oxford Logic Series*. Claredon Press, Oxford, 1977.

[Gir71]   J-Y. Girard. Une extension de l'interpretation de godel a l'analyse, et son application a l'elimination des coupures dans l'analyse et la theorie des types. In *2nd Scandinavian Logic Symp.*, pages 63–69. NY:Springer-Verlag, 1971.

[Hey66]   A. Heyting. *Intuitionism*. North-Holland, Amsterdam, 1966.

[Kle52]   Stephen C. Kleene. *Introduction to Metamathematics*. Princeton:van Nostrand, 1952.

[LS86]   J. Lambeck and P. Scott. *Introduction to higher order categorical logic*. Cambridge University Press, Cambridge, 1986.

[ML82]   P. Martin-Lof. Constructive mathematics and computer programming. In *Sixth International Congress for Logic, Methodology, and Philosophy of Science*, pages 153–75. Amsterdam:North Holland, 1982.

[ML84]   P. Martin-Lof. *Intuitionistic Type Theory*. Bibioplois, Napoli, 1984.

[Rus03]   B. Russell. Mathematical logic as based on a theory of types. *Am. J. Math.*, 30:222–62, 1903.

[Sco70]   D. Scott. Constructive validity. In *Symp. on Automatic Demonstration, Lecture Notes in Math.*, volume 125, pages 237–275. Springer-Verlag, 1970.

[Tai67]   W. Tait. Intensional interpretation of functionals of finite type. In *J. Symbolic Logic*, volume 32(2), pages 187–199, 1967.

[Tar44]   A. Tarski. The semantic conception of truth and the foundations of semantics. *Philos. and Phenom. Res.*, 4:341–376, 1944.

[Tro73]   A. Troelstra. *Metamathematical Investigation of Intuitionistic Mathematics*. Springer-Verlag, New York, 1973.

[vD80]   D. van Daalen. *The Language Theory of AUTOMATH*. PhD thesis, Tech. University of Edinburgh, 1980.

Jay Moore presented the fruits of 18 year's work on producing rabbits automatically. Being aware of the need for a solid foundation, he showed us the most important part of his system, written in LISP, viz. the

CONS - TABLE

The Addition of Bounded Quantification
and
Partial Functions
to
A Computational Logic
and
Its Theorem Prover

Robert S. Boyer and J. Strother Moore[1]
ICSCA-CMP-52   January, 1988

The research reported here was supported by the Venture Research Unit of British Petroleum, Ltd., London, National Science Foundation Grant MCS-8202943, and Office of Naval Research Contract N00014-81-K-0634.

Institute for Computing Science and Computer Applications
The University of Texas at Austin
Austin, Texas 78712

[1]Moore's current address is Computational Logic, Inc., Suite 290, 1717 West Sixth Street, Austin, TX 78703.

Abstract

We describe an extension to our quantifier-free computational logic to provide the expressive power and convenience of bounded quantifiers and partial functions. By *quantifier* we mean a formal construct which introduces a *bound* or *indicial* variable whose *scope* is some subexpression of the quantifier expression. A familiar quantifier is the Σ operator which sums the values of an expression over some range of values on the bound variable. Our method is to represent expressions of the logic as objects in the logic, to define an interpreter for such expressions as a function in the logic, and then define quantifiers as "mapping functions." The novelty of our approach lies in the formalization of the interpreter and its interaction with the underlying logic. Our method has several advantages over other formal systems that provide quantifiers and partial functions in a logical setting. The most important advantage is that proofs not involving quantification or partial recursive functions are not complicated by such notions as "capturing," "bottom," or "continuity." Naturally enough, our formalization of the partial functions is nonconstructive. The theorem prover for the logic has been modified to support these new features. We describe the modifications. The system has proved many theorems that could not previously be stated in our logic. Among them are:

- classic quantifier manipulation theorems, such as

$$\sum_{i=0}^{n} g(i)+h(i) = \sum_{i=0}^{n} g(i) + \sum_{i=0}^{n} h(i);$$

- elementary theorems involving quantifiers, such as the Binomial Theorem:

$$(a+b)^n = \sum_{i=0}^{n} \binom{n}{i} a^i b^{n-i};$$

- elementary theorems about "mapping functions" such as:

$$(\text{FOLDR 'PLUS 0 L}) = \sum_{i \in L} i;$$

- termination properties of many partial recursive functions such as the fact that an application of the partial function described by

```
(LEN X)
⇐
(IF (EQUAL X NIL)
    0
    (ADD1 (LEN (CDR X))))
```

terminates if and only if the argument ends in `NIL`;

- theorems about functions satisfying unusual recurrence equations such as the 91-function and the following list reverse function:

```
(RV X)
⇐
(IF (AND (LISTP X) (LISTP (CDR X)))
    (CONS (CAR (RV (CDR X)))
          (RV (CONS (CAR X)
                    (RV (CDR (RV (CDR X)))))))
    X) .
```

1. Introduction

The research reported here was motivated by a desire to add the expressive power of quantifiers to the logic mechanized by the theorem prover described in [1, 2, 8]. By *quantifier* we mean a formal construct which introduces a *bound* or *indicial* variable whose *scope* is limited to some given subformula or subterm, which we here call the *body*, of the quantified expression.

Everyday mathematics makes frequent use of a wide variety of quantifiers. Among them are:

$\sum_{v \in s} f(v)$

$\prod_{v \in s} f(v)$

$\{v \mid p(v)\}$

$\bigcup_{v \in s} f(v)$

Such constructs are also common in computer programming: all high level programming languages provide convenient "iterative forms:" the FORTRAN DO-loop, the Pascal *for*-statement, the Interlisp FOR statement, the Maclisp LOOP statement. As evidence for the power and convenience of such iterative forms, in the code for our theorem prover we use the LOOP construct more often than the procedure definition construct.

We limit our attention to bounded quantification, that is, quantification where the bound variable ranges over some finite sequence. It turns out that the formalization we employ also gives us partial recursive functions, though we do not focus on that aspect of the solution yet.

The logic to which we will add quantifiers is described in detail in [1] and amended slightly in [2]. The theorem prover for that logic is described in [1, 2, 8]. In section 2 we outline the necessary background information, where we also give an annotated list of references to representative applications. Section 2 can be summarized as follows: The logic is a quantifier-free first-order logic providing for the definition of total recursive functions on finite, inductively constructed data objects such as numbers, atomic symbols, and ordered pairs. The logic resembles Pure Lisp. The theorem prover is a large and complicated computer program that can discover some proofs in the logic. The theorem prover consists of 570,000 bytes of source code and is the product of 15 years work by the two authors. Under the guidance of human users the theorem prover has checked proofs of such theorems as Gauss' law of quadratic reciprocity and Gödel's incompleteness theorem. The logic has proved useful in formalizing the properties of computer programs, algorithms, and systems. The theorem prover has proved many algorithms and computer programs correct, has verified the correctness of digital hardware designs, and has been used to investigate various properties of system designs.

Logic is a vehicle. Ours is a truck. It is not particularly small or elegant, but it is capable of hauling a lot of cargo. A major constraint in our formalization of quantifiers was to take advantage of the existing logic and theorem prover. Quantifiers and partial functions are, in essence, just mechanisms for controlling the application of the elementary operators of the underlying theories (e.g., arithmetic, list processing, etc.). To build a formal system or mechanical theorem prover for the manipulation of quantifiers or partial functions without extensive support for the elementary theories is akin to building a vehicle with no room for passengers or cargo. Indeed, we believe it is a mistake to let the provisions for the sophisticated features impair the simplicity of the elementary theories they are designed to support. Even in theorems involving quantifiers, the vast majority of the logical manipulations are concerned with the quantifier-free expressions inside the quantifier bodies: precisely the kind of expressions our existing theorem prover was designed to manipulate.

In this introduction we motivate our introduction of quantifiers, briefly sketch the formalization used, and illustrate the new theory by exhibiting both schematic and concrete theorems about quantifiers and partial recursive functions. In succeeding sections we give background information, present the formal details of our new theory, construct several proofs in it, briefly sketch the changes made in the existing theorem prover to support the quantified theory, and show many beautiful results proved by the system.

Suppose the user of the logic desires to discuss the list obtained by doubling the elements of L. The expression (DOUBLE-LIST L) denotes such a list, if the user has defined DOUBLE-LIST as

Definition.
(DOUBLE-LIST L)
=
(IF (NLISTP L)
　　NIL
　　(CONS (TIMES 2 (CAR L))
　　　　　(DOUBLE-LIST (CDR L)))).

For example, (DOUBLE-LIST '(1 2 3 4)) = '(2 4 6 8).

A useful theorem about DOUBLE-LIST is that it "distributes" over the list concatenation function APPEND:

Theorem.
(DOUBLE-LIST (APPEND A B))
=
(APPEND (DOUBLE-LIST A)
　　　　(DOUBLE-LIST B)).

However, suppose that in addition the user wished to refer to the list obtained by adding 1 to every element of L. To do so he would have to define the function ADD1-LIST, so that (ADD1-LIST '(1 2 3 4)) = '(2 3 4 5). Should it be necessary to use the fact that ADD1-LIST distributes over APPEND, that fact would have to be proved. One is tempted to say "proved again." But since DOUBLE-LIST and ADD1-LIST are different function symbols, the first lemma cannot be used to shorten the proof of the second.

In the quantified version of our logic we permit the user to write such expressions as:

　　　(for X in L collect (TIMES 2 X))

and

　　　(for X in L collect (ADD1 X)).

The first expression is equivalent to (DOUBLE-LIST L) and the second is equivalent to (ADD1-LIST L).

It is possible to state very general lemmas about quantifiers. Consider for example the schematic form:

```
(for V in (APPEND A B) collect body(V))
=
(APPEND (for V in A collect body(V))
        (for V in B collect body(V))),
```

where *body* is understood here to be a second order variable. (Our formalization does not introduce such variables or other new syntactic classes. We adopt this notation now only for expository purposes.) This lemma is easy to prove because no time is wasted considering special properties of the particular *body* used. This lemma is more useful than the fact that DOUBLE-LIST distributes over APPEND since it also handles the analogous property for ADD1-LIST and other such functions.

The introduction of quantifiers has three major attractions: First, quantifiers are conceptually clarifying. Logical relationships that would otherwise be buried inside of recursive definitions are lifted out into the open. The users and readers of the logic need no longer invent and remember names for many "artificial" recursive functions. Second, it is possible to state general purpose, schematic theorems about quantifiers, thus reducing the number of theorems needed. Third, these schematic theorems are generally easier to prove than the corresponding theorems about recursively defined instances of the quantifiers because irrelevant concepts have been abstracted out of the theorems. Thus, quantifiers are a boon to the reader, to the writer, and to the theorem prover.

The quantifiers most commonly found in formal systems are the universal and existential quantifiers, $\forall$ and $\exists$, of predicate calculus and the λ-expression of lambda-calculus. In [22] Morse defines a formal system in which new quantifiers can be introduced. Such classical formal treatments of quantifiers include the new class of "bound" or "indicial" variables, "quantifier" symbols for which some "argument" slots are known to contain bound variables and others to contain terms in which the variables may or may not be considered bound by the quantifier, and higher-order "schematic" variables to permit the statement of general lemmas. For example, in the expression:

$$\sum_{v \varepsilon s(u,v)} f(v)$$

the "Σ" is a "quantifier" symbol with three argument slots. The first, here occupied by the first occurrence of "v," is an "indicial variable" slot, indicating that "v" is the variable bound by this quantifier. The second, here occupied by the term "s(u,v)," is "normal" in the sense that occurrences of "v" in this term are not bound by this quantifier. The third, here occupied by the term "f(v)," is the "body" of the quantifier and occurrences of "v" here are bound. The rule of instantiation is changed so that substitution only replaces "free" variables and has additional restrictions to avoid "capturing." New rules of inference are added to permit renaming of bound variables and schematic instantiation.

We find such elaborations of elementary logic unattractive for three reasons. First, it is surprisingly easy to get the rules wrong and produce an inconsistent logic. For example, Alonzo Church writes "Especially difficult is the matter of a correct statement of the rule of substitution for functional variables," and he observes that Hilbert, Ackermann, Carnap, and Quine all published incorrect statements of the rule ([12], pp. 289). A. P. Morse (private communication) has observed that Kelley incorrectly states the rule for instantiating the axiom of comprehension in [17].[2] Second, the elaborations complicate the proofs of theorems that can be stated and proved in far simpler systems. Finally, the impact of such elaborations on an existing theorem prover for a simpler logic are enormous. In our system, code for choosing proof tactics is often mingled with code for carrying out logical transformations justified by rules of inference. Such elaborations as enumerated above require modifying virtually every program in the system. For example, many (if not most) of our programs "know" the structure of terms and would have to be reprogrammed to accommodate bound variable slots. Many of our programs explore "virtual" terms that are specified as instantiations of a given term under a given substitution. Such programs carry out the substitution "on the fly" and thus would be affected by a change in the rule of instantiation.

We have discovered a device for obtaining the power of bounded quantification while avoiding many of these problems. Its great advantage is that to introduce quantifiers we did not have to change either the syntax or the rules of inference of the logic. Instead, we introduced FOR as a new function symbol and added some new axioms to the logic to define it. The impact of this approach is tremendous: the old version of the theorem prover is sound for the quantified version of the logic and proofs of quantifier-free formulas are not complicated by the provisions for quantifiers.

Our syntax for quantified expressions is borrowed from Teitleman's FOR operator in Interlisp [28]. The expression:

```
(for X in (APPEND U V)
     when (MEMBER X B)
     collect (TIMES X C))
```

is formally represented in the logic and in the implementation by:

```
(FOR 'X
     (APPEND U V)
     '(MEMBER X B)
     'COLLECT
     '(TIMES X C)
     (LIST (CONS 'B B) (CONS 'C C))).
```

FOR is a function of six arguments. In common usage the first, third, fourth and fifth are explicit constants supplying the *bound variable symbol*, an s-expression to be treated as a *conditional* expression, an *operator* indicating what should be done on each iteration, and an s-expression to be treated as the *body*. The second argument is the range of values the bound variable is to take on. The last argument is an association list mapping the free variables in the conditional and body s-expressions to their values. FOR maps over the range, binding the bound variable successively to the elements of the range, and performs the indicated operation on the result of evaluating the body whenever the conditional expression evaluates to true.

For example, to determine the value of the preceding FOR expression, we map over the

---

[2]We ourselves have never made so many mistakes in coding our system as we have in the few pages of code surrounding our treatment of FOR.

elements of `(APPEND U V)`. For each such element we first determine whether the value of `'(MEMBER X B)` is true; in this evaluation, we want `'X` to have as its value the current member of `(APPEND U V)`, but for `'B` to have as its value `B`. If the evaluation of `'(MEMBER X B)` is true, then we accumulate into a list the result of evaluating `'(TIMES X C)`. During this latter evaluation, we want `'X` to have as its value the current member of `(APPEND U V)`, and we want `'C` to have `C` as its value. When we have finished mapping over `(APPEND U V)`, we return the list of "accumulated" results.

The formal definition of `FOR` is:

Definition.
```
(FOR V L COND OP BODY A)
    =
(IF (NLISTP L)
    (QUANTIFIER-INITIAL-VALUE OP)
    (IF (EVAL COND (CONS (CONS V (CAR L)) A))
        (QUANTIFIER-OPERATION OP
            (EVAL BODY (CONS (CONS V (CAR L)) A))
            (FOR V (CDR L) COND OP BODY A))
        (FOR V (CDR L) COND OP BODY A))).
```

The definitions of `QUANTIFIER-INITIAL-VALUE` and `QUANTIFIER-OPERATION` may be found in Section 7. The definition of `EVAL` is given in Section 6. `(QUANTIFIER-INITIAL-VALUE OP)` defines the value of each quantifier operation on the empty range. For example, `(QUANTIFIER-INITIAL-VALUE 'SUM)` is 0 and `(QUANTIFIER-INITIAL-VALUE 'ALWAYS)` is `T`. `(QUANTIFIER-OPERATION OP X Y)` performs the indicated operation at each iteration. For example, `(QUANTIFIER-OPERATION 'SUM X Y)` is `(PLUS X Y)` and `(QUANTIFIER-OPERATION 'ALWAYS X Y)` is `(AND X Y)`.

This approach to quantification is well known in the Lisp community. So what is new? It is our formal treatment of the key concept underlying the above definition of `FOR`, namely `EVAL`. Formalizing an interpreter for a language within the language is a subtle task that easily leads to formal theories that are either too powerful (i.e., inconsistent) or too weak.

`EVAL` is a function that takes an s-expression and an association list (or *alist*) pairing quoted variable symbols to values and returns the value of the given s-expression under the assignments in the alist.[3] For example, we wish to have the theorem that:

```
(EVAL '(TIMES X Y) σ) = (TIMES X Y)
```

provided σ assigns `'X` the value `X` and `'Y` the value `Y`. However, one must be careful to avoid introducing inconsistency by making `EVAL` "too powerful." For example, if we have, for every n-ary function symbol `fn`:

```
(EVAL '(fn x₁ ... xₙ) A)
=
(fn (EVAL 'x₁ A) ... (EVAL 'xₙ A))
```

then a contradiction arises if it is possible to define

---

[3]In our formalization, `EVAL` takes an additional flag argument which we have here suppressed. Strictly speaking `(EVAL x va)` is an abbreviation for `(EVAL T x va)`.

```
      (RUSSELL X) = (NOT (EVAL X NIL))
```
and
```
      (CONST) = '(RUSSELL (CONST)).
```
For then
```
      (RUSSELL (CONST))
   =  (NOT (EVAL (CONST) NIL))
   =  (NOT (EVAL '(RUSSELL (CONST)) NIL))
   =  (NOT (RUSSELL (EVAL '(CONST) NIL)))
   =  (NOT (RUSSELL (CONST))).
```
But neither the definition of RUSSELL nor of CONST is, by itself, "bad." RUSSELL is just an abbreviation for a simple expression involving previously introduced functions. CONST is defined to be a list constant.

Brutal solutions to this problem, such as disallowing the use of EVAL in definitions or preventing EVAL from being able to evaluate 'EVAL expressions, prevent the conventional use of quantifiers. The former suggestion disallows the definition of FOR; the latter prevents nested FORs since the outer FOR would be evaluating the inner one with EVAL and the inner one involves EVAL.

Such paradoxes arise in naive formulations of higher order logic, set theory, and the semantics of lambda calculus. A mechanism must be introduced to prevent these formal systems from being "too powerful." This mechanism is frequently quite artificial (e.g., hierarchies of types, subscripts on variable and function symbols, notions such as continuity and unusual objects such as $\bot$ etc.) and so clumsy that its presence is frequently ignored in simple theorems (where it would otherwise dominate the proof process) or is suppressed by informal syntactic conventions. Of course, in the formal logic -- as implemented in our machine -- the mechanism cannot be suppressed and its clumsiness is reflected both in the code and in the proofs produced. The evaluation of the relative clumsiness of logics is certainly in part aesthetic; however, we have extensively experimented with proofs involving $\bot$, both by hand and with theorem-proving programs. Our conclusion is that rigorous attention to the potential presence of $\bot$ is very difficult. The difficulty stems primarily from the fact that in the usual axiomatizations, almost any function can surprisingly return $\bot$ if one of its arguments is $\bot$. The simplest symbols, such as = and -> usually have duals: those that "respect" $\bot$ and those that do not. The possibility of $\bot$'s presence haunts every proof step. In our system, it can be very difficult to prove things about functions that are not total, but the fact that some functions are not total does not complicate one bit the proofs of simple theorems about total functions. Although the logical theories about $\bot$ are extremely beautiful as mathematical logics, we have found these logics to be vastly easier to study than to use in practice.

Our solution to the logical difficulties of defining an interpreter is to axiomatize within the logic a nonconstructive function, here called V&C, which takes a quoted expression, an alist, and (implicitly) a set of recurrence equations constituting the definitions of all the non-primitive functions, and which either returns a pair <v, c> specifying the value and cost in function calls of evaluating the expression or F if no cost is sufficient. In other words, V&C solves the halting problem for partial recursive functions. While no such recursive function exists, the axiom characterizing V&C is satisfied by one and only one function. Having defined V&C, we define EVAL in such a way that

>   (EVAL ' (fn x_1 ... x_n) A)
>   =
>   (fn (EVAL 'x_1 A) ... (EVAL 'x_n A))

holds for every provably total function fn, though of course not for every function, in particular, not for RUSSELL above.

The presence of V&C within the logic permits us to address ourselves formally to termination questions directly. For example, using V&C we can introduce a recurrence equation which does not always terminate -- a condition that prevents the equation's admission as a recursive definition under the logic's principle of definition -- and explore the logical properties of the equation, including its termination properties.

Unlike the Scott-Strachey approach [27, 14], our system does not actually provide *functions* as objects. We merely provide *descriptions of* or *recipes for computing* functions as objects. Nevertheless, we can describe any partial recursive function and address ourselves to the proof of its properties. Furthermore, the rules for proving properties of (descriptions of) functions are very similar to those used in the Scott-Strachey system. Within the framework of a formal, logical system, it matters little in practice whether the formulas are thought of as talking about functions or their descriptions (if the underlying rules are the same): proofs are syntactic.

We discuss our termination proofs after we have introduced V&C formally. We now continue with our discussion of quantifiers.

How, in this formalism, do we state theorems about quantifiers, e.g., theorems apparently requiring the use of second order variables? Consider the familiar theorem:

>   (for I in L sum (PLUS $g(I)$ $h(I)$))
>   =
>   (PLUS (for I in L sum $g(I)$)
>   (for I in L sum $h(I)$)),

where *g* and *h* are second order. The statement of this theorem in our formulation is:

>   **Theorem.** SUM-DISTRIBUTES-OVER-PLUS:
>   (FOR I L COND 'SUM (LIST 'PLUS G H) A)
>   =
>   (PLUS (FOR I L COND 'SUM G A)
>   (FOR I L COND 'SUM H A)).

We prove SUM-DISTRIBUTES-OVER-PLUS below. For the time being, let us assume that we have proved the following fact about EVAL:

>   **Theorem.** EVAL-DISTRIBUTES-OVER-PLUS:
>   (EVAL (LIST 'PLUS X Y) A)
>   =
>   (PLUS (EVAL X A) (EVAL Y A)).

Proof. The proof is by induction on L. In the base case, where L is empty, both sides reduce to 0, by expanding the definition of FOR and (QUANTIFIER-INITIAL-VALUE 'SUM).

In the induction step, assume the theorem holds for L and prove that it holds for (CONS K L). Let σ be (CONS (CONS I K) A). The induction step breaks into two cases according to whether the condition COND evaluates to F. The two cases are similar and we show only the case where the condition is non-F. We will transform the left-hand side of our induction conclusion into the right-hand side:

```
(FOR I (CONS K L) COND 'SUM (LIST 'PLUS G H) A)
  =                                                [1]
(PLUS (EVAL (LIST 'PLUS G H) σ)
      (FOR I L COND 'SUM (LIST 'PLUS G H) A))
  =                                                [2]
(PLUS (PLUS (EVAL G σ) (EVAL H σ))
      (FOR I L COND 'SUM (LIST 'PLUS G H) A))
  =                                                [3]
(PLUS (PLUS (EVAL G σ) (EVAL H σ))
      (PLUS (FOR I L COND 'SUM G A)
            (FOR I L COND 'SUM H A)))
  =                                                [4]
(PLUS (PLUS (EVAL G σ)
            (FOR I L COND 'SUM G A))
      (PLUS (EVAL H σ)
            (FOR I L COND 'SUM H A)))
  =                                                [5]
(PLUS (FOR I (CONS K L) COND 'SUM G A)
      (FOR I (CONS K L) COND 'SUM H A)).
```

Step 1 is the expansion of the definitions of FOR and QUANTIFIER-OPERATION. Step 2 is by EVAL-DISTRIBUTES-OVER-PLUS. Step 3 is the use of the induction hypothesis. Step 4 is simple arithmetic and step 5 is by the definitions of FOR and QUANTIFIER-OPERATION again. Q.E.D.

The proof just given can be constructed automatically by the unmodified version of our theorem prover, given the definition of FOR and the assumed property of EVAL. Furthermore, once this theorem has been proved as a rewrite rule, it can be instantiated and used by a standard term rewrite system. For example, consider the term

```
(for K in (FROM-TO 0 N)
     when (PRIME K)
     sum (PLUS K (SQ K))).
```

This term is an abbreviation for:

```
(FOR 'K (FROM-TO 0 N)
     '(PRIME K)
     'SUM '(PLUS K (SQ K))
     NIL).
```

Call this the "target" term. The left-hand side of the theorem SUM-DISTRIBUTES-OVER-PLUS,

```
(FOR I L COND 'SUM (LIST 'PLUS G H) A)
```

matches the target term under the instantiation that replaces I with 'K, L with (FROM-TO 0 N), COND with '(PRIME K), G with 'K, H with '(SQ K), and A with NIL. Thus we can replace the target with the instantiation of the right-hand side of SUM-DISTRIBUTES-OVER-PLUS, which may be abbreviated:

```
(PLUS (for K in (FROM-TO 0 N)
          when (PRIME K)
          sum K)
      (for K in (FROM-TO 0 N)
          when (PRIME K)
          sum (SQ K))).
```

Thus, our formalization of FOR permits the statement, proof, and use of "schematic" lemmas without any change in the logic.

Recall the primary advantage of introducing FOR as an ordinary function symbol: the existing theorem prover is sound for the quantified logic. While the existing theorem prover may not be very "smart" about quantified expressions, its proofs of unquantified theorems remain unchanged and its manipulations of quantified formulas are correct. To our surprise, the system can prove a wide variety of theorems about quantifiers and it has successfully applied those theorems in other proofs.

We have added several new proof techniques explicitly for dealing with FOR, EVAL, and V&C. We describe them briefly in this paper and illustrate several mechanical proofs, including a proof of the Binomial Theorem and some termination proofs.

2. Background: The Unquantified Logic, Its Theorem Prover and Capabilities

Readers already familiar with our logic and theorem prover can skip this section.

We here describe the unquantified logic and its theorem prover. In so doing we familiarize the reader with the working logic. We also put into perspective one of the major constraints on our quantifier work: the new theory and theorem prover should be as rugged and practicable as the old.

In [1, 2, 8] we describe a quantifier-free first-order logic and a large and complicated computer program that proves theorems in that logic. The major application of the logic and theorem prover is the formal verification of properties of computer programs, algorithms, system designs, etc. In this section we describe the logic and the theorem prover briefly and we list some of the major applications.

2.1. The Unquantified Logic

A complete and precise definition of the logic can be found in Chapter III of [1] together with the minor revisions detailed in section 3.1 of [2].

We use the prefix syntax of Pure Lisp [21] to write down terms. For example, we write (PLUS I J) where others might write PLUS(I,J) or I+J.

The logic is first-order, quantifier free, and constructive. It is formally defined as an extension of propositional calculus with variables, function symbols, and the equality relation. We add axioms defining the following:

- The 0-ary Boolean functions TRUE and FALSE. We abbreviate the terms (TRUE) and (FALSE) as T and F respectively;
- The if-then-else function, IF, with the property that (IF x y z) is z if x is F and y otherwise;
- the Boolean "connector functions" AND, OR, NOT, and IMPLIES; for example, (NOT p) is T if p is F and F otherwise;
- the equality function EQUAL, with the property that (EQUAL x y) is T or F according to whether x is y;
- inductively constructed objects, including:
  - Natural Numbers. Natural numbers are built from the constant (ZERO) by successive applications of the constructor function ADD1. The function NUMBERP recognizes natural numbers, e.g., is T or F according to whether its argument is a natural number or not. The function SUB1 returns the predecessor of a non-0 natural number.
  - Ordered Pairs. Given two arbitrary objects, the function CONS returns an ordered pair containing them. The function LISTP recognizes such pairs. The functions CAR and CDR return the two components of such a pair. They return 0 if given a non-pair.
  - Literal Atoms. Given an arbitrary object, the function PACK constructs an atomic symbol with the given object as its "print name." LITATOM recognizes such objects and UNPACK returns the print name.

  We call each of the classes above a "shell." T and F are each considered the elements of two singleton shells. Axioms insure that all shell classes are disjoint;
- the definitions of several useful functions, including:
  - LESSP which, when applied to two natural numbers, returns T or F according to whether the first is smaller than the second;
  - LEX2, which, when applied to two pairs of naturals, returns T or F according to whether the first is lexicographically smaller than the second; and
  - COUNT which, when applied to an inductively constructed object, returns its "size;" for example, the COUNT of an ordered pair is one greater than the sum of the COUNTs of the components.

The logic provides a principle under which the user can extend it by the addition of new shells. By instantiating a set of axiom schemas the user can obtain a set of axioms describing a new class of inductively constructed n-tuples with type-restrictions on each component. For each shell there is a recognizer (e.g., LISTP for the ordered pair shell), a constructor (e.g., CONS), an optional empty object (e.g., there is none for the ordered pairs but (ZERO) is the empty natural number), and n accessors (e.g., CAR and CDR).

The logic provides a principle of recursive definition under which new function symbols may be introduced. Consider the definition of the list concatenation function:

Definition.
```
(APPEND X Y)
   =
(IF (LISTP X)
    (CONS (CAR X) (APPEND (CDR X) Y))
    Y) .
```

The equations submitted as definitions are accepted as new axioms under certain conditions that guarantee that one and only one function satisfies the equation. One of the conditions is that certain derived formulas be theorems. Intuitively, these formulas insure that the recursion "terminates" by exhibiting a "measure" of the arguments that decreases, in a well-founded sense, in each recursion. A suitable derived formula for APPEND is:

```
(IMPLIES (LISTP X)
         (LESSP (COUNT (CDR X))
                (COUNT X))).
```

However, in general the user of the logic is permitted to choose an arbitrary measure function (COUNT was chosen above) and one of several relations (LESSP above).

The rules of inference of the logic, in addition to those of propositional calculus and equality, include mathematical induction. The formulation of the induction principle is similar to that of the definitional principle. To justify an induction schema it is necessary to prove certain theorems that establish that, under a given measure, the inductive hypotheses are about "smaller" objects than the conclusion.

Using induction it is possible to prove such theorems as the associativity of APPEND:

Theorem.
```
(EQUAL (APPEND (APPEND A B) C)
       (APPEND A (APPEND B C))).
```

2.2. The Mechanization of the Unquantified Logic

The theorem prover for the unquantified logic, as it stood in 1979, is described completely in [1]. Many improvements have been added since. In [2] we describe a "metafunction" facility which permits the user to define new proof procedures in the logic, prove them correct mechanically, and have them used efficiently in subsequent proof attempts. During the period 1980-1985 a linear arithmetic decision procedure was integrated into the rule-driven simplifier. The problems of integrating a decision procedure into a heuristic theorem prover for a richer theory are discussed in [8]. The theorem prover is briefly sketched here.

The theorem prover is a computer program that takes as input a term in the logic and repeatedly transforms it in an effort to reduce it to non-F. The theorem prover employs eight basic transformations:
- decision procedures for propositional calculus, equality, and linear arithmetic;
- term rewriting based on axioms, definitions and previously proved lemmas;
- application of verified user-supplied simplifiers called "metafunctions;"
- renaming of variables to eliminate "destructive" functions in favor of "constructive" ones;
- heuristic use of equality hypotheses;
- generalization by the replacement of terms by type-restricted variables;
- elimination of apparently irrelevant hypotheses; and
- mathematical induction.

The theorem prover contains many heuristics to control the orchestration of these basic techniques.

In a shallow sense, the theorem prover is fully automatic: the system accepts no advice or directives from the user once a proof attempt has started. The only way the user can alter the behavior of the system during a proof attempt is to abort the proof attempt. However, in a deeper sense, the theorem prover is interactive: the system's behavior is influenced by the data base of lemmas which have already been formulated by the user and proved by the system. Each conjecture, once proved, is converted into one or more "rules" which guide the theorem prover's actions in subsequent proof attempts.

A data base is thus more than a logical theory: it is a set of rules for proving theorems in the given theory. The user leads the theorem prover to "difficult" proofs by "programming" its rule base. Given a goal theorem, the user generally discovers a proof himself, identifies the key steps in the proof, and then formulates them as lemmas, paying particular attention to their interpretation as rules.

The key role of the user in our system is guiding the theorem prover to proofs by the strategic selection of the sequence of theorems to prove and the proper formulation of those theorems. Successful users of the system must know how to prove theorems in the logic and must understand how the theorem prover interprets them as rules.

2.3. Capabilities of the Unquantified Theorem Prover

What can be formalized in the unquantified logic? What can be proved by the unquantified version of the theorem prover? We indicate answers to these questions by discussing some of the applications of that theorem prover.

Below is an annotated list of selected references to theorems proved by the system. The reader should understand, in view of the foregoing remarks on the role of the user, that -- for the deep theorems at least -- the theorem prover did not so much *discover* proofs as *check* proofs sketched by the user.

- **Elementary List Processing**: Many elementary theorems about list processing are discussed among the examples in [1]. The appendix includes theorems proved about such concepts as concatenation, membership, permuting (including reversing and sorting) and tree exploration.

- **Elementary Number Theory**: Euclid's Theorem and the existence and uniqueness of prime factorizations are proved in [1]. A version of the pigeon hole principle and Fermat's theorem are proved in [6]. Wilson's Theorem is proved in [23]. Finally, Gauss' Law of Quadratic Reciprocity has been checked; the theorem, its definitions, and the lemmas suggested by Russinoff are included among the examples in the standard distribution of the theorem-proving system.

- **Metamathematics**: The soundness and completeness of a decision procedure for propositional calculus, similar to the Wang algorithm, is proved in [1]. The soundness of an arithmetic simplifier for the logic is proved in [2]. The Turing completeness of Pure LISP is proved in [10]. The recursive unsolvability of the halting problem for Pure LISP is proved in [7]. The Tautology Theorem, i.e., that every tautology has a proof in Shoenfield's formal system, is proved in [24]. The Church-Rosser theorem is proved in [25]. Gödel's incompleteness theorem is proved in [26].

- **Communications Protocols**: Safety properties of two transport protocols, the Stenning protocol and the "NanoTCP" protocol, are proved in [13].

- **Concurrent Algorithms**: A mechanized theory of "simple" sorting networks and a proof of the equivalence of sequential and parallel executions of an insertion sort program are described in [18]. A more general treatment of sorting networks and an equivalence proof for a bitonic sort are given in [15]. A proof of the optimality of a given transformation for introducing concurrency into sorting networks is described in [19].

- **Fortran Programs**: A verification condition generator for a subset of ANSI Fortran 66 and 77 is presented in [3]. The same paper describes the correctness proof of a Fortran implementation of the Boyer-Moore fast string searching algorithm. A correctness proof for a Fortran implementation of an integer square root algorithm based on Newton's method is described in [4]. The proof of a linear time majority vote algorithm in Fortran is given in [5].

- **Real Time Control**: A simple real time control problem is considered in [11]. The paper presents a recursive definition of a "simulator" for a simple physical system -- a vehicle attempting to navigate a straightline course in a varying cross-wind. Two theorems are proved about the simulated vehicle: the vehicle does not wander outside of a certain corridor if the wind changes "smoothly" and the vehicle homes to the proper course if the wind stays steady for a certain amount of time.

- **Assembly Language**: A simple assembly language for a stack machine is formalized in [1]. The book also gives a correctness proof for a function that compiles expressions into that assembly language. In our standard benchmark of definitions and theorems is a collection that defines another simple assembly language, including "jump" and "move to memory" instructions, and proves the correctness of a program that iteratively computes the sum of the integers from 0 to n. The correctness proof is complicated by the fact that the instructions are fetched from the same memory being modified by the execution of the program. The list of events is included in the standard distribution of our theorem-proving system.

- **Hardware Verification**: The correctness of a ripple carry adder is given in [16]. The adder is a recursively defined function which maps a pair of bit vectors and an input carry bit to a bit vector and an output carry bit. The theorem establishes that the natural number interpretation of the output is the Peano sum of the natural number interpretations of the inputs, with appropriate consideration of the carry flags. An analogous result is proved for twos-complement integer arithmetic. The recursive description of the circuit can be used to generate an adder of arbitrary width. A 16-bit wide version is shown. Propagate-generate and conditional-sum adders have also been proved correct. Also in [16] is the correctness proof of the combinational logic for a 16-bit wide arithmetic logical unit providing the standard operations on bit vectors, natural numbers, and integers. The dissertation then presents a recursively described microcoded cpu of about 2000 gates called the FM8501 and proves that the device correctly implements an instruction set defined by a high-level interpreter.

3. The Formal Definition of V&C

In order to add the power of quantifiers and partial functions we extend the logic of [1] by (a) adopting the abbreviation conventions of [2], (b) adding definitions of several recursive functions, (c) adding several simple axioms defining functions that map between syntactic objects (e.g., function symbols) and objects in the logic (e.g., LITATOM constants), (d) adding an axiom describing the uncomputable function V&C, and then (e) defining several useful functions on top of V&C. In this section we take steps (a)-(d).

Technically, the extended logic remains first-order (though we have some of the power of second order variables and functional objects) and quantifier free (though we have some of the power of quantifiers). However, the extended logic is non-constructive.

3.1. Explicit Values, Abbreviations and Quotations

We start with the logic described in Chapter III of [1].[4] We add to that logic a new convention for writing down certain constants. The convention is, essentially, the "quote" or "dot" notation of Lisp.

In the "formal syntax" of the logic every term is either a variable symbol or is the application of an n-ary function symbol fn to n other terms, t_1, ..., t_n, written (fn t_1 ... t_n).

The "extended syntax" of the logic provides succinct abbreviations for certain constants (i.e., variable-free terms), namely those composed entirely of shell constructors and empty shell objects. We call such terms *explicit value terms*. See [2] for details.

Here are some examples of explicit value terms displayed in the formal syntax:

(ADD1 (ADD1 (ZERO)))

(CONS (TRUE) (CONS (FALSE) (ZERO)))

(PACK (CONS (ADD1 (ZERO)) (ZERO)))

Explicit value terms play a key role in our formalization of quantifiers and partial functions because they are used to encode the terms of the logic as objects in the logic. Before discussing the "quotation" of terms we illustrate the notation in which explicit value terms are usually displayed.

Nests of ADD1's around (ZERO) are abbreviated by natural numbers in decimal notation. Thus, the term (ADD1 (ADD1 (ZERO))) may be abbreviated 2.

Literal atoms constructed from certain lists of ASCII character codes are abbreviated by quoted symbols. For example, the term (PACK (CONS 65 (CONS 66 (CONS 67 0)))) may be abbreviated 'ABC. (The ASCII codes for the letters "A", "B" and "C" are, respectively, 65, 66, and 67.) The term 'NIL is further abbreviated NIL.

Terms of the form (CONS t_1 (CONS t_2 ... (CONS t_n NIL) ...)) may be abbreviated (LIST t_1 t_2 ... t_n).

Finally, lists of explicit values may be abbreviated with the "dot notation" of Pure Lisp. For example, the explicit value term:

(LIST (CONS 'X 7)

---

[4]Actually, we have revised the logic in three ways that are unimportant to the thrust of the current work. (1) We have abandoned the old convention for writing down explicit LITATOMS and adopt a new one described here. (2) NIL is no longer the bottom object of the LITATOM shell -- the shell has no bottom object now. (3) The default value returned when CAR or CDR is applied to a non-LISTP is 0, now, instead of NIL. These changes to the theory were described in [2].

```
            (CONS 'Y 8)
            (CONS 'Z 9))
```
may be abbreviated ' ((X . 7) (Y . 8) (Z . 9)). The explicit term
```
      (LIST 'PLUS
            (LIST 'ADD1 'X)
            'Y)
```
may be abbreviated ' (PLUS (ADD1 X) Y).

The "quote notation" just illustrated has a remarkable relationship to the formal syntax of the logic itself.

The formation rules for the functions and variable symbols of our language are such that to each symbol, **sym**, there corresponds a **LITATOM** which we write '**sym**. For example, X is a variable symbol and 'X or (PACK (CONS 88 0)) is a **LITATOM**. ADD1 is a function symbol and 'ADD1 is a **LITATOM**.

To each term, t, there corresponds an explicit value term, 't, which may be written down by writing down t in the formal syntax and preceding it with a single quote mark. For example, (ADD1 X) is a term in the logic, and ' (ADD1 X) is an explicit value term, namely (CONS 'ADD1 (CONS 'X NIL)), or, using fewer abbreviations:

```
      (CONS (PACK (CONS 65
                        (CONS 68
                              (CONS 68 (CONS 49 0))))))
            (CONS (PACK (CONS 88 0))
                  (PACK (CONS 78
                              (CONS 73 (CONS 76 0)))))))).
```

We call 't a "quotation" of t. The quotation of a term is an explicit value term that "represents" the given term. We define the notion precisely in [2]. It turns out that terms have many quotations. For example, each of the explicit value terms below is a quotation of (PLUS 1 X):

    ' (PLUS (ADD1 (ZERO)) X)

    ' (PLUS (ADD1 (QUOTE 0)) X)

    ' (PLUS (QUOTE 1) X)

The reader should note that the notion of "quotation" is not, technically, an extension to the logic, merely a convention for referring to certain constants in it.

3.2. The Subfunctions of V&C

We extend the logic by the definition of several recursive functions. These definitions are all admissible under the definitional principle. These functions are auxilliary to **V&C**; the reader may wish to study them only after reading the definition of **V&C** in the next subsection.

(ASSOC X ALIST) returns the first pair in **ALIST** whose **CAR** is **X**, or **F** if no such pair exists:

Definition.
```
(ASSOC X ALIST)
  =
(IF (NLISTP ALIST)
    F
    (IF (EQUAL X (CAAR ALIST))
        (CAR ALIST)
        (ASSOC X (CDR ALIST)))).
```

(MEMBER X L) returns T or F according to whether X is an element of L:

Definition.
```
(MEMBER X L)
  =
(IF (NLISTP L)
    F
    (IF (EQUAL X (CAR L))
        T
        (MEMBER X (CDR L)))).
```

(STRIP-CARS L) returns a list of the successive CARs of the elements of L:

Definition.
```
(STRIP-CARS L)
  =
(IF (NLISTP L)
    NIL
    (CONS (CAAR L) (STRIP-CARS (CDR L)))).
```

(SUM-CDRS L) returns the sum of the natural numbers in the CDRs of the elements of L:

Definition.
```
(SUM-CDRS L)
  =
(IF (NLISTP L)
    0
    (PLUS (CDAR L) (SUM-CDRS (CDR L)))).
```

(PAIRLIST L1 L2) returns the list of pairs of corresponding elements of L1 and L2:

Definition.
```
(PAIRLIST L1 L2)
  =
(IF (LISTP L1)
    (CONS (CONS (CAR L1) (CAR L2))
          (PAIRLIST (CDR L1) (CDR L2)))
    NIL).
```

(FIX-COST VC N) treats VC as though it is either a "value-cost" pair or F. If VC is a "value-cost" pair, then FIX-COST adds N into the second element of the pair; otherwise, FIX-COST returns F.

Definition.
(FIX-COST VC N)
=
(IF VC
    (CONS (CAR VC) (PLUS N (CDR VC)))
    F).

In addition we add axioms characterizing four new functions. These functions are essentially just tables that give information about the LITATOMs in the logic corresponding to function symbols in the language. These four functions could be defined for any given extension of the logic. But because the logic may be extended by the user with the shell and definitional principles, these functions are in fact characterized by axiom schemas.

(SUBRP X) is T or F according to whether X is the LITATOM corresponding to one of the primitive function symbols (listed below) or a constructor, recognizer, bottom, or accessor function symbol of a shell. E.g., (SUBRP 'CAR) is T but (SUBRP 'REVERSE) is F. The primitive function symbols are ADD-TO-SET, AND, APPEND, APPLY-SUBR, ASSOC, BODY, COUNT, DIFFERENCE, EQUAL, FALSE, FALSEP, FIX, FIX-COST, FORMALS, GEQ, GREATERP, IF, IMPLIES, LENGTH, LEQ, LESSP, MAX, MEMBER, NLISTP, NOT, OR, ORDINALP, ORDP, ORD-LESSP, PAIRLIST, PLUS, QUANTIFIER-INITIAL-VALUE, QUANTIFIER-OPERATION, QUOTIENT, REMAINDER, STRIP-CARS, SUBRP, SUM-CDRS, TIMES, TRUE, TRUEP, UNION, and ZEROP. The decision as to which functions are primitive is somewhat *ad hoc* and is based upon implementation considerations.

(APPLY-SUBR FN ARGS) "applies" the primitive function or shell function denoted by FN to the appropriate number of elements of ARGS. E.g., (APPLY-SUBR 'CDR (LIST X)) is (CDR X) and (APPLY-SUBR 'EQUAL (LIST X Y)) is (EQUAL X Y). APPLY-SUBR is so defined just on the LITATOMs for which SUBRP is T.

For every user defined function introduced with a definition of the form (fn x_1 ... x_n) = body we have:

(FORMALS 'fn) = '(x_1 ... x_n)

and

(BODY 'fn) = 'body.

Thus

(FORMALS 'APPEND) = '(X Y)

(BODY 'APPEND) = '(IF (LISTP X)
                         (CONS (CAR X)
                               (APPEND (CDR X) Y))
                         Y)

To be perfectly precise, the body in the right-hand side above may differ from that given in two minor ways. One is related to the handling of abbreviations. The other permits the user to define a symbol to be the result returned by EVALuating a given body. Neither is important to the current discussion. See the user's manual [9] for details. If no definition has yet been made for a function symbol corresponding to a LITATOM, then no facts about the values of SUBRP, FORMALS, APPLY-SUBR, or BODY for that LITATOM are yet given.

3.3. The Axiom for V&C

V&C is axiomatized as a function of three arguments, FLG, X, and VA. X is treated either as (a quotation of) a term or else a list of (quotations of) terms, depending on FLG. VA is an association list assigning values to (the quotations of) variable symbols. V&C returns the value and cost of X under VA, if one exists, and F otherwise. Informally, the cost of evaluating an expression is the number of function symbols that must be applied to produce the value with a call-by-value interpreter. If V&C returns F we say X is *undefined* under VA.

There are six cases to consider when X is a term: it is a variable, a constant of some non-LISTP type, a constant embedded in a QUOTE form, an IF expression, an application of a SUBRP or an application of a (presumably) defined function.

Whenever it is necessary to evaluate a subterm of X recursively, we ask whether the result is F and if so return F. Otherwise, the result is a pair containing value and cost components. The value component is used in the determination of the value of X and the cost component is added into the cost of X. STRIP-CARS is used to collect together the value components of a list of evaluated arguments. SUM-CDRS is used to sum their cost components. FIX-COST is used to increment the cost of a recursively obtained "pair," conditional upon the "pair" being a pair rather than F.

The FLG argument is a technical device to handle mutual recursion; if FLG is 'LIST, X represents a list of terms, otherwise, X represents a single term.

Below is the axiom characterizing V&C. Following the conventions of Lisp, comments are delimited on the left by ; and on the right by end-of-line.

Axiom.
```
(V&C FLG X VA)
   =
(IF (EQUAL FLG 'LIST)

        ;X is a list of terms. Return a list of value-cost
        ;"pairs" -- some "pairs" may be F.

        (IF (NLISTP X)
            NIL
            (CONS (V&C T (CAR X) VA)
                  (V&C 'LIST (CDR X) VA)))

      ;Otherwise, consider the cases on the X.

    (IF (LITATOM X)                        ;Variable
        (CONS (CDR (ASSOC X VA)) 0)

    (IF (NLISTP X)                         ;Constant
        (CONS X 0)

    (IF (EQUAL (CAR X) 'QUOTE)             ;QUOTEd
        (CONS (CADR X) 0)
```

```
        (IF (EQUAL (CAR X) 'IF)                  ; IF-expr
```

; If the test of the IF is defined, test the value and
; interpret the appropriate branch. Then, if the branch
; is defined, increment its cost by that of the test plus
; one. If the test is undefined, X is undefined.

```
            (IF (V&C T (CADR X) VA)
                (FIX-COST
                  (IF (CAR (V&C T (CADR X) VA))
                      (V&C T (CADDR X) VA)
                      (V&C T (CADDDR X) VA))
                  (ADD1 (CDR (V&C T (CADR X) VA))))
                F)
```

; Otherwise, X is the application of a SUBRP or
; defined function. If some argument is undefined, so is X.

```
(IF (MEMBER F (V&C 'LIST (CDR X) VA))
    F

(IF (SUBRP (CAR X))                              ; SUBRP
```

; Apply the primitive to the values of the arguments and
; let the cost be one plus the sum of the argument costs.

```
            (CONS (APPLY-SUBR (CAR X)
                              (STRIP-CARS (V&C 'LIST (CDR X) VA)))
                  (ADD1 (SUM-CDRS (V&C 'LIST (CDR X) VA))))

                                                 ; Defined fn
```

; Interpret the BODY on the values of the arguments
; and if that is defined increment the cost by one plus
; the sum of the argument costs.

```
            (FIX-COST
              (V&C T (BODY (CAR X))
                     (PAIRLIST
                       (FORMALS (CAR X))
                       (STRIP-CARS (V&C 'LIST (CDR X) VA))))
              (ADD1
                (SUM-CDRS
                  (V&C 'LIST (CDR X) VA)))))))))))
```

We also add the axioms that (SUBRP 'V&C) = F, that (FORMALS 'V&C) = ' (FLG X VA) and that the BODY of 'V&C is the quotation of the term on the right-hand side of the equal sign in the axiom above.

We make the following claim about V&C. Consider the primitive recursive function that attempts to compute the value of an expression X, under an assignment VA of values to its variables, using the recurrence equations specified by BODY, but which counts the total number of function applications and IF tests used but "fails" if that count exceeds a specified limit n. Call the function Ψ and suppose that when it succeeds it returns a singleton set, {v}, containing the computed value and when it fails it returns the empty set ϕ. Consider any expression x and assignment va. Suppose that there exists an n such that $\Psi(x,va,n)=\{v\}$. Let k be the least such n. Then (V&C T x va) = <v,k>. If, on the other hand, there exists no such n, (V&C T x va) = F. The nonconstructive assumption in our extended logic is that it is mathematically meaningful to discuss a function that determines whether, for some n, the primitive recursive function Ψ returns non-ϕ.

3.4. Window Dressings

Two trivial but useful theorems about V&C are:

Theorem.
```
(V&C 'LIST L VA)
=
(IF (NLISTP L)
    NIL
    (CONS (V&C T (CAR L) VA)
          (V&C 'LIST (CDR L) VA)))
```
That is, the V&C of a list of expressions is the list of V&C's.

We can define the auxiliary function V&C-APPLY (see below) so that the following formula is also a theorem:

Theorem.
```
(V&C T X VA)
=
(IF (LITATOM X)
    (CONS (CDR (ASSOC X VA)) 0)
    (IF (NLISTP X)
        (CONS X 0)
        (IF (EQUAL (CAR X) 'QUOTE)
            (CONS (CADR X) 0)
            (V&C-APPLY (CAR X)
                       (V&C 'LIST (CDR X) VA)))))
```

This theorem tells us that the V&C of an expression can be determined by considering four cases. The first three (variable, constant, and QUOTEd constant) are straightforward. The fourth, function application, is much simpler than perhaps is apparent from the axiom for V&C: the V&C of (fn t_1 ... t_n) is a function only of fn and the V&C's of the t_i's. This holds whether fn is IF, a SUBRP, or a non-SUBRP. The function that determines the V&C of an application is V&C-APPLY, defined immediately below. V&C-APPLY expects as it first argument FN the name of a function and as its second argument ARGS a list of value-cost pairs.

Definition.
```
(V&C-APPLY FN ARGS)
=
(IF (EQUAL FN 'IF)
```
   ; In the case of IF, we check the first argument, i.e. the
   ; first element of ARGS. If that first argument is F
   ; we return F. Otherwise, we examine the CAR of the first
   ; argument for the value of the test: if the value is non-F, we
   ; choose the second argument and otherwise we choose the
   ; third argument. If the chosen argument is F, we return F;
   ; otherwise, we return the pair resulting from adding one plus the
   ; cost of the test into the CDR of the chosen argument.

```
    (IF (CAR ARGS)
        (FIX-COST (IF (CAAR ARGS)
                      (CADR ARGS)
                      (CADDR ARGS))
                  (ADD1 (CDAR ARGS)))
        F)
(IF (MEMBER F ARGS)
```
   ; In the non-IF case, we return F if any of the arguments
   ; are F.

```
    F
(IF (SUBRP FN)
```
   ; In the case of a SUBRP, we just invoke APPLY-SUBR and
   ; and make the cost one plus the cost of the arguments.

```
    (CONS (APPLY-SUBR FN
                      (STRIP-CARS ARGS))
          (ADD1 (SUM-CDRS ARGS)))
```
   ; In the general case, we evaluate with V&C the BODY
   ; of FN in an environment in which the FORMALS of FN
   ; are bound to the corresponding values in ARGS.
   ; If V&C returns a value-cost pair, we add
   ; in one plus the costs of the arguments.

```
    (FIX-COST
      (V&C T
           (BODY FN)
           (PAIRLIST
             (FORMALS FN)
             (STRIP-CARS ARGS)))
      (ADD1 (SUM-CDRS ARGS)))))))
```

Another important result is that neither the definedness nor the value of a function application is affected by the particular costs of the arguments, provided all the arguments are defined. Another way to put this is that we can replace any "actual" expression by one that always has the same value without affecting the definedness or value of the result. Formally:

Theorem. EQ-ARGS-GIVE-EQ-VALUES:
```
(IMPLIES
  (AND (NOT (EQUAL FN 'QUOTE))
       (NOT (MEMBER F (V&C 'LIST ARGS1 VA1)))
       (NOT (MEMBER F (V&C 'LIST ARGS2 VA2)))
       (EQUAL (STRIP-CARS (V&C 'LIST ARGS1 VA1))
              (STRIP-CARS (V&C 'LIST ARGS2 VA2))))
  (AND (IFF
          (V&C T (CONS FN ARGS1) VA1)
          (V&C T (CONS FN ARGS2) VA2))
       (EQUAL
          (CAR (V&C T (CONS FN ARGS1) VA1))
          (CAR (V&C T (CONS FN ARGS2) VA2))))).
```

We now introduce some abbreviations. Suppose ′fn is a LITATOM corresponding to an n-ary function symbol fn, ′(v_1 ... v_n) is a list of n distinct LITATOM constants, and ′body is some constant. By

$$(fn\ v_1\ ...\ v_n) \Leftarrow body$$

we mean

$$(SUBRP\ 'fn) = F$$
$$\wedge\ (FORMALS\ 'fn) = '(v_1\ ...\ v_n)$$
$$\wedge\ (BODY\ 'fn) = 'body.$$

Observe that for all user-defined functions

Definition.
$$(fn\ v_1\ ...\ v_n) = body$$

we have

$$(fn\ v_1\ ...\ v_n) \Leftarrow body.$$

A *semi-concrete alist* corresponding to a substitution $\{<v_1,t_1>, ..., <v_n,t_n>\}$ is a term of the form (LIST (CONS ′v_1 t_1) ... (CONS ′v_n t_n)). A *standard alist* on a set of variables is a semi-concrete alist corresponding to the identity substitution on those variables.

For example, (LIST (CONS ′X (ADD1 I)) (CONS ′Y (G Z))) is a semi-concrete alist corresponding to the substitution $\{<X, (ADD1\ I)>, <Y, (G\ Z)>\}$. The term (LIST (CONS ′X X) (CONS ′Y Y)) is a standard alist on $\{X,\ Y\}$.

If t is a term and σ is a term, then by [t,σ] we mean (V&C T ′t σ). When σ is a standard alist on the variables of t we write merely [t]. We write *v.vc* as an abbreviation for the value component, i.e., (CAR vc), and *c.vc* as an abbreviation for the cost component, i.e., (CDR vc). We sometimes write (CONS v c) as <v,c>.

Thus, [(APPEND A B)] is an abbreviation for

```
(V&C T '(APPEND A B)
     (LIST (CONS 'A A)
           (CONS 'B B))).
```

This notation is potentially confusing because while we think of t as a *term* it "becomes" a *constant* in [t]. Care must be exercised when doing substitutions. An example where such care is taken may be found in the proof of APP-IS-PARTIALLY-APPEND below, in the formulation of the induction hypothesis.

Let τ be any substitution. We write t/τ to denote the result of applying τ to term t. Let σ be the semi-concrete alist corresponding to τ. Then [t]/τ is [t,σ].

For example, suppose τ is {<A, (CDR A)>, <B, B>}, t = (APPEND A B), and σ is (LIST (CONS 'A (CDR A)) (CONS 'B B)). Then

$$[t]/\tau$$
=
```
(V&C T '(APPEND A B)
      (LIST (CONS 'A A)
            (CONS 'B B)))/τ
```
=
```
(V&C T '(APPEND A B)
      (LIST (CONS 'A (CDR A))
            (CONS 'B B)))
```
=
[t,σ].

This is a trivial consequence of the definitions of "standard" and "semi-concrete" alists and our [...] notation; it has nothing whatsoever to do with V&C.

We use the notation $fn\langle vc_1, \ldots, vc_n\rangle$ to denote (V&C-APPLY 'fn (LIST vc_1 ... vc_n)). Note that for all function symbols, [(fn t_1 ... t_n)] = $fn\langle [t_1], \ldots, [t_n]\rangle$.

4. Theorems about Partial Functions

We have now a logic obtained from our unquantified logic by the addition of a few axioms. The rules of inference are the same as before. We now show, without proof, a few theorems about V&C to illustrate various aspects of its definition and use.

Suppose
```
(APP X Y)
  ⇐
(IF (EQUAL X (QUOTE NIL))
    Y
    (CONS (CAR X) (APP (CDR X) Y))).
```
This supposition describes a (partial) function. Consider for a moment the recurrence equation analogous to the prescription above[5]

```
Definition?
(APP X Y)
  =
(IF (EQUAL X NIL)
    Y
    (CONS (CAR X) (APP (CDR X) Y))).
```

---

[5]When used as terms, NIL, 'NIL and (QUOTE NIL) are all abbreviations for the same LITATOM.

The recurrence above is similar to APPEND's, but terminates when X is NIL instead of when X is not a LISTP. This equation is inadmissible under the principle of definition because there is no measure of the arguments that decreases in a well-founded sense. In particular, 0 is not NIL and (CDR 0) is 0. Were the above equation an axiom we could derive:

(APP 0 1) = (CONS 0 (APP 0 1)),

contradicting the theorem Y ≠ (CONS X Y). Nevertheless, with V&C we can investigate the partial function described by this equation.

Here are some theorems about the "partial function" APP:

Theorem.
[(APP X Y)]≠F ↔ (PROPERP X)

Theorem.
[(APP X Y)]≠F
→
V.[(APP X Y)] = (APPEND X Y).

The first theorem can be read "(APP X Y) is defined if and only if X is a proper list." A list is proper iff "it ends in a NIL," i.e., the first non-LISTP in its CDR chain is NIL. The second theorem can be read "If (APP X Y) is defined then its value is (APPEND X Y)."

An alternative to the notion of cost in the formalization of an interpreter for partial functions is to introduce a special object, say ⊥, that is used as the "value" of undefined interpretations. The definition of the interpreter then passes this value up when it arises in the interpretation of subexpressions. We rejected this approach because ⊥ clutters the statements of virtually all the theorems about interpretations. For example, in the alternative formalization of the definedness condition for (APP X Y) one must include the conditions that no element of X is ⊥, no CDR of X is ⊥ and that Y is not ⊥.[6]

For admissible definitions not involving V&C the V&C theorems are even simpler. Consider APPEND. We have:

Theorem.
[(APPEND X Y)]≠F
∧
V.[(APPEND X Y)] = (APPEND X Y).

That is, the partial function described by

---

[6]In our paper on the mechanical proof of the unsolvability of the halting problem, [7], we formalized Pure Lisp with an interpretation that used ⊥ as described above. The theorem we proved, while valid, was technically inadequate as a formalization of the alleged result because it admitted a trivial proof if one was permitted to construct a Pure Lisp program whose representation included the object ⊥. Our oversight was pointed out by a University of Texas graduate student, Jonathan Bellin, and was easily repaired. However, we cite this as an example of the difficulty of coping with ⊥ formally. The corrected statement of the unsolvability of the halting problem may be found in the standard distribution of our program.

```
(APPEND X Y)
    ⇐
(IF (LISTP X)
    (CONS (CAR X) (APPEND (CDR X) Y))
    Y)
```

always terminates and is APPEND.

We next consider the partial function described by:

```
(RUSSELL) ⇐ (NOT (RUSSELL)).
```

We can prove:

Theorem.
`[(RUSSELL)] = F`

That is, the partial function RUSSELL is everywhere undefined.

We have also dealt with total functions that are uniquely defined by equations that are simply inadmissible under our principle of definition. Consider for example the 91-function:

Definition?
```
(F91 X)
  =
(IF (LESSP 100 X)
    (DIFFERENCE X 10)
    (F91 (F91 (PLUS X 11))))
```

This definition is inadmissible because no measure can be proved to be decreasing in the outermost recursive call above. The reason is that the derived formulas must be proved *before* the new axiom is admitted but any justification of the outermost recursion above must involve properties of F91.

But we can suppose:

```
(F91 X)
   ⇐
(IF (LESSP 100 X)
    (DIFFERENCE X 10)
    (F91 (F91 (PLUS X 11)))).
```

We can then prove the well-known facts about F91:

Theorem.
[(F91 X)] ≠ F
∧
v.[(F91 X)] = (G91 X),

where (G91 X) is defined to be (IF (LESSP 100 X) (DIFFERENCE X 10) 91).

The most complicated inadmissible function we have investigated with V&C is the unusual list reverse function first shown to us by Rod Burstall, and attributed by Manna [20] to Ashcroft.

```
(RV L)
  ⇐
(IF (LISTP L)
    (IF (LISTP (CDR L))
        (CONS (CAR (RV (CDR L)))
              (RV (CONS (CAR L)
                        (RV (CDR (RV (CDR L)))))))
        (CONS (CAR L) 'NIL))
    'NIL)
```

Our theorem prover has proved

Theorem.
[(RV X)] ≠ F
∧
v.[(RV X)] = (REVERSE X).

5. Proofs about Partial Functions

In this section we prove some of the foregoing theorems to illustrate the simplicity of the logic. We also use these proofs to develop and illustrate the rules for manipulating [...]-expressions.

Theorem.
[(RUSSELL)] = F

Proof. If [(RUSSELL)] ≠ F then the interpretation of the BODY of 'RUSSELL is also non-F and has smaller cost:[7]

  c.[(RUSSELL)] > c.[(NOT (RUSSELL))].

But the cost of the application of a SUBRP is greater than the cost of its argument (provided the argument is defined). Hence:

  c.[(NOT (RUSSELL))] > c.[(RUSSELL)]

Contradiction. Thus, [(RUSSELL)]=F. **Q.E.D.**

We next prove a lemma about APP.

Lemma. APP-0-LOOPS:
APP⟨<0,1>,<Y,0>⟩ = F

The intent of this lemma is to say that APP does not terminate when the value of its first argument is 0. This is true because the CDR of a non-LISTP -- and thus of 0 -- is 0.[8]

Proof. Assume the contrary; i.e., APP⟨<0,1>, <Y,0>⟩ ≠ F. Let σ be (LIST (CONS 'X 0) (CONS 'Y Y)). Then

  c.APP⟨<0,1>, <Y,0>⟩
    >   [1]

---

[7]In fact, the cost of interpreting the body of RUSSELL is one less than interpreting the call, but it is not necessary that we concern ourselves with the particular costs involved.

[8]The statement above actually specifies, in addition, that the cost of the first argument be 1. This statement of the lemma suits our current purposes and is easy to prove.

```
C.[(IF (EQUAL X 'NIL)
       Y
       (CONS (CAR X) (APP (CDR X) Y))),σ]
>                                                    [2]
C.[(CONS (CAR X) (APP (CDR X) Y)),σ]
=                                                    [3]
C.CONS⟨[(CAR X),σ],[(APP (CDR X) Y),σ]⟩
=                                                    [4]
C.CONS⟨[(CAR X),σ],APP⟨[(CDR X),σ],[Y,σ]⟩⟩
=                                                    [5]
C.CONS⟨[(CAR X),σ],APP(<0,1>,<Y,0>)⟩
>                                                    [6]
C.APP⟨<0,1>,<Y,0>⟩.
```

Step 1 is via the definition of V&C-APPLY. Step 2 is by the observation that the cost of a defined IF-expression is greater than the cost of the appropriate branch. In the application above we observe that (EQUAL X 'NIL) is defined and has F as its value under σ. Steps 3 and 4 are by appeal to the relation between V&C and V&C-APPLY. Step 5 is by the definition of V&C. Finally, step 6 is via the observation that the cost of a defined SUBRP application is greater than the cost of each argument. Observe that we have again arrived at a contradiction. Hence, APP⟨<0,1>,<Y,0>⟩=F. Q.E.D.

Using the above lemma we can prove:

Theorem. APP-IS-PARTIALLY-APPEND:
[(APP X Y)]≠F
→
V.[(APP X Y)] = (APPEND X Y)

Proof. We induct on X.

Base Case: (NLISTP X). If X is 'NIL then both sides of the conclusion reduce to Y. Therefore, suppose X is non-'NIL and consider [(APP X Y)].

```
[(APP X Y)] ≠ F
↔                                                    [1]
[(IF (EQUAL X (QUOTE NIL))
     Y
     (CONS (CAR X)
           (APP (CDR X) Y)))]≠F
↔                                                    [2]
[(CONS (CAR X)
       (APP (CDR X) Y))]≠F
↔                                                    [3]
[(APP (CDR X) Y)]≠F
↔                                                    [4]
APP⟨[(CDR X)],[Y]⟩≠F
↔                                                    [5]
APP⟨<0,1>,<Y,0>⟩≠F
```

which contradicts APP-0-LOOPS. Step 1 is justified by the fact that the application of a non-SUBRP is defined if and only if the arguments and the body are defined. Step 2 is justified by the fact that an IF is defined if and only if the test and the appropriate branch are defined. Step 3 uses the fact that every SUBRP is defined if and only if the arguments are. Steps 4 and 5 are just the definition of V&C.

Induction Step. We assume `(LISTP X)`. Let σ be a semi-concrete alist corresponding to {<X, (CDR X)>, <Y,Y>}. Our induction hypothesis is:

Induction Hypothesis
`[(APP X Y),σ]≠F`
→
`V.[(APP X Y),σ] = (APPEND (CDR X) Y)`

Note that the instantiation does not hit the `'X` inside the `'(APP X Y)` inside `[(APP X Y)]`. To get this effect, we transform this hypothesis to the equivalent:

Induction Hypothesis
`[(APP (CDR X) Y)]≠F`
→
`V.[(APP (CDR X) Y)] = (APPEND (CDR X) Y)`

using `EQ-ARGS-GIVE-EQ-VALUES`.

We assume `[(APP X Y)]≠F` and consider `[(APP X Y)]`, using the same rules used in the base case:

`[(APP X Y)]≠F`
↔
`[(IF (EQUAL X 'NIL)`
`    Y`
`    (CONS (CAR X)`
`          (APP (CDR X) Y)))]≠F`
↔
`[(CONS (CAR X) (APP (CDR X) Y))]≠F`
↔
`[(APP (CDR X) Y)]≠F`.

We can thus detach the conclusion of our induction hypothesis:

`V.[(APP (CDR X) Y)] = (APPEND (CDR X) Y)`.

Then, appealing to the just derived chain of definedness results we can derive the value of `(APP X Y)`:

`V.[(APP X Y)]`
=   [1]
`V.[(IF (EQUAL X 'NIL)`
`       Y`
`       (CONS (CAR X)`
`             (APP (CDR X) Y)))]`
=   [2]
`V.[(CONS (CAR X) (APP (CDR X) Y))]`
=   [3]
`V.CONS⟨[(CAR X)],[(APP (CDR X) Y)]⟩`
=   [4]
`(CONS V.[(CAR X)] V.[(APP (CDR X) Y)])`
=   [5]
`(CONS (CAR X) V.[(APP (CDR X) Y)])`
=   [6]
`(CONS (CAR X) (APPEND (CDR X) Y))`
=   [7]
`(APPEND X Y)`.

Step 1 uses the observation that if the application of a non-`SUBRP` is defined, then its value is the value of the body. Step 2 uses the corresponding rule for `IF`. Step 3 is by the previously mentioned relation between `V&C` and `V&C-APPLY`. Step 4 is by the observation that, for `SUBRP` applications that are defined, the value of the application is the primitive function applied to the values of the arguments. Step 6 uses the induction hypothesis. Step 7 is by the definition of `APPEND`. Q.E.D.

The reader should not be discouraged by the length of the proof just presented. The length is a reflection of the fact that we have carefully presented each step. The proof is not deep or complicated. Indeed, it is just the mechanical application of a set of very useful rules for manipulating definedness conditions, and value and cost expressions. We summarize the rules informally here:

Definedness: A variable or `QUOTE`d constant is always defined. An `IF`-expression is defined when the test and the appropriate branch are. The call of a `SUBRP` other than `IF` is defined if and only if all the arguments are. Finally, a call of a non-`SUBRP` is defined if and only if all of the arguments are defined and the body is defined.

Value Expressions: The value of a variable or `QUOTE`d constant is straightforward. The value of a defined `IF`-expression is the value of the appropriate branch, depending on the value of the test. The value of a defined `SUBRP` call is the corresponding primitive function applied to the values of the arguments. The value of a defined non-`SUBRP` call is the value of the body.

Cost Expressions: The cost of a variable or `QUOTE`d constant is 0. The cost of a defined `IF`-expression is greater than the costs of both the test and the appropriate branch. The cost of a defined `SUBRP` call other than `IF` is greater than the cost of each argument. The cost of a defined non-`SUBRP` call is greater than the cost of each argument and the cost of the body.

This collection of rules can be expressed as theorems. For example, the definedness condition for calls of `SUBRP`s may be written:

Theorem.
```
(IMPLIES
   (AND (NOT (EQUAL FN 'IF))
        (SUBRP FN))
   (IFF (V&C T (CONS FN ARGS) A)
        (NOT (MEMBER F (V&C 'LIST ARGS A))))).
```

The formal statement of the "definedness condition for `SUBRP`s" as a theorem in the logic may look inelegant. One might have expected a *metatheorem*:

Metatheorem.
If `fn` is a primitive function symbol other than `IF`, then
  $[(\text{fn } t_1 \ldots t_n), \sigma] \neq F$
  if and only if
  $[t_1, \sigma] \neq F \land \ldots \land [t_n, \sigma] \neq F$.

However, when applied to quoted terms the theorem above leads directly to the desired conclusions. The `SUBRP` hypothesis is relieved by computation given any quoted function symbol and the (`V&C 'LIST ...`) and `MEMBER` expressions expand appropriately on quoted argument lists.

For example, observe how the theorem handles the formula:

    [(CONS (CAR X) (APP (CDR X) Y))]≠F.

Let σ be the standard alist (LIST (CONS 'X X) (CONS 'Y Y)). By the abbreviation conventions the above formula is equivalent to:

    (V&C T '(CONS (CAR X)
                  (APP (CDR X) Y))
          σ)≠F
↔
    (V&C T (CONS 'CONS
                 '((CAR X) (APP (CDR X) Y)))
          σ)≠F.

By the definedness condition for SUBRP calls, above, it is equivalent to

    (NOT (MEMBER F (V&C 'LIST
                        '((CAR X) (APP (CDR X) Y))
                        σ))),

which by the definitions of MEMBER and V&C is equivalent to:

    (NOT (MEMBER F
           (LIST (V&C T '(CAR X) σ)
                 (V&C T '(APP (CDR X) Y) σ))))
↔
    (V&C T '(CAR X) σ)≠F
    ∧
    (V&C T '(APP (CDR X) Y) σ)≠F
↔
    [(CAR X),σ]≠F ∧ [(APP (CDR X) Y)]≠F
↔
    [(CAR X)]≠F ∧ [(APP (CDR X) Y)]≠F.

The last line is justified by the fact that if an alist (σ) contains a binding of a variable ('Y) not occurring in the term ((CAR X)), then that binding may be dropped. We show the formal statement of such a theorem later.

The corresponding "value theorem for SUBRP calls" is

Theorem.
    (IMPLIES (AND (SUBRP FN)
                  (V&C T (CONS FN ARGS) A))
             (EQUAL
               (CAR (V&C T (CONS FN ARGS) A))
               (APPLY-SUBR FN
                           (STRIP-CARS
                             (V&C 'LIST ARGS A))))).

Once again, when this rule is applied to a quoted term the unfamiliar function symbols APPLY-SUBR, STRIP-CARS and (V&C 'LIST ...) expand out and the rule permits us to behave just as though we had:

Metatheorem.
For every SUBRP fn, including IF, if
[(fn t_1 ... t_n),σ]≠F, then
V.[(fn t_1 ... t_n),σ]
  =
(fn V.[t_1,σ] ... V.[t_n,σ]).

A cost-manipulation theorem is shown below. It is the rule that relates the cost of a defined call of a non-SUBRP to the cost of the body.

Theorem.
```
(IMPLIES
   (AND (NOT (EQUAL FN 'QUOTE))
        (NOT (SUBRP FN))
        (V&C T (CONS FN ARGS) A))
   (GREATERP
      (CDR (V&C T (CONS FN ARGS) A))
      (CDR (V&C T (BODY FN)
                    (PAIRLIST (FORMALS FN)
                              (STRIP-CARS
                                 (V&C 'LIST ARGS A))))))).
```
All of the theorems shown above may be proved in a straightforward way from the axiom defining V&C and the definitions of its subfunctions.

Using the above rules we can prove the following metatheorem, which is the first step towards the most important metatheorem in our implementation of the modified theorem prover. We are interested in a syntactically defined class of terms with the property that, if t is in the class, then [t]≠F and v.[t] = t.

Call a term *primitive* if it is composed entirely of variable symbols, constants, QUOTEd constants, and applications of SUBRPs to such terms. (LISTP X) and (CONS (CAR X) 'NIL) are examples of primitive terms. Observe that:

[(LISTP X)] ≠ F

V.[(LISTP X)] = (LISTP X)

[(CONS (CAR X) 'NIL)] ≠ F

V.[(CONS (CAR X) 'NIL)] = (CONS (CAR X) NIL).

It is easy to prove, by induction on the structure of primitive terms, that if t is primitive [t]≠F and v.[t] = t. The key observation is that a call of a SUBRP ' fn is defined if the arguments are and that the value of the call is the application of the function fn to the values of the arguments.

We would like to widen the syntactic class to include user defined functions. At this point, we will show how to include all of the admissible functions that do not involve V&C and its dependents. We eventually expand the class still further to include some uses of V&C. We call the expanded class the *tame* terms.

Using the techniques illustrated above, we can prove:

Theorem. APPEND-X-Y-IS-TAME:
[(APPEND X Y)]≠F
∧
V.[(APPEND X Y)] = (APPEND X Y).

The proof is by induction on X by CDR and follows exactly the outline of the proof for APP-IS-PARTIALLY-APPEND. The proof is left to the reader.

Note that the lemma, as stated, does not tell us about arbitrary APPEND expressions, just '(APPEND X Y). It is useful to "lift" the lemma to arbitrary APPEND expressions. Suppose we have APPEND-X-Y-IS-TAME and wish to prove:

Theorem. APPEND-IS-TAME:
(IMPLIES
   (AND (V&C T U A)
        (V&C T V A))
   (AND (V&C T (LIST 'APPEND U V) A)
        (EQUAL
           (CAR (V&C T (LIST 'APPEND U V) A))
           (APPEND (CAR (V&C T U A))
                   (CAR (V&C T V A)))))),

which might be abbreviated:

Metatheorem.
If [u]≠F and [v]≠F then
[(APPEND u v)]≠F
and
V.[(APPEND u v)] = (APPEND V.[u] V.[v]).

Note that this theorem lets us do for APPEND exactly what we can do for SUBRPS: Provided the argument expressions are defined, a call of APPEND is defined and has as its value the APPEND of the values of its arguments. Intuitively, this property means we could include APPEND among the function symbols permitted in "primitive" terms.

Proof of APPEND-IS-TAME. The proof is immediate from APPEND-X-Y-IS-TAME and the previously shown EQ-ARGS-GIVE-EQ-VALUES, by instantiating the variables in the latter lemma as follows:

```
ARGS1:    '(X Y)
VA1:      (LIST (CONS 'X X) (CONS 'Y Y))
ARGS2:    (LIST U V)
VA2:      A
FN:       'APPEND
```
Q.E.D.

Observe that the proof of APPEND-IS-TAME from APPEND-X-Y-IS-TAME is not concerned with APPEND, just V&C. That is, we could similarly "lift" analogous theorems about other function symbols.

An analogous theorem can be proved about each admissible function symbol that does not rely (at any level) upon V&C. In particular, from the properties of the "primitives" and the "tameness" of the subfunctions of an admissible function, we can prove the "tameness" of each admissible function. We complete our detailed discussion of proofs about partial functions by illustrating this claim.

The function we will focus on is REVERSE:

Definition.
(REVERSE X)
=
(IF (LISTP X)
    (APPEND (REVERSE (CDR X))
            (CONS (CAR X) NIL))
    NIL) .

We will prove

Theorem. REVERSE-X-IS-TAME:
[(REVERSE X)]≠F
$\wedge$
v.[(REVERSE X)] = (REVERSE X) .

Proof. We induct on X. The base case, when (LISTP X) = F, is trivial.

In the induction step we assume (LISTP X) = T and the induction hypothesis (which we simplify, as before, by moving the substitution {<X, (CDR X)>} inside the quoted expression using EQ-ARGS-GIVE-EQ-VALUES):

Induction Hypothesis.
[(REVERSE (CDR X))]≠F
$\wedge$
v.[(REVERSE (CDR X))] = (REVERSE (CDR X)) .

We consider the definedness condition first.

[(REVERSE X)]≠F
$\leftrightarrow$
[(IF (LISTP X)
     (APPEND (REVERSE (CDR X))
             (CONS (CAR X) 'NIL))
     'NIL)]≠F
$\leftrightarrow$
[(APPEND (REVERSE (CDR X))
         (CONS (CAR X) 'NIL))]≠F

Since

[(REVERSE (CDR X))]≠F

by the induction hypothesis, and

[(CONS (CAR X) 'NIL)]≠F

since the expression is primitive, we get, from APPEND-IS-TAME, that

[(APPEND (REVERSE (CDR X))
         (CONS (CAR X) 'NIL))]≠F

and hence [(REVERSE X)]≠F. Furthermore,

v.[(REVERSE X)]
=
v.[(APPEND (REVERSE (CDR X))
           (CONS (CAR X) 'NIL))]

which, by APPEND-IS-TAME,

>   =
>   (APPEND v.[(REVERSE (CDR X))]
>   v.[(CONS (CAR X) 'NIL)])
>   =
>   (APPEND (REVERSE (CDR X))
>   (CONS (CAR X) NIL))
>   =
>   (REVERSE X)

Q.E.D.

The other theorems of the previous section have similar proofs. For example in proving that (F91 X) is defined and has as its value (G91 X), the proof is by an induction in which one assumes two instances of the conjecture, one for X replaced by (PLUS X 11) and the other for X replaced by (G91 (PLUS X 11)), under the hypothesis that X≤100. The measure justifying this induction is (DIFFERENCE 101 X). The proof is straightforward by the techniques developed.

The unquantified version of our theorem prover can construct these proofs from the axiom for V&C and the definitions shown. It is necessary for the user to guide the theorem prover by the appropriate choice of lemmas to prove first.

6. EVAL and APPLY

Recall our interest in EVAL: we use it in the definition of FOR to evaluate the conditional and body expressions. At first sight, an appropriate definition of (EVAL 't σ) is v.[t,σ], i.e.,

> **Impression:**
> (EVAL X A) = (CAR (V&C T X A)).

However, recall that in our proof of

> **Theorem.** SUM-DISTRIBUTES-OVER-PLUS:
> (FOR I L P 'SUM (LIST 'PLUS G H) A)
> =
> (PLUS (FOR I L P 'SUM G A)
>   (FOR I L P 'SUM H A)).

we assumed the following fact about EVAL:

> **Lemma.** EVAL-DISTRIBUTES-OVER-PLUS:
> (EVAL (LIST 'PLUS X Y) A)
> =
> (PLUS (EVAL X A) (EVAL Y A)).

But is it the case that v.[(PLUS x y)] = (PLUS v.[x] v.[y])? It certainly is if x and y are defined. But if x is not defined then [(PLUS x y)] is undefined. Thus, the left-hand value expression above becomes v.F, which happens to be 0. But the right-hand side above is (PLUS v.[x] v.[y]), which is (PLUS 0 v.[y]), not 0.

We could correct the situation by defining (CAR x), i.e., v.x, to be ⊥ on non-lists and define PLUS and all other functions to return ⊥ when one of their arguments is ⊥. But we then lose the familiar elementary properties of many functions. For example, (TIMES 0 X) = 0 would no longer be a theorem. In addition, then all our proofs about such elementary functions, even proofs not involving partial functions, would have to consider ⊥. We believe this is too high a price to pay for convenient quantifier manipulation.

But having EVAL-DISTRIBUTES-OVER-PLUS be an unconditional equality gives us powerful and easily used rules like the unconditional SUM-DISTRIBUTES-OVER-PLUS. We achieve this by defining EVAL in a more complicated way than merely the CAR of V&C.

Definition.
```
(EVAL FLG X A)
   =
(IF (EQUAL FLG 'LIST)
    (IF (NLISTP X)
        NIL
        (CONS (EVAL T (CAR X) A)
              (EVAL 'LIST (CDR X) A)))
 (IF (LITATOM X)   (CDR (ASSOC X A))
 (IF (NLISTP X)    X
 (IF (EQUAL (CAR X) 'QUOTE) (CADR X)
    (APPLY (CAR X)
           (EVAL 'LIST (CDR X) A)))))),
```
where APPLY is as defined below.

The FLG argument plays the same role in EVAL as it does in V&C. We henceforth ignore it, sometimes even writing (EVAL t a) for (EVAL T t a). Observe that for every function symbol fn we have:

```
(EVAL (LIST 'fn X1 ... Xn) A)
=
(APPLY 'fn (LIST (EVAL X1 A) ... (EVAL Xn A))) .
```

Without even knowing the definition of APPLY this insures several very elegant theorems about EVAL, for example:

Theorem. Irrelevant bindings can be deleted:
```
(IMPLIES (NOT (MEMBER V (FREE-VARS X)))
         (EQUAL (EVAL X (CONS (CONS V VAL) A))
                (EVAL X A))),
```

Theorem. Substitution of equal EVALs:
```
(IMPLIES (EQUAL (EVAL X A) (EVAL Y A))
         (EQUAL (EVAL (SUBSTITUTE Y X Z) A)
                (EVAL Z A))),
```
where FREE-VARS returns the free variables in the quotation of a term and (SUBSTITUTE Y X Z) substitutes Y for X in Z. These theorems can be proved by the unquantified version of the theorem prover from the definition of EVAL without any knowledge of APPLY. In particular, the definition of EVAL makes it clear that the value of an s-expression denoting a function application is entirely determined by the function applied and the (recursively obtained) values of the argument s-expressions.

We wish it to be the case that

    `(APPLY 'PLUS (LIST X Y)) = (PLUS X Y)`

We can arrange this for `'PLUS` and for every other total function in the logic by defining:

Definition.
```
(APPLY FN ARGS)
   =
(CAR (V&C-APPLY FN (PAIRLIST ARGS 0)))
```

For example, by `APPEND-X-Y-IS-TAME`, we get

```
  (APPLY 'APPEND (LIST X Y))
= V.APPEND⟨<X,0>,<Y,0>⟩
= V.[(APPEND X Y)]
= (APPEND X Y).
```

For partial functions introduced with "⇐" and then proved total, such as the unusual reverse function `RV`, we have analogous simple theorems relating the result of `APPLY` to the application of the corresponding total function. For example,

```
  (APPLY 'RV (LIST X))
= V.RV⟨<X,0>⟩
= V.[(RV X)]
= (REVERSE X).
```

But we do not automatically get, for all function symbols `fn`,

    `(APPLY 'fn (LIST X1 ... Xn)) = (fn X1 ... Xn).`

For example, it is not the case that:

    `(APPLY 'V&C (LIST FLG X VA)) = (V&C FLG X VA).`

7. The Definition of the Quantifier Function FOR

Having defined `EVAL` and `APPLY`, we then introduce `FOR` as shown in the Introduction.

The two main subfunctions of `FOR`, in addition to `EVAL`, are defined as follows:

Definition.
```
(QUANTIFIER-INITIAL-VALUE OP)
   =
(CDR (ASSOC OP '((ADD-TO-SET . NIL)
                 (ALWAYS . *1*TRUE)
                 (APPEND . NIL)
                 (COLLECT . NIL)
                 (COUNT . 0)
                 (DO-RETURN . NIL)
                 (EXISTS . *1*FALSE)
                 (MAX . 0)
                 (SUM . 0)
                 (MULTIPLY . 1)
                 (UNION . NIL))))
```

Definition.
```
(QUANTIFIER-OPERATION OP X Y)
  =
(IF (EQUAL OP 'ADD-TO-SET)  (ADD-TO-SET X Y)
(IF (EQUAL OP 'ALWAYS)      (AND X Y)
(IF (EQUAL OP 'APPEND)      (APPEND X Y)
(IF (EQUAL OP 'COLLECT)     (CONS X Y)
(IF (EQUAL OP 'COUNT)       (IF X (ADD1 Y) Y)
(IF (EQUAL OP 'DO-RETURN)   X
(IF (EQUAL OP 'EXISTS)      (OR X Y)
(IF (EQUAL OP 'MAX)         (MAX X Y)
(IF (EQUAL OP 'SUM)         (PLUS X Y)
(IF (EQUAL OP 'MULTIPLY)    (TIMES X Y)
(IF (EQUAL OP 'UNION)       (UNION X Y)
                            0)))))))))))
```

When FOR runs, it can be thought of "doing" something with the result of evaluating the fifth argument, provided that the evaluation of the second argument is true. Here is an intuitive characterization of what each quantifier does. ADD-TO-SET collects up the results into a list without duplication. ALWAYS is our universal quantifier; it ANDs the results together. APPEND appends the results together. COLLECT collects up the results. COUNT simply counts the number of non-F results. DO-RETURN returns the first result. EXISTS is our existential quantifer; it ORs the results together. MAX returns the maximum result, or 0 if there were none. SUM adds the results together. TIMES multiplies the results together. UNION unions the results together.

8. Theorems about Quantifiers

In this section we show many simple theorems about FOR that illustrate the power of the notation. We start with theorems that can be proved from the definition of FOR without knowledge of EVAL.

Theorem.
```
(FOR X (APPEND A B) COND 'COLLECT BODY ALIST)
  =
(APPEND (FOR X A COND 'COLLECT BODY ALIST)
        (FOR X B COND 'COLLECT BODY ALIST))
```

Theorem.
```
(FOR X (APPEND A B) COND 'COUNT BODY ALIST)
  =
(PLUS (FOR X A COND 'COUNT BODY ALIST)
      (FOR X B COND 'COUNT BODY ALIST))
```

Theorem.
```
(FOR X (APPEND A B) COND 'ADD-TO-SET BODY ALIST)
  =
(UNION (FOR X A COND 'ADD-TO-SET BODY ALIST)
       (FOR X B COND 'ADD-TO-SET BODY ALIST))
```

Theorem.
```
(FOR X (APPEND A B) COND 'DO-RETURN BODY ALIST)
  =
(IF (FOR X A (LIST 'QUOTE T) 'EXISTS COND ALIST)
    (FOR X A COND 'DO-RETURN BODY ALIST)
    (FOR X B COND 'DO-RETURN BODY ALIST))
```

Theorem.
```
(IMPLIES
  (MEMBER OP '(ALWAYS MAX EXISTS SUM
               APPEND MULTIPLY UNION))
  (EQUAL
    (FOR X (APPEND A B) COND OP BODY ALIST)
    (QUANTIFIER-OPERATION OP
       (FOR X A COND OP BODY ALIST)
       (FOR X B COND OP BODY ALIST))))
```

The next group of theorems are schematic in nature. Note however that we do not need second order variables to state these theorems. Note also that they are simple equalities and are not encumbered by hypotheses about the well-definedness of the expressions to which they are applied. Thus, these theorems are easily used in simplification. Their proofs require knowledge of EVAL and APPLY.

Theorem.
```
(FOR X R COND 'SUM (LIST 'PLUS G H) ALIST)
  =
(PLUS (FOR X R COND 'SUM G ALIST)
      (FOR X R COND 'SUM H ALIST))
```

Theorem.
```
(FOR X R COND 'MULTIPLY
              (LIST 'TIMES G H) ALIST)
  =
(TIMES (FOR X R COND 'MULTIPLY G ALIST)
       (FOR X R COND 'MULTIPLY H ALIST))
```

Theorem.
```
(FOR X R COND 'ALWAYS (LIST 'AND G H) ALIST)
  =
(AND (FOR X R COND 'ALWAYS G ALIST)
     (FOR X R COND 'ALWAYS H ALIST))
```

Theorem.
```
(FOR X R COND 'EXISTS (LIST 'OR G H) ALIST)
  =
(OR (FOR X R COND 'EXISTS G ALIST)
    (FOR X R COND 'EXISTS H ALIST))
```

The following theorem may be read "if the bound variable does not occur freely in the body of a FOR then the body is constant." That is, one can instead evaluate the body of the FOR without concern for the bound variable's values and use the result of the evaluation as the constant value of the body.

Theorem.
```
(IMPLIES
   (NOT (MEMBER X (FREE-VARS BODY)))
   (EQUAL (FOR X R COND OP BODY ALIST)
          (FOR X R COND OP
               (LIST 'QUOTE (EVAL BODY ALIST))
               ALIST)))
```

A similar theorem can be proved about the conditional expression.

There is a class of theorems about constant bodies. For example:

Theorem.
```
(FOR X R COND 'SUM (LIST 'QUOTE BODY) ALIST)
=
(TIMES BODY
       (FOR X R (LIST 'QUOTE T)
            'COUNT COND ALIST))
```

Finally, we can prove theorems that allow us to manipulate the range of a quantifier. We illustrate such a theorem when we discuss the proof of the Binomial Theorem.

Using `APPLY` we can also define "mapping functions" similar to those in such languages as SASL [29] and Lisp. For example:

Definition.
```
(FOLDR OP K LST)
=
(IF (NLISTP LST)
    K
    (APPLY OP (LIST (CAR LST)
                    (FOLDR OP K (CDR LST))))).
```
For example, (FOLDR 'PLUS 0 '(1 2 3 4 5)) = 1+2+3+4+5+0 = 15.

Among the theorems the system can prove about `FOLDR` are:

Theorem.
```
(FOLDR OP K (APPEND A B))
=
(FOLDR OP (FOLDR OP K B) A)
```

Theorem.
(FOLDR 'CONS B A) = (APPEND A B)

Theorem.
(FOLDR 'AND T LST) = (for P in LST always P)

Theorem.
(FOLDR 'PLUS 0 LST) = (for I in LST sum I)

In the last two theorems above we use the abbreviation convention introduced informally in the introduction. We can describe the convention precisely now. If *cond* and *body* are terms and σ is a standard alist on the variables in *cond* and *body*, then when we write

(for *v* in *r* when *cond* *op* *body*)

it is an abbreviation for

    (FOR ′v r ′cond ′op ′body σ).

When *cond* is T we often omit it and the when "key-word."

9. The Modified Theorem Prover

Perhaps the major appeal of the logic we have presented is that our existing mechanical theorem prover is sound for it. Furthermore, that theorem prover is capable of proving the foregoing theorems from the axioms and definitions for V&C, EVAL, and FOR. However, the theorem prover's performance can be improved greatly by building in some of the properties of these three function symbols. We discuss in this section several of the improvements we have made.

Most of our improvements are based on the metatheoretic notion of a "tame" term. For every tame term t we have the metatheorem v.[t] = t. A term is *tame* if it is a variable, an explict value, the application of a "total" function to tame terms, a term of the form (V&C T ′t alist) or (EVAL T ′t alist) where t and alist are tame, or a term of the form (FOR v r ′cond op ′body alist) where each of v, r, cond, op, body and alist are tame.

We classify each function symbol as to whether it is total or not at the time it is introduced, as a function of the previously introduced functions. Intuitively, fn is total if its body is tame, which means, roughly, that every function called in the body is total. However, the body may involve recursive calls of fn. Do we assume fn is total when we determine whether its body is tame? At first glance the answer seems to be "yes, because we have proved, during the admission of the function, that every recursive call of fn decreases a measure of the arguments in a well-founded sense." But consider calls of fn occurring inside of quoted expressions given to EVAL. Those calls have not been checked. For example, assuming fn total and then asking if its body is tame would result in the following function being considered total:

    Definition.
    (RUSSELL) = (NOT (EVAL ′(RUSSELL) NIL)),

since, if RUSSELL is considered total then the EVAL expression above is tame. Therefore, in the definition of "total" we do not use the notion of "tame" and instead use the notion of "super-tame" which means that fn is considered total outside of EVAL expressions but not inside. Here are the precise definitions of "total" and "super-tame."

All the primitives except V&C, V&C-APPLY, EVAL, APPLY and FOR are *total*. A function defined by (fn x_1 ... x_n)=body is *total* iff body is super-tame with respect to fn.

A term is *super-tame* with respect to fn iff it is a tame term (under the assumption that fn is not total) or it is a call of a total function or fn on super-tame terms with respect to fn.[9]

Every function definable in our old logic is total. In addition, functions in the new logic that

---

[9]This definition is somewhat more conservative than is justified. For example, we could in some cases permit calls of fn inside of EVALs.

involve V&C, EVAL and FOR are total provided the interpreted arguments are the quotations of tame terms.

The fundamental theorem about tame terms is

Metatheorem.
If t is a tame term and σ is a semi-concrete alist corresponding to a substitution τ on the variables of t

then
   [t,σ]≠F
and
   V.[t,σ] = t/τ.

When we discussed proofs of theorems about partial functions we illustrated the proof of the metatheorem. We proved that REVERSE expressions have the tameness property above, given the tameness property for APPEND. The proof was by induction by CDR on the argument of REVERSE. More generally, any newly admitted total function can be proved to have the tameness property, given the tameness property of all the previously admitted total functions. The proof is by induction on the measure justifying the newly admitted function. The only problematic part of the proof is that we included among the tame terms applications of V&C to the quotations of tame terms. Proving the tameness property for such applications of V&C itself is simple given the following fundamental property of V&C: If (V&C T X A) is non-F then [(V&C T X A)] is non-F and has (V&C T X A) as its value. The property can be proved by induction on the cost component of (V&C T X A). It is, in addition, the case that if (V&C T X A) is F then so is [(V&C T X A)].

We use the metatheorem in several ways. An obvious one is that whenever the theorem prover encounters a term of the form:

   (CAR (V&C T 't σ))

where t is a tame term and σ is a semi-concrete alist corresponding to a substitution τ on the variables of t, it is replaced by t/τ.

We have similar simplification routines for V&C-APPLY (on total functions) EVAL, and APPLY (on total functions). The most complicated simplifier is for the FOR function.

When the theorem prover encounters a term of the form:

   (FOR (QUOTE v) r
        (QUOTE cond)
        op
        (QUOTE body)
        alist)

where v is a variable symbol, cond and body are tame terms, and alist a semi-concrete alist corresponding to a substitution τ on the variables in cond and body we: instantiate cond and body with τ (deleting any pair of the form <v, t>), rewrite the instantiated terms to obtain cond' and body', and then, provided the results are tame terms, return:

   (FOR (QUOTE v) r

```
          (QUOTE cond')
          op
          (QUOTE body')
          alist')
```

where `alist'` is a standard alist on the variables in `cond'` and `body'`. We take care, when rewriting `cond` and `body` to rename `v` if there are hypotheses about `v`. In addition, we then assume the hypothesis `(MEMBER v r)` when rewriting `cond` and we assume that and `cond'` when rewriting `body`.[10]

In all we added about 10 pages of Lisp code to the theorem prover to support the simplification of expressions involving V&C and its cousins. However, the reader is reminded that it was unnecessary to change or even inspect any existing code; we merely added new simplifiers for the new function symbols.

For information on how to obtain a copy of the Common Lisp version of the theorem prover write to the authors at Computational Logic, Inc., Suite 290, 1717 West Sixth Street, Austin, TX 78703.

10. Proof of the Binomial Theorem

In this section we prove the Binomial Theorem:

$$(a+b)^n = \sum_{i=0}^{n} \binom{n}{i} a^i b^{n-i};$$

In our notation, the Binomial Theorem is:

Theorem.
```
(EQUAL (EXP (PLUS A B) N)
       (for I in (FROM-TO 0 N) sum
          (TIMES (BC N I)
                 (EXP A I)
                 (EXP B (DIFFERENCE N I)))))
```

where `(FROM-TO I J)` is the list of the natural numbers from `I` to `J`, `(TIMES i j k)` is an abbreviation for `(TIMES i (TIMES j k))` and the binomial coefficient is defined recursively as:

Definition.
```
(BC N M)
=
(IF (ZEROP M)
    1
    (IF (LESSP N M)
        0
        (PLUS (BC (SUB1 N) M)
              (BC (SUB1 N) (SUB1 M)))))
```

---

[10]Recall the previously mentioned litany of well-known mathematicians who got the rules wrong when dealing with the instantiation of higher-order variables. The metatheorems that establish the rules for simplifying inside the body of FORs are exactly the places one would expect such mistakes to be made. Despite our caution we goofed here the first time we implemented the simplification. We neglected the possibility that the user-supplied alist of the FOR might contain a binding for the indicial variable -- a binding that is completely irrelevant under the axioms but which had effect in our implementation. Our error was caught by a Matt Kaufmann, a colleague at the University of Texas.

Proof of the Binomial Theorem. We induct on N. The base case, when N is 0, is trivial; both sides reduce to 1.

In the induction step we know N>0 and we assume:

Induction Hypothesis.
```
(EQUAL (EXP (PLUS A B) (SUB1 N))
       (for I in (FROM-TO 0 (SUB1 N))
            sum
            (TIMES (BC (SUB1 N) I)
                   (EXP A I)
                   (EXP B
                        (DIFFERENCE (SUB1 N) I)))))
```

As noted previously, the substitution of (SUB1 N) for N technically changes only the alist of the FOR, not the quoted body expression above. However, as we have done in our previously shown proofs, we can drive that substitution in, since both the body and the substituted terms are tame. In our implementation this transformation is carried out by the previously mentioned FOR simplifier, when it instantiates the quoted body of the FOR, rewrites the result, and quotes it again.

We now prove the induction step by deriving the left-hand side of the Binomial Theorem from the right-hand side, assuming the inductive hypothesis above and N>0. We will use standard arithmetic notation for PLUS, TIMES, EXP, and DIFFERENCE. After the derivation we comment upon each step. The derivation is somewhat long because we show each step.

```
(for I in (FROM-TO 0 N)
     sum (BC N I)*A^I*B^(N-I))
=                                                            [1]
(for I in (CONS 0 (FROM-TO 1 N))
     sum (BC N I)*A^I*B^(N-I))
=                                                            [2]
(BC N 0)*A^0*B^(N-0)
    + (for I in (FROM-TO 1 N)
           sum (BC N I)*A^I*B^(N-I))
=                                                            [3]
B^N + (for I in (FROM-TO 1 N)
           sum (BC N I)*A^I*B^(N-I))
=                                                            [4]
B^N + (for I in (FROM-TO 1 N)
           sum [(BC N-1 I)+(BC N-1 I-1)]
                *
                A^I*B^(N-I))
=                                                            [5]
B^N + (for I in (FROM-TO 1 N)
           sum (BC N-1 I)*A^I*B^(N-I)
                +
                (BC N-1 I-1)*A^I*B^(N-I))
=                                                            [6]
B^N + (for I in (FROM-TO 1 N)
           sum (BC N-1 I)*A^I*B^(N-I))
    + (for I in (FROM-TO 1 N)
           sum (BC N-1 I-1)*A^I*B^(N-I))
=                                                            [7]
```

```
(for I in (FROM-TO 0 N)
    sum (BC N-1 I)*A^I*B^(N-I))
+
(for I in (FROM-TO 1 N)
    sum (BC N-1 I-1)*A^I*B^(N-I))

=                                                    [8]
(for I in (APPEND (FROM-TO 0 N-1) (LIST N))
    sum (BC N-1 I)*A^I*B^(N-I))
+
(for I in (FROM-TO 1 N)
    sum (BC N-1 I-1)*A^I*B^(N-I))
=                                                    [9]
(for I in (FROM-TO 0 N-1)
    sum (BC N-1 I)*A^I*B^(N-I))
+
(for I in (LIST N)
    sum (BC N-1 I)*A^I*B^(N-I))
+
(for I in (FROM-TO 1 N)
    sum (BC N-1 I-1)*A^I*B^(N-I))
=                                                    [10]
(for I in (FROM-TO 0 N-1)
    sum (BC N-1 I)*A^I*B^(N-I))
+
(for I in (FROM-TO 1 N)
    sum (BC N-1 I-1)*A^I*B^(N-I))
=                                                    [11]
(for I in (FROM-TO 0 N-1)
    sum (BC N-1 I)*A^I*B*B^((N-1)-I))
+
(for I in (FROM-TO 1 N)
    sum (BC N-1 I-1)*A^I*B^(N-I))
=                                                    [12]
B*(for I in (FROM-TO 0 N-1)
     sum (BC N-1 I)*A^I*B^((N-1)-I))
+
(for I in (FROM-TO 1 N)
    sum (BC N-1 I-1)*A^I*B^(N-I))
=                                                    [13]
B*(for I in (FROM-TO 0 N-1)
     sum (BC N-1 I)*A^I*B^((N-1)-I))
+
(for I in (FROM-TO 0 N-1)
    sum (BC N-1 I)*A^(I+1)*B^(N-(I+1)))
=                                                    [14]
B*(for I in (FROM-TO 0 N-1)
     sum (BC N-1 I)*A^I*B^((N-1)-I))
+
(for I in (FROM-TO 0 N-1)
    sum (BC N-1 I)*A*A^I*B^((N-1)-I))
=                                                    [15]
B*(for I in (FROM-TO 0 N-1)
     sum (BC N-1 I)*A^I*B^((N-1)-I))
+
A*(for I in (FROM-TO 0 N-1)
     sum (BC N-1 I)*A^I*B^((N-1)-I))
```

```
                =                                              [16]
(A+B)*(for I in (FROM-TO 0 N-1)
        sum (BC N-1 I)*A^I*B^((N-1)-I))
                =                                              [17]
(A+B)*(A+B)^(N-1)
                =                                              [18]
(A+B)^N
```
Q.E.D.

Step 1 is the expansion of (FROM 0 N).

Step 2 is the expansion of FOR. The first term in the resulting formula is the body of the FOR with I replaced by 0. That term is produced by the EVAL simplifier since the body is tame.

In step 3 the instantiated body is simplified to B^N, using simple arithmetic.

Step 4 is the expansion of (BC N I) inside the body of the FOR. This is done by the FOR simplifier, when it rewrites the body under the hypothesis that I is a member of the range. The definition of BC has two "base" cases, one where N is 0 and the other where I exceeds N. We are not in the former because N>0. We are not in the latter because I is a member of (FROM-TO 1 N). Thus, the BC expression expands to the sum of two recursive calls.

Step 5 is further simplification inside the body of the FOR. We distribute the multiplication over the addition of the two BC calls.

Step 6 is an application of the quantifier rewrite rule that the sum of a PLUS is the PLUS of the sums.

In step 7 we extend the range of the first for from (FROM-TO 1 N) to (FROM-TO 0 N) by observing that at I=0 the extended for sums in the B^N term added explicitly to the earlier for.

Step 8 is the expansion of (FROM-TO 0 N) at the high end.

Step 9 distributes for over an APPENDed range.

Step 10 drops the middle for of the previous formula because it is equal 0. The simplification is done by expanding the definition of for and using the EVAL simplifier on the instantiated body; when I=N the body of the for is 0 because of the definition of BC.

Step 11 is arithmetic simplification inside the body of the first quantifier.

Step 12 is an appeal to a FOR lemma that permits factors not containing the bound variable to be moved outside of sums. Observe that the first for in the resulting formula is the right hand side of the induction hypothesis. We are not yet ready to use the induction hypothesis however; we wish to manipulate the second for in formula 13 to make the same term appear there.

In step 13 we apply a FOR lemma that shifts the range down by 1 but increments each occurrence of the bound variable by 1. The theorem can be stated:

Theorem.

```
(IMPLIES (AND (LITATOM V)
              (NOT (ZEROP J))
              (NOT (ZEROP K)))
         (EQUAL (FOR V (FROM-TO J K) COND OP BODY ALIST)
                (FOR V (FROM-TO (SUB1 J) (SUB1 K))
                     (SUBSTITUTE (LIST 'ADD1 V) V COND)
                     OP
                     (SUBSTITUTE (LIST 'ADD1 V) V BODY)
                     ALIST)))
```

Step 14 is arithmetic simplification inside the body of the second for.

Step 15 brings out a constant factor again, here an A. Note that the two fors in the resulting formula are identical: they are the right hand side of the induction hypothesis.

In step 16 we apply the distribution law of multiplication over addition.

In step 17 we appeal to the induction hypothesis.

In step 18 we use the definition of exponentiation.

Our mechanical proof uses the same reasoning as that shown above, but the steps are in a slightly different order.

The reader is encouraged to note that even though the proof involves several interesting quantifier manipulation techniques, the most commonly used manipulations are the expansion of recursive definitions and the simplification of list processing and arithmetic expressions both inside of and outside of the quantifiers.

11. Conclusion

We have described an extension to our computational logic and its supporting theorem prover that provides the power of partial functions and quantification over finite domains.

The extension consists of the following steps, starting with the logic described in [1]
1. adopt the notational conventions of [2];
2. add definitions for the functions ASSOC, PAIRLIST, MEMBER, FIX-COST, STRIP-CARS and SUM-CDRS;
3. add axioms to define the functions SUBRP, APPLY-SUBR, FORMALS and BODY -- these functions could be defined as simple tables for a given definitional/shell extension of the logic;
4. add an axiom characterizing the function V&C, an interpreter for the logic which returns the value and cost of any expression in the logic or F if the expression has no interpretation -- V&C is not a computable function but is uniquely characterized by the axiom given; and
5. define a variety of useful functions in terms of V&C, namely, V&C-APPLY, EVAL, APPLY, and FOR.

The most attractive feature of our extension is that it does not alter the term structure of our language, the axioms already present, or the rules of inference. There are two advantages to this. First, the statements and proofs of theorems not involving partial functions or quantified expressions are unaffected by the provision of these features. Second, the existing mechanical theorem prover is sound for the extended logic; changes made in support of the extension were concerned entirely with simplifiers for handling the new function symbols, not consideration of the correctness of existing code.

These considerations are important because a logic or mechanical theorem prover that supports quantification or partial functions is merely an academic exercise unless it provides extensive support for the primitive theories of arithmetic, sequences, trees, etc. Quantifiers and partial functions are used to discuss the operations and objects in those theories. Even proofs involving extensive quantifier manipulation, such as the Binomial Theorem, are usually dominated by the quantifier-free manipulations at the core. We believe it is a mistake to sacrifice the simplicity of the core theories for the sake of quantifiers or partial functions.

That said, however, it is important that the provisions for new features not be so protective of the primitives that it is awkward to use the new features. We have addressed this concern in this paper by using the new features to state and prove theorems that could not previously be stated in our logic.

We have shown how the termination properties of many partial recursive functions could be stated in terms of V&C and proved formally in the extended logic. We are unaware of any other mechanical proof of, say, the correctness of the unusual reverse function RV.

We have shown how schematic quantifier manipulation laws can be stated, proved and used in the logic. We used such laws in the proof of the Binomial Theorem. We are unaware of any other mechanical proof of this theorem.

We have described several simplification techniques that are useful in manipulating V&C, EVAL and FOR expressions. We have implemented these techniques in an experimental extension to our mechanical theorem prover. We have demonstrated these techniques at work in the proof of the Binomial Theorem.

In summary, we believe we have produced a practical extension of our logic and theorem prover that supports partial functions and bounded quantification.

References

1. R. S. Boyer and J S. Moore. *A Computational Logic.* Academic Press, New York, 1979.

2. R. S. Boyer and J S. Moore. Metafunctions: Proving Them Correct and Using Them Efficiently as New Proof Procedures. In *The Correctness Problem in Computer Science*, R. S. Boyer and J S. Moore, Eds., Academic Press, London, 1981.

3. R. S. Boyer and J S. Moore. A Verification Condition Generator for FORTRAN. In *The Correctness Problem in Computer Science*, R. S. Boyer and J S. Moore, Eds., Academic Press, London, 1981.

4. R. S. Boyer and J S. Moore. The Mechanical Verification of a FORTRAN Square Root Program. SRI International, 1981.

5. R. S. Boyer and J S. Moore. MJRTY - A Fast Majority Vote Algorithm. Technical Report ICSCA-CMP-32, Institute for Computing Science and Computer Applications, University of Texas at Austin, 1982.

6. R. S. Boyer and J S. Moore. "Proof Checking the RSA Public Key Encryption Algorithm". *American Mathematical Monthly 91*, 3 (1984), 181-189.

7. R. S. Boyer and J S. Moore. "A Mechanical Proof of the Unsolvability of the Halting Problem". *JACM 31*, 3 (1984), 441-458.

8. R. S. Boyer and J S. Moore. Integrating Decision Procedures into Heuristic Theorem Provers: A Case Study with Linear Arithmetic. In *Machine Intelligence 11*, Oxford University Press, (to appear, 1987).

9. R. S. Boyer and J S. Moore. A User's Manual for the Boyer-Moore Theorem Prover Second Edition: The Quantified Theory. Institute for Computer Science, University of Texas at Austin, (to appear, 1987).

10. R. S. Boyer and J S. Moore. A Mechanical Proof of the Turing Completeness of Pure Lisp. In *Automated Theorem Proving: After 25 Years*, W.W. Bledsoe and D.W. Loveland, Eds., American Mathematical Society, Providence, R.I., 1984, pp. 133-167.

11. R. S. Boyer, M. W. Green and J S. Moore. The Use of a Formal Simulator to Verify a Simple Real Time Control Program. Technical Report ICSCA-CMP-29, University of Texas at Austin, 1982.

12. A. Church. *Introduction to Mathematical Logic.* Princeton University Press, Princeton, New Jersey, 1956.

13. Benedetto Lorenzo Di Vito. Verification of Communications Protcols and Abstract Process Models. PhD Thesis ICSCA-CMP-25, Institute for Computing Science and Computer Applications, University of Texas at Austin, 1982.

14. M.J.C. Gordon. *The Denotational Description of Programming Languages.* Springer-Verlag, New York, 1979.

15. Huang, C.-H., and Lengauer, C. The Automated Proof of a Trace Transformation for a Bitonic Sort. Tech. Rept. TR-84-30, Department of Computer Sciences, The University of Texas at Austin, Oct., 1984.

16. Warren A. Hunt, Jr. FM8501: A Verified Microprocessor. University of Texas at Austin, December, 1985.

17. J. Kelley. *General Topology.* D. van Nostrand, Princeton, New Jersey, 1955.

18. Lengauer, C. "On the Role of Automated Theorem Proving in the Compile-Time Derivation of Concurrency". *Journal of Automated Reasoning 1*, 1 (1985), 75-101.

19. Lengauer, C., and Huang, C.-H. A Mechanically Certified Theorem about Optimal Concurrency of Sorting Networks, and Its Proof. Tech. Rept. TR-85-23, Department of Computer Sciences, The University of Texas at Austin, Oct., 1985.

20. Z. Manna. *Mathematical Theory of Computation.* McGraw-Hill Book Company, New York, New York, 1974.

21. J. McCarthy, et al.. *LISP 1.5 Programmer's Manual.* The MIT Press, Cambridge, Massachusetts, 1965.

22. A. P. Morse. *A Theory of Sets.* Academic Press, New York, 1965.

23. David M. Russinoff. A Mechanical Proof of Wilson's Theorem. Department of Computer Sciences, University of Texas at Austin, 1983.

24. N. Shankar. "Towards Mechanical Metamathematics". *Journal of Automated Reasoning 1*, 1 (1985).

25. N. Shankar. A Mechanical Proof of the Church-Rosser Theorem. Tech. Rept. ICSCA-CMP-45, Institute for Computing Science, University of Texas at Austin, 1985.

26. N. Shankar. Checking the proof of Godel's incompleteness theorem. Institute for Computing Science, University of Texas at Austin, 1986.

27. J. E. Stoy. *Denotational Semantics: The Scott-Strachey Approach to Programming Language Theory.* The MIT Press, Cambridge, Massachusetts, 1977.

28. W. Teitelman. INTERLISP Reference Manual. Xerox Palo Alto Research Center, 3333 Coyote Hill Road, Palo Alto, Ca., 1978.

29. D. A. Turner. "A New Implementation Technique for Applicative Languages". *Software -- Practice and Experience 9* (1979), 31-49.

Part II

Design Calculi

The design of programs within a calculus of formal rules has similarities to the design of proofs within a logical system. However, while in a logical system mainly logical propositions are manipulated and transformed by logical rules, in the design of programs special notational forms are manipulated and transformed. Nevertheless this can be seen as a special application of logics.

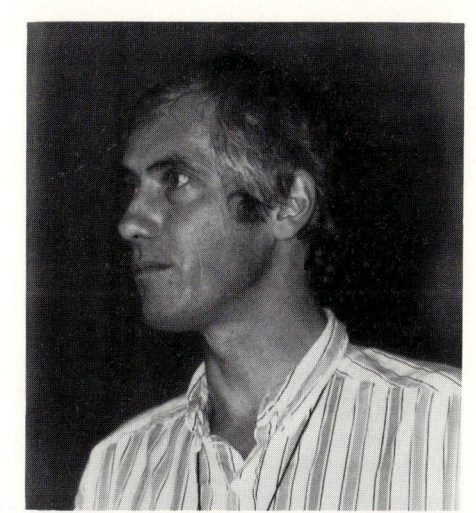

R.S. Bird

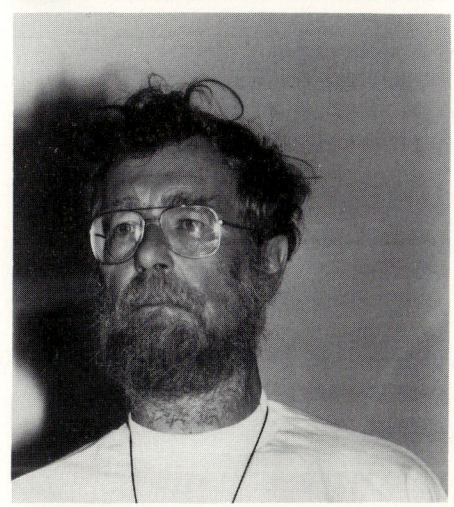

E.W. Dijkstra

C.A.R. Hoare

Richard Bird's calculus admits a first formalization of the concepts of hats and rabbits: A hat is simply viewed as a list of rabbits:

$$\textbf{type } hat = [\,rabbit\,]$$

To shorten the notation, we introduce special squiggles for these concepts:

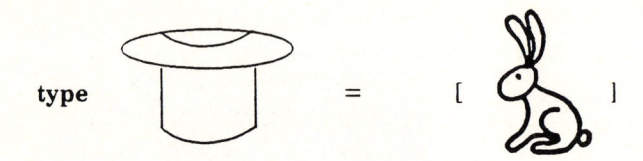

$$\textbf{type } 🎩 = [\,🐰\,]$$

During his lectures, Bird kept track of the number of rabbits he pulled out of the hat. In his formalism this can be expressed by the function:

$$rabbitcount = \uparrow/ \cdot +/* \cdot (k_1*)* \cdot inits$$

which for a sequence of rabbits counts the number of rabbits in it.

It is an easy exercise, the reader may use Bird's calculus, to derive from this specification the more efficient version:

$$rabbitcount = +/ \cdot k_1*$$

Lectures on Constructive Functional Programming

Richard S. Bird
Programming Research Group
11 Keble Rd., Oxford OX1 3QD, UK

Abstract

The subject of these lectures is a calculus of functions for deriving programs from their specifications. This calculus consists of a range of concepts and notations for defining functions over various data types — including lists, trees, and arrays — together with their algebraic and other properties. Each lecture begins with a specific problem, and the theory necessary to solve it is then developed. In this way we hope to show that a functional approach to the problem of systematically calculating programs from their specifications can take its place alongside other methodologies.

Acknowledgements

Much of the following material was developed in collaboration with Lambert Meertens of the CWI, Amsterdam, to whom I am grateful for both support and friendship.

I would also like to acknowledge the contributions of Roland Backhouse, Jeremy Gibbons, Geraint Jones, Andrew Kay, Oege de Moor, Doaitse Swierstra, and Chris Wright, all of whom have suggested important ideas or improvements. Any failure of understanding or deficiencies in presentation remain, of course, my sole responsibility. Detailed references, including related work, are given at the end of each lecture.

1 Basic concepts

1.0 Problem

Consider the following simple identity:

$$(a_1 \times a_2 \times a_3) + (a_2 \times a_3) + a_3 + 1 = ((1 \times a_1 + 1) \times a_2 + 1) \times a_3 + 1$$

This equation generalises in the obvious way to n values $a_1, a_2, \ldots, a_n$ and we will refer to it subsequently as **Horner's rule**. As we shall see, Horner's rule turns out to be quite useful in our calculus. The reason is that the interpretation of $\times$ and $+$ need not be confined to the usual multiplication and addition operations of arithmetic. The essential constraints are only that both operations are associative, $\times$ has identity element 1, and $\times$ distributes through $+$.

The problem we address in this lecture is to develop suitable notation for expressing Horner's rule concisely.

1.1 Functions

Except where otherwise stated all functions are assumed to be *total*. The fact that a function f has source type α and target type β will be denoted in the usual way by $f : \alpha \to \beta$. We shall say that f takes arguments in α and returns results in β.

Functional application is written without brackets; thus $f\,a$ means $f(a)$. Functions are curried and application associates to the left, so $f\,a\,b$ means $(f\,a)b$ and not $f(a\,b)$. Where convenient we will write $f_a\,b$ as an alternative to $f\,a\,b$. Functional application is more binding than any other operation, so $f\,a \oplus b$ means $(f\,a) \oplus b$ and not $f(a \oplus b)$.

Functional composition is denoted by a centralised dot ($\cdot$). We have

$$(f \cdot g)a = f(g\,a)$$

Various symbols will be used to denote general binary operators, in particular, $\oplus$, $\otimes$, and $\circledast$ will be used frequently. No particular properties of an operator should be inferred from its shape. For example, depending on the context, $\oplus$ may or may not denote a commutative operation.

Binary operators can be *sectioned*. This means that $(a\oplus)$ and $(\oplus a)$ both denote functions. The definitions are:

$$\begin{aligned}(a\oplus)\,b &= a \oplus b \\ (\oplus b)\,a &= a \oplus b\end{aligned}$$

Thus, if $\oplus$ has type $\oplus : \alpha \times \beta \to \gamma$, then we have

$$(a\oplus) : \beta \to \gamma$$
$$(\oplus b) : \alpha \to \gamma$$

for all a in α and b in β.

For example, one way of stating that functional composition is associative is to write

$$(f \cdot) \cdot (g \cdot) = ((f \cdot g) \cdot)$$

To improve readability we shall often write sections without their full complement of brackets. For example, the above equation can be written as

$$(f \cdot) \cdot (g \cdot) = (f \cdot g) \cdot$$

The identity element of $\oplus : \alpha \times \alpha \to \alpha$, if it exists, will be denoted by $id_\oplus$. Thus,

$$a \oplus id_\oplus = id_\oplus \oplus a = a$$

However, the identity element of functional composition (over functions of type $\alpha \to \alpha$) will be denoted by id_α. Thus

$$id_\alpha \, a = a$$

for all a in α.

The constant valued function $K : \alpha \to \beta \to \alpha$ is defined by the equation

$$K \, a \, b = a$$

for all a in α and b in β. We sometimes write K_a as an alternative to $K \, a$.

1.2 Lists

Lists are finite sequences of values of the same type. We use the notation $[\alpha]$ to describe the type of lists whose elements have type α. Lists will be denoted using square brackets; for example $[1, 2, 1]$ is a list of three numbers, and $[[1], [1, 2], [1, 2, 1]]$ is a list of three lists of numbers. The function $[\cdot] : \alpha \to [\alpha]$ maps elements of α into singleton lists. Thus

$$[\cdot]a = [a]$$

The primitive operation on lists is concatenation, denoted by the sign $+\!\!+$. For example:

$$[1] +\!\!+ [2] +\!\!+ [1] = [1, 2, 1]$$

Concatenation is an associative operation, that is,

$$x + \!\!\!+\, (y + \!\!\!+\, z) = (x + \!\!\!+\, y) + \!\!\!+\, z$$

for all lists x, y and z in $[\alpha]$.

In the majority of situations (though not all) it is convenient to assume the existence of a special list, denoted by $[\,]$ and called the *empty* list, which acts as the identity element of concatenation. Thus,

$$x + \!\!\!+\, [\,] = [\,] + \!\!\!+\, x = x$$

for all x in $[\alpha]$. To distinguish this possibility, we shall let $[\alpha]$ denote the type of lists over α including $[\,]$, and $[\alpha]^+$ the type of lists over α excluding $[\,]$.

In order to define functions on lists, we shall make the following assumption. Suppose $f : \alpha \to \beta$ and $\oplus : \beta \times \beta \to \beta$ is associative with identity element $id_\oplus$. Then the three equations

$$\begin{aligned} h[\,] &= id_\oplus \\ h[a] &= f\,a \\ h(x + \!\!\!+\, y) &= h\,x \oplus h\,y \end{aligned}$$

specify a unique function $h : [\alpha] \to \beta$. In the case that $id_\oplus$ is not defined, we also suppose that the last two equations by themselves determine a unique function $h : [\alpha]^+ \to \beta$.

A function h satisfying the above three equations will be called a *homomorphism*. Homomorphisms will be discussed in the next lecture. One simple example of a homomorphism is provided by the function $\# : [\alpha] \to N$ which returns the *length* of a list. Here, N denotes the natural numbers $\{0, 1, \ldots\}$. We have

$$\begin{aligned} \#[\,] &= 0 \\ \#[a] &= 1 \\ \#(x + \!\!\!+\, y) &= \#x + \#y \end{aligned}$$

Observe that $+$ is associative with 0 as its identity element.

1.3 Bags and sets

By definition, a (finite) *bag* is a list in which the order of the elements is ignored. Bags are constructed by adding the rule that $+\!\!\!+$ is commutative as well as associative. Also by definition, a (finite) *set* is a bag in which repetitions of elements are ignored. Sets are constructed by adding the rule that $\mathbin{+\!\!+}$ is idempotent as well as commutative and associative. As we shall see, much of the theory developed below holds for bags and sets as well as lists.

In the main we shall use the single operator $\mathbin{+\!\!+}$ for all three structures, relying on context to resolve ambiguity. However, in order to distinguish different uses in one and the same expression, we shall sometimes use $\uplus$ (bag union) for the concatenation operator on bags, and $\cup$ (set union) for the same operator on sets. Singleton bags are denoted by $\lbag a \rbag$ and singleton sets by $\{a\}$.

We can define functions on bags by making an assumption similar to that for lists. Suppose $f : \alpha \to \beta$ and $\oplus : \beta \times \beta \to \beta$ is an associative and commutative operator with identity element $id_\oplus$. Then we assume that the three equations

$$\begin{aligned} h \lbag \, \rbag &= id_\oplus \\ h \lbag a \rbag &= f \, a \\ h(x \uplus y) &= h \, x \oplus h \, y \end{aligned}$$

define a unique function $h : \lbag \alpha \rbag \to \beta$. A similar assumption is made for sets, except that we also require $\oplus$ to be idempotent.

For example, the *size* of a bag is the number of elements it contains, counting repetitions. It can be defined by the equations

$$\begin{aligned} \# \lbag \, \rbag &= 0 \\ \# \lbag a \rbag &= 1 \\ \#(x \uplus y) &= \#x + \#y \end{aligned}$$

However, although $+$ is associative and commutative, it is not idempotent, so the same equations do not define the size function on sets.

1.4 Map

The operator $*$ (pronounced 'map') takes a function on its left and a list on its right. Informally, we have

$$f * [a_1, a_2, \ldots, a_n] = [f \, a_1, f \, a_2, \ldots, f \, a_n].$$

Formally, we specify $f *$ by three equations

$$\begin{aligned} f * [\,] &= [\,] \\ f * [a] &= [f \, a] \\ f * (x \mathbin{+\!\!+} y) &= (f * x) \mathbin{+\!\!+} (f * y) \end{aligned}$$

The function $f*$ is similarly defined on bags and sets.

An important property of $*$ is that it distributes (backwards) through functional composition:

$$(f \cdot g)* = (f*) \cdot (g*)$$

This fact will be referred to as the $*$ *distributivity* rule. Its use in calculations is so frequent that we shall sometimes employ it without explicit mention.

1.5 Reduce

The operator $/$ (pronounced 'reduce') takes a binary operator on its left and a list on its right. Informally, we have

$$\oplus/[a_1, a_2, \ldots, a_n] = a_1 \oplus a_2 \oplus \cdots \oplus a_n$$

Formally, we specify $\oplus/$, where $\oplus$ is associative, by three equations

$$\begin{aligned} \oplus/[\,] &= id_\oplus \quad &\text{(if } id_\oplus \text{ exists)} \\ \oplus/[a] &= a \\ \oplus/(x \mathbin{+\!\!+} y) &= (\oplus/x) \oplus (\oplus/y) \end{aligned}$$

If $\oplus$ is commutative as well as associative, then $\oplus/$ can be applied to bags; and if $\oplus$ is also idempotent, then $\oplus/$ can be applied to sets.

If $\oplus$ does not have an identity element, then we can regard $\oplus/$ as a function of type $\oplus/ : [\alpha]^+ \to \alpha$. Alternatively, we can invent an extra value and adjoin it to α. Provided a little care is taken, so-called 'fictitious' identity elements can always be added to a domain. For example, the minimum operator $\downarrow$ defined by

$$\begin{aligned} a \downarrow b &= a \quad \text{if } a \leqslant b \\ &= b \quad \text{otherwise} \end{aligned}$$

has no identity element in R (the domain of real numbers). However, the fictitious number ∞ can be adjoined to R. The only property attributed to ∞ is that

$$a \downarrow \infty = \infty \downarrow a = a$$

for all a in $R \cup \{\infty\}$. In this way, inconsistency is avoided.

Two useful functions where we choose not to invent identity elements are given by

$$\begin{aligned} head &= \ll/ \\ last &= \gg/ \end{aligned}$$

where the operators $\ll$ ('left') and $\gg$ ('right') are defined by

$$\begin{aligned} a \ll b &= a \\ a \gg b &= b \end{aligned}$$

The function *head* selects the first element of a non-empty list, while *last* selects the last element. Both $\ll$ and $\gg$ are associative but neither possesses an identity element. Both operators are idempotent, but neither is commutative, so *head* and *last* are not defined on bags and sets.

1.6 Promotion

The equations defining $f*$ and $\oplus/$ can be expressed as identities between functions. They come in three groups:

empty rules

$$\begin{aligned} f* \cdot K[\,] &= K[\,] \\ \oplus/ \cdot K[\,] &= id_\oplus \end{aligned}$$

one-point rules

$$\begin{aligned} f* \cdot [\cdot] &= [\cdot] \cdot f \\ \oplus/ \cdot [\cdot] &= id_\alpha \end{aligned}$$

join rules

$$\begin{aligned} f* \cdot \mathbin{+\!\!+}/ &= \mathbin{+\!\!+}/ \cdot (f*)* \\ \oplus/ \cdot \mathbin{+\!\!+}/ &= \oplus/ \cdot (\oplus/)* \end{aligned}$$

The interesting rules here are the last two, since they are not simple transcriptions of the third equations for $f*$ and $\oplus/$. A rough and ready justification of the join rule for $f*$ is as follows:

$$\begin{aligned} & f * \mathbin{+\!\!+}/[x_1, x_2, \ldots, x_n] \\ =\ & f * (x_1 \mathbin{+\!\!+} x_2 \mathbin{+\!\!+} \cdots \mathbin{+\!\!+} x_n) \\ =\ & (f*x_1) \mathbin{+\!\!+} (f*x_2) \mathbin{+\!\!+} \cdots \mathbin{+\!\!+} (f*x_n) \\ =\ & \mathbin{+\!\!+}/[f*x_1, f*x_2, \ldots, f*x_n] \\ =\ & \mathbin{+\!\!+}/(f*) * [x_1, x_2, \ldots, x_n] \end{aligned}$$

A similar justification can be given for the join rule for $\oplus/$. We shall refer to these two rules as *map promotion* and *reduce promotion* respectively.

The nomenclature is historical and is intended to express the idea that an operation on a compound structure can be 'promoted' into its components.

The map and promotion rules are often applied in sequence. Consider the following little calculation:

$$\begin{aligned}
\oplus/ \cdot f* \cdot +\!\!+/ \cdot g* &= \quad \text{map promotion} \\
&\quad \oplus/ \cdot +\!\!+/ \cdot f** \cdot g* \\
&= \quad \text{reduce promotion} \\
&\quad \oplus/ \cdot \oplus/* \cdot f** \cdot g* \\
&= \quad *\text{ distributivity} \\
&\quad \oplus/ \cdot (\oplus/ \cdot f* \cdot g)*
\end{aligned}$$

These three steps will, in future, be compressed into one under the name *map and reduce promotion*.

1.7 Directed reductions

We now introduce two more operators $\nrightarrow$ (pronounced 'left-to-right reduce', or just 'left reduce') and $\nleftarrow$ ('right-to-left reduce') which are closely related to $/$. Informally, we have

$$\begin{aligned}
\oplus \nrightarrow_e [a_1, a_2, \ldots, a_n] &= ((e \oplus a_1) \oplus a_2) \oplus \cdots \oplus a_n \\
\oplus \nleftarrow_e [a_1, a_2, \ldots, a_n] &= a_1 \oplus (a_2 \oplus \cdots \oplus (a_n \oplus e))
\end{aligned}$$

In particular, we have

$$\begin{aligned}
\oplus \nrightarrow_e [\,] &= e \\
\oplus \nleftarrow_e [\,] &= e
\end{aligned}$$

Thus, the parameter e (called the *starting value* or *seed*) defines the value of the reduction on empty lists.

Notice in a left-reduce that the brackets group from the left, and in a right-reduce they group from the right. Since an order of association is provided, the operator $\oplus$ of a left or right-reduction need not be associative. In fact, in a left-reduce we can have $\oplus : \beta \times \alpha \to \beta$ and in a right-reduce $\oplus : \alpha \times \beta \to \beta$. Thus, for a given seed e in β, the types of $\nrightarrow_e$ and $\nleftarrow_e$ are

$$\begin{aligned}
\nrightarrow_e &: (\beta \times \alpha \to \beta) \to [\alpha] \to \beta \\
\nleftarrow_e &: (\alpha \times \beta \to \beta) \to [\alpha] \to \beta
\end{aligned}$$

Formally, we can define $\oplus\nrightarrow_e$ on lists by two equations:

$$\begin{aligned}
\oplus \nrightarrow_e [\,] &= e \\
\oplus \nrightarrow_e (x +\!\!+ [a]) &= (\oplus \nrightarrow_e x) \oplus a
\end{aligned}$$

These equations are different in form to previous definitions. However, since it is intuitively clear that every non-empty list can be expressed uniquely in the form $x \mathbin{+\!\!+} [a]$, these two equations are sufficient to specify $\oplus \not{\to} e$ uniquely. (This point is dealt with in the third lecture). A similar definition holds for $\oplus \not{\leftarrow} e$.

Both kinds of reduction can be applied to bags and sets provided $\oplus$ satisfies additional conditions, designed to ensure that the result of a directed reduction is independent of any particular representation of the bag or set. For $\oplus \not{\to} e$ to be defined on bags we require that

$$(b \oplus a_1) \oplus a_2 = (b \oplus a_2) \oplus a_1$$

for all b in β and a_1, a_2 in α. For sets we need the extra condition

$$(b \oplus a) \oplus a = b \oplus a$$

Similar conditions are required for right-reductions. These remarks are given for completeness for we shall not apply directed reductions to bags or sets.

It is convenient for some purposes to define a more restricted form of directed reduction in which the seed is omitted. Informally, we have that

$$\oplus \not{\to} [a_1, a_2, \ldots, a_n] = ((a_1 \oplus a_2) \oplus a_3) \oplus \cdots \oplus a_n$$
$$\oplus \not{\leftarrow} [a_1, a_2, \ldots, a_n] = a_1 \oplus (a_2 \oplus \cdots \oplus (a_{n-1} \oplus a_n))$$

Note that the type of $\oplus$ in this kind of directed reduce must be of the form $\oplus : \alpha \times \alpha \to \alpha$. The value of $\oplus \not{\to} [\,]$ is not defined unless $\oplus$ possesses a unique *left-identity* element, i.e. a value e satisfying

$$e \oplus a = a$$

for all a. If such a value exists and is unique, we can set

$$\oplus \not{\to} [\,] = e$$

Similarly, $\oplus \not{\leftarrow} [\,]$ is defined only if $\oplus$ has a unique right identity element.

There are a number of properties relating the various forms of directed reduction. For example, we have

$$(\oplus \not{\to}) \cdot ([a] \mathbin{+\!\!+}) = \oplus \not{\to} a$$
$$(\oplus \not{\leftarrow}) \cdot (\mathbin{+\!\!+} [a]) = \oplus \not{\leftarrow} a$$

Other properties will be considered in a later lecture. For the present we give just one illustration of the use of left-reduce.

Recall from the first section that the right-hand side of Horner's rule reads

$$(((1 \times a_1 + 1) \times a_2 + 1) \times \cdots + 1) \times a_n + 1$$

This expression can be written using a left-reduce:

$$\circledast \mathop{/\!\!\!/}_1 [a_1, a_2, \ldots, a_n]$$

where the operator $\circledast$ is defined by

$$a \circledast b = (a \times b) + 1$$

It is interesting to compare this with another form of Horner's rule:

$$(a_1 \times a_2 \times a_3) + (a_2 \times a_3) + a_3 = ((a_1 \times a_2 + a_2) \times a_3 + a_3$$

Here, the general form of the right-hand side can be written as

$$\circledast \mathop{/\!\!\!/} [a_1, a_2, \ldots, a_n],$$

where, this time, $\circledast$ is defined by

$$a \circledast b = (a \times b) + b$$

1.8 Accumulations

With each form of directed reduction over lists there corresponds a form of computation called an *accumulation*. These forms are expressed with the operators $/\!\!\!/\!\!\!/$ ('left-accumulate') and $/\!\!\!/\!\!\!/$ ('right-accumulate') and are defined informally by

$$\oplus \mathop{/\!\!\!/\!\!\!/} e\, [a_1, a_2, \ldots, a_n] = [e, e \oplus a_1, \ldots, ((e \oplus a_1) \oplus a_2) \oplus \cdots \oplus a_n]$$
$$\oplus \mathop{/\!\!\!/\!\!\!/} e\, [a_1, a_2, \ldots, a_n] = [a_1 \oplus (a_2 \oplus \cdots \oplus (a_n \oplus e)), \ldots, a_n \oplus e, e]$$

Formally, we have

$$\begin{aligned} \oplus \mathop{/\!\!\!/\!\!\!/} e\, [] &= [e] \\ \oplus \mathop{/\!\!\!/\!\!\!/} e\, ([a] \mathbin{+\!\!+} x) &= [e] \mathbin{+\!\!+} (\oplus \mathop{/\!\!\!/\!\!\!/} e \oplus a\, x) \end{aligned}$$

Alternatively, we can define a left-accumulation by

$$\begin{aligned} \oplus \mathop{/\!\!\!/\!\!\!/} e\, [] &= [e] \\ \oplus \mathop{/\!\!\!/\!\!\!/} e\, (x \mathbin{+\!\!+} [a]) &= (\oplus \mathop{/\!\!\!/\!\!\!/} e\, x) \mathbin{+\!\!+} [b \oplus a] \\ &\text{where } b = \mathit{last}(\oplus \mathop{/\!\!\!/\!\!\!/} e\, x) \end{aligned}$$

Yet a third way of defining $\oplus\!\!\!/\!\!\!/_e$ will be given in the next section. The definitions of the other accumulation operators are similiar and we omit details.

Observe from the above equations that $\oplus\!\!\!/\!\!\!/_e\,x$ can be evaluated with n calculations of $\oplus$, where $n = \#x$. For example, the list $[0!, 1!, \ldots, n!]$ of the first $(n+1)$ factorial numbers can be computed by evaluating

$$\times \!\!\!/\!\!\!/_1 [1, 2, \ldots, n]$$

This requires $O(n)$ steps, whereas the alternative

$$fact * [0, 1, \ldots, n],$$

where $fact\ k = \times/[1, 2, \ldots, k]$, requires $O(n^2)$ steps. Also amusing is the fact that

$$\div \!\!\!/\!\!\!/_1 [1, \ldots, n] = [\frac{1}{0!}, \ldots, \frac{1}{n!}]$$

Note that

$$\oplus\!\!/\!_e = last \cdot \oplus\!\!\!/\!\!\!/_e$$

so left-reductions can be defined in terms of left-accumulations. On the other hand, we also have

$$\oplus\!\!\!/\!\!\!/_e = \otimes\!\!/\!_{[e]}$$

where

$$x \otimes a = x +\!\!\!+ [last\ x \oplus a]$$

Hence left-accumulations can be defined in terms of left-reductions.

1.9 Segments

A list y is a *segment* of x if there exist u and v such that $x = u +\!\!\!+ y +\!\!\!+ v$. If $u = [\,]$, then y is an *initial segment*, and if $v = [\,]$, then y is a *final segment*.

The function *inits* returns the list of initial segments of a list, in increasing order of length. The function *tails* returns the list of final segments of a list, in decreasing order of length. Thus, informally, we have

$$\begin{aligned} inits[a_1, a_2, \ldots, a_n] &= [[\,], [a_1], [a_1, a_2], \ldots, [a_1, a_2, \ldots, a_n]] \\ tails[a_1, a_2, \ldots, a_n] &= [[a_1, a_2, \ldots, a_n], [a_2, a_3, \ldots, a_n], \ldots, [\,]] \end{aligned}$$

The functions $inits^+$ and $tails^+$ are similar, except that the empty list does not appear in the result.

These four functions can be defined by accumulations. For example,

$$\begin{aligned} \mathit{inits} &= (+\!\!+\!\!\#_{[\,]}) \cdot [\cdot]* \\ \mathit{inits}^+ &= (+\!\!+\!\!\#) \cdot [\cdot]* \end{aligned}$$

Alternatively, we can define these functions by explicit recursion equations. For example:

$$\begin{aligned} \mathit{tails}[\,] &= [[\,]] \\ \mathit{tails}(x +\!\!+ [a]) &= (+\!\!+[a]) * \mathit{tails}\, x +\!\!+ [[\,]] \end{aligned}$$

The following result shows another way we can define accumulations.

Accumulation lemma

$$\begin{aligned} (\oplus\!\!\#\!e) &= (\oplus\!\!\!\not\!\!e)* \cdot \mathit{inits} \\ (\oplus\!\!\#) &= (\oplus\!\!\!\not\!\!\,)* \cdot \mathit{inits}^+ \end{aligned}$$

There are similar equations for right-accumulations. The accumulation lemma is used frequently in the derivation of efficient algorithms for problems about segments. On lists of length n, evaluation of the left-hand side requires $O(n)$ computations involving $\oplus$, while the right-hand side requires $O(n^2)$ computations.

The functions segs returns a list of all segments of a list, and segs^+ returns a list of all non-empty segments. A convenient definition is

$$\mathit{segs} = +\!\!+\!/ \cdot \mathit{tails}* \cdot \mathit{inits}$$

For example,

$$\mathit{segs}[1,2,3] = [[\,],[1],[\,],[1,2],[2],[\,],[1,2,3],[2,3],[3],[\,]]$$

Notice that the empty list $[\,]$ appears four times in $\mathit{segs}[1,2,3]$ (and not at all in $\mathit{segs}^+[1,2,3]$). The order in which the elements of $\mathit{segs}\,x$ appear is not important for our purposes and we shall make no use of it. In effect, we regard $\mathit{segs}\,x$ as a bag of lists. This identification can be made explicit by introducing a 'bagifying' function

$$\mathit{bag} = \uplus/ \cdot \{\cdot\}*$$

which converts a list into a bag of its elements (and is the identity function on bags). We can then define

$$\mathit{bagsegs} = \mathit{bag} \cdot \mathit{segs}$$

However, explicit use of *bag* can be avoided in many examples. Consider a function of the form
$$P = \oplus/ \cdot f* \cdot bagsegs$$
where we must have that $\oplus$ is commutative as well as associative. We can calculate

$$\begin{array}{rl} P = & \text{definition of } bagsegs \\ & \oplus/ \cdot f* \cdot \uplus/ \cdot \{\cdot\}* \cdot segs \\ = & \text{map and reduce promotion} \\ & \oplus/ \cdot (\oplus/ \cdot f* \cdot \{\cdot\})* \cdot segs \\ = & \text{one-point rules} \\ & \oplus/ \cdot f* \cdot segs \end{array}$$

and so *bagsegs* can be replaced by *segs*.

1.10 Horner's rule

Now let us return to the problem posed at the beginning. Horner's rule can be expressed as an equation

$$\oplus/ \cdot \otimes/* \cdot tails = \circledast\!\!\not/e$$

where $e = id_\otimes$ and $a \circledast b = (a \otimes b) \oplus e$. Horner's rule is valid provided $\otimes$ distributes (backwards) over $\oplus$, that is,

$$(a \oplus b) \otimes c = (a \otimes c) \oplus (b \otimes c)$$

for all a, b and c of the appropriate type. This condition is equivalent to the assertion that the equation

$$(\oplus/x) \otimes c = \oplus/(\otimes c) * x$$

holds for all non-empty x. If we also assume that $id_\oplus$ is a *left-zero* of $\otimes$, i.e.,

$$id_\oplus \otimes a = id_\oplus$$

for all a, then the restriction to non-empty lists can be dropped.

Horner's rule is proved by induction. The idea is to show that

$$f = \oplus/ \cdot \otimes/* \cdot tails$$

satisfies the equations

$$\begin{array}{rl} f[] & = e \\ f(x +\!\!+ [a]) & = f\,x \circledast a \end{array}$$

from which we can deduce that $f = \oplus\!\!\!/\!\!\!\!\!\nearrow_e$. The proof of Horner's rule makes use of the recursive characterisation of *tails* given in the previous section. We shall leave details to the reader.

Horner's rule can be generalised in a number of ways, all of which depend on the assumption that $\otimes$ distributes backwards over $\oplus$. First of all, if d is a left-zero of $\otimes$, then we have

$$(\oplus\!\!\!/\!\!\!\!\!\nearrow_d) \cdot (\otimes\!\!\!/\!\!\!\!\!\nearrow_e)* \cdot tails = \circledast\!\!\!/\!\!\!\!\!\nearrow_{d \oplus e}$$

where $a \circledast b = (a \otimes b) \oplus e$. Thus the operators $\oplus$ and $\otimes$ involved in Horner's rule need not be associative.

Second, we have

$$\oplus\!/ \cdot (\otimes\!/ \cdot f*)* \cdot tails = \circledast\!\!\!/\!\!\!\!\!\nearrow_e$$

where $e = id_\otimes$ and $a \circledast b = (a \otimes f\,b) \oplus e$. This particular form of Horner's rule will be used in the next lecture.

Third, we have that the equation

$$\oplus\!/ \cdot \otimes\!/* \cdot tails^+ = \circledast\!\!\!/\!\!\!\!\!\nearrow$$

holds over all non-empty lists. Here, $a \circledast b = (a \otimes b) \oplus b$. In this formulation we do not require that $id_\otimes$ be defined.

1.11 Application

Let us give one application of Horner's rule. There is a famous problem, called the *maximum segment sum (mss)* problem, which is to compute the maximum of the sums of all segments of a given sequence of numbers, positive, negative or zero. In symbols

$$mss = \uparrow\!/ \cdot +\!/* \cdot segs$$

Direct evaluation of the right-hand side of this equation requires $O(n^3)$ steps on a list of length n. There are $O(n^2)$ segments and each can be summed in $O(n)$ steps, giving $O(n^3)$ steps in all. Using Horner's rule it is easy to calculate an $O(n)$ algorithm:

$$
\begin{array}{rl}
mss = & \text{definition} \\
 & \uparrow\!/ \cdot +\!/* \cdot segs \\
= & \text{definition of } segs \\
 & \uparrow\!/ \cdot +\!/* \cdot +\!\!+\!/ \cdot tails* \cdot inits \\
= & \text{map and reduce promotion} \\
 & \uparrow\!/ \cdot (\uparrow\!/ \cdot +\!/* \cdot tails)* \cdot inits
\end{array}
$$

$$\begin{aligned}&= \text{Horner's rule with } a \circledast b = (a+b) \uparrow 0\\&\quad \uparrow/\cdot \circledast \not{\hspace{-2pt}/}_0 * \cdot \mathit{inits}\\&= \text{accumulation lemma}\\&\quad \uparrow/\cdot \circledast\not{\hspace{-2pt}/}_0\end{aligned}$$

Horner's rule is applicable because $+$ distributes through $\uparrow$, and $0 = id_+$. The result is a linear time algorithm.

An interesting variation of the problem is not so well-known. It is to compute the maximum segment *product*. In symbols

$$msp = \uparrow/\cdot \times/* \cdot segs$$

Since $\times$ does not distribute through $\uparrow$ for negative numbers, the previous derivation does not work. However, we do have

$$\begin{aligned}(a \uparrow b) \times c &= (a \times c) \uparrow (b \times c) \quad \text{if } c \geqslant 0\\(a \uparrow b) \times c &= (a \times c) \downarrow (b \times c) \quad \text{if } c \leqslant 0\end{aligned}$$

where $\downarrow$ takes the minimum of its two arguments. A similar pair of equations holds for $(a \downarrow b) \times c$. These facts are enough to ensure that, with suitable cunning, Horner's rule can be made to work. The idea is to define $\oplus$ by

$$(a_1, b_1) \oplus (a_2, b_2) = (a_1 \downarrow a_2, b_1 \uparrow b_2)$$

and $\otimes$ by

$$\begin{aligned}(a, b) \otimes c &= (a \times c, b \times c) \quad \text{if } c \geqslant 0\\&= (b \times c, a \times c) \quad \text{otherwise}\end{aligned}$$

Then, using the observations about $\uparrow$ and $\downarrow$ given above, we have that

$$((a_1, b_1) \oplus (a_2, b_2)) \otimes c = ((a_1, b_1) \otimes c) \oplus ((a_2, b_2) \otimes c)$$

and so $\otimes$ distributes backwards through $\oplus$.

Now define

$$f\,x = (\downarrow/\times/* \mathit{segs}\,x, \uparrow/\times/* \mathit{segs}\,x)$$

We claim (without proof) that

$$f = \oplus/\cdot (\otimes\not{\hspace{-2pt}/}_e)* \cdot \mathit{segs}$$

where $e = (1, 1)$. Using the generalisation of Horner's rule cited in the previous section, a similar calculation to before shows that

$$f = \oplus/\cdot \otimes\not{\hspace{-2pt}/}_e$$

where $\circledast$ is defined by
$$(a, b) \circledast c = ((a, b) \otimes c) \oplus e$$
Hence we have
$$msp = \pi_2 \cdot \oplus/ \cdot \circledast /\!\!/ e$$
where $\pi_2(a, b) = b$. Again this is a linear time algorithm.

1.12 Segment decomposition

The sequence of calculation steps given in the derivation of the *mss* problem arises frequently. Here is the essential idea expressed as a general theorem.

Theorem 1 (Segment decomposition) *Suppose S and T are defined by*
$$\begin{aligned} S &= \oplus/ \cdot f* \cdot segs \\ T &= \oplus/ \cdot f* \cdot tails \end{aligned}$$
If T can be expressed in the form $T = h \cdot \circledast /\!\!/ e$, then we have
$$S = \oplus/ \cdot h* \cdot \circledast /\!\!/ e$$

Proof

We calculate

$$\begin{aligned} S &= & & \text{given} \\ & & \oplus/ \cdot f* \cdot segs & \\ &= & & \text{definition of } segs \\ & & \oplus/ \cdot f* \cdot +\!\!+/ \cdot tails* \cdot inits & \\ &= & & \text{map and reduce promotion} \\ & & \oplus/ \cdot (\oplus/ \cdot f* \cdot tails)* \cdot inits & \\ &= & & \text{hypothesis on } T \\ & & \oplus/ \cdot (h \cdot \circledast /\!\!/ e)* \cdot inits & \\ &= & & *\text{ distributivity} \\ & & \oplus/ \cdot h* \cdot \circledast /\!\!/ e * \cdot inits & \\ &= & & \text{accumulation lemma} \\ & & \oplus/ \cdot h* \cdot \circledast /\!\!/ e & \end{aligned}$$

□

1.13 References

Much of the foregoing theory is introduced in

[1] Bird, R.S. An introduction to the theory of lists. *Logic of Programming and Calculi of Discrete Design*, (edited by M. Broy), NATO ASI Series F Vol 36, Springer-Verlag, Berlin (1987) 3-42.

An earlier account, using somewhat different syntactic conventions, is in

[2] Meertens, L.G.L.T Algorithmics - towards programming as a mathematical activity. *Proc. CWI Symp. on Mathematics and Computer Science*, CWI Monographs, North-Holland, 1 (1986) 289-334.

An alternative treatment of some of the concepts, stressing the use of the map and reduction operators in functional programming, is in the recent textbook

[3] Bird, R.S. and Wadler, P.L. *Introduction to Functional Programming*. Prentice Hall International, Hemel Hempstead, UK, (1988)

The maximum segment sum problem is well-known and is discussed in, among other places,

[4] Bentley, J.L. *Programming Pearls* (Chapter 7) Addison-Wesley, Reading, Mass, USA (1986)

[5] Gries, D. A note on a standard strategy for developing loop invariants and loops. *Science of Computer Programming*, Vol 4, 2 (1982) 207-214

The maximum product problem appears as Exercise 47 in

[6] Rem, M. Small programming exercises. *Science of Computer Programming*, Vol 10, 2 (1988)

2 Homomorphisms

2.0 Problem

Given is a sequence x and a predicate p. Required is an efficient algorithm for computing some longest segment of x, all of whose elements satisfy p.

2.1 Monoids and homomorphisms

An algebra $(\beta, \oplus, id_\oplus, i)$ is called a *monoid* over α if $i : \alpha \to \beta$ and $\oplus : \beta \times \beta \to \beta$ is an associative operator with identity element $id_\oplus$. In particular, $([\alpha], +\!\!+, [], [\cdot])$ is a monoid over α for any α. The algebra $(N, +, 0, K_1)$ is also a monoid over α for any α.

Given monoids $(\beta, \oplus, id_\oplus, i)$ and $(\gamma, \otimes, id_\otimes, j)$ over α, a function $h : \beta \to \gamma$ is called a *homomorphism* if it satisfies the three equations

$$\begin{aligned} h\, id_\oplus &= id_\otimes \\ h(i\, a) &= j\, a \\ h(x \oplus y) &= h\, x \otimes h\, y \end{aligned}$$

Our basic assumption about the particular monoid $([\alpha], +\!\!+, [], [\cdot])$ is the property that for each monoid $(\beta, \oplus, id_\oplus, i)$ over α there is a unique homomorphism h from $[\alpha]$ to β. Such a monoid is called the *free monoid* over α.

The following lemma gives a useful characterisation of homomorphisms on lists.

Lemma 2 *Let h be the unique homomorphism from $[\alpha]$ to the monoid $(\beta, \oplus, id_\oplus, f)$. Then $h = \oplus/ \cdot f*$.*

Proof. Using the definitions of map and reduce we have

$$(\oplus/ \cdot f*)[\,] = \oplus/[\,] = id_\oplus$$

and

$$(\oplus/ \cdot f*)[a] = \oplus/[f\, a] = f\, a$$

and

$$\begin{aligned} (\oplus/ \cdot f*)(x +\!\!+ y) &= \oplus/(f * x +\!\!+ f * y) \\ &= ((\oplus/ \cdot f*)x) \oplus ((\oplus/ \cdot f*)y) \end{aligned}$$

Thus $\oplus/ \cdot f*$ is a homomorphism from $[\alpha]$ to β. But, since there is exactly one homomorphism from $[\alpha]$ to β, we have $h = \oplus/ \cdot f*$. □

2.2 General equations

Not all functions on lists are homomorphisms. It is instructive to determine the conditions under which a set of equations of the form

$$\begin{aligned} h[\,] &= e \\ h[a] &= f\, a \\ h(x +\!\!+ y) &= H(x, y, h\, x, h\, y) \end{aligned}$$

determines a unique function h.

Consider the equations

$$\begin{aligned} h'[\,] &= ([\,], e) \\ h'[a] &= ([a], f\,a) \\ h'(x \mathbin{+\mkern-8mu+} y) &= h'\,x \oplus h'\,y \end{aligned}$$

where $\oplus$ is defined by

$$(x, u) \oplus (y, v) = (x \mathbin{+\mkern-8mu+} y, H(x, y, u, v))$$

Since we have

$$h = \pi_2 \cdot h'$$

where $\pi_2(a, b) = b$, it follows that h is a well-defined function if h' is.

In order to determine the conditions under which the above equations determine h', let β be the smallest set of values such that

1. $([\,], e)$ is in β;

2. $([a], f\,a)$ is in β for all a in α;

3. $(x, u) \oplus (y, v)$ is in β whenever (x, u) and (y, v) are.

Now, by our basic assumption, h' is uniquely determined if $\oplus$ is associative with identity element $([\,], e)$. We must therefore have:

1. $H(x, [\,], u, e) = u$

2. $H([\,], x, e, u) = u$

3. $H(x \mathbin{+\mkern-8mu+} y, z, H(x, y, u, v), w) = H(x, y \mathbin{+\mkern-8mu+} z, u, H(y, z, v, w))$

for all (x, u) and (y, v) in β. These three conditions (the *consistency conditions*) determine the properties that H and e must satisfy in order for the equations for h to determine h completely.

Let us consider one example. Take $e = [\,]$ and

$$\begin{aligned} H(x, y, u, v) &= u \mathbin{+\mkern-8mu+} v \quad \text{if } u = x \\ &= u \quad\quad\;\;\, \text{otherwise} \end{aligned}$$

The verification of the first two consistency conditions on e and H is left to the reader. The third condition does *not* hold unless it is the case that $\#x \geqslant \#u$ for all (x, u) in β. This condition is satisfied if

$$\#f\,a \leqslant 1$$

for all a. In particular, if we take

$$\begin{aligned} f\,a &= [a] \quad \text{if } p\,a \\ &= [] \quad \text{otherwise} \end{aligned}$$

for an arbitrary predicate p, then the consistency conditions are satisfied. With this definition of f, the value of $h\,x$ is just the longest initial segment of x all of whose elements satisfy p. In symbols:

$$h = \uparrow_{\#}/ \cdot all\ p\triangleleft \cdot inits$$

As a last point, we show that h is not a homomorphism. For concreteness take $p = even$, the predicate that determines whether a number is even. Suppose

$$h(x \mathbin{+\!\!+} y) = h\,x \oplus h\,y$$

for some operator $\oplus$. Since $h[2,1] = 2, h[4] = [4]$, and $h[2] = [2]$, we have

$$\begin{aligned} h[2,1,4] &= h[2,1] \oplus h[4] \\ &= [2] \oplus [4] \\ &= h[2] \oplus h[4] \\ &= h[2,4] \end{aligned}$$

This is a contradiction, since $h[2,1,4] = [2]$ and $h[2,4] = [2,4]$.

2.3 Examples

Let us now consider some examples of homomorphisms on lists.

(1) First of all, the function $\#$ is a homomorphism:

$$\# = +/ \cdot K_1 *$$

(2) Second, the function *reverse* which reverses the order of the elements in a list is a homomorphism:

$$reverse = \widetilde{+\!\!+}/ \cdot [\cdot]*$$

where $x \mathbin{\widetilde{+\!\!+}} y = y \mathbin{+\!\!+} x$. (In general, we define $\widetilde{\oplus}$ by the equation $x \mathbin{\widetilde{\oplus}} y = y \oplus x$.) Of course, on bags and sets, where $\widetilde{+\!\!+} = +\!\!+$, the function *reverse* is just the identity function.

(3) The function *sort* which reorders the elements of a list into ascending order is a homomorphism:

$$sort = ⫲/ \cdot [\cdot]*$$

Here, ⫲ (pronounced 'merge') is defined by the equations

$$
\begin{aligned}
x \mathbin{⫲} [\,] &= x \\
[\,] \mathbin{⫲} y &= y \\
([a] \mathbin{+\!\!+} x) \mathbin{⫲} ([b] \mathbin{+\!\!+} y) &= [a] \mathbin{+\!\!+} (x \mathbin{⫲} ([b] \mathbin{+\!\!+} y)) \quad \text{if } a \leqslant b \\
&= [b] \mathbin{+\!\!+} (([a] \mathbin{+\!\!+} x) \mathbin{⫲} y) \quad \text{otherwise}
\end{aligned}
$$

Thus, $x \mathbin{⫲} y$ is the result of merging two sorted lists x and y. Since ⫲ is both associative and commutative, the function *sort* can be applied to bags. By defining a variant of ⫲ that removes duplicates, so that the operation is also idempotent, we can sort sets.

(4) Two useful homomorphisms are *all* and *some*:

$$
\begin{aligned}
all\ p &= \wedge/ \cdot p* \\
some\ p &= \vee/ \cdot p*
\end{aligned}
$$

Here, $\wedge$ is logical conjunction and $\vee$ is logical disjunction. The function *all p* applied to a list x returns *True* if every element of x satisfies the predicate p, and *False* otherwise. The function *some p* applied to x returns *True* if at least one element of x satisfies p, and *False* otherwise. Since conjunction and disjunction are associative, commutative and idempotent operations, *all* and *some* can be applied to bags and sets as well as lists.

(5) The function $split : [\alpha]^+ \to \alpha \times [\alpha]$, which splits a non-empty list into its first element and the remainder, is a homomorphism:

$$
\begin{aligned}
split[a] &= (a, [\,]) \\
split(x \mathbin{+\!\!+} y) &= split\ x \oplus split\ y
\end{aligned}
$$

where we define $\oplus$ by

$$(a, x) \oplus (b, y) = (a, x \mathbin{+\!\!+} [b] \mathbin{+\!\!+} y)$$

In particular, we can define

$$tail = \pi_2 \cdot split$$

Unlike *head* (which is $\pi_1 \cdot split$), the function *tail* is not a homomorphism. Note that the homomorphisms described in this example are homomorphisms on the *semigroup* $([\alpha]^+, +\!\!+, [\cdot])$.

Using *split*, we can define the function *tails* of the last lecture as a homomorphism
$$tails = \oplus/ \cdot f*$$
where
$$\begin{aligned} f\, a &= [[a], []] \\ xs \oplus ys &= (+\!\!+z) * xs +\!\!+ tail\, zs \quad \text{where } (z, zs) = split\, ys \end{aligned}$$

A simple calculation shows that $id_\oplus = [[]]$, so we have $tails[\,] = [[]]$, as expected.

2.4 All applied to

In order to be able to describe functions such as *tails* a little more concisely, it is useful to introduce an operator $\circ$ (pronounced 'all applied to') defined by
$$\begin{aligned} [\,]^\circ\, a &= [\,] \\ [f]^\circ\, a &= [f\, a] \\ (fs +\!\!+ gs)^\circ\, a &= (fs^\circ\, a) +\!\!+ (gs^\circ\, a) \end{aligned}$$

Less formally, we have
$$[f, g, \ldots, h]^\circ\, a = [f\, a, g\, a, \ldots, h\, a]$$

Thus $\circ$ takes a sequence of functions and a value and returns the result of applying each function to the value. Note that $(^\circ a)$ is a homomorphism. Note also that the notation $[\cdot]$ we have been using so far can be rewritten as $[id]^\circ$.

We can now write, for example,
$$tails = \oplus/ \cdot [[id]^\circ, [\,]^\circ]^\circ *$$

2.5 Conditional expressions

So far, we have been using the notation
$$\begin{aligned} h\, x &= f\, x \quad \text{if } p\, x \\ &= g\, x \quad \text{otherwise} \end{aligned}$$

to describe functions defined by cases. From now on, we shall also use the McCarthy conditional form

$$h = (p \rightarrow f, g)$$

to describe the same function.

There are a number of well-known laws about conditional forms, the most important of which are:

$$\begin{aligned} h \cdot (p \rightarrow f, g) &= (p \rightarrow h \cdot f, h \cdot g) \\ (p \rightarrow f, g) \cdot h &= (p \cdot h \rightarrow f \cdot h, g \cdot h) \\ (p \rightarrow f, f) &= f \end{aligned}$$

(Remember, all functions are assumed to be *total*, so these laws need no qualifications about definedness.)

2.6 Filter

The operator ◁ (pronounced 'filter') takes a predicate p and a list x and returns the sublist of x consisting, in order, of all those elements of x that satisfy p. Using the new notations just introduced, we can define $p◁$ as a homomorphism

$$p◁ = +\!\!+/ \cdot (p \rightarrow [id]°, []°)*$$

In effect, $p◁x$ is obtained by replacing each element a of x by $[a]$ if $p\,a$ holds, and $[\,]$ otherwise, and then concatenating the resulting lists. Note that $p◁$ can be applied to bags and sets as well as lists.

An easy calculation shows that the following rule (which we will call *filter promotion*) holds:

$$(p◁) \cdot +\!\!+/ = +\!\!+/ \cdot (p◁)*$$

Another rule, whose proof is also left to the reader, is the *map-filter swap* rule:

$$p◁ \cdot f* = f* \cdot (p \cdot f)◁$$

2.7 Cross-product

If $\oplus$ is a binary operator, then $\mathsf{X}_\oplus$ is a binary operator that takes two lists x and y and returns a list of values of the form $a \oplus b$ for all a in x and b in y. For example:

$$[a, b]\,\mathsf{X}_\oplus\,[c, d, e] = [a \oplus c, b \oplus c, a \oplus d, b \oplus d, a \oplus e, b \oplus e]$$

Formally, we define $\mathsf{X}_\oplus$ by three equations:

$$\begin{aligned} x \mathsf{X}_\oplus [\,] &= [\,] \\ x \mathsf{X}_\oplus [a] &= (\oplus a) * x \\ x \mathsf{X}_\oplus (y +\!\!+ z) &= (x \mathsf{X}_\oplus y) +\!\!+ (x \mathsf{X}_\oplus z) \end{aligned}$$

Thus $(x \mathsf{X}_\oplus)$ is a homomorphism (on lists, bags or sets) for every x.

There are a number of useful properties of $\mathsf{X}_\oplus$. We shall state them without proof.

First of all, $\mathsf{X}_\oplus$ is associative if $\oplus$ is, and commutative if $\oplus$ is. It is not, in general, idempotent if $\oplus$ is.

Next, $[\,]$ is the zero element of $\mathsf{X}_\oplus$, that is,

$$[\,] \mathsf{X}_\oplus x = x \mathsf{X}_\oplus [\,] = [\,]$$

for all x.

We also have the *cross promotion* rules:

$$\begin{aligned} f *\! * \cdot \mathsf{X}_{+\!\!+}/ &= \mathsf{X}_{+\!\!+}/ \cdot f *\! *\! * \\ \oplus/* \cdot \mathsf{X}_{+\!\!+}/ &= \mathsf{X}_\oplus/ \cdot \oplus/*\! * \end{aligned}$$

Finally, we have that if $\otimes$ distributes through $\oplus$, then

$$\oplus/ \cdot \mathsf{X}_\otimes/ = \otimes/ \cdot \oplus/*$$

This result says that the sum of the products is the product of the sums. We shall call it the *cross-distributivity* rule.

The particular operator $\mathsf{X}_{+\!\!+}$ has many uses. For example, the *cartesian product* function $cp : [[\alpha]] \to [[\alpha]]$, defined by

$$cp = \mathsf{X}_{+\!\!+}/ \cdot [id]^\circ *\! *$$

takes a list of lists and returns a list of lists of elements, one from each component. For example,

$$cp[[a, b], [c], [d, e]] = [[a, c, d], [b, c, d], [a, c, e], [b, c, e]]$$

Second, the list *subs* x of all subsequences of x can be defined as the homomorphism

$$subs = \mathsf{X}_{+\!\!+}/ \cdot [[\,]^\circ, [id]^\circ]^\circ *$$

For example

$$subs[a,b,c] = \mathsf{X}_{+\!\!+}/[[[\,],[a]],[[\,],[b]],[[\,],[c]]]$$

and the expression on the right simplifies to

$$[[\,],[a],[b],[a,b],[c],[a,c],[b,c],[a,b,c]]$$

Third, we have

$$(all\ p \to [id]^\circ,[\,]^\circ) = \mathsf{X}_{+\!\!+}/ \cdot (p \to [[id]^\circ]^\circ,[\,]^\circ)*$$

This technical result means that we can write $all\ p\triangleleft$ as follows:

$$\begin{aligned} all\ p\triangleleft &= +\!\!+/ \cdot (all\ p \to [id]^\circ,[\,]^\circ)* \\ &= +\!\!+/ \cdot (\mathsf{X}_{+\!\!+}/ \cdot (p \to [[id]^\circ]^\circ,[\,]^\circ)*)* \end{aligned}$$

This daunting expression will make another appearance in the next section but one.

2.8 Selection operators

Suppose f is a numeric valued function. We want to define an operator $\Uparrow_f$ such that

1. $\Uparrow_f$ is associative, commutative and idempotent;

2. $\Uparrow_f$ is *selective* in that

$$x \Uparrow_f y = x \quad \text{or} \quad x \Uparrow_f y = y$$

3. $\Uparrow_f$ is *maximising* in that

$$f(x \Uparrow_f y) = f x \uparrow f y$$

If f is an injective function, then the above three conditions specify $\Uparrow_f$ completely (actually, idempotence follows from selectivity). If, however, f is not injective, then the value of $x \Uparrow_f y$ is not specified when $x \neq y$ but $f x = f y$. For example, the value of

$$[1,2] \Uparrow_\# [3,4]$$

is not determined by the above conditions, beyond the fact that it must be one of $[1,2]$ or $[3,4]$.

There are two ways to resolve such under-specifications. One is to forgo commutativity, defining for instance a *left-biased* version of $\uparrow_f$:

$$\begin{aligned} x \uparrow_f y &= x \quad \text{if } fx \geqslant fy \\ &= y \quad \text{otherwise} \end{aligned}$$

This solution is not very satisfactory because the calculation of expressions such as

$$\uparrow_\#/ \cdot p \triangleleft \cdot segs$$

depends artificially on the precise order in which the function *segs* returns the list of segments of x (a feature which we said in the last lecture we would ignore).

The alternative is to let $\uparrow_f$ stand for $\uparrow_{f'}$, where f' is an injective function, the precise nature of which we are not interested in, that respects the ordering on values given by f, that is,

$$fx < fy \quad \text{implies} \quad f'x < f'y$$

If necessary to ease a calculation, we can always introduce *refinements* of f (i.e. a function that respects the ordering of f but may introduce further distinctions), provided such refinements are consistent with all previous ones.

One particular refinement of $\uparrow_\#$ is especially useful and we impose it at the outset. We shall assume that $+\!\!+$ distributes through $\uparrow_\#$, in other words:

$$\begin{aligned} x +\!\!+ (y \uparrow_\# z) &= (x +\!\!+ y) \uparrow_\# (x +\!\!+ z) \\ (x \uparrow_\# y) +\!\!+ z &= (x +\!\!+ z) \uparrow_\# (y +\!\!+ z) \end{aligned}$$

Such a refinement arises if, for example, we always select the *lexicographically* least sequence as the value of $x \uparrow_\# y$ when $\#x = \#y$.

Since we mainly do calculations at the function level, we would like to write the above distributive rules in the form

$$\begin{aligned} (x+\!\!+) \cdot \uparrow_\#/ &= \uparrow_\#/ \cdot (x+\!\!+)* \\ (+\!\!+x) \cdot \uparrow_\#/ &= \uparrow_\#/ \cdot (+\!\!+x)* \end{aligned}$$

The missing piece which enables the two forms to be connected (without restricting ourselves to non-empty lists) concerns the fictitious value $\omega = \uparrow_\#/[\,]$. This is *not* the empty list, but a very short list satisfying $\#\omega =$

$-\infty$. In other words, we want to suppose that ω is the zero element of $+\!\!+$. This decision can be couched in algebraic language: we suppose that $([\alpha], +\!\!+, \uparrow_\#, [\,], \omega)$ is a *semiring*. In general, a semiring $(S, \times, +, id_\times, id_+)$ is a set S closed under two associative operations $\times$ and $+$, with $+$ also commutative, such that $\times$ distributes over $+$. Moreover, the identity element of $+$ is the zero element of $\times$.

Let us put these assumptions to work in a short calculation:

$$\begin{aligned}
& \uparrow_\#/ \cdot all\ p \triangleleft \\
=\ & \text{daunting expression for } all\ p \triangleleft \text{ from Section 2.7} \\
& \uparrow_\#/ \cdot +\!\!+/ \cdot (\times_{+\!\!+}/ \cdot (p \to [[id]^\circ]^\circ, [\,]^\circ)*)* \\
=\ & \text{reduce promotion} \\
& \uparrow_\#/ \cdot (\uparrow_\#/ \cdot \times_{+\!\!+}/ \cdot (p \to [[id]^\circ]^\circ, [\,]^\circ)*)* \\
=\ & \text{semiring assumption and cross-distributivity} \\
& \uparrow_\#/ \cdot (+\!\!+/ \cdot \uparrow_\#/ * \cdot (p \to [[id]^\circ]^\circ, [\,]^\circ)*)* \\
=\ & * \text{ distributivity} \\
& \uparrow_\#/ \cdot (+\!\!+/ \cdot (\uparrow_\#/ \cdot (p \to [[id]^\circ]^\circ, [\,]^\circ)*)* \\
=\ & \text{conditionals} \\
& \uparrow_\#/ \cdot (+\!\!+/ \cdot (p \to \uparrow_\#/ \cdot [[id]^\circ]^\circ, \uparrow_\#/ \cdot [\,]^\circ)*)* \\
=\ & \text{empty and one-point rules} \\
& \uparrow_\#/ \cdot (+\!\!+/ \cdot (p \to [id]^\circ, K_\omega)*)*
\end{aligned}$$

We shall use this result in the next section.

2.9 Solution

The problem we started the lecture with was to compute the longest segment of a list, all of whose elements satisfied some given property p. In symbols, we want to compute f, where

$$f = \uparrow_\#/ \cdot all\ p \triangleleft \cdot segs$$

Let us calculate:

$$\begin{aligned}
& \uparrow_\#/ \cdot all\ p \triangleleft \cdot segs \\
=\ & \text{segment decomposition} \\
& \uparrow_\#/ \cdot (\uparrow_\#/ \cdot all\ p \triangleleft \cdot tails)* \cdot inits \\
=\ & \text{result at end of last section} \\
& \uparrow_\#/ \cdot (\uparrow_\#/ \cdot (+\!\!+/ \cdot (p \to [id]^\circ, K_\omega)*)* \cdot tails)* \cdot inits
\end{aligned}$$

$$= \text{Horner's rule with } x \circledast a = (x + \!\!\!+ (p\, a \to [a], \omega)) \uparrow_\# []$$
$$\uparrow_\#/ \cdot \circledast \not{+}_{[]} * \cdot inits$$
$$= \text{accumulation lemma}$$
$$\uparrow_\#/ \cdot \circledast \not{+}_{[]}$$

Finally, we can simplify $x \circledast a$ to

$$x \circledast a = (p\, a \to x +\!\!\!+ [a], [])$$

This is a linear time algorithm (in the number of calculations of p).

The derivation of the above program might seem a little elaborate, bringing in cross-products, semirings, fictitious elements and so on, just to crack a small walnut. The central aspect, namely that

$$\uparrow_\#/ \cdot \text{all } p \triangleleft \cdot \text{tails}$$

can be expressed as a left-reduction, can be established quite quickly by an induction proof, one that avoids all talk of zero elements of concatenation. However, it is instructive to see a second application of Horner's rule.

2.10 References

Further discussion of some of the operators introduced above is in:

[1] Bird, R.S. A calculus of functions for program derivation. *Proc. Institute of Declarative Programming*, University of Texas, USA, 1987. (Also available as a Programming Research Group Monograph PRG-64, Oxford, UK.)

An extensive discussion of homomorphisms on trees, lists, bags and sets is in:

[2] Backhouse, R. An exploration of the Bird-Meertens formalism. (*Unpublished draft*), Dept. of Computer Science, Groningen University, The Netherlands. (1988)

3 Left reductions

3.0 Problem

Given is a list of lists of numbers. Required is an efficient algorithm for computing the minimum of the maximum numbers in each list. More succinctly,

we want to compute
$$minimax = \downarrow\!/ \cdot \uparrow\!/*$$
as efficiently as possible.

3.1 Left reductions

We characterised $\oplus\!\not/e$ in the first lecture by two equations
$$\begin{aligned} \oplus\!\not/e\,[\,] &= e \\ \oplus\!\not/e\,(x +\!\!+ [a]) &= (\oplus\!\not/e\,x) \oplus a \end{aligned}$$
More generally, we have that $\oplus\!\not/e$ satisfies the three equations
$$\begin{aligned} \oplus\!\not/e\,[\,] &= e \\ \oplus\!\not/e\,[a] &= e \oplus a \\ \oplus\!\not/e\,(x +\!\!+ y) &= \oplus\!\not/e_{e'}\,y \quad \text{where } e' = \oplus\!\not/e\,x \end{aligned}$$
Equivalently, setting $f\,e = \oplus\!\not/e$, we have
$$\begin{aligned} f\,e\,[\,] &= e \\ f\,e\,[a] &= e \oplus a \\ f\,e\,(x +\!\!+ y) &= f(f\,e\,x)\,y \end{aligned}$$
In order to show that these equations determine a unique function, suppose $e : \beta$ and $\oplus : \beta \times \alpha \to \beta$. Define the homomorphism h by
$$\begin{aligned} h\,[\,] &= id_\beta \\ h\,[a] &= (\oplus a) \\ h(x +\!\!+ y) &= h\,x\,;\,h\,y \end{aligned}$$
where $(;)$ is defined by $f\,;\,g = g \cdot f$. Thus h is the unique homomorphism
$$h : ([\alpha], +\!\!+, [\,], [\cdot]) \to (\beta \to \beta, ;, id_\beta, g)$$
where $g\,a = (\oplus a)$. Now we have
$$\oplus\!\not/e\,x = h\,x\,e$$
and so $\oplus\!\not/e$ is a well-defined function.

The basic reason why left reductions are important in our calculus (and analogous remarks apply to right reductions) is as follows. Consider a set of equations of the form
$$\begin{aligned} f\,[\,] &= e \\ f(x +\!\!+ [a]) &= F(a, x, f\,x) \end{aligned}$$

We claim that
$$f = \pi_2 \cdot \oplus\!\!\not\!/_{e'}$$
where
$$\begin{aligned} e' &= ([], e) \\ (x, u) \oplus a &= (x \mathbin{+\!\!+} [a], F(a, x, u)) \end{aligned}$$

In brief, every set of equations of the above form can be expressed in terms of a suitable left reduction.

The relationship between homomorphisms, left-reductions, and right-reductions can be interpreted in terms of the different ways we can view lists. The 'monoid' view of lists is to say that every list is either (i) the empty list; (ii) a singleton list; or (iii) the concatenation of two (non-empty) lists. The primary mechanism for defining functions with this view is the homomorphism. Another view of lists is to say that every list is either (i) the empty list; or (ii) of the form $x \mathbin{+\!\!+} [a]$ for some list x and value a. The primary mechanism in this case is the left reduction.

Yet a third view of lists is to say that every list is either (i) the empty list; or (ii) of the form $[a] \mathbin{+\!\!+} x$ for some a and list x. The primary mechanism here is the right reduction. In the majority of functional programming languages, it is this third view that prevails. One of the reasons concerns the possibility of defining functions on *infinite* lists, a reason that we will not go into here. Fortunately, we can define left reductions with this view as well. We have

$$\begin{aligned} \oplus\!\!\not\!/_e\, [] &= e \\ \oplus\!\!\not\!/_e\, ([a] \mathbin{+\!\!+} x) &= \oplus\!\!\not\!/_{e'}\, x \quad \text{where } e' = e \oplus a \end{aligned}$$

We leave the verification of this fact to the reader.

3.2 Loops

In the functional approach to program derivation, the final product of a calculation is an expression denoting a mathematical function. This expression still has to be translated into a specific programming language in order for it to be executable by computer. One obvious candidate is a functional programming language, such as ML or Miranda[1]. However, there is no reason why the final expression should not be translated into a conventional imperative language. For example, a left reduction can easily be translated into a loop. Using hopefully straightforward notation, the value $\oplus\!\!\not\!/_e\, x$ is the result delivered by the following imperative program:

---
[1] Miranda is a trademark of Research Software Ltd.

```
|[ var a; a := e;
   for b in x
   do a := a oplus b;
   return a ]|
```

Here, the 'generator' `b in x` successively assigns to b the elements of x in order from left to right.

3.3 Left-zeros

Both the imperative and functional implementations of left reductions require that the argument list be traversed in its entirety. Such a traversal can be cut short if we recognize the possibility that an operator may have *left-zeros*. By definition, ω is a left-zero of $\oplus$ if

$$\omega \oplus a = \omega$$

for all a. An operator may have none, one or many different left-zeros. If ω is a left-zero of $\oplus$, then

$$\oplus \!\not{}_\omega\, x = \omega$$

for all x. Since

$$\oplus \!\not{}_e\, (x \mathbin{+\!\!+} y) \;=\; \oplus \!\not{}_{e'}\, y \quad \text{where } e' = \oplus \!\not{}_e\, x$$

it follows that

$$\oplus \!\not{}_e\, (x \mathbin{+\!\!+} y) = \oplus \!\not{}_e\, x$$

whenever the right-hand side is a left-zero of $\oplus$. In words, evaluation of a left-reduction can be terminated on encountering a left-zero.

Suppose $lzero_\oplus$ is a predicate that determines whether its argument is a left-zero of $\oplus$. Using hopefully equally straightforward notation as before, we then have that $\oplus \!\not{}_e\, x$ can be evaluated by the program

```
|[ var a; a := e;
   for b in x while not lzero(a)
   do a := a oplus b;
   return a ]|
```

Before seeing an application of this idea we need a simple yet powerful result.

Lemma 3 (Specialisation) *Every homomorphism on lists can be expressed as a left (or also a right) reduction. More precisely,*

$$\oplus/ \cdot f* = \odot \not{\hspace{-2pt}/} e$$

where $e = id_\oplus$ and

$$a \odot b = a \oplus f\, b$$

We omit the simple proof.

3.4 Minimax

Let us return to the problem of computing

$$minimax = \downarrow/ \cdot \uparrow/*$$

efficiently. Using the specialisation lemma, we can write

$$minimax = \odot \not{\hspace{-2pt}/} \infty$$

where ∞ is the identity element of $\downarrow/$, and

$$a \odot x = a \downarrow (\uparrow/x)$$

Since $\downarrow$ distributes through $\uparrow$ we have

$$a \odot x = \uparrow/(a\downarrow) * x$$

Using the specialisation lemma a second time, we have

$$a \odot x = \oplus_a \not{\hspace{-2pt}/}_{-\infty}\, x$$

where $-\infty$ is the identity element of $\uparrow$ and

$$b \oplus_a c = b \uparrow (a \downarrow c)$$

Now, a is a left-zero of $\oplus_a$ (and so, by the way, is ∞), and $-\infty$ is a left-zero of $\odot$. This means we can implement $(minimax\ xs)$, where xs is a list of lists, by the loop

```
|[ var a; a:= infinity;
   for x in xs while a <> -infinity
   do a := a odot x;
   return a ]|
```

where the assignment `a := a odot x` can be implemented by the loop

```
|[ var b; b:= -infinity;
   for c in x while b <> a
   do b := b max (a min c);
   a := b ]|
```

3.5 The alpha-beta algorithm

We now generalise the minimax problem to trees. Consider the data-type

$$tree ::= Tip\ num\,|\,Fork\ [tree]$$

The syntax of this declaration is that of the functional language Miranda, and it is also employed in the notation of Bird and Wadler (reference [2] of Lecture 1). It says that ($Tip\ n$) is a tree for each number n, and that ($Fork\ ts$) is a tree whenever ts is a sequence of trees. The primitive functions Tip and $Fork$ are called the *constructors* of the type $tree$.

We wish to calculate an efficient algorithm for computing a function $eval : tree \to num$, where

$$\begin{aligned} eval(Tip\ n) &= n \\ eval(Fork\ ts) &= \uparrow/(-eval) * ts \end{aligned}$$

Here we use the notation $-f$ for the function defined by $(-f)a = -(f\ a)$.

Using the specialisation lemma on the right-hand side of the second equation for $eval$, we obtain

$$eval(Fork\ ts) = \oplus \not\!/_{-\infty}\ ts$$

where

$$a \oplus t = a \uparrow (-eval\ t)$$

We now expand this last equation by considering the two possible forms for a tree t:

$$\begin{aligned} a \oplus (Tip\ n) &= a \uparrow (-n) \\ a \oplus (Fork\ ts) &= a \uparrow (-(\uparrow/(-eval) * ts)) \end{aligned}$$

The last equation can now be simplified using the laws

$$\begin{aligned} -(a \uparrow b) &= (-a) \downarrow (-b) \\ a \uparrow (b \downarrow c) &= (a \uparrow b) \downarrow (a \uparrow c) \end{aligned}$$

We obtain
$$a \oplus (Fork\ ts) = \downarrow/(a\uparrow) * eval * ts$$

After using the $*$ distributivity law, the right-hand side of this equation is also a candidate for specialisation. We have
$$a \oplus (Fork\ ts) = \otimes a \not\mathrel{\rightarrow}_\infty ts$$

where
$$b \otimes_a t = b \downarrow (a \uparrow eval\ t)$$

Furthermore, since
$$\begin{aligned} eval\ t &= \infty \downarrow (-\infty \uparrow eval\ t) \\ &= \infty \otimes_{-\infty} t \end{aligned}$$

we have —without inventiveness— reduced the problem of calculating $eval\ t$ to that of evaluating $b \otimes_a t$ for values of a and b.

Let us now expand the definition of $b \otimes_a t$ in a similar way as we did for $a \oplus t$. We obtain
$$\begin{aligned} b \otimes_a (Tip\ n) &= b \downarrow (a \uparrow n) \\ b \otimes_a (Fork\ ts) &= b \downarrow (a \uparrow (\uparrow/(-eval) * ts)) \end{aligned}$$

In oder to simplify the right-hand side of this last equation, we need the dual distributive law
$$b \downarrow (a \uparrow c) = (b \downarrow a) \uparrow (b \downarrow c)$$

and the fact that evaluation of $b \otimes_a t$ is required only for values of a and b satisfying $a = a \downarrow b$; in other words, for $a \leqslant b$. In such a case we have
$$b \downarrow (a \uparrow c) = a \uparrow (b \downarrow c)$$

by commutativity of $\downarrow$.

We then obtain
$$b \otimes_a (Fork\ ts) = a \uparrow (\uparrow/(b\downarrow) * (-eval) * ts)$$

Using specialisation yet a third time, we obtain
$$b \otimes_a (Fork\ ts) = \oplus_b \not\mathrel{\rightarrow}_a ts$$

where
$$\alpha \oplus_b t = \alpha \uparrow (b \downarrow (-eval\ t))$$
At this point, the seemingly endless succession of expansion and specialisation steps can be stopped. A short calculation using the given properties of $-, \uparrow$ and $\downarrow$ yields
$$\alpha \oplus_\beta t = -(-\alpha) \otimes_{(-\beta)} t$$
Introducing
$$bval\ \alpha\ \beta\ t = \beta \otimes_\alpha t$$
and putting the resulting equations together, we obtain

$$\begin{array}{rcl}
eval\ t & = & bval\ (-\infty)\ \infty\ t \\
bval\ \alpha\ \beta\ (Tip\ n) & = & \beta \downarrow (\alpha \uparrow n) \\
bval\ \alpha\ \beta\ (Fork\ ts) & = & \oplus_\beta \not{\hspace{-2pt}\uparrow}_\alpha\ ts \\
\alpha' \oplus_\beta t & = & -bval(-\beta)(-\alpha')t
\end{array}$$

Finally, we bring on the left-zeros. We only need to observe that β is a left-zero of $\oplus_\beta$. This follows from the definition of $\oplus_\beta$ and the absorbtive law
$$\beta \uparrow (\beta \downarrow \gamma) = \beta$$
Incorporating this optimisation yields the alpha-beta algorithm.

The various axioms concerning $(\uparrow, \downarrow, -, \infty, -\infty)$ used in the above derivation are precisely those of a Boolean algebra.

3.6 References

An alternative, and arguably less satisfactory, treatment of the alpha-beta algorithm occurs in

[1] Bird, R.S. and Hughes, R.J.M. The alpha-beta algorithm: an exercise in program transformation. *Information Processing Letters*, 24 (1987) 53-57.

The importance of the purely algebraic notion of left-zeros and its consequences for optimisation was discussed in

[2] Meertens, L. First steps towards the theory of Rose trees. *(Unpublished draft)*, CWI, Amsterdam, 1988.

This paper also contains another treatment of the alpha-beta algorithm.

4 Arrays

4.0 Problem

Given is a two-dimensional array x with elements in the set $\{0,1\}$. Required is an efficient algorithm for computing the area of the largest rectangle (i.e. contiguous subarray) of x, all of whose elements are 1.

4.1 Arrays

In this lecture we consider only two-dimensional arrays. Whereas lists are constructed in terms of a single total operator $+\!\!+$, arrays are constructed using two *partial* operators, $\ominus$ (pronounced 'above') and ϕ (pronounced 'beside'). The intention is that $x \ominus y$ denotes the array obtained by placing array x directly above array y, and $x \phi y$ is the array obtained by placing x to the left of y. The array $x \ominus y$ is defined just in the case that x and y have the same *width* (or number of columns); similarly, $x \phi y$ is defined just in the case that x and y have the same *height* (or number of rows).

Both $\ominus$ and ϕ are associative operators. If the widths of x, y and z are equal, then

$$x \ominus (y \ominus z) = (x \ominus y) \ominus z$$

Similarly, if x, y and z all have the same height, then

$$x \phi (y \phi z) = (x \phi y) \phi z$$

One further equation satisfied by $\ominus$ and ϕ is as follows: if all of $x \ominus y$, $u \ominus v$, $x \phi u$, and $y \phi v$ are defined, then we have

$$(x \ominus y) \phi (u \ominus v) = (x \phi u) \ominus (y \phi v)$$

We shall refer to this property by saying that $\ominus$ *abides* with ϕ (the name *abide* is simply an abbreviation of 'above-beside'). It can be pictured as

$$\left(\begin{array}{c|c} x & u \\ \hline y & v \end{array} \right) = \left(\begin{array}{c|c} x & u \\ \hline y & v \end{array} \right)$$

In the next section we shall formalise the definition of arrays as an algebra based on two partial binary operations satisfying the associativity and abides conditions.

The type of arrays with elements from α will be denoted by $|\alpha|$, and the function which returns a singleton array will be denoted by $|\cdot|$. Thus, $|a|$

denotes a singleton array for each a in α. However, in displayed examples we shall use round brackets to indicate arrays. For example, the array

$$\begin{pmatrix} 1 & 2 & 3 \\ 4 & 5 & 6 \\ 7 & 8 & 9 \end{pmatrix}$$

is described by the formula

$$(|1| \phi |2| \phi |3|) \ominus (|4| \phi |5| \phi |6|) \ominus (|7| \phi |8| \phi |9|)$$

among others.

By definition, a *row vector* is an array of unit height, and a *column vector* is an array of unit width.

Note, finally, that we choose not to define the concept of an empty array.

4.2 Binoids and homomorphisms

The formal definition of arrays is in terms of a certain kind of algebra which, for lack of standard terminology, we shall call a *binoid*. By definition, $(\beta, \oplus, \otimes, i)$ is a binoid over α whenever $i : \alpha \to \beta$ is a total function, and $\oplus, \otimes : \beta \times \beta \to \beta$ are partial operators such that the following conditions hold.

1. $(i\,a \oplus i\,b)$ and $(i\,a \otimes i\,b)$ are defined for all a, b in α;

2. $\oplus$ is associative in the sense that, if $x \oplus y$ and $y \oplus z$ are defined, then both of $(x \oplus y) \oplus z$ and $x \oplus (y \oplus z)$ are defined and

$$(x \oplus y) \oplus z = x \oplus (y \oplus z)$$

3. Similarly, $\otimes$ is associative in the sense that, if $x \otimes y$ and $y \otimes z$ are defined, then
$$(x \otimes y) \otimes z = x \otimes (y \otimes z)$$

4. $\oplus$ abides with $\otimes$ in the sense that, if all of $x \oplus y, u \oplus v, x \otimes u, y \otimes v$ are defined, then

$$(x \oplus y) \otimes (u \oplus v) = (x \otimes u) \oplus (y \otimes v)$$

Here are three examples of binoids.

Example 1. Let $\oplus : \beta \times \beta \to \beta$ be a total, associative, and commutative operator. Then $\oplus$ abides with itself, and so $(\beta, \oplus, \oplus, i)$ is a binoid over α for all $i : \alpha \to \beta$.

Example 2. Recall that the operator $\ll$ is defined by $a \ll b = a$. Let $\oplus : \beta \times \beta \to \beta$ be associative. Then $(\beta, \oplus, \ll, i)$ is a binoid over α for all total $i : \alpha \to \beta$. In particular, $\oplus$ abides with $\ll$ since both sides of

$$(a \oplus b) \ll (c \oplus d) = (a \ll c) \oplus (b \ll d)$$

reduce to $a \oplus b$. Similarly, $(\beta, \oplus, \gg, i)$ is a binoid over α, where $a \gg b = b$.

Example 3. Define the partial operator $\bullet$ by the equation

$$a \bullet b = a \quad \text{if } a = b$$

Then $(N, +, \bullet, K_1)$ is a binoid over α for all α. Note, in particular that $(K_1\, a \bullet K_1\, b)$ is defined for all a and b, and the abides condition

$$(x + y) \bullet (u + v) = (x \bullet u) + (y \bullet v),$$

holds whenever $x \bullet u$ and $y \bullet v$ are defined, that is, when $x = u$ and $y = v$.

A homomorphism from a binoid $(\beta, \oplus, \otimes, i)$ over α to a binoid $(\gamma, \odot, \diamond, j)$ over α is a total function $h : \beta \to \gamma$ satisfying the following equations:

$$\begin{aligned} h(i\,a) &= j\,a \\ h(x \oplus y) &= h\,x \odot h\,y \quad \text{provided } x \oplus y \text{ is defined} \\ h(x \otimes y) &= h\,x \diamond h\,y \quad \text{provided } x \otimes y \text{ is defined} \end{aligned}$$

The array binoid $(|\alpha|, \ominus, \phi, |\cdot|)$ is now defined to be the *free* binoid over α. Thus, for each binoid $(\beta, \oplus, \otimes, i)$ over α there is a unique homomorphism from $|\alpha|$ to β.

Two particularly important homomorphisms are ht and wd, returning the height and width of an array. These are the homomorphisms from $|\alpha|$ to the binoids $(N, +, \bullet, K_1)$ and $(N, \bullet, +, K_1)$ respectively, where $\bullet$ is as defined in Example 3 above. It follows from the definition of homomorphism that if $x \ominus y$ is defined, then $wd\,x = wd\,y$; similarly, if $x \phi y$ is defined, then $ht\,x = ht\,y$. The converse implications also hold: if $wd\,x = wd\,y$, then $x \ominus y$ is defined, and if $ht\,x = ht\,y$, then $x \phi y$ is defined. The proof of this fact is omitted.

Weak binoids and homomorphisms

As defined, homomorphisms are total functions. It is useful to weaken the definition of both binoid and homomorphism to allow for partial functions on arrays. By definition, a *weak* binoid over α is an algebra $(\beta, \oplus, \otimes, i)$ satisfying all the binoid conditions except the first: it is not required that $i\,a \oplus i\,b$ and $i\,a \otimes i\,b$ be defined for all a and b in α. For example, $(N, +, \bullet, id_N)$ is a weak binoid over N. It is not a binoid because $(id_N\,a \bullet id_N\,b)$ is defined only if $a = b$. Clearly, every binoid is also a weak binoid.

Let $(\beta, \oplus, \otimes, i)$ be a weak binoid. Writing $x \sqsubseteq y$ to denote the assertion that $x = y$ whenever x is defined, consider the set H of partial functions $h : |\alpha| \to \beta$ satisfying the inequations

$$\begin{aligned} h|a| &\sqsubseteq i\,a \\ h(x \ominus y) &\sqsubseteq h\,x \oplus h\,y \\ h(x \phi y) &\sqsubseteq h\,x \otimes h\,y \end{aligned}$$

The set H is not empty because it contains the everywhere undefined function. Furthermore, it is a consequence of the definition of $|\alpha|$ as the free binoid over α that for any two functions h_1, h_2 in H we have

$$h_1\,x \sqsubseteq h_2\,x \text{ or } h_2\,x \sqsubseteq h_1\,x$$

for all arrays x. Thus, H contains a unique function $h = \sup H$ such that for all h_1 in H and arrays x we have

$$h_1\,x \sqsubseteq h\,x$$

We call such an h the *weak homomorphism* from $|\alpha|$ to β. Clearly, if a weak homomorphism is total, then it is a homomorphism.

4.3 Map and reduce

The same symbol $*$ is used for mapping over arrays as for mapping over lists. Suppose $f : \alpha \to \beta$. Then $f* : |\alpha| \to |\beta|$ is defined to be the unique homomorphism from $|\alpha|$ to the binoid $(|\beta|, \ominus, \phi, |\cdot| \cdot f)$. It satisfies the three equations:

$$\begin{aligned} f * |a| &= |f\,a| \\ f * (x \ominus y) &= (f * x) \ominus (f * y) \\ f * (x \phi y) &= (f * x) \phi (f * y) \end{aligned}$$

The $*$ distributive law

$$(f \cdot g)* = f* \cdot g*$$

is valid for arrays as well as lists.

The analogue of $\oplus/$ for arrays is a reduction $(\oplus, \otimes)/$ involving two operators. Suppose that $(\alpha, \oplus, \otimes, id_\alpha)$ is a weak binoid over α. Then $(\oplus, \otimes)/$ is defined to be the weak homomorphism from $|\alpha|$ to α. It satisfies the three inequations:

$$(\oplus, \otimes)/|a| \sqsubseteq a$$
$$(\oplus, \otimes)/(x \ominus y) \sqsubseteq ((\oplus, \otimes)/x) \oplus ((\oplus, \otimes)/y)$$
$$(\oplus, \otimes)/(x \phi y) \sqsubseteq ((\oplus, \otimes)/x) \otimes ((\oplus, \otimes)/y)$$

Note that the operator $\oplus$ which replaces the 'above' operator $\ominus$ comes first in the reduction, and the operator $\otimes$ which replaces the 'beside' operator ϕ comes second.

For example, $(+,+)/$ sums the elements in an array of numbers, and $(\vee, \vee)/$ determines whether there exists a true entry in an array of booleans. Both these functions are total. The binoid conditions are satisfied because $+$ and $\vee$ are commutative and associative operators,

On the other hand, the functions $(+, \bullet)/$ and $(\bullet, +)/$ are partial. For example, $(+, \bullet)/x$ is defined only if x is an array of numbers with the property that all elements in a given row are equal. It follows that the particular functions

$$ht = (+, \bullet)/ \cdot K_1*$$
$$wd = (\bullet, +)/ \cdot K_1*$$

are total.

The top-left element of an array is given by

$$topleft = (\ll, \lll)/$$

Similarly, we can define reductions that return each of the other corner elements. Example 2 above shows that the binoid conditions are satisfied.

The identity function on arrays is given by

$$id = (\ominus, \phi)/ \cdot |\cdot|*$$

In general, $(\ominus, \phi)/x$ is defined only if x is an array of arrays with the property that each row of x consists of arrays of the same width, and each column of x consists of arrays of the same height.

The companion function

$$tr = (\phi, \ominus)/ \cdot |\cdot|*$$

defines the operation of array transposition. A simple but important fact is that tr is its own inverse, that is,

$$tr \cdot tr = id$$

4.4 Promotion

The one-point and promotion rules for lists have counterparts in the theory of arrays. (There is no analogue of the empty rule because we have not defined the concept of an empty array.) These rules are:

one-point rules

$$f* \cdot |\cdot| = |\cdot| \cdot f$$
$$(\oplus, \otimes)/ \cdot |\cdot| = id$$

promotion rules

$$f* \cdot (\ominus, \phi)/ = (\ominus, \phi)/ \cdot f**$$
$$(\oplus, \otimes)/ \cdot (\ominus, \phi)/ \sqsubseteq (\oplus, \otimes)/ \cdot (\oplus, \otimes)/*$$

Notice that the last rule is an inequation rather than an equation since the left-hand side may not be defined for a given array.

We also have two rules involving transposition:

transpose rules

$$f* \cdot tr = tr \cdot f*$$
$$(\oplus, \otimes)/ \cdot tr = (\otimes, \oplus)/$$

To illustrate the transpose rules, we can calculate:

$$
\begin{array}{rl}
tr \cdot tr = & \text{definition of } tr \\
& (\phi, \ominus)/ \cdot |\cdot|* \cdot tr \\
= & \text{map transpose rule} \\
& (\phi, \ominus)/ \cdot tr \cdot |\cdot|* \\
= & \text{reduce transpose rule} \\
& (\ominus, \phi)/ \cdot |\cdot|* \\
= & \text{definition of } id \\
& id
\end{array}
$$

4.5 Zip

Let us return for the moment to lists. For each binary operator $\oplus : \alpha \times \beta \to \gamma$ we define a partial operator $Y_\oplus$ (pronounced 'zip with $\oplus$') informally by the equation

$$[a_1, a_2, \ldots, a_n] \, Y_\oplus \, [b_1, b_2, \ldots, b_n] = [a_1 \oplus b_1, a_2 \oplus b_2, \ldots, a_n \oplus b_n]$$

Thus, $x \, Y_\oplus \, y$ is defined only in the case that $\#x = \#y$. The type of $Y_\oplus$ is given by

$$Y_\oplus : [\alpha] \times [\beta] \to [\gamma]$$

Among the many properties that $Y_\oplus$ enjoys is the fact that $Y_\oplus$ is associative if $\oplus$ is; similarly, $Y_\oplus$ is commutative and/or idempotent if $\oplus$ is.

Formally, we can specify $Y_\oplus$ by three equations:

$$
\begin{array}{rcl}
[\,] \, Y_\oplus \, [\,] & = & [\,] \\
[a] \, Y_\oplus \, [b] & = & [a \oplus b] \\
(x \mathbin{+\!\!+} y) \, Y_\oplus \, (u \mathbin{+\!\!+} v) & = & (x \, Y_\oplus \, u) \mathbin{+\!\!+} (y \, Y_\oplus \, v) \quad \text{if } \#x = \#u \wedge \#y = \#v
\end{array}
$$

The third equation is just the condition that $Y_\oplus$ abides with $\mathbin{+\!\!+}$.

The operator $Y_\oplus$ can also be defined on arrays of the same shape, that is, of the same height and width. We have

$$
\begin{array}{rcl}
|a| \, Y_\oplus \, |b| & = & |a \oplus b| \\
(x \ominus y) \, Y_\oplus \, (u \ominus v) & = & (x \, Y_\oplus \, u) \ominus (y \, Y_\oplus \, v) \\
(x \phi y) \, Y_\oplus \, (u \phi v) & = & (x \, Y_\oplus \, u) \phi (y \, Y_\oplus \, v)
\end{array}
$$

The last two equations are asserted only in the case that x is the same shape as u, and y is the same shape as v. So, $\ominus$ abides with $Y_\oplus$, and so does ϕ.

Some useful examples of this operator are as follows. First, the function

$$rows = (\ominus, Y_\phi)/ \cdot \|\cdot\|*$$

converts an array into a column vector whose entries are row vectors, one for each row of the array. For example:

$$rows \begin{pmatrix} 1 & 2 & 3 \\ 4 & 5 & 6 \\ 7 & 8 & 9 \end{pmatrix} = \begin{pmatrix} \{1 \ 2 \ 3\} \\ \{4 \ 5 \ 6\} \\ \{7 \ 8 \ 9\} \end{pmatrix}$$

Similarly, the function

$$cols = (Y_\ominus, \phi)/ \cdot \|\cdot\|*$$

converts an array into a row vector, each entry being a column vector.

The related functions

$$\begin{aligned} \textit{listrows} &= (+\!\!+, \mathsf{Y}\!\!+\!\!+)/ \cdot [\![\cdot]\!]* \\ \textit{listcols} &= (\mathsf{Y}\!\!+\!\!+, +\!\!+)/ \cdot [\![\cdot]\!]* \end{aligned}$$

each convert an array into a list of lists. The function *listrows* turns an array into a list of rows, each row being a list of entries from a row of the array. The function *listcols* turns the array into a list of columns. Two useful identities are:

$$\begin{aligned} (\oplus, \otimes)/ &= \oplus/ \cdot \otimes/* \cdot \textit{listrows} \\ (\oplus, \otimes)/ &= \otimes/ \cdot \oplus/* \cdot \textit{listcols} \end{aligned}$$

4.6 Row and column reductions

The general array reduction $(\oplus, \otimes)/$ does not prescribe any particular order of application of the operators $\oplus$ and $\otimes$. It is also useful to introduce sequential forms of reduction, namely $/^R$ and $/^C$, that operate along rows or columns. The effect of a row reduction $/^R$ is illustrated by

$$\oplus/^R \begin{pmatrix} 1 & 2 & 3 \\ 4 & 5 & 6 \\ 7 & 8 & 9 \end{pmatrix} = \begin{pmatrix} 1 \oplus 2 \oplus 3 \\ 4 \oplus 5 \oplus 6 \\ 7 \oplus 8 \oplus 9 \end{pmatrix}$$

Thus, $\oplus/^R x$ returns a column vector. Similarly,

$$\oplus/^C \begin{pmatrix} 1 & 2 & 3 \\ 4 & 5 & 6 \\ 7 & 8 & 9 \end{pmatrix} = \begin{pmatrix} 1 \oplus 4 \oplus 7 & 2 \oplus 5 \oplus 8 & 3 \oplus 6 \oplus 9 \end{pmatrix}$$

Thus $\oplus/^C x$ returns a row vector.

Formally, we can define

$$\begin{aligned} \oplus/^R &= (\ominus, \mathsf{Y}_\oplus)/ \cdot |\cdot|* \\ \oplus/^C &= (\mathsf{Y}_\oplus, \phi)/ \cdot |\cdot|* \end{aligned}$$

In particular, these equations can be used to justify the following alternative definitions of *rows* and *cols*:

$$\begin{aligned} \textit{rows} &= \phi/^R \cdot |\cdot|* \\ \textit{cols} &= \ominus/^C \cdot |\cdot|* \end{aligned}$$

We also have the identity

$$\oplus/^R = tr \cdot \oplus/^C \cdot tr$$

We shall also define directed versions of these array reductions: in particular, $\not{\oplus}^R$ denotes a left–to–right row reduction, and $\not{\oplus}^C$ denotes a top–to–bottom column reduction. For example,

$$\oplus\not{/}^C \begin{pmatrix} 1 & 2 & 3 \\ 4 & 5 & 6 \\ 7 & 8 & 9 \end{pmatrix} = \begin{pmatrix} (1 \oplus 4) \oplus 7 & (2 \oplus 5) \oplus 8 & (3 \oplus 6) \oplus 9 \end{pmatrix}$$

Row and column accumulations

Similarly, we can define row and column accumulations on arrays. These are denoted by $\#^R$ and $\#^C$, and their effect is illustrated by the following examples:

$$\oplus\#^R \begin{pmatrix} 1 & 2 & 3 \\ 4 & 5 & 6 \\ 7 & 8 & 9 \end{pmatrix} = \begin{pmatrix} 1 & 1 \oplus 2 & (1 \oplus 2) \oplus 3 \\ 4 & 4 \oplus 5 & (4 \oplus 5) \oplus 6 \\ 7 & 7 \oplus 8 & (7 \oplus 8) \oplus 9 \end{pmatrix}$$

$$\oplus\#^C \begin{pmatrix} 1 & 2 & 3 \\ 4 & 5 & 6 \\ 7 & 8 & 9 \end{pmatrix} = \begin{pmatrix} 1 & 2 & 3 \\ 1 \oplus 4 & 2 \oplus 5 & 3 \oplus 6 \\ (1 \oplus 4) \oplus 7 & (2 \oplus 5) \oplus 8 & (3 \oplus 6) \oplus 9 \end{pmatrix}$$

Thus, if $\oplus : \alpha \times \alpha \to \alpha$, then

$$\oplus\#^R, \oplus\#^C : |\alpha| \to |\alpha|$$

Array accumulations are related to list accumulations by the equations

$$\begin{array}{rcl} \textit{listrows} \cdot (\oplus\#^R) & = & (\oplus\#)* \cdot \textit{listrows} \\ \textit{listcols} \cdot (\oplus\#^C) & = & (\oplus\#)* \cdot \textit{listcols} \end{array}$$

In order to relate array accumulations to array reductions, in the way that list accumulations were related to list reductions in the first lecture, we need to consider the array analogues of *inits* and *tails*. This we do next.

4.7 Tops and bottoms

There are four reasonable ways of dissecting an array: we shall call them *tops*, *bottoms*, *lefts* and *rights*. Two of them are illustrated by the following examples:

$$\textit{lefts} \begin{pmatrix} 1 & 2 & 3 \\ 4 & 5 & 6 \\ 7 & 8 & 9 \end{pmatrix} = \left(\begin{pmatrix} 1 \\ 4 \\ 7 \end{pmatrix} \begin{pmatrix} 1 & 2 \\ 4 & 5 \\ 7 & 8 \end{pmatrix} \begin{pmatrix} 1 & 2 & 3 \\ 4 & 5 & 6 \\ 7 & 8 & 9 \end{pmatrix} \right)$$

$$\textit{tops} \begin{pmatrix} 1 & 2 & 3 \\ 4 & 5 & 6 \\ 7 & 8 & 9 \end{pmatrix} = \begin{pmatrix} \begin{pmatrix} 1 & 2 & 3 \end{pmatrix} \\ \begin{pmatrix} 1 & 2 & 3 \\ 4 & 5 & 6 \end{pmatrix} \\ \begin{pmatrix} 1 & 2 & 3 \\ 4 & 5 & 6 \\ 7 & 8 & 9 \end{pmatrix} \end{pmatrix}$$

The essential points here are that *lefts* and *rights* each return a single row, while *tops* and *bottoms* each return a single column.

We can give the definition of *lefts* and *tops* in terms of accumulations:

$$\begin{aligned} \textit{lefts} &= (\phi \#^R) \cdot \textit{cols} \\ \textit{tops} &= (\ominus \#^C) \cdot \textit{rows} \end{aligned}$$

These equations should be compared to the definition

$$\textit{inits}^+ = (+\!\!\!+\#) \cdot [\cdot]*$$

of Lecture 1.

As one might expect, there is a multitude of relationships between the various forms of array reductions, array accumulations, and the four dissection functions introduced above. In particular, we have the:

orthogonal rules

$$\begin{aligned} \oplus/^C * \cdot \textit{lefts} &= \textit{lefts} \cdot \oplus/^C \\ \oplus/^R * \cdot \textit{tops} &= \textit{tops} \cdot \oplus/^R \end{aligned}$$

— plus ten similar equations obtained by replacing *lefts* by *rights* and *tops* by *bottoms*, or by replacing $/^C$ and $/^R$ by the associated directed reductions or accumulations.

We also have the following analogues of the accumulation lemma of Lecture 1.

accumulation lemmas

$$\begin{aligned} (\oplus \#^C) * \cdot \textit{tops} &= \textit{rows} \cdot (\oplus \#^C) \\ (\oplus \#^R) * \cdot \textit{lefts} &= \textit{cols} \cdot (\oplus \#^R) \end{aligned}$$

4.8 Rectangles

By definition, a *rectangle* of an array x is a contiguous subarray of x. Thus, rectangles are to arrays as segments are to lists. In this section we put the four dissection functions *tops*, *bottoms*, *lefts*, and *rights* together in order to define the rectangles of an array.

First of all, we give some arrays of arrays that will prove useful. The *top-lefts* (*topls*) of an array is defined by

$$topls = (\ominus, \phi)/ \cdot tops* \cdot lefts$$

This is a total function since $(\ominus, \phi)/$ is applied to an array (of arrays) each column of which has the same width, and each row the same height. For example:

$$topls \begin{pmatrix} 1 & 2 & 3 \\ 4 & 5 & 6 \\ 7 & 8 & 9 \end{pmatrix} = \begin{pmatrix} \begin{pmatrix} 1 \\ 1 \\ 4 \\ 1 \\ 4 \\ 7 \end{pmatrix} & \begin{pmatrix} 1 & 2 \\ 1 & 2 \\ 4 & 5 \\ 1 & 2 \\ 4 & 5 \\ 7 & 8 \end{pmatrix} & \begin{pmatrix} 1 & 2 & 3 \\ 1 & 2 & 3 \\ 4 & 5 & 6 \\ 1 & 2 & 3 \\ 4 & 5 & 6 \\ 7 & 8 & 9 \end{pmatrix} \end{pmatrix}$$

Similarly, the *bottom-rights* (*botrs*) of an array is defined by

$$botrs = (\ominus, \phi)/ \cdot bottoms* \cdot rights$$

The *horizontal-segments* (*hsegs*) of an array is defined by

$$hsegs = (\ominus, \phi)/ \cdot bottoms* \cdot tops$$

and the *vertical-segments* (*vsegs*) by

$$vsegs = (\ominus, \phi)/ \cdot rights* \cdot lefts$$

We can put these functions together to define the rectangles of an array:

$$rects = (\ominus, \phi)/ \cdot botrs* \cdot topls$$

Thus, *rects* returns an array whose elements are the rectangles of a given array. We shall see in the next section that there are various equivalent ways to define *rects*; in particular,

$$rects = (\ominus, \phi)/ \cdot hsegs* \cdot vsegs$$

defines exactly the same function.

4.9 BRTL rules

It is an inevitable consequence of the extra dimensionality provided by arrays that the number of possible algebraic identities goes up by a multiplicative factor. Too many identities are almost as much a problem in program calculation as too few. In this section we describe, in effect, no fewer than ten additional equations. Fortunately, they come in logical groupings.

We start with the fact that

$$(\ominus, \phi)/ \cdot tops* \cdot lefts = (\ominus, \phi)/ \cdot lefts* \cdot tops$$

There are three additional equations of this kind: we can replace *tops* by *bottoms* and *lefts* by *rights*.

From these four equations we can generate four more. Two of them are:

$$(\ominus, \phi)/ \cdot vsegs* \cdot tops = (\ominus, \phi)/ \cdot tops* \cdot vsegs$$
$$(\ominus, \phi)/ \cdot hsegs* \cdot lefts = (\ominus, \phi)/ \cdot lefts* \cdot hsegs$$

The two additional ones are obtained by replacing *tops* by *bottoms* and *lefts* by *rights*.

Finally, to the above eight there can now be added:

$$(\ominus, \phi)/ \cdot botrs* \cdot topls = (\ominus, \phi)/ \cdot vsegs* \cdot hsegs$$
$$(\ominus, \phi)/ \cdot vsegs* \cdot hsegs = (\ominus, \phi)/ \cdot hsegs* \cdot vsegs$$

That gives ten. A good way to remember these identities, particularly the last two, is to see that the relative order of *bottoms* (B) and *tops* (T), and the relative order of *rights* (R) and *lefts* (L) remain unchanged throughout all the equations. For example, the last two rules can be captured with the abbreviations

$$BR \cdot TL = RL \cdot BT$$
$$RL \cdot BT = BT \cdot RL$$

Similar abbreviations hold for the other rules.

For a sample proof we shall tackle the fifth equation. For convenience, we introduce the additional abbreviations: θ for $(\ominus, \phi)/$ and V for *vsegs*. The following chain of equational reasoning, which is given without comments, uses the reduce promotion rule in both directions. This is safe since all functions are total.

$$\begin{aligned}
\theta \cdot V* \cdot T &= \theta \cdot (\theta \cdot R* \cdot L)* \cdot T \\
&= \theta \cdot \theta* \cdot R** \cdot L* \cdot T \\
&= \theta \cdot \theta \cdot R** \cdot L* \cdot T \\
&= \theta \cdot R* \cdot \theta \cdot L* \cdot T \\
&= \theta \cdot R* \cdot \theta \cdot T* \cdot L \\
&= \theta \cdot \theta \cdot R** \cdot T* \cdot L \\
&= \theta \cdot \theta* \cdot R** \cdot T* \cdot L \\
&= \theta \cdot (\theta \cdot R* \cdot T)* \cdot L \\
&= \theta \cdot (\theta \cdot T* \cdot R)* \cdot L \\
&= \theta \cdot \theta* \cdot T** \cdot R* \cdot L \\
&= \theta \cdot \theta \cdot T** \cdot R* \cdot L \\
&= \theta \cdot T* \cdot \theta \cdot R* \cdot L \\
&= \theta \cdot T* \cdot V
\end{aligned}$$

4.10 Rectangle decomposition

The segment decomposition theorem of Lecture 1 has the following counterpart in the theory of arrays.

Theorem 4 (Rectangle decomposition) *Suppose R and B are total functions defined by*

$$\begin{aligned}
R &= (\oplus, \otimes)/ \cdot f* \cdot rects \\
B &= (\oplus, \otimes)/ \cdot f* \cdot bottoms
\end{aligned}$$

If B can be expressed in the form $B = g \cdot \circledast\!\!\!/\!\!\!/^C$, then

$$R = (\oplus, \otimes)/ \cdot h* \cdot rows \cdot (\circledast\!\!\!/\!\!\!/^C)$$

where h is defined by

$$h = (\oplus, \otimes)/ \cdot g* \cdot vsegs$$

Proof

We shall need the following observation about $rects$:

$$\begin{aligned}
rects &= \text{one definition of } rects \\
& (\ominus, \phi)/ \cdot vsegs* \cdot hsegs \\
&= \text{definition of } hsegs \\
& (\ominus, \phi)/ \cdot vsegs* \cdot (\ominus, \phi)/ \cdot bottoms* \cdot tops \\
&= \text{map and reduce promotion} \\
& (\ominus, \phi)/ \cdot ((\ominus, \phi)/ \cdot vsegs* \cdot bottoms)* \cdot tops \\
&= BRTL \text{ rule} \\
& (\ominus, \phi)/ \cdot ((\ominus, \phi)/ \cdot bottoms* \cdot vsegs)* \cdot tops
\end{aligned}$$

We shall also need the following orthogonal reduction rule, whose proof is left to the reader:

$$(\circledast \not{f}^C)* \cdot vsegs = vsegs \cdot (\circledast \not{f}^C)$$

Now we argue:

$$\begin{aligned}
R &= \text{observation} \\
& (\oplus, \otimes)/ \cdot f* \cdot (\ominus, \phi)/ \cdot ((\ominus, \phi)/ \cdot bottoms* \cdot vsegs)* \cdot tops \\
&= \text{map and reduce promotion} \\
& (\oplus, \otimes)/ \cdot ((\oplus, \otimes)/ \cdot f* \cdot (\ominus, \phi)/ \cdot bottoms* \cdot vsegs)* \cdot tops \\
&= \text{map and reduce promotion} \\
& (\oplus, \otimes)/ \cdot ((\oplus, \otimes)/ \cdot ((\oplus, \otimes)/ \cdot f* \cdot bottoms)* \cdot vsegs)* \cdot tops \\
&= \text{assumption on } B \\
& (\oplus, \otimes)/ \cdot ((\oplus, \otimes)/ \cdot (g \cdot (\circledast \not{f}^C))* \cdot vsegs)* \cdot tops \\
&= * \text{ distributivity} \\
& (\oplus, \otimes)/ \cdot ((\oplus, \otimes)/ \cdot g* \cdot (\circledast \not{f}^C)* \cdot vsegs)* \cdot tops \\
&= \text{orthogonal reduction rule cited above} \\
& (\oplus, \otimes)/ \cdot ((\oplus, \otimes)/ \cdot g* \cdot vsegs \cdot (\circledast \not{f}^C))* \cdot tops \\
&= * \text{ distributivity; setting } h = (\oplus, \otimes)/ \cdot g* \cdot vsegs \\
& (\oplus, \otimes)/ \cdot h* \cdot (\circledast \not{f}^C)* \cdot tops \\
&= \text{accumulation lemma} \\
& (\oplus, \otimes)/ \cdot h* \cdot rows \cdot (\circledast \not{f}^C)
\end{aligned}$$

□

The computational advantage of applying the rectangle decomposition theorem is that if h (which is essentially a problem about the segments of a list — see below) can be computed in linear time, and if values of $\otimes$ can be computed in constant time, then R can be computed in time proportional to the number of elements in the given array.

We can formulate the rectangle decomposition theorem in terms of lists in the following way (the proof is omitted):

Corollary 5 *Suppose R and B are as defined above. If B can be written in the form*

$$B = g \cdot \textit{listrow} \cdot \circledast /\!\!/^C,$$

where listrow converts a row vector into a list of its elements, then

$$R = \oplus/ \cdot h* \cdot \textit{listrows} \cdot (\circledast /\!\!/^C)$$

where

$$h = \otimes/ \cdot g* \cdot \textit{segs}$$

4.11 Horner's rule

In order to apply the rectangle decomposition theorem, we need to express

$$B = (\oplus, \otimes)/ \cdot f* \cdot \textit{bottoms}$$

in terms of a column reduction. Since *bottoms* returns a column vector, the operator $\otimes$ plays no part in the array reduction. More precisely, if *listcol* converts a single column into a list of its elements, then

$$B = \oplus/ \cdot \textit{listcol} \cdot f* \cdot \textit{bottoms}$$

Consider now the particular case $f = (\otimes, \odot)/$, which can be considered to be one version of Horner's rule for arrays. Under the conditions that: (i) $\otimes$ distributes (backwards) through $\oplus$; and (ii) $\odot$ abides with $\oplus$, we can show that

$$\oplus/ \cdot \textit{listcol} \cdot f* \cdot \textit{bottoms} = \odot/ \cdot \textit{listrow} \cdot \circledast /\!\!/^C$$

where $\circledast$ is defined (as in the version of Horner's rule for non-empty lists) by

$$a \circledast b = (a \otimes b) \oplus b$$

We shall illustrate Horner's rule rather than give a formal proof. Consider the array

$$x = \begin{pmatrix} 1 & 2 \\ 3 & 4 \\ 5 & 6 \end{pmatrix}$$

The left-hand side of Horner's rule applied to x gives

$$((1 \otimes 3 \otimes 5) \odot (2 \otimes 4 \otimes 6)) \oplus ((3 \otimes 5) \odot (4 \otimes 6)) \oplus (5 \odot 6)$$

Using the fact that $\oplus$ abides with $\odot$, we can write this in the form

$$((1 \otimes 3 \otimes 5) \oplus (3 \otimes 5) \oplus 5) \odot ((2 \otimes 4 \otimes 6) \oplus (4 \otimes 6) \oplus 6)$$

Now, assuming $\otimes$ distributes over $\oplus$, we can write the above expression in the form

$$((((1 \otimes 3) \oplus 3) \otimes 5) \oplus 5) \odot ((((2 \otimes 4) \oplus 4) \otimes 6) \oplus 6)$$

Using the definition of $\circledast$, this simplifies to

$$((1 \circledast 3) \circledast 5) \odot ((2 \circledast 4) \circledast 6)$$

and thus to

$$(\odot/ \cdot \textit{listrow} \cdot \circledast \!\not{f}^C)x$$

where x is the original array.

4.12 Application

At long last we are in a position to make progress on the problem posed at the beginning of this lecture. The problem is to compute R, where

$$R = \uparrow/ \cdot \textit{area}* \cdot \textit{filled} \triangleleft \cdot \textit{bag} \cdot \textit{rects},$$

given that R is applied to arrays whose elements are 1 or 0. Since we have not defined the filter operation on arrays (and cannot reasonably do so if the result is to be an array), we must first make a bag out of the array of rectangles, by applying

$$\textit{bag} = (\uplus, \uplus)/ \cdot \wr \cdot \int *,$$

in order to filter out those rectangles we do not want.

The functions *filled* and *area* can be defined by

$$\begin{aligned}\textit{filled} &= (\wedge, \wedge)/ \cdot (=1)* \\ \textit{area} &= (+, +)/ \cdot K_1*\end{aligned}$$

It is possible to make a convenient simplification and eliminate the filter from the specification of R. Define a modified addition operator $\oplus$ by the equation
$$a \oplus b = 0 \quad \text{if } a = 0 \vee b = 0$$
$$= a + b \quad \text{otherwise}$$
The operator $\oplus$ is both associative and commutative. If we define
$$area' = (\oplus, \oplus)/$$
then it is easy to show, provided x is an array over $\{0, 1\}$, that
$$area'\, x = area\, x, \quad \text{if } filled\, x$$
$$= 0 \quad \text{otherwise}$$
Thus we can eliminate the filter, and reformulate the problem as one of computing R, where
$$R = (\uparrow, \uparrow)/ \cdot (\oplus, \oplus)/* \cdot rects$$
For an array filled with zeros, the new version of R returns zero (while the previous version returned $-\infty$); otherwise the functions are the same.

The new form of R is such that we can try to apply the rectangle decomposition theorem of the previous section. This means that we have to express
$$B = \uparrow/ \cdot listcol \cdot (\oplus, \oplus)/* \cdot bottoms$$
in the form
$$B = g \cdot listrow \cdot \circledast \not{/}^c$$
for suitable g and $\circledast$.

A good place to start is to try and use Horner's rule. The first condition of Horner's rule, namely that $\oplus$ distributes through $\uparrow$, is easily seen to be satisfied. Unfortunately, the second condition, which is that $\oplus$ abides with $\uparrow$, is not satisfied.

All is not lost, however, because we have not yet used the fact that we are only considering arrays over $\{0, 1\}$. The first crucial observation is that, provided x is an array over $\{0, 1\}$, we have
$$(\oplus, \oplus)/x = width\, x \times (\oplus, \downarrow)/x$$
This restriction on x is sufficient to ensure that the reduction $(\oplus, \downarrow)/x$ is well-defined. The abides condition for $\oplus$ and $\downarrow$, namely that
$$(a \oplus b) \downarrow (c \oplus d) = (a \downarrow c) \oplus (b \downarrow d),$$

holds if
$$(a = 0 \lor b = 0 \lor a = b) \land (c = 0 \lor d = 0 \lor c = d)$$
and the restriction on x guarantees that this condition is satisfied. If x is an array over $\{0, 1\}$ we therefore have
$$B\,x = \textit{width}\,x \times C\,x$$
where
$$C = \uparrow\!/ \cdot \textit{listcol} \cdot (\oplus, \downarrow)/\ast \cdot \textit{bottoms}$$
Furthermore — and this is the crux — under the same assumption about the elements of x, we have that $\downarrow$ abides with $\uparrow$. This gives us Horner's rule for C and we can write
$$C = \downarrow\!/ \cdot \textit{listrow} \cdot \circledast \!\!\not{/}^C$$
where $\circledast$ is defined by
$$a \circledast b = (a \oplus b) \uparrow b$$
Equivalently, we have
$$\begin{aligned} a \circledast b &= 0 && \text{if } b = 0 \\ &= a + b && \text{otherwise} \end{aligned}$$
Finally, we obtain
$$B = g \cdot \textit{listrow} \cdot \circledast \!\!\not{/}^C$$
where
$$g\,x = \#x \times \downarrow\!/x$$
This is the desired form for B.

Now, using the rectangle decomposition theorem, we obtain
$$R = \uparrow\!/ \cdot h\ast \cdot \textit{listrows} \cdot (\circledast \!\!\not{/}^C)$$
where
$$h = \uparrow\!/ \cdot g\ast \cdot \textit{segs}$$
The definition of h has a simple intuitive interpretation. Think of a sequence x of nonnegative numbers as representing a *histogram*. Then $h\,x$ denotes the largest rectangular area under the histogram x. In the final lecture we shall show how to compute h in linear time. Since $\circledast$ is computable in constant time, it follows that R can be computed in time proportional to the number of entries in the array.

4.13 References

The largest filled rectangle problem was invented as a generalisation of a similar problem about largest filled *squares*. This largest filled square problem was posed and solved in

[1] Gries, D. A note on a standard strategy for developing loop invariants and loops. *Science of Computer Programming* 2 (1982) 207-214

After solving the largest filled rectangle problem, the author learnt of another solution (expressed as a five-pass algorithm) described in

[2] Dean Brock, J. Finding the largest empty rectangle on a grated surface. *Proc. 4th Annual Symp. on Theoretical Aspects of Computer Science, Passau, W. Germany* — in LNCS, No. 247, Springer-Verlag, Berlin, (1987) 66-75.

5 Trees

(*Note:* The material of this section is the result of joint work with Jeremy Gibbons of the PRG, Oxford. For reasons of space, most of the ideas are sketched only briefly. A fuller account will appear elsewhere.)

5.0 Problem

Define a *heap* to be a labelled binary tree t with the property that for each subtree t' of t, the label of t' is a number which is no greater than the labels of all subtrees of t'. Required is an efficient algorithm for converting a sequence of numbers x into a heap whose inorder traversal is x.

5.1 Trees

The type of labelled binary trees (henceforth, just called *trees*) with labels from α will be denoted by $\langle \alpha \rangle$. This type is specified by a free algebra generated from elements of α under the assignment $\langle \cdot \rangle : \alpha \to \langle \alpha \rangle$ which maps elements of α to singleton trees. The constituents of this algebra are:

(1) Two partial operations $\swarrow$ (pronounced 'under') and $\searrow$ (pronounced 'over') such that $\swarrow$ *associates* with $\searrow$, in the sense that

$$(x \swarrow y) \searrow z = x \swarrow (y \searrow z)$$

whenever both sides are defined.

(2) Two predicates *noleft* and *noright* such that $x \swarrow y$ is defined just in the case that *noleft y* holds, and $x \searrow y$ is defined just in the case that *noright x* holds. Moreover, we suppose that

$$
\begin{aligned}
\textit{noleft} \langle a \rangle &= \textit{True} \\
\textit{noleft}(x \swarrow y) &= \textit{False} \\
\textit{noleft}(x \searrow y) &= \textit{noleft } x
\end{aligned}
$$

$$
\begin{aligned}
\textit{noright} \langle a \rangle &= \textit{True} \\
\textit{noright}(x \swarrow y) &= \textit{noright } y \\
\textit{noright}(x \searrow y) &= \textit{False}
\end{aligned}
$$

Another way of putting these conditions is to say that *noleft x* holds just in the cases that x is a singleton tree, or x is of the form $\langle a \rangle \searrow y$. Similarly, *noright x* holds just in the cases that x is a singleton tree, or x is of the form $y \swarrow \langle a \rangle$. It follows that the expression

$$x \swarrow y \searrow z$$

is well-defined just in the case that y is a singleton tree.

Let us relate these operations on trees to the usual pictures. For example, the tree

$$(\langle a \rangle \swarrow \langle b \rangle \searrow \langle c \rangle) \swarrow \langle d \rangle \searrow \langle e \rangle$$

can be drawn in the following way:

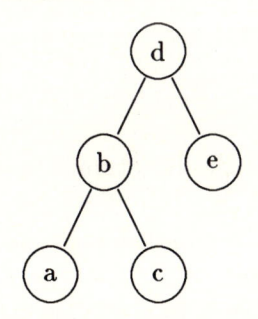

On the other hand, the tree

$$\langle a \rangle \swarrow \langle b \rangle \searrow (\langle c \rangle \swarrow \langle d \rangle \searrow \langle e \rangle)$$

can be pictured as follows:

```
       b
      / \
     a   d
        / \
       c   e
```

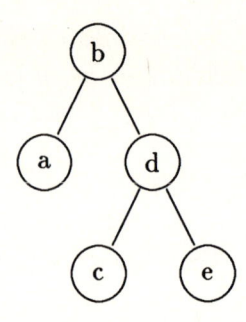

We have not yet defined the notion of an empty tree. If we wish to have such a tree, then we can denote it by $\langle\,\rangle$ and suppose that $\langle\,\rangle$ is the unique left identity of $\swarrow$ and the unique right identity of $\searrow$. Thus

$$\langle\,\rangle \swarrow x = x$$
$$x \searrow \langle\,\rangle = x$$

for all non-empty trees x. We also suppose that $x \swarrow \langle\,\rangle$ and $\langle\,\rangle \searrow x$ are undefined, for otherwise

$$x \swarrow (\langle\,\rangle \searrow y) \neq (x \swarrow \langle\,\rangle) \searrow y$$

and so $\swarrow$ and $\searrow$ no longer associate.

5.2 An alternative view

An alternative, and more common, view of labelled binary trees is in terms of a ternary constructor *Bin*. This view is captured in the type declaration

$$tree\,\alpha ::= Nil \mid Bin\,(tree\,\alpha)\,\alpha\,(tree\,\alpha)$$

(The syntax used here is that of the functional language Miranda; it is also used in the text [3] cited in Lecture 1.) This declaration defines a tree to be either the empty tree *Nil*, or a tree *Bin x a y* with left subtree x, label a, and right subtree y.

We can move from the ternary view to the binary view by using the equivalences

$$Nil \equiv \langle\,\rangle$$
$$Bin\,x\,a\,y \equiv x \swarrow \langle a \rangle \searrow y$$

A slightly different view of trees excludes the empty tree. This view recognises trees as being of one of the following forms:

$$\langle a \rangle$$
$$x \swarrow \langle a \rangle$$
$$\langle a \rangle \searrow y$$
$$x \swarrow \langle a \rangle \searrow y$$

The advantage of viewing labelled binary trees in terms of two partial binary operators, rather than a single total ternary operator, is primarily that we can set up the notion of reduction on trees in a simple manner. However, each view of trees has its advantages and disadvantages, so we shall employ whichever is the more convenient in a given situation.

5.3 Map and reduce

The next move, which should be familiar by now, is to define the map and reduction operators for trees. The definition of $*$ is given by three equations:

$$\begin{aligned} f * \langle a \rangle &= \langle f\, a \rangle \\ f * (x \swarrow y) &= (f * x) \swarrow (f * y) \\ f * (x \searrow y) &= (f * x) \searrow (f * y) \end{aligned}$$

For reduction we need two operators $\oplus$ and $\otimes$ such that $\oplus$ associates with $\otimes$. We then define

$$\begin{aligned} (\oplus, \otimes)/\langle a \rangle &= a \\ (\oplus, \otimes)/(x \swarrow y) &= ((\oplus, \otimes)/x) \oplus ((\oplus, \otimes)/y) \\ (\oplus, \otimes)/(x \searrow y) &= ((\oplus, \otimes)/x) \otimes ((\oplus, \otimes)/y) \end{aligned}$$

These equations define reduction over non-empty trees. If, in addition, $\oplus$ has a unique left identity element e, and e is also the unique right identity element of $\otimes$, then we can set

$$(\oplus, \otimes)/\langle\,\rangle = e$$

Let us now consider some examples of reduction.

(1) The *label* of a tree is given by

$$label = (\gg, \ll)/$$

The operator $\gg$ associates with $\ll$, for both sides of

$$a \gg (b \ll c) = (a \gg b) \ll c$$

simplify to b. Note, however, that $\ll$ does *not* associate with $\gg$, that is,

$$a \ll (b \gg c) \neq (a \ll b) \gg c$$

Here, the left-hand side reduces to a, but the right-hand side reduces to c.

(2) The inorder traversal of a tree is defined by

$$inorder = (+\!\!+, +\!\!+)/ \cdot [\cdot]*$$

(3) The size of a tree is defined by

$$size = (+, +)/ \cdot K_1*$$

(4) The function *member x*, which determines whether x appears as a label in a given tree, is defined by

$$member\ x = (\vee, \vee)/ \cdot (= x)*$$

In the examples above there is only one operator in the reduction, and this operator is associative. The reduction is well-defined because an associative operator associates with itself. Moreover, each operator possesses an identity element (which is therefore the unique left and right identity element of the operator), and so each of the above functions is defined on the empty tree.

Here are some examples where the operators in a reduction are not the same.

(5) The *depth* of a tree is defined by

$$depth = (\oplus, \widetilde{\oplus})/ \cdot K_1*$$

where the operator $\oplus$ is defined by

$$a \oplus b = (1 + a) \uparrow b$$

and, as usual, $a \widetilde{\oplus} b = b \oplus a$. Neither $\oplus$ nor $\widetilde{\oplus}$ is associative, but nevertheless $\oplus$ associates with $\widetilde{\oplus}$. The proof of this fact is left to the reader.

(6) A similar function is *heaporder*, defined by
$$heaporder = (\oplus, \widetilde{\oplus})/ \cdot [\cdot]*$$
where $\oplus$ is defined by
$$x \oplus ([a] \mathbin{+\!\!+} y) = [a] \mathbin{+\!\!+} (x \mathbin{\mathbb{M}} y)$$
We leave to the reader the proof that $\oplus$ associates with $\widetilde{\oplus}$, and that $[\,]$ is the unique left identity of $\oplus$ (and therefore the unique right identity of $\widetilde{\oplus}$). Thus, we have
$$heaporder\langle\,\rangle = [\,]$$
An alternative definition of *heaporder* can be based on the ternary view of trees:

$$\begin{aligned}
heaporder\,\langle\,\rangle &= [\,] \\
heaporder\,(x \mathbin{\swarrow} \langle a \rangle \mathbin{\searrow} y) &= [a] \mathbin{+\!\!+} (heaporder\,x \mathbin{\mathbb{M}} heaporder\,y)
\end{aligned}$$

By definition, a tree x is a heap if *heaptree* x holds, where
$$heaptree = nondec \cdot heaporder$$
Here, *nondec* is a predicate that determines whether a sequence is in non-decreasing order. An alternative definition of *heaptree* is given by the equations:

$$\begin{aligned}
heaptree\langle a \rangle &= True \\
heaptree(x \mathbin{\swarrow} y) &= heaptree\,x \wedge heaptree\,y \wedge label\,x \geqslant label\,y \\
heaptree(x \mathbin{\searrow} y) &= heaptree\,x \wedge heaptree\,y \wedge label\,x \leqslant label\,y
\end{aligned}$$

5.4 Accumulations

Let us now very briefly consider accumulations on trees. There are two kinds: upwards (or towards the root) and downwards (or towards the leaves). For reasons of space we consider only the first kind.

An upwards accumulation (on non-empty trees) is denoted by $\curlywedge$, and takes a pair of operators $(\oplus, \otimes)$ as its left argument, and a tree x as its right argument. The result is a tree of the same shape as x. The function $up = (\oplus, \otimes)\curlywedge$ is defined by the equations:

$$\begin{aligned}
up\langle a \rangle &= \langle a \rangle \\
up(x \mathbin{\swarrow} \langle a \rangle) &= up\,x \mathbin{\swarrow} \langle b \oplus a \rangle \\
up(\langle a \rangle \mathbin{\searrow} y) &= \langle a \otimes c \rangle \mathbin{\searrow} up\,y \\
up(x \mathbin{\swarrow} \langle a \rangle \mathbin{\searrow} y) &= up\,x \mathbin{\swarrow} \langle b \oplus a \otimes c \rangle \mathbin{\searrow} up\,y \\
&\quad \text{where } b = label(up\,x) \text{ and } c = label(up\,y)
\end{aligned}$$

For example, the function *subtrees* with type

$$subtrees : \langle \alpha \rangle \to \langle\langle \alpha \rangle\rangle$$

can be defined by

$$subtrees = (\downarrow, \searrow) \lambda \cdot \langle \cdot \rangle *$$

The expression *subtrees x* evaluates to a tree of exactly the same shape as x but whose labels are the subtrees of x. In particular,

$$label * subtrees\ x = x$$

We shall use this result below.

The accumulation lemma for trees states that

$$(\oplus, \otimes) \lambda = (\oplus, \otimes)/ * \cdot subtrees$$

The expression on the left can be computed in time linear in the size of the tree, whereas the expression on the right takes quadratic time in the worst case.

For example, the function

$$treesizes = size* \cdot subtrees$$

can be re-expressed as

$$treesizes = (+, +) \lambda \cdot K_1 *$$

and therefore can be computed in linear time. (We leave the reader to formulate and prove the necessary subsidiary identity that enable the second definition of *treesizes* to be calculated from the first.)

5.5 Building a heap

The problem stated at the beginning was to build a heap whose inorder traversal was a given sequence. We are required, therefore, to construct a function *heap* satisfying the equations

$$\begin{aligned} inorder(heap\ x) &= x \\ heaptree(heap\ x) &= True \end{aligned}$$

for all lists x. In words, the first equation says that *heap* is a right-inverse of *inorder*, while the second says that *heap* must return a tree satisfying the heap condition. Note that *inorder* is surjective, but not injective. For example, both the trees

$$\langle 1 \rangle \searrow (\langle 1 \rangle \searrow \langle 2 \rangle) \quad \text{and} \quad \langle 1 \rangle \swarrow \langle 1 \rangle \searrow \langle 2 \rangle$$

produce the inorder traversal $[1, 1, 2]$. Moreover, both trees are heaps, so the specification of *heap* does not determine the function uniquely. Indeterminacy arises because there is a choice as to the relative placement of equal values.

To determine a constructive definition of *heap*, we can look for a solution of the form

$$heap = \oplus / \cdot f*$$

In other words, we can look for a definition as a homomorphism over lists. Using the specification of *heap*, it is possible to calculate the values of f and $\oplus$. We obtain that $f = \langle \cdot \rangle$ and that $\oplus$ is determined by the equation

$$
\begin{aligned}
(x \swarrow \langle a \rangle \searrow y) \oplus (u \swarrow \langle b \rangle \searrow v) &= x \swarrow \langle a \rangle \searrow (y \oplus (u \swarrow \langle b \rangle \searrow v)) && \text{if } a < b \\
&= ((x \swarrow \langle a \rangle \searrow y) \oplus u) \swarrow \langle b \rangle \searrow v && \text{otherwise}
\end{aligned}
$$

together with the condition that $\langle \rangle = id_\oplus$. We leave to the reader the proof that this definition of *heap* meets its specification.

In this solution, indeterminacy is resolved by placing equal values to the left. More precisely, suppose we define the *right-spine* of a tree by the equation

$$rspine = (\gg, +\!\!+)/ \cdot [\cdot]*$$

Informally, the right-spine of a tree is the sequence of labels obtained by starting at the root and proceeding along the right branches to the rightmost tip. Then our definition of *heap* is such that $rspine(heap\ x)$ is a sequence in strictly increasing order.

5.6 Solution as a left reduction

The definition of *heap* as a homomorphism does not prescribe an order of computation. To obtain a sequential algorithm we can specialise the definition to a left reduction:

$$heap = \otimes \!\!\not\!\!\rightarrow_{\langle\rangle}$$

where $x \otimes b = x \oplus f\, b$. Simplification yields:

$$\begin{aligned}
\langle\rangle \otimes b &= \langle b\rangle \\
(x \swarrow \langle a\rangle \searrow y) \otimes b &= x \swarrow \langle a\rangle \searrow (y \otimes b) && \text{if } a < b \\
&= (x \swarrow \langle a\rangle \searrow y) \swarrow \langle b\rangle && \text{otherwise}
\end{aligned}$$

A pictorial interpretation of $\otimes$ is as follows. If x is the heap

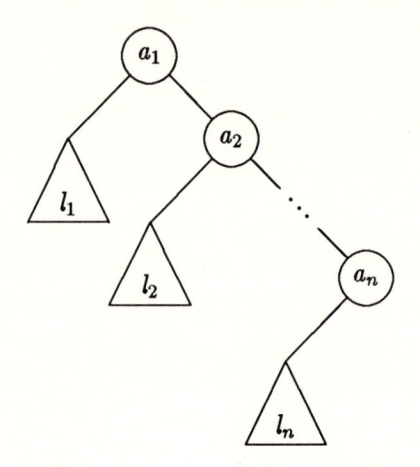

then $x \otimes b$ will be the heap

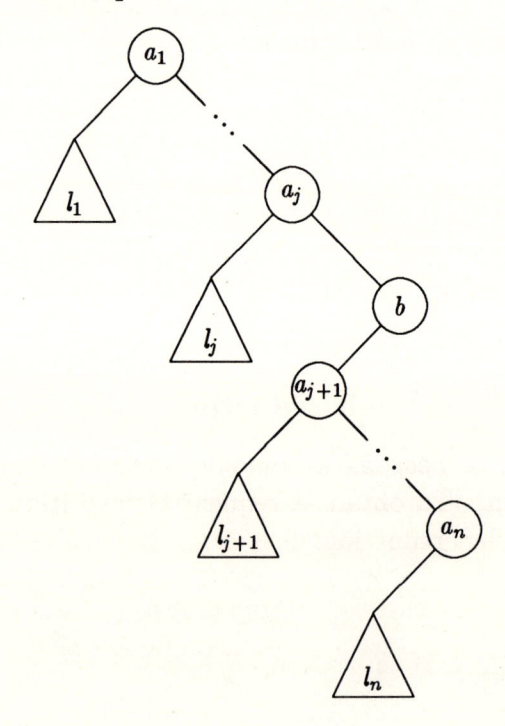

where j is defined by the condition $a_j < b \leqslant a_{j+1}$.

The running time of this algorithm is $O(N^2)$, where N is the length of the argument. Each element b may be compared with every label in the right spine, and the right spine can increase by one in length at each step. A more efficient algorithm can be obtained by comparing b with labels in the right spine, starting with the rightmost label and proceeding to the root. The amount of processing done at each step is then proportional to the change in length of the right spine. This gives a linear time algorithm for building the heap.

To implement the above idea we need a change in representation. Consider the function cut defined informally by the equation

$$cut(x_1 \searrow (x_2 \searrow (\ldots \searrow x_n))) = [x_1, x_2, \ldots, x_n]$$

where each x_j is such that $noright\ x_j$ holds. Thus, cut takes an arbitrary tree and returns a sequence of trees obtained by removing every right branch along the right spine. It is easy to check that cut is a bijective function. If we define

$$paste = \searrow \#\langle\,\rangle$$

then cut and $paste$ are inverse functions, that is,

$$\begin{aligned} cut \cdot paste &= id_{[\langle\alpha\rangle]} \\ paste \cdot cut &= id_{\langle\alpha\rangle} \end{aligned}$$

To implement the change in representation, we can modify the definition of $heap$ by writing

$$heap = paste \cdot \odot \#_{[\,]}$$

where $\odot$ is specified by the equation

$$(cut\ x) \odot b = cut(x \otimes b)$$

Putting it another way, if $\odot$ and $\otimes$ are related by the above equation, then

$$cut \cdot \otimes \#\langle\,\rangle = \odot \#\, cut\langle\,\rangle$$

and so, by applying $paste$ to both sides, we get the new equation for $heap$.

To complete the change in representation, it remains to synthesise a constructive definition of $\odot$ from its specification. Omitting details, we can calculate that

$$\begin{aligned} [\,] \odot b &= [\langle b \rangle] \\ ([x \swarrow \langle a \rangle] \mathbin{+\!\!+} xs) \odot b &= [x \swarrow \langle a \rangle] \mathbin{+\!\!+} (xs \odot b) && \text{if } a < b \\ &= [paste([x \swarrow \langle a \rangle] \mathbin{+\!\!+} xs) \swarrow \langle b \rangle] && \text{otherwise} \end{aligned}$$

This effects the change in representation but, in order to achieve the desired increase in efficiency, we still need to change the order in which the elements of the left-hand argument of $\odot$ are processed.

5.7 Prefix and suffix

Let us introduce four new operators on lists. They are $\lrcorner$ ('take prefix'), $\urcorner$ ('drop prefix'), $\llcorner$ ('take suffix') and $\ulcorner$ ('drop suffix'). Each operator takes a predicate on the left and a list on the right. The definitions of $p \lrcorner x$ and $p \llcorner x$ are:

$$p \lrcorner x = \uparrow_{\#}/\, all\ p \triangleleft inits\ x$$
$$p \llcorner x = \uparrow_{\#}/\, all\ p \triangleleft tails\ x$$

Both operations can be implemented efficiently so that the number of calculations of p equals one more than the number of elements in the result.

The remaining two operators are defined by the equations:

$$(p \lrcorner x) + \!\!+ (p \urcorner x) = x$$
$$(p \ulcorner x) + \!\!+ (p \llcorner x) = x$$

Thus $p \urcorner x$ is what remains when $p \lrcorner x$ is removed from x. A similar statement holds for $p \ulcorner x$.

We state without proof the following lemma.

Lemma 6 *Let x be a sequence and p a predicate such that $p * x$ is non-increasing (taking False $<$ True). Then*

$$p \lrcorner x = \bar{p} \ulcorner x$$

where $\bar{p}$ is the negation of p.

5.8 A linear algorithm

We can now use the newly introduced operators in the construction of a linear time algorithm for our problem about building a heap. Recall that, currently, we have

$$heap = paste \cdot \odot \!\not\!\!\!\!/\, []$$

where

$$paste = \searrow \!\!\!\!+\!\!\!\!/\, \langle\rangle$$

and
$$\begin{aligned}[] [\,] \odot b &= [\langle b \rangle] \\ ([x \mathbin{\swarrow} \langle a \rangle] \mathbin{+\!\!+} xs) \odot b &= [x \mathbin{\swarrow} \langle a \rangle] \mathbin{+\!\!+} (xs \odot b) && \text{if } a < b \\ &= [\mathit{paste}([x \mathbin{\swarrow} \langle a \rangle] \mathbin{+\!\!+} xs) \mathbin{\swarrow} \langle b \rangle] && \text{otherwise} \end{aligned}$$

Using the operators $\lrcorner$ and $\ulcorner$, we can rewrite the definition of $\odot$ in the form

$$xs \odot b = (p_b \lrcorner\, xs) \mathbin{+\!\!+} [\mathit{paste}(p_b \ulcorner xs) \mathbin{\swarrow} \langle b \rangle]$$

where the predicate p_b is defined by

$$p_b(x \mathbin{\swarrow} \langle a \rangle) = (a < b)$$

Since, by the heap assumption, $p_b * xs$ is non-increasing, we have that

$$xs \odot b \;=\; (\bar{p}_b \ulcorner xs) \mathbin{+\!\!+} [\mathit{paste}(\bar{p}_b \llcorner xs) \mathbin{\swarrow} \langle b \rangle]$$

With the new definition of $\odot$, the function *heap* can be computed in linear time.

5.9 Application

The representation of sequences by heaps has a number of uses, of which we give just one brief illustration. The problem that arose in the last lecture, namely to compute the area of the largest rectangle under a histogram, can be formulated as a function

$$\begin{aligned} \mathit{mra} &= \uparrow\!/ \cdot \mathit{area}\!* \cdot \mathit{segs} \\ \mathit{area}\, x &= \#x \times \downarrow\!/x \end{aligned}$$

The function *mra* can be computed in linear time by converting the given list into a heap, multiplying each element by the size of the subheap below that element, and taking the maximum of the results. In symbols, we have

$$\begin{aligned} \mathit{mra} &= (\uparrow, \uparrow)/ \cdot \mathit{area}'\!* \cdot \mathit{subtrees} \cdot \mathit{heap} \\ \mathit{area}'\, x &= \mathit{size}\, x \times \mathit{label}\, x \end{aligned}$$

Proof of this claim is omitted. Now, suppose we define

$$\mathit{areas} = \mathit{area}'\!* \cdot \mathit{subtrees}$$

Using the results about *subtrees* cited above, we can then calculate

$$\begin{aligned} \mathit{areas}\, x &= (\mathit{size} * \mathit{subtrees}\, x) \curlyvee_\times (\mathit{label} * \mathit{subtrees}\, x) \\ &= ((+,+) \barwedge K_1 * x) \curlyvee_\times x \end{aligned}$$

Thus *areas* can be computed in linear time. It follows, finally, that

$$mra = (\uparrow, \uparrow)/ \cdot areas \cdot heap$$

can also be computed in linear time.

5.10 References

The idea of using heaps to solve certain problems about segments can be found in

[1] De Moor, O. and Swierstra, D. The low segment problem. Presentation at WG2.1, Rome, March 1988.

The largest rectangle under a histogram is a generalisation of Problem 40 in

[2] Rem, M. Small programming exercises. *Science of Computer Programming*. 1987.

Rem's problem is to compute the size of the largest square under a histogram; in symbols,

$$\uparrow/ \cdot \#* \cdot p\triangleleft \cdot segs,$$

where $p\,x = (\downarrow/x \geqslant \#x.)$

Edsger Dijkstra also produces an infinite stream of rabbits, but at a much slower pace. This is because he handcarves his rabbits. The purpose is to keep them from wearing off too quickly, since he is fond of re-usable rabbits, i.e. rabbits that can be pulled out of the hat over and over again.

On a Problem Transmitted by Doug McIlroy

Prof. Dr. Edsger W. Dijkstra
Dept. of Computer Sciences
The University of Texas at Austin
Austin, TX 78712-1188
USA

During the recent meeting of IFIP Working Group 2.3 on "Programming Methodology", Doug McIlroy (AT&T) told me the following

Theorem Let a big rectangle R be tiled into small rectangles r. Then

$$(\underline{A}r :: P.r) \Rightarrow P.R$$, where

P.q ≡ (rectangle q has a side of integer length).

My quick consideration that this might be a theorem was as follows. Let each side of each small rectangle be a multiple of $1/p$. Then

(0) having an integer side, each small rectangle r has an area that is a multiple of $1/p$

(1) hence   R   has an area — the sum of areas of small rectangles — that is a multiple of $1/p$

(2) each side of R — being sums of sides of small rectangles — is a multiple of $1/p$.

(3) combining (1) and (2) we conclude for p a prime that R has a side of integer length.

So far so good. But even the consideration that with sufficiently large prime p each real value can be approximated arbitrarily closely by a multiple of $1/p$ does not make this a proof. Before I had designed a proof, Doug told me the argument that I shall now develop.

The argument takes for granted that each small rectangle has sides parallel to those of the big one.

How do we formally express that the little rectangles r partition the big one R ? Just stating that the sum of the areas of the little ones equals the area of the big one does not suffice for then the jigsaw puzzle need not fit. The claim that the little rectangles have been so positioned in the plane as to form a tiling of R is equivalent to the statement

(0)   ($\underline{\text{SUM}}$ r:: $\iint_r$ f.x.y dx dy) = ($\iint_R$ f.x.y dx dy) for any f.

Remark This characterization of the r's forming a tiling of R may surprise the reader at first sight but it is the only compact way in which I can characterize that fact. That the tiling implies (0) is a direct consequence of the definition of the integral - we know it more generally as "splitting the range" -, but (0) is also a sufficient condition. With f=0 inside R and f=1 outside R it expresses that no r lies outside R. With f=1 inside R but outside all r's and f=0 elsewhere, it expresses that R is covered by the r's, etc. (End of Remark).

But if (0) is $\underline{\text{the}}$ characterization of a tiling there is only one thing we can do:

firstly, we must think of a constraint such that a sum meets the constraint if all summands do, and secondly, we must find such an f that for any rectangle q with sides horizontal or vertical

(1)   (q has a side of integer length) ≡

($\iint_q$ f.x.y dx dy) meets the constraint).

Let us focus on the constraint first. Being positive works only for non-empty sums, but being ≥ 0 would do. Being congruent 0 **mod** p would do; but meeting the constraint should say something about one of the sides. By choosing p prime, our quick consideration led to some sort of conclusion, but we saw that that argument was a dead end: the p was too arbitrary. Why don't we try the simplest constraint we can think of, viz. being equal to zero?

This choice pins down requirement (1) on f : for any rectangle q with sides horizontal or vertical, f should satisfy

(2)   (q has a side of integer lenght) ≡
       $(\iint_q f.x.y \; dx \; dy) = 0$,

or, a little bit more explicitly

(2')   (q's horizontal side is of integer length) ∨
       (q's vertical side is of integer length)   ≡
       $(\iint_q f.x.y \; dx \; dy) = 0$,

The latter formulation suggests to rewrite the right-hand side as a disjunction of two terms, dependent on the horizontal and the vertical dimension of q only. Because a product is zero iff a factor of it is zero, we would like to write the double integral as the product of two single integrals. This we can achieve by choosing for f.x.y the product of two factors, dependent on x and y respectively. In order to maintain the symmetry we choose for f with some h

       f.x.y = h.x • h.y
Then
       $(\iint f.x.y \; dx \; dy) = (\int h.x \; dx) \cdot (\int h.y \; dy)$

and (2) is now satisfied provided h satisfies

(3)   (b-a is integer) ≡ $(\int_a^b h.x \; dx) = 0$

Can we find such an h ? With h = H' we can rewrite (3) as the conjunction of

(4a)   (b-a is integer) $\Rightarrow$ H.b = H.a   and

(4b)   (b-a is integer) $\Leftarrow$ H.b = H.a

Relation (4a) is satisfied by any H with period 1. Because we wish to define h by h = H', H should also be differentiable. So far H.x = sin.(2π x) would do the job, but fails to satisfy (4b), which requires all values in a period to be distinct. A moment's reflexion tells us that no real, differentiable, and periodic function meets that requirement, but that in the complex plane there is no problem: for instance

$$H.x = e^{2\pi i x}$$

meets all our requirements. (Any differentiable function with period 1 whose period traces a nonintersecting cyclic path in the complex plane will do.)

*   *
*

The above proof design has been recorded for a number of reasons. Doug McIlroy showed me this proof as a surprising example of how effective complex numbers can be in solving a problem in real numbers. He pulled $e^{2\pi i(x+y)}$ out of a hat. The above design makes it quite clear why a detour via the complex plane is so appropriate.

Another reason to record this design is that each next step of design is sweetly reasonable after the decision to characterize the tiling by (0). I am convinced that the elegance of the final argument and the compelling nature of its design are an immediate consequence of the choice of (0): it is noncombinatorial and lends itself to manipulation. I am also convinced that this is an instance of a very general observation.

Austin, 21. November 1987

A computing scientist's approach to a once-deep theorem of Sylvester's

Prof. Dr. Edsger W. Dijkstra
Dept. of Computer Sciences
The University of Texas at Austin
Austin, TX 78712-1188, USA

Well, actually it wasn't Sylvester's theorem, it was only his conjecture - dating from the year 1893 -, and it remained so for more than 40 years until T. Gallai (alias Grünwald) "finally succeeded, using a rather complicated argument" [Coxeter]. We shall derive (essentially) the simple argument of L.M. Kelly (1948).

Theorem Consider a finite number of distinct points in the real Euclidean plane; these points are collinear or there exists a straight line through exactly 2 of them.

To see that this is a truly geometrical theorem and not a combinatorial one, we slightly rephrase the setting. Let us assume for a moment that collinearity of points in the Euclidean plane is fully captured by

(i) any pair of points is collinear, and if two collinear triples have two points in common, their four points are collinear.

Let us rephrase this: replace "points" by "people", "lines" by "clubs" and "collinear" by "club-sharing" (i.e. belonging to one and the same club). Club membership is postulated to satisfy the analogue of (i):

(ii) any pair of people is club-sharing, and if two club-sharing triples have two people in common, their four people are club-sharing.

The analogue of Sylvester's theorem would state for a finite population: all people belong to one and the same club or there exists a club with exactly 2 members. Its falsity is shown by the following counterexample of 7 people - numbered from 0 through 6 - with the following 7 clubs: {013}, {124}, {235}, {346}, {450}, {561}, and {602}. Postulate (ii) is satisfied because each of the 21 pairs of people occurs in exactly 1 club. Thus we have established that Sylvester's theorem is truly a geometrical one; let us now try to prove it.

Being computing scientists, we love constructive arguments, i.e. we like to show that something exists by designing an algorithm that computes such a thing. We therefore propose to design an algorithm that computes a line that passes through exactly 2 of the points from a given finite, non-collinear set of distinct points. (Legenda: from here on we no longer repeat that the points are distinct, nor that they belong to the given, non-collinear set.)

More precisely, we have to design an algorithm that operates on a variable q of type: line and establishes the post-condition R , given by

R: q passes through exactly 2 of the points

The simplest idea is to initialize q by the line through 2 arbitrary points. (This is always possible because, the given set being non-collinear, there are at least 3 points.) If q goes through 3 or more points, it has to be changed, otherwise it can be accepted as final value. That is, with invariant P given by

P: q passes through $\geq$ 2 points

we propose as first approximation of our algorithm

```
    establish P by initialization of q
;  do q passes through ≥ 3 points →
        change q under invariance of P
    od
```

Because

$$P \wedge \neg (q \text{ passes through} \geq 3 \text{ points}) \Rightarrow R$$

we are done when the algorithm terminates.

Our remaining task is to ensure that it does terminate. To that end we have to exploit the finiteness of the given set and its non-collinearity. Because the exploitation of finiteness is absolutely standard, we first focus our attention on what we con conclude form the non-collinearity. From the latter we can draw <u>only one</u> conclusion in connection with q , viz. the existence of a point through which q does not pass. That is, we propose to introduce a variable E of type: point , and to strengthen P to P1

P1:
    q passes through ≥ 2 points ∧
    q does not pass through E

The new approximation of our algorithm is

```
    establish P1 by initializing q and E
;  do q passes through ≥ 3 points →
        {?} change q and E under invariance of P1
    od
```

(Ignore for a moment the assertion "{?}"; the important thing to realize is that with the feasibility of maintaining the stronger P1, the non-collinearity of the given set has been exhausted.)

In the current stage of program design, our only option is a further refinement of the as yet rather nondeterministic

(0)   "change q and E under invariance of P1"

Because we may have to reduce its nondeterminism lest the algorithm fails to terminate, let us investigate its freedom: what precondition {?} can we guarantee? We know of the existence of 4 points, viz. E and the three points on the current q . Because the new q has to pass through ≥ 2 points and has to differ from the old q , the new q passes through the old E and one of the 3 points on the old q ; in each case, one of the remaining 2 points on the old q has to be chosen as the new E . In summary: for the new pair (q, E) we have 6 possibilities.

For the termination argument we need a variant function of the pair (q, E); because the number of points is finite, the number of pairs (q, E) satisfying P1 is finite, and any function of the pair (q, E) that decreases at each change will do.

What is the simplest function of a line and a point (not on that line) that we can think of? The Euclidean distance between the two!

Let us investigate whether we can refine (0) so as to decrease the distance between q and E. Let us name the three points on the old q: A, B, C, so that A becomes the new E. With that convention, the refinement of (0) that decreases the distance of the pair (q, E) as much as possible is

(1)   q, E := of BE and CE the nearest to A, A

Finally we derive a condition on A as our choice for the new E from the requirement that the variant function decreases. With

```
      h = distance between E and q
      b = distance between A and BE
      c = distance between A and CE
```

the required decrease of the variant function is expressed by

(2)   b **min** c < h

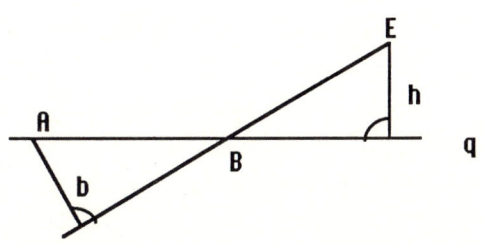

In order to derive (2), we proceed as follows

```
          b min c < h
   =          {definition of min}
          b < h   v   c < h
   =          {similar triangles, see figure}
          AB < EB   v   AC < EC
   ⇐          {monotonicity of + } (See Note)
          AB + AC < EB + EC
   ⇐          {P1 ⇒ BC < EB + EC, i.e. the strict triangular
              inequality} (See Note)
          AB + AC ≤ BC
   =          {AB + AC ≥ BC, i.e. triangular inequality}
          AB + AC = BC
   =          {AB, AC and BC denote unsigned lengths}
          on q, A lies between B and C.
```

Hence, with for A the point between the two others, (1) does the job. And this concludes our proof of Sylvester's theorem.

Note Since steps that express equivalence don't destroy information, the others need some more justification. We all know the mononicity of ≥, i.e. no one doubts

$$x \geq x' \land y \geq y' \Rightarrow x + y \geq x' + y' ;$$
its contrapositive yields the equivalent
$$x < x' \lor y < y' \Leftarrow x + y < x' + y'$$
and that is what we used.

To justify the next step, a second look at our demonstrandum (2) suffices: since it is impossible to demonstrate (2) for h = 0, we have to use once more that q does not pass through E . Since E occurs in this calculation in the combinations EB and EC, we translate this into the nondegeneracy of triangle BEC. The step eliminates E from the rest of the calculation. (End of Note.)

For the sake of completeness we point out that, after the choice of the variant function, we have made two silent choices. We have chosen -as usual- to decrease the variant function; because of the finiteness, successfully increasing it would also have yielded a valid termination argument. With a huge h and ABC close together, however, the distance between E and q cannot be increased, which settles this silent choice. Moreover, we could have grouped our 6 cases differently, viz. by common new q instead of by common new E. We could have said "Let us name the three points so that AE becomes the new q" and instead of (1) we would have come up with
    q, E := AE, of B and C the nearest to AE
It does not work.

                    ★   ★
                              ★

A few methodological remarks are in order, because the theorem certainly deserves the name of a once-deep theorem: after 1933, when Karamata and Erdös revived interest in the problem [Coxeter], it took another fifteen years before L.M. Kelly made essentially the above use of the Euclidean distance and found the simple argument.

It was very gratifying to see that, once the decision had been taken to tackle this problem as a programming task, the job of designing the program was all but standard. I have used this problem in oral examinations for a course on "Mathematical Methodology" for Computing Science graduates. Some needed more prompting or more time than others, but none of them needed any prompting to come up with the Euclidean distance between q and E as candidate for the variant function. They knew that the argument required a variant function and they all suggested the Euclidean distance without hesitation. And that was Kelly's great invention!

A fringe benefit of proving the theorem by designing a program is that it takes away the surprise that in such a non-metric context a metric concept such as the Euclidean distance enters the picture. We all know that a monotonic function of an acceptable variant is again an acceptable variant and that the challenge always is to find a nice one. It is very much like the freedom to choose the most convenient coordinate system.

Acknowledgement That the distance from points to lines through other points could be used in the proof was told to me by Bernhard von Stengel; he told me to look at the shortest such distance. (End of Acknowledgement.)

*   *

*

For Sylvester's theorem to be true it is essential that the points are distinct. (Consider a non-degenerate triangle with each vertex coinciding with a triple of points.) Replace "any 2 points are distinct" by "through any 2 points passes only one straight line". The latter can be generalized to one dimension more "through any 3 points passes only one plane", i.e. "no 3 points are collinear". And now we are ready to generalize Sylvester's theorem to three dimensions:

Theorem Consider in the real three-dimensional Euclidean space a finite number of points such that no 3 of them are collinear; these points are coplanar or there exists a plane through exactly 3 of them.

(In the three-dimensional case, just requiring that the points be distinct is not enough: consider two non-intersecting, nonparallel lines with 4 distinct points on each.)

Proof sketch Select one of the points and a plane outside. Project, with the selected point as centre, the remaining points on the selected plane, to which projection Sylvester's theorem is applied. (End of Proof sketch.)

*   *

*

Coxeter mentions no more-dimensional generalization of Sylvesters's theorem. Maybe he did not think it sufficiently interesting. Maybe he could not comfortably generalize because none of his formulations mentions explicitly that the points have to be distinct.

Coxeter's passage is interesting for historical reasons. He quotes Sylvesters's original statement of the problem:

> *"Prove that it is not possible to arrange any finite number of real points so that a right line through every two of them shall pass [sic] through a third, unless they all lie in the same right line."*

Fortunately we don't formulate problems like that anymore. I could not read it and ended up looking up "unless" in the COD, which gave two interpretations "if not" (which boils down to ∨) and "except when" (which boils down to "≢"). I felt excused. (Actually, Sylvester used "unless" in the meaning of "∨".)

A few lines further, Coxeter gives credit to T. Motzkin (1951): "Sylvester's 'negative' statement was rephrased 'positively' by Motzkin:

If n points in the real plane are not on one straight line, then there exists a straight line containing exactly two of the points."

It is not quite clear for which achievement Motzkin receives credit. He replaces Sylvester's contorted

¬(A line: line passes ≥ 2: line passes ≥ 3)

thanks to de Morgan by

(E line: line passes ≥ 2: line passes < 3)

which can be simplified (arithmetically!) to

(E line:: line passes = 2)

which in the statement of the theorem is certainly a simplification. (But note that in the proof one immediate uses

line passes = 2 ≡ (line passes ≥ 2) ∧ ¬(line passes ≥3).)

Or did Motzkin get credit for replacing Sylvester's disjunction by an implication? You never know with Coxeter. (I dislike in Motzkin's formulation, besides the dangling "n", the implication: compared to Sylvester's disjunction, I consider that a step backwards. Please note that the implicative formulation introduced - in "*not* on a straight line" - a negation.)

Coxeter's section opens with a quotation from G.H. Hardy (1940):

> "Reductio ad absurdum, which Euclid loved so much, is one of a mathematician's finest weapons. It is a far finer gambit than any chess gambit: a chess play may offer the sacrifice of a pawn or even a piece, but a mathematician offers the game."

No matter how hard I try, almost half a century later I am unable to give even a mildly sensible interpretation to the above quotation of Hardy's, but, in 1961, Coxeter evidently felt he could: his proof gloriously ends with the now infamous "which is absurd".

(Coxeter focusses his attention on the pair (q,E) with minimum distance and derives a contradiction from the assumption that that q passes through at least 3 points. The choice of the pair with minimum distance is overspecific: it is only a device to construct the avoidable contradiction. Tellingly, he concludes

> "This completes the proof that there is always a line containing exactly two of the points. Of course, there may be more that one such line […]".)

Fascinating to analyse mathematical style from such a recent past!

Reference
Coxeter, FRS, H.S.M. "Introduction to Geometry", 2nd ed., John Wiley & Sons, Inc. New York etc., pp 65-66

Austin, 5 February 1988

The derivation of a proof by J.C.S.P. van der Woude

Prof. Dr. Edsger W. Dijkstra
Dept. of Computer Sciences
The University of Texas at Austin
Austin, TX 78712-1188
USA

In the following

• P and Q will be used to denote predicates on some space.

• X and Y will be used to denote functions from the natural number to predicates on that space; accordingly, X.i ($0 \leq i$) and Y.i ($0 \leq i$) denote predicate sequences.

• f will be used to denote a predicate transformer, i.e. a function from predicates to predicates.

• square brackets will be used to denote universal quantification of the enclosed predicate over the space in question.

With the above notational conventions we give the following definitions

- "sequence X.i ($0 \leq i$) is monotonic" means
  "sequence X.i ($0 \leq i$) is weakening or strengthening".

- "sequence X.i ($0 \leq i$) is weakening" means
  (A i, j: $0 \leq i < j$: [X.i $\Rightarrow$ X.j])

- "sequence X.i ($0 \leq i$) is strenghthening" means
  (A i, j: $0 \leq i < j$: [X.i $\Leftarrow$ X.j])

- "predicate transformer f is monotonic" means
  [P $\Rightarrow$ Q] $\Rightarrow$ [f.P $\Rightarrow$ f.Q] for all P, Q.

- "predicate transformer f is finitely conjunctive" means
  $[f.(P \wedge Q) \equiv f.P \wedge f.Q]$ for all P, Q.

- "predicate transformer f is **or**-continuous" means
  $[f.(\mathbf{E}\ i: 0 \leq i: X.i) \equiv (\mathbf{E}\ i: 0 \leq i: f.(X.i))]$ for any monotonic sequence $X.i\ (0 \leq i)$

- "predicate transformer f is **and**-continuous" means
  $[f.(\mathbf{A}\ i: 0 \leq i: X.i) \equiv (\mathbf{A}\ i: 0 \leq i: f.(X.i))]$ for any monotonic sequence $X.i\ (0 \leq i)$

We can now formulate the

Theorem For any predicate transformer f
(0)   (f is finitely conjunctive) $\wedge$ (f is **or**-continuous) $\Rightarrow$
      (f is **and**-continuous).

Here, we shall sketch the simple part of the proof and shall derive the exciting part (which we owe to J.C.S.P. van der Woude).

Proof Under the truth of the antecedent of (0) we have to show for monotonic $X.i\ (0 \leq i)$

(1) $[f.(\mathbf{A}\ i: 0 \leq i: X.i) \equiv (\mathbf{A}\ i: 0 \leq i: f.(X.i))]$

To begin with we recall that —not proved here— because f is finitely conjunctive, f is monotonic. We now distinguish two cases.

<u>X.i $(0 \leq i)$ is weakening</u>   Because f is monotonic, also the predicate sequence $f.(X.i)\ (0 \leq i)$ is weakening; consequently —not shown here— both sides of (1) are equivalent to $f.(X.0)$. This concludes the first case.

<u>X.i $(0 \leq i)$ is strenghthening</u>   Because f is monotonic —not shown here— LHS(1) $\Rightarrow$ RHS(1) and we are left with the proof obligation

(2) $[f.(A\ i:\ 0 \le i:\ X.i) \Leftarrow (A\ i:\ 0 \le i:\ f.(X.i))]$

for strengthening X.i (0 ≤ i) and an f that is finitely conjunctive and **or**-continuous.

Meeting the obligation of showing (2) is the exciting part of the proof. Reduced to its bare essentials, it consists of one definition and about a dozen simple steps. But in presenting just that irrefutable formal argument, we would pull several rabbits out of the magical hat. The proof is exciting because of the existence of heuristic considerations that quite effectively buffer these shocks of invention. For that reason, we shall develop this proof instead of just presenting it. To aid the reader in parsing the interleaved presentation of heuristic considerations and proof fragments, the latter will be indented. Here we go!

For the sake of brevity we shall omit from here on the ranges 0 ≤ i and 0 ≤ j, which are to be understood. We begin with a general remark about the exploitation of **or**-continuity. The **or**-continuity of f states

(3) $[f.(E\ i\ ::\ Y.i) \equiv (E\ i::\ f.(Y.i))]$

for any monotonic sequence Y.i. For a strengthening sequence Y.i, just monotonicity of f suffices for (3) to hold, and for constant sequences Y.i, (3) holds for any f. The relevant conclusion from these observations is that, if f's **or**-continuity is going to be exploited -and it is a safe assumption that it has to- a truly weakening sequence has to enter the picture.

Armed with this insight, we return to our demonstrandum (2). The simplest way of demonstrating an implication is to start at one side and then to repeatedly manipulate the expression (while either weakening or strengthening is allowed) until the other side is reached. So, let us try that. That decision being taken, at which side should we start?

Both sides are built from the "familiar" universal quantification and the "unfamiliar" application of f, about which our knowledge is limited, the only difference being that, at the two sides, they occur in opposite order. In such a situation, the side with the "unfamiliar" operation as the outer one counts as the more complicated one and is therefore the preferrred starting point. In our case, it is the consequent

(4)   f. (A̱i:: X.i)

so let us start from there. The formal challenge of manipulating (4) while exploiting what we know about f should provide the heuristic guidance as to in which direction to proceed.

Rewriting (4) so as to exploit f's **or**-continuity would require rewriting its argument (A̱i:: X.i) as an existential quantificaiton over a truly weakening sequence, but how to do that -I tried in vain- is not clear at all. So, let us try to exploit at this stage f's finite conjunctivity, i.e. let us introduce a P and Q such that

   [(A̱i:: X.i) ≡ P ∧ Q]

For one of the conjuncts, say P, we may choose any predicate implied by (A̱i:: X.i); the law of instantiation tells us that any X.j would do. (Note that this choice is less restrictive than it might seem: because X.i is a strengthening sequence, any finite conjunction of some X.i's yields some X.j.) We could therefore consider for some j the introduction of a predicate Q constrained by

   [(A̱i:: X.i) ≡ X.j ∧ Q]

But the introduction of one predicate Q for one specific j is unlikely to do the job: for one thing, the universal quantifications in the demonstrandum don't change their value if the range 0 ≤ i is replaced by j < i. This observation suggests, instead of the introduction of a single predicate Q, a predicate sequence Y.i, constrained by

(5) $(Aj:: [(Ai:: X.i) \equiv X.j \wedge Y.j])$.

The introduction of the sequence Y.j will turn out to be the major invention of the proof under design. For the time being, we don't define Y -as would be done immediately in a "bottom-up" proof- but only collect constraints on Y, of which (5) is the first one. We do so in the hope that, eventually, we can construct a Y that meets all the constraints.

A minor problem with the use of (5) as a rewrite rule is that it equates an expression not depending on j with one that formally does depend on j. The formal dependence upon j that would thus be introduced can be eliminated by quantifying over j; because we are rewriting a consequent, we use existential quantification because that yields a formally weaker expression -the range being non-empty!- than universal quantification (and the weaker the consequent, the lighter the task ahead of us). In short, we propose to start our proof under design with

```
      f.(Ai:: X.i)
   =    {(5) and range of j non-empty}
      (Ej:: f.(X.j ∧ Y.j))
   =    {f is finitely conjunctive}
(6)   (Ej:: f.(X.j) ∧ f.(Y.j))
```

So far, so good! We have not yet exploited f's **or**-continuity and we cannot do so before we have an existential quantification over a truly weakening sequence. In (6) we do have an existential quantification (albeit, as yet, over a constant sequence) and, with X.i a (truly) strengthening sequence, there is a fair chance that (5) permits a (truly) weakening sequence Y.j. So let us introduce the second constraint on Y

(7)   sequence Y.j (0 ≤ j) is weakening

as a next step towards the use of f's **or**-continuity, i.e. the use of (3) as a rewrite rule.

Comparison of the right-hand side of (3) with (6) shows that we can use (3) as rewrite rule only after we have succeeded in removing in (6) the first conjunct f.(X.j) from the term. We cannot just omit it, as that would weaken the expression and, heading for an antecedent, we are not allowed to do that. We may strengthen it; in particular, strengthening it to something independent of j would allow us to take the constant conjunct outside the existential quantification of (6). In order to strengthen f.(X.j) to something that is independent of j, we propose to quantify universally over j. That is, at (6) we propose to continue our proof under design with

```
       (Ej:: f.(X.j) ∧ f.(Y.j))
   ⇐   {instantiation, monotonicity of ∧, E}
       (Ej:: (Ai:: f.(X.i)) ∧ f.(Y.j))
   =   {∧ distributes over E}
       (Ai:: f.(X.i)) ∧ (Ej:: f.(Y.j))
   =   {(3) and (7), i.e. the use of or-continuity}
(8)    (Ai:: f.(X.i)) ∧ f.(Ej:: Y.j)
```

So far, so very good! Note that the left conjunct of (8) is the antecedent of (2) we are heading for! Again, we cannot just omit the second conjunct in (8) as that would weaken the expression; the second conjunct has to be subsumed —i.e. implied— by the first one. By the looks of it we can equate (8) with its first conjunct on just the monotonicity of f and some implicative relation between X and Y —which will emerge as our third and last constraint on Y— . But be careful! If the range of i were empty, the first conjunct of (8) would yield true, whereas (8) would yield f.(Ej:: Y.j) and there is no reason to assume these equivalent. Somewhere along the completion of our formal argument, we have to exploit the non-emptiness of i's range. As we can do it immediately, let us do it immediately. In short, we propose to continue our proof under design at (8) with

      $(\mathbf{A}i:: f.(X.i)) \wedge f.(\mathbf{E}.j:: Y.j)$
=   {range of i non-empty}
      $(\mathbf{A}i:: f.(X.i) \wedge f.(\mathbf{E}.j:: Y.j))$
=   {monotonicity of f and (9)}
      $(\mathbf{A}i:: f.(X.i))$

with, as our third and last constraint on Y,

(9) $(\mathbf{A}i:: [X.i \Rightarrow (\mathbf{E}.j:: Y.j)])$

But for the demonstration of the existence of Y, we have completed the proof in seven steps (six of which are equivalences). Now for the existence of a Y satisfying (5), (7) and (9).

In order to ease satisfaction of (9), we define Y as the weakest solution of (5), i.e. we define Y.j for any j by

(10) $[Y.j \equiv (\mathbf{A}i:: X.i) \vee \neg X.j]$

In order to verify that this Y indeed satisfies (5), we observe for any j

      $X.j \wedge Y.j$
=   {(10)}
      $X.j \wedge ((\mathbf{A}i:: X.i) \vee \neg X.j)$
=   {$\wedge$ distributes over $\vee$}
      $(X.j \wedge (\mathbf{A}i:: X.i)) \vee (X.j \wedge \neg X.j)$
=   {j in i's range; predicate calculus}
      $(\mathbf{A}i:: X.i)$

In order to verify that condition (7) is met, i.e. that Y.j $(0 \leq i)$ is indeed weakening, we observe for any j and k

```
        [Y.j ⇒ Y.k]
    =   {(10)}
        [(Ai:: X.i) ∧ ¬X.j) ⇒ (Ai:: X.i) ∧ ¬X.k)]
    ⇐   {monotonicity of ∧}
        [¬X.j ⇒ ¬X.k ]
    =   {counterpositive}
        [X.j ⇐ X.k]
    ⇐   {X.i (0 ≤ i) is strengthening}
        [j < k]
```

Finally, in order to verify that Y satisfies (9), we observe

```
        (Ej:: Yj)
    =   {(10)}
        (Ej:: (Ai:: X.i) ∨ ¬X.j)
    =   {j's range is not empty}
        (Ai:: X.i) ∨ (Ej:: ¬X.j)
    =   {de Morgan}
        (Ai:: X.i) ∨ ¬ (Aj:: X.j)
    =   {Excluded Middle}
        true
```

And this concludes the exciting part.

(End of Proof.)

Van der Woude's proof is very beautiful and I think it worthwhile to ponder over the question why this is so. It is beautiful in the way in which the proof has been divided into two parts, with Y and its three properties forming the interface between them. It is a meaningful division in the sense that our dealing with f is entirely confined to the first part. Also, the interface between the two parts is the right one, void of any overspecification: it only mentions the existence of a Y with the properties relevant for the first part. Finally, the second part, which no longer deals with f but is concerned with the existence of a Y, is pleasingly constructive. It is really a beautifully structured argument.

I think also our derivation of the proof very beautiful. The development of the first part, which deals with f, is fully driven by the need to exploit that f is given to be finitely conjunctive and **or**-continuous, and the interface was constructed as we went along. Furthermore, the second part, which constructs a Y meeting the three requirements, does so in the most straightforward manner without pulling a single rabbit out of a hat; finally it contains three mutually independent verifications that the Y constructed meets the three requirements indeed. A very nice disentanglement!

Remark I would like to draw attention to the second step of the final calculation, which establishes $[(\mathbf{E}j:: Y.j) \equiv true]$. Because this cannot be established if the range for j is empty —existential quantification over an empty range yields false—, the calculation has to exploit that j's range is not empty. The knowledge that disjunction distributes over existential quantification only in the case of a non-empty range —and this belongs to the general knowledge the predicate calculator should have at his disposal— all but dictates that second step. (End of Remark.)

Finally, I would like to point out that, though carried out in great detail, the whole formal proof consists of fewer that twenty steps: the whole calculation is really quite short. I beg the reader to remember this whenever he is faced with a defence of informality on the supposed grounds that formal proofs are too lengthy and too tedious to be of any practical value. This supposition is wrong.

Austin, 27. January 1988

Tony Hoare presented the smell of categories. A very important construction in this setting is the pullout:

However, Hoare's main aim was to move argumentation to as high a level as possible. In particular, rather than arguing about functions via their application, one should reason about them as objects in their own right. For the purpose of rabbit processing this means that the rabbits should be expelled and only hats should be used. But then the pullout construction requires the concept of higher order hats:

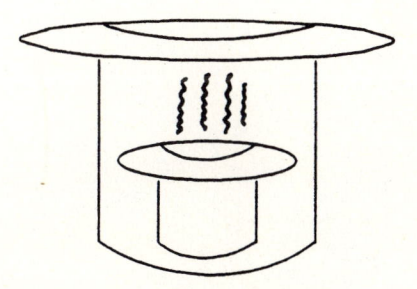

Now we have achieved the goal: Only the smell of rabbits is left.

Notes on an Approach to Category Theory for Computer Scientists

C.A.R. Hoare

Introduction

These notes have been designed for the benefit of theoretical computer scientists who are not sure whether they want to study category theory, and who are too busy to devote the long period of continuous study required to master the subject from standard texts. The notes are therefore structured into three independent chapters, of which the earlier ones are the simplest and most clearly relevant to computer science. Each chapter introduces a number of essential categorical concepts, illustrates them by examples intended to be familiar to computer scientists, and presents theorems describing their most important properties. Each chapter may therefore be studied at widely separated intervals of time; further, the material of each chapter is organised so that there is no need to finish one chapter (or even one section) before starting the next. Finally, the reader who decides to abandon the study of category theory before completing the notes will still have obtained benefit from the effort expended.

Why is category theory so difficult? The actual definition of a category is hardly more complicated than that of other algebraic structures such as groups, rings, or fields. The properties of categorical constructions are no different in principle from familiar algebraic properties such as associativity, commutivity, and distributivity. The real problem is just that categorical definitions and their properties are so much more complicated than computer scientists are used to. For example, the adjunction is one of the most important concepts of category theory, and one of the most relevant to applications in computer science. However one of the simpler definitions of an adjunction requires six free variables (two categories, two functors, and two natural transformations) and four bound variables (two objects and two arrows). Even apparently simpler definitions and theorems usually contain an alternation of universal and existential quantifiers. The existential quantifiers often take the complicated forms "There exists exactly (or at most) one x such that ...". The complication and unfamiliarity of the formulae make it difficult to acquire and develop the kind of instinctive skill at pattern-matching that makes algebraic calculation such an effective method of mathematical reasoning. An expert in category theory tackles this problem with the aid of diagrams; but the art of diagram chasing is itself skill that must be learnt, and so presents a hurdle for the beginner.

These notes attempt to solve the problem in a different way. The detailed treatment of category theory is postponed to the last section within each chapter. The main part of each chapter is devoted to three simple special cases, sets, preorders, and monoids, each of which has an independent interest for computer science. Because each case is a category, it permits the definition of many of the important categorical concepts, and formulation of their properties as theorems. But in each case, the definitions, the theorems and the proofs are much simpler than for categories in general. For example, an adjunction between sets is nothing more than an isomorphism. Its definition requires at most four free variables (two sets and two functions) and two bound variables (one member from each set). An adjunction between preorders is nothing more than a Galois connection, or a Scott retraction (projection-embedding pair); its definition requires the same four free variables and two bound ones but uses inequalities instead of equations. For an adjunction between monoids, two more free variables are required, namely the unit and counit of the adjunction, but these are simple arrows rather than families. The objective of presenting these simpler cases is to familiarise a reader with the general pattern of the definition, so that the extra formal complexity of the general categorical adjunction will seem acceptable, perhaps desirable, but certainly inevitable. The same gentle approach is taken to the definition of the other major categorical concepts, namely functors, limits, and natural transformations. There is, of course, a danger of confusion in using the same technical terms with different definitions in each chapter. The essential unity of the definitions can be made apparent only by studying the general categorical concept.

These notes include an excessive number of examples to illustrate each definition. There is no need to study, understand, or check the details of more than one example from each list. The reason for the length of the list is to enable each reader to select from it a few cases which are already familiar or interesting, which will help in memorising the definition and recalling it when needed. The length of the list may also be taken as evidence of the value and relevance of the definition being illustrated. Standard texts on category theory also have long lists of examples, but they are nearly all drawn from advanced algebra (or even algebraic topology), so they are not generally accessible to computer scientists.

It is not the purpose of these notes to explain why a computer scientist might derive benefit and also pleasure from the study of category theory. In fact, the benefit will probably be confined to a small group of theoretical computer scientists, who are engaged in clarification of the relationships between large-scale mathematical structures, theories, languages, and formal systems. I have found the theory useful in development of my understanding of the relationship between specifications, designs, correctness proofs, and programming languages of various kinds. In particular, I have been able to examine and explain various methods of proving the correctness of data representations, and check their validity in the context of different programming languages. This is a topic which has interested me since long before I heard of category theory; and I was lucky to find such a directly relevant application so quickly. I can wish my reader similar good fortune, but cannot promise it.

In my view, category theory is quite the most general and abstract branch of pure mathematics. Almost every structure in mathematics can be regarded as a category, usually in several different ways. If it is not a category, then it is a functor or a limit or a natural transformation or an adjunction. New categories can be constructed in dozens of interesting ways from old categories, or relations between them. The extreme reflexiveness and self-applicability of category theory is an inexhaustible source of confusion, or of delight, or of both. But the corollary of a high degree of generality and abstraction is that the theory gives almost no assistance in solving the more specific problems within any of the subdisciplines to which it applies. It is a tool for the generalist, of little benefit to the practitioner or the specialist – except one who specialises (often quite narrowly) in category theory itself.

In summary, perhaps category theory bears the same relation to practical computer science as topology does to engineering mathematics. Topology provides a valuable general framework for analysis; and analysis establishes the validity of the methods of calculus; and it is only these that are used by engineers to solve practical problems. Similarly, category theory provides a general framework for theories of programming; such theories form the basis of the design and definition of programming languages and their associated software engineering methods. It is only the methods and languages that are used by practicing programmers, who need know nothing of the underlying theories.

The chain from theory to application is long and has many links; but that is characteristic of all mature scientific disciplines. It would be a grave mistake to allow the chain to be broken at any point. That seems to me a good reason for encouraging a select few among theoretical computer scientists to take the trouble of mastering category theory.

Summary

The first chapter is a brief survey of set theory. It shows that the class of functions between sets is a category with a very rich structure, and that a set itself is a very impoverished category. The next chapter introduces the definition of a preorder. Within a pre-order, simple and familiar definitions are given of the basic categorical concepts: equivalence, initial and final objects, products and co-products, limits and co-limits, functors and adjunctions. Another simple class of category is a monoid, within which it is possible to define the concepts of a natural transformation and give a more general definition of an adjunction. That is the topic of the third chapter.

Most of what I know of category theory has been gleaned from the following books. They are recommended as references and selective further reading for those who wish to obtain a full understanding of the subject.

Bibliography

R. Goldblatt, Topoi: The Categorial Analysis of Logic; North Holland, Revised Edition, 1984.

E.G. Manes and M.A. Arbib, Algebraic Approaches to Program Semantics; Springer-Verlag, 1986.

Saunders MacLane, Categories for the Working Mathematician; Springer-Verlag, 1971.

J. Lambek and P.J. Scott, Introduction to Higher Order Categorical Logic; Cambridge University Press, 1986.

H. Herrlich and G.E. Strecker, Category Theory, Second Edition, Helderman Verlag, Berlin 1979.

D.E. Rydeheard and R.M. Burstall, Computational Category Theory. Prentice-Hall, 1988.

Acknowledgements

To Roland Backhouse, Michael Barr, Richard Bird, Paul Gardiner, John Gray, Jeremy Jacob, Claire Martin, Oege de Moor, Lars Olsen, Mike Spivey, George Strecker and Charles Wells. By their efforts, the reader has been spared many inaccuracies and infelicities. The author is grateful to the Admiral R. Inman Chair of Computing Science at the University of Texas in Austin, which provided the opportunity to begin a study of Category Theory.

0 SETS

0.1 Introduction

A *set* is a collection of *members*. A set may be defined by the *comprehension* notation $\{x \mid Px\}$, where P is some property enjoyed by all members of the set, but not by anything outside the set. A finite set may be defined by enumeration of its members; for example, the five vowels of the English alphabet are $\{\text{"a"}, \text{"e"}, \text{"i"}, \text{"o"}, \text{"u"}\}$. The notation "$x \in s$" states that x is a member of s. The negation of this is denoted "$x \notin s$". The list "$x \in s$ and $y \in s$, and ... and $z \in s$" is abbreviated to "$x, y, \ldots, z \in s$".

A set s is a *subset* of a set t if all members of s are also members of t. Formally, the subset relation $\subseteq$ between sets is defined

$$s \subseteq t \;\;\hat{=}\;\; (x \in s \text{ implies } x \in t, \text{ for all } x).$$

Two sets are equal if and only if they have the same members:

$$s = t \;\;\text{iff}\;\; (s \subseteq t \text{ and } t \subseteq s), \qquad \text{all sets } s \text{ and } t.$$

There is no way to prove this assertion; it must simply be accepted as an axiom of set theory. The same is true of many of the assertions made hereafter.

Examples

X0 $\{\}$ is the empty set. The notation suggests an enumeration of its members, of which there are none. An alternative definition is by comprehension $\{\} \;\hat{=}\; \{x \mid x \neq x\}$. Since $\{\}$ has no members, $x \in \{\}$ is always false; so $\{\}$ is trivially a subset of every set.

X1 $\{0\}$ is the set containing just one object, namely the number zero. More generally, if x is an object, $\{x\}$ is called the *unitset* of x, and contains x as its only member. It may also be defined by comprehension:

$$\{x\} \;\;\hat{=}\;\; \{y \mid y = x\}.$$

X2 A set is itself an object, and may therefore be a member of another set. For example, $\{\{\}\}$ is the set which contains the empty set as its only member. It is important to distinguish a unitset from its only member. For example, $\{\{\}\}$ has one member, whereas $\{\}$ has none.

X3 $\{0,1\}$ is the set containing just the natural numbers 0 and 1. Its definition by comprehension is $\{0,1\} \triangleq \{y \mid y = 0 \text{ or } y = 1\}$.

X4 N is the set containing all natural numbers $\{0,1,2,\ldots\}$.

X5 Any subset of a set is a set.

In the following examples, s and t are assumed to be sets.

X6 $(s \cup t)$ is the union of s and t, and is defined as

$$\{x \mid x \in s \text{ or } x \in t\}.$$

X7 $(s \cap t)$ is the intersection of s and t, defined as

$$\{x \mid x \in s \text{ and } x \in t\}.$$

X8 The *powerset* of s is the set of all subsets of s. Among its members is both $\{\}$ and s itself.

$$\mathsf{P}s \triangleq \{r \mid r \subseteq s\}.$$

X9 If $t \in \mathsf{P}s$, then its complement $\neg t$ is defined

$$\neg t \triangleq \{x \mid x \in s \text{ and } x \notin t\}.$$

Note that the definition of the complement is relative to some expressed or implied universe s, of which its argument is understood to be a subset.

X10 If s is a set of sets, its union $\bigcup s$ is the set containing all members of any of its members

$$\bigcup s \triangleq \{x \mid \text{there is a } y \in s \text{ such that } x \in y\}.$$

Similarly, the intersection of any *nonempty* family of sets is defined

$$\bigcap s \triangleq \{x \mid x \in y, \text{ for all } y \in s\}.$$

It is tempting to try to extend this defnition to empty families by the convention

$$\bigcap \{\} = \{x \mid x = x\},$$

i.e., the set containing absolutely everything. Unfortunately such a universal set does not exist (see X13 below).

If $x \in s$ and $y \in t$, we can form the pair (x,y). Two such pairs are equal only if both components are equal:

$$(x,y) = (x',y') \quad \text{iff} \quad x = x' \text{ and } y = y'.$$

Note that the order of a pair is significant: for example (0,1) differs from (1,0), and both of these differ from {0,1}(which equals {1,0}).

X11 Pairs are considered as objects capable of membership in sets. In particular, $(s \times t)$ is the (cartesian) *product* of s and t. It contains all pairs (x,y), where x is a member of s and y is a member of t:

$$s \times t \triangleq \{(x,y) \mid x \in s \text{ and } y \in t\}.$$

In a programming language like PASCAL, an ordered pair is a record with two fields, one of type s and the other of type t; and a cartesian product can be declared as a record type

record *fst* : s;   *snd* : t **end**,

where *fst* and *snd* are field names used to select the two components of the record. In LISP, a pair is constructed by the *cons* function.

X12 $(s+t)$ is the *coproduct* of s and t. It is often called the direct or disjoint sum or discriminated union. In PASCAL, its members are called variant records. The coproduct may be defined as a set of pairs. Each pair consists of a tag, which is either 0 or 1; and its second component is a value from either s or t. If the tag is 0 the value is a member of s, and if the tag is 1, the value is a member of t.

$$(s+t) \triangleq \{(w,x) \mid (w = 0 \text{ and } x \in s) \text{ or } (w = 1 \text{ and } x \in t)\}.$$

X13 (counterexample). There is no set of all sets. If there were, it would contain as a subset the *Russell* set, defined as the set of all sets which are not members of themselves:

$$\textit{Russell} \triangleq \{x \mid x \notin x\}.$$

The question can then be asked "Is *Russell* a member of itself?" If the answer is "yes", then it must satisfy the defining property of the Russell set, namely that it is *not* a member of itself. If the answer is "no" then it must fail to satisfy the defining property; consequently it *is* a member of itself. In both cases, the assumption that the collection of all sets is itself a set leads to a contradiction, and must be rejected.

This collection is therefore called a *class*. Classes are not objects, and they are not capable of being members of sets, although they may be members of other classes. Thus the same set notations will be used for describing classes. A collection of sets that may be a set or a class will be called a *family*.

0.2 Functors on sets

A *functor* is an object with three components written $(f : s \to t)$, where

> s is a set called the *source* of the functor,
>
> t is a set called the *target* of the functor,
>
> f is a total function, which maps each member x of s to a member of t. This member is denoted (fx), using simple juxtaposition to denote application of a function f to an argument x. Such juxtaposition will bind more tightly than all other infix operators introduced later.

The condition that $(f : s \to t)$ is a functor may be formalised:

$$x \in s \text{ implies } fx \in t, \qquad \text{for all } x.$$

The functions f and f' are the same if they give the same result for all arguments:

$$f = f' \quad \text{iff} \quad (fx = f'x, \text{ for all } x).$$

The functors $(f : s \to t)$ and $(f' : s' \to t')$ are the same if and only if $f = f'$ and $s = s'$ and $t = t'$. Thus the types of the argument and result are an essential part of a functor. If s is a subset of t, and fx is in s, then fx is also in t. However the functors $(f : r \to s)$ and $(f : r \to t)$ are quite different (unless, of course, $s = t$). In this respect, functors are like functions in a strictly typed programming language.

In order to reduce the weight of notation, we shall often write "Let $f : s \to t$" in place of "Let $(f : s \to t)$ be a functor". Furthermore, in the scope of such a declaration, the functor $(f : s \to t)$ will be abbreviated to just f.

We shall use lambda-notation to denote the function part of a functor. If x is any variable ranging over members of s, and $\ldots x \ldots$ is any expression taking a value in t whenever x takes a value in s, then $(\lambda x \ldots x \ldots)$ is the function that maps each y in s to $\ldots y \ldots$; and consequently $((\lambda x \ldots x \ldots) : s \to t)$ is a functor.

A *bifunctor* is defined as a functor whose source is a cartesian product; it therefore has two arguments. The function part f of a bifunctor with source $r \times s$ is written with a pair of arguments (x, y), where x ranges over members of r and y over members of s. Let "$\ldots x \ldots y \ldots$" be an expression which (under these constraints on x and y) takes values in the set t. Then $((\lambda(x, y) \ldots x \ldots y \ldots) : r \times s \to t)$ defines a bifunctor.

Examples

In the following examples r, s, t, u stand for sets.

X0 I_s is the *identity* functor on s. It is defined

$$I_s \triangleq ((\lambda x.x) : s \to s).$$

This is an example of an *endofunctor*, one whose source and target are the same.

X1 Another example of an endofunctor is the successor function on natural numbers

$$\sigma \triangleq ((\lambda n.n + 1) : \mathsf{N} \to \mathsf{N}).$$

X2 For each set s there exists exactly one total function from s to $\{0\}$, namely the constant function $(\lambda x.0)$. The corresponding family of functors (one for each set s) is defined

$$!_s \triangleq ((\lambda x.0) : s \to \{0\}).$$

X3 For each $y \in t$, we can define the constant functor

$$K_t(y) \triangleq ((\lambda x.y) : \{0\} \to t).$$

Every functor from $\{0\}$ to a set t is a constant functor of this kind, and there exists exactly one such functor for each member of t.

X4 A function from $\{\}$ to any set t can never be applied (because $\{\}$ has no members). For each set t there is exactly one such functor with source $\{\}$ and target t. This is denoted

$$i_t \;\triangleq\; ((\lambda x.x):\{\}\to t).$$

X5 (counterexample) If s is any nonempty set, there is *no* total function from s to the empty set. This is a fundamental difference between the empty set and all other sets. It breaks the symmetry suggested by X2 and X4 between $\{\}$ and $\{0\}$.

X6 0th is defined as the bifunctor which maps each pair of type $s \times t$ onto its first component. In LISP this is called *car*.

$$0^{th} \;\triangleq\; ((\lambda(x,y).x):s\times t\to s).$$

X7 Its partner (the *cdr* of LISP) is defined

$$1^{st} \;\triangleq\; ((\lambda(x,y).y):s\times t\to t).$$

The previous two functors should really be subscripted by s and t; but this is too cumbersome for frequent use.

X8 The functor Δ_s makes two copies of its argument, gathering them as a pair:

$$\Delta_s \;\triangleq\; (\lambda x.(x,x):s\to(s\times s)).$$

A similar action is performed by the *fork* of UNIX, which splits the current state of the machine into two, and permits each copy to be updated concurrently.

X9 There is a functor $(\lambda x.(0,x):s\to(s+t))$, which maps each member of s to the corresponding member of the coproduct set $s+t$ (0.1, X12).

X10 Its partner is defined as $(\lambda y.(1,y):t\to(s+t))$.

X11 The analogue of Δ_s for coproducts is Δ'_s, which removes the tag from an argument of type $(s+s)$

$$\Delta'_s \;\triangleq\; (\lambda(w,x).x:(s+s)\to s).$$

Let $f : s \to t$ and $g : t \to u$. Then the *composition* of f and g is also a functor; it may be written $f;g$ or $g \circ f$, and is defined

$$f;g \triangleq ((\lambda x.g(fx)) : s \to u).$$

Note that composition is undefined unless the target of one functor is the same as the source of the other. Important properties of functorial composition are

$$I_s; f = f = f; I_t, \qquad \text{for all } f : s \to t.$$
$$f;(g;h) = (f;g);h \qquad \text{(associativity)}.$$

Taking advantage of associativity, chains of compositions are usually written without brackets, $f;g;h$.

X12 The functor $!_s; K_t(y)$ maps every member of s to the constant y, being a member of t. Every constant functor may be *factored through* $\{0\}$ in this way.

Let $f : s \to t$ and $g : u \to v$. Then we can define functors operating on the products and coproducts of their sources and targets. This illustrates the principle that for each data structuring method there is a corresponding method of structuring programs which operate on that data.

X13 $f \times g$ is a bifunctor expecting a pair of arguments. It applies f to one component and g to the other, and delivers the two results as a pair. It may be implemented in a programming language by concurrent execution of f and g on disjoint areas of the machine state.

$$f \times g \triangleq (\lambda(x,y).(fx, gy) : (s \times u) \to (t \times v)).$$

X14 The functor $f + g$ expects an argument of type $(s + u)$. It first tests the tag; if this is 0, the function f is evaluated; or if it is 1, the function g is evaluated. In either case, the same tag is put back onto the answer. The selection of exactly one of the two alternatives is similar to that provided by a conditional or case statement in a programming language.

$$f + g \triangleq (\lambda(w,x). \text{ if } w = 0 \text{ then } (0, fx) \text{ else } (1, gx) : (s + u) \to (t + v)).$$

X15 Let $y \in s$ and $f : s \to s$. Then we define by induction a functor $(g : \mathbf{N} \to s)$, which when applied to any natural number n delivers the result of applying f n times to y.

$$K_\mathbf{N}(0); g = K_s(y) \qquad \text{(i.e., } g0 = y\text{)}$$
$$\sigma; g = g; f \qquad \text{(i.e., } g(n+1) = f(gn)\text{)}.$$

It is a fundamental property of natural numbers that there is exactly one function g that satisfies this pair of equations. Functions defined in this way are said to be *primitive recursive*; they are total functions, and when calculated, they always terminate. Using higher order functors (described in the next section), all total functions of practical significance can be defined by primitive recursion.

0.3 Higher order functors

Functors are themselves objects which may be collected into a set. For any pair of sets s and t, we define their *homset* as the set of functors with source s and target t:

$$[s \to t] \;\triangleq\; \{x \mid \exists g.\; x = (g : s \to t)\}.$$

Since this is a set, we may define *higher order* functors, which take such homsets as their source or target (or both). Such functors expect functors as arguments or deliver functors as results (or both).

X1 For each s and t, we define the *evaluation* bifunctor ε_{st}; it expects its first argument to be a functor, and delivers the result of applying this to the second argument. It plays much the same role as *eval* in LISP, but does not require the first argument to be coded as a list.

$$\varepsilon_{st} \;\triangleq\; ((\lambda(f,x).fx) : ([s \to t] \times s) \to t).$$

X2 For each pair of sets s and t, the functor η_{st} expects an argument from the set s, and delivers as its result a functor. This functor in turn expects an argument of type t and delivers as its result a pair consisting of the values of both the arguments previously supplied:

$$\eta_{st} \;\triangleq\; (\lambda x.(\lambda y.(x,y)) : s \to [t \to (s \times t)]).$$

X3 Let $f : s \to t$ and $g : u \to v$. Then we can define a functor which expects as argument a functor $h : t \to u$, and envelopes it by f and g. It is called a *hom-functor*:

$$(f \Rightarrow g) \;\triangleq\; ((\lambda h.f; h; g) : [t \to u] \to [s \to v]).$$

A similar facility is offered by a class with **inner** in SIMULA 67. The class is called by prefixing its name to a user block. The class provides the appropriate initialisation (f) and finalisation (g) for some new data object, and the user block is executed in between. This facility is used in the implementation of abstract data types, where correct initialisation (f) is required to establish an invariant, and finalisation (g) may be used to return resources to an operating system, from which they have been initially acquired.

X4 Let $f : (s \times t) \to u$. Then $\theta_{stu} f$ (known as "curried f") is a functor which expects an argument from s and delivers as result a functor; this expects an argument from t, and delivers the result of applying f to the pair of arguments previously supplied.

$$\theta_{stu} f \;\triangleq\; (\lambda x.(\lambda y.f(x,y))) : s \to [t \to u]).$$

For example, the η functor is a curried *cons*:

$$\eta_{st} = \theta_{st(s \times t)}(I_{s \times t}).$$

X5 The operation θ_{stu} has an inverse $\check{\theta}_{stu}$, known as "uncurry". Let $g : s \to [t \to u]$. Then $\check{\theta}_{stu} g$ expects a pair of arguments from $s \times t$, and calculates its result by feeding them one at a time to f:

$$\check{\theta}_{stu} g \;\triangleq\; (\lambda(x,y).((gx)y) : (s \times t) \to u).$$

Functors may be used to assist in the definition of sets.

X6 The *image* of a functor ($f : s \to t$) is that subset of the members of t which can be obtained by applying f to some member of s:

$$im\; f \;\triangleq\; \{y \mid \text{there is an } x \in s \text{ such that } fx = y\}.$$

If $im\; f$ contains the whole of the target set t, then f is said to be a *surjective* functor, or a *surjection*.

X7 Conversely, for any subset s of t, there is a functor which maps each member of s to itself in t. It is called the *inclusion* functor:

$$\subseteq_{st} \;\triangleq\; ((\lambda x.x) : s \to t).$$

Clearly $\subseteq_{ss}$ is the same as I_s; but $\subseteq_{st}$ differs from $\subseteq_{su}$ whenever t differs from u. Furthermore, the inclusion functor is an *injection*, in the sense that it maps different members of its source to different members of its target. All category-theoretic properties of subsets may be expressed more generally as properties of injective functors.

X8 Let $y \in t$. Then the inverse image of y through f is the set $f^{-1}y$ of members of s which f maps to y:

$$f^{-1}y \triangleq \{x \mid fx = y\}.$$

X9 The set of all inverse images through $(f : s \to t)$ is defined

$$\text{quot } f \triangleq \{f^{-1}y \mid y \in \text{im } f\}.$$

This is a *quotient* (or partition) of s, in the sense that

(1) It is a subset of the powerset $\mathbf{P}s$

(2) It does not have $\{\}$ as a member

(3) Every member of s is a member of exactly one set in the partition.

X10 Conversely, let t be any quotient of the set s. Then there exists a functor $(f : s \to t)$ which maps each member of s to the (unique by (X9, 3)) member of the quotient to which it belongs. It is the only functor with the property that

$$fx = y \quad \text{iff } x \in y, \qquad \text{for all } x \in s \text{ and } y \in t.$$

Furthermore f is a surjection, and $\text{quot } f = t$. Thus every quotient defines a surjection, and vice-versa. All category-theoretic properties of quotients can be expressed more generally as properties of surjective functors.

An *equivalence* relation over s is defined as a reflexive transitive and symmetric relation on members of s, i.e., it satisfies

$x \simeq x$ \hfill (reflexivity)

if $x \simeq y$ and $y \simeq z$ then $x \simeq z$ \hfill (transitivity)

if $x \simeq y$ then $y \simeq x$ \hfill (symmetry).

Any quotient q of s defines an equivalence relation over the members of s, by which each set in q contains all members of s which are equivalent to each other:

$$x \simeq y \text{ in } q \triangleq \exists z \in q.\, x \in z \text{ and } y \in z, \qquad \text{for all } x, y \in s. \qquad (*)$$

Conversely any equivalence relation $\simeq$ over s can be used to define a quotient of s, denoted by $(s/\simeq)$. For each x in s, the equivalence class surrounding x is defined

$$[x]_\simeq \triangleq \{y \mid y \simeq x\},$$

where the subscript $\simeq$ is usually omitted. The corresponding quotient is the set of sets

$$s/\simeq \triangleq \{[x]_\simeq \mid x \in s\}.$$

Furthermore, the equivalence relation (*) defined by this quotient is exactly the one we started with. This shows that a study of equivalence relations is mathematically the same as the study of quotients; and both are included in the study of surjective functors.

An endofunctor of s simultaneously defines a quotient of s (its inverse images) and a subset of s (its image). An interesting special case is an endofunctor $(f : s \to s)$, whose image contains a representative member (necessarily unique) from each set of the quotient, or more formally:

$$fx \in f^{-1}(fx), \qquad \text{for all } x \in s.$$

From this it follows that

$$f(fx) = fx, \qquad \text{i.e., } f;f = f.$$

A functor with this property is called an *idempotent*.

The definitions of products and coproducts may be extended with the aid of functors to an arbitrary number of components.

X11 Let $f : r \to F$, where F is some family of sets (for example, the class of all sets). The *coproduct* (or colimit or dependent sum) of f is defined as the discriminated union of all the sets in the image of f, where the tags are drawn from the set r:

$$\sum f \triangleq \{(x,y) \mid x \in r \text{ and } y \in fx\}.$$

If $r = \{0,1\}$ and $f0 = s$ and $f1 = t$, then the definition of $\sum f$ reduces exactly to our previous definition (0.1 X12) of $(s+t)$.

If F contains Σf for *all* f in $[r \to F]$ then F is said to be *r-cocomplete*. A family which is r-cocomplete for all sets r is called simply cocomplete (without qualification). If r is restricted to finite or countable sets, then the family is called finitely or countably cocomplete.

X12 Let $f : r \to F$. Then the *product* (or limit or dependent product) of f is defined as the set of functors:

$$\Pi f \; \triangleq \; \{g \mid \forall x \in r. \; gx \in fx\}.$$

For example, if $r = \{0,1\}$ and $f0 = s$ and $f1 = t$ then

$$\Pi f = \{g \mid g0 \in s \text{ and } g1 \in t\}. \qquad \ldots(1)$$

Each g in this set defines a pair $(g0, g1)$, where $g0 \in s$ and $g1 \in t$. Furthermore, each pair (x, y) in $s \times t$ defines a functor g

$$g \; \triangleq \; (\lambda z. \text{ if } z = 0 \text{ then } x \text{ else } y) : \{0,1\} \to s \times t.$$

Thus it is possible to regard (or even define) an ordered pair as a functor whose source is $\{0,1\}$; and in this view Πf defined in (1) is the same as (0.1 X11) the binary product $s \times t$.

The definition of *r-complete* (or *complete*) families of sets is similar to that for cocomplete families, using products instead of coproducts.

X13 Let $s \in \mathbf{P}t$, and define the *characteristic function* of s as

$$\chi s \; \triangleq \; ((\lambda x. \text{ if } x \in s \text{ then } 1 \text{ else } 0) : t \to \{0,1\}).$$

So χ itself is a functor from $\mathbf{P}t \to [t \to \{0,1\}]$.

X14 Let $f : t \to \{0,1\}$, and define the *comprehension* of f as

$$\psi f \; \triangleq \; \{x \mid fx = 1\}.$$

So ψ itself is a functor from $[t \to \{0,1\}]$ to $\mathbf{P}t$. Clearly $\psi(\chi s) = s$ and $\chi(\psi f) = f$.

0.4 Isomorphisms

Let $f : s \to t$ and $g : t \to s$. If $f;g = I_s$ then f is said to be a *left inverse* of g and g is a *right inverse* of f. If in addition f has a left inverse g' then $g = g'$. In this case, g is said to be simply the *inverse* of f, written $\check{f}$. A functor f can never have more than one inverse.

Other properties of inverses are

$$\check{I}_s = I_s, \qquad (\check{\check{f}}) = f,$$

$\overset{\smile}{f;g} = \check{g}; \check{f}$ (note the reversal).

A functor which has an inverse is called an *isomorphism*. If there exists an isomorphism $(f : s \to t)$ then the source s and target t are said to be *isomorphic*, abbreviated $s \simeq t$. This is an equivalence relation. An important property of isomorphism is that it is respected (preserved) by the most interesting set-theoretic constructions:

If $s \simeq t$ then

$s \times u \simeq t \times u$ and $u \times s \simeq u \times t$

and $s + u \simeq t + u$ and $[s \to u] \simeq [t \to u]$, etc.

Examples

X0 I_s is its own inverse.

X1 So is the swapping functor $(\lambda(x,y).(y,x) : r \times s \to s \times r)$.

X2 $\lambda(x,y).((x,0^{th}y), 1^{st}y) : r \times (s \times t) \to (r \times s) \times t$ has inverse
$\lambda(y,z).(0^{th}y,(1^{st}y,z)) : (r \times s) \times t \to r \times (s \times t)$.

X3 $((\lambda x.0) : [\{\} \to s] \to \{0\})$ has inverse $((\lambda y.i_s) : \{0\} \to [\{\} \to s])$.
Indeed the source and target contain exactly one member each.

X4 $((\lambda f.f0) : [\{0\} \to s] \to s)$ has inverse $(\lambda x.(\lambda y.x) : s \to [\{0\} \to s])$.
This is a formal statement of the relation between members of a set and the constant functors into that set.

X5 $(\lambda f.(f0, f1) : [\{0,1\} \to s] \to (s \times s))$ has inverse
$(\lambda(x,y).\lambda z.\text{if } z = 0 \text{ then } x \text{ else } y : (s \times s) \to [\{0,1\} \to s])$.

X6 $(\theta_{rst} : [(r \times s) \to t] \to [r \to [s \to t]])$ has inverse (0.3, X4, X5)
$(\check{\theta}_{rst} : [r \to [s \to t]] \to [(r \times s) \to t])$.

X7 $(\lambda f.(\lambda x.0^{th}(fx), \lambda x.1^{st}(fx))) : [r \to (s \times t)] \to ([r \to s] \times [r \to t])$ has inverse $(\lambda(g,h).\lambda x.(gx, hx)) : ([r \to s] \times [r \to t]) \to [r \to (s \times t)]$.

X8 $[s \to \{0,1\}]$ is isomorphic to the powerset of s (by 0.3 X13 and X14).

X9 (counterexample). There is no isomorphism between s and its powerset.

In set theory, two sets are isomorphic if and only if they have the same number of members, i.e., the same cardinality. Indeed, the cardinal numbers are often defined as the equivalence classes associated with isomorphism, or even with a representative member of each class, e.g.,

$0 = \{\}$
$1 = \{0\}$
$2 = \{0,1\}$
$s \times t$ (the product) $= s \times t$
t^s (the exponent) $= [s \to t]$.

Under this interpretation, the isomorphisms listed above establish the following familiar laws of cardinal arithmetic, which are valid also for infinite cardinals:

$$x \times y = y \times x, \quad x \times (y \times z) = (x \times y) \times z,$$
$$x^0 = 1, \quad x^1 = x, \quad x^2 = x \times x,$$
$$z^{(x \times y)} = (z^x)^y, \quad (x \times y)^z = x^z \times y^z.$$

There are a number of equivalent ways of determining whether a function is an isomorphism.

(0) A functor between sets is an isomorphism if and only if it is a *bijection*, i.e., it is both an injection and a surjection.

(1) If $(f : s \to t)$ has an inverse, then for each y in t the equation

$$fx = y$$

has a unique solution in s for x (namely $\check{f}y$). Conversely, the existence of all such unique solutions guarantees the existence of an inverse.

(2) If $(g : t \to s)$ has an inverse, then for each x in s the equation

$$x = gy$$

has a unique solution in t for y (namely $\breve{g}x$). Conversely, the existence of all such unique solutions ensures the existence of an inverse.

(3) Let f and g be mutual inverses. Then

$$fx = y \quad \text{iff} \quad x = gy, \qquad \text{for all } x \in s \text{ and } y \in t \qquad (*)$$

Proof: Assume $x = gy$.

$$
\begin{aligned}
& & fx & = f(gy) \\
& \{\text{def;}\} & & = (g; f)y \\
& \{g; f = I_t\} & & = y.
\end{aligned}
$$

The other half of the proof is similar. □

Conversely, $(*)$ implies that f and g are mutual inverses.

Proof: Substitute fx for y in $(*)$.

$$
\begin{aligned}
x & = g(fx), && \text{all } x \in s \\
  & = (f; g)x.
\end{aligned}
$$

Therefore $f; g = I_s$. The other half of the proof is similar. □

The existence of five equivalent definitions for an isomorphism is an indication of the importance of the concept. They also serve as a pattern for the even more important definition of an adjunction in category theory. For this reason, laws of this general form $(*)$ above will in future be called *adjunctive*.

0.5 Sets and categories

Let F be a family of functors with the following closure properties:

(1) If $(f : s \to t) \in F$ then $I_s, I_t \in F$.
(2) If $(f : s \to t), (g : t \to u) \in F$ then $((f; g) : s \to u) \in F$.

Then F is called a *concrete category*. The members of F are called the *arrows* of the category, denoted $|F|$; and the *objects* of the category are defined as the family of sets

$$\|F\| = \{s \mid I_s \in |F|\}.$$

The *source* function (written as an overbar leftward arrow $\overleftarrow{}$) maps each functor to the object which is its source, and the *target* function ($\overrightarrow{}$) maps it to its target:

$$\overleftarrow{(f : s \to t)} = s, \qquad \overrightarrow{(f : s \to t)} = t.$$

In algebraic formulae, it is convenient to ignore the distinction between objects and identity functions, so that the identity law takes the form

$$p;\overrightarrow{p} \;=\; p \;=\; \overleftarrow{p};p.$$

The following families of functors provide examples of concrete categories. In each case, the two closure properties are easy to check.

X0 The family of all functors, which has all sets as its objects. Following categorical tradition of naming a category from its objects, it is called *SET*. All concrete categories are subfamilies of *SET*.

X1 The family of all injective functors and the family of all surjective functors, which have the same objects as *SET*.

X2 The set of all finite functions, which has all finite sets as its objects.

X3 The set of all computable functions on computable sets.

X4 The family of all functors whose source and target have at least n members.

An *abstract* category has many of the mathematical properties of a concrete category, but its objects are not necessarily sets and its arrows are not necessarily functors. Each arrow is like a functor, in that it has a source and target which are objects, and two compatible arrows can be composed; but unlike a functor an arrow cannot be applied to an argument.

More formally a category C is defined as a mathematical structure $(\|C\|, |C|, I, ;, \leftarrow, \rightarrow)$ where

$\|C\|$ is the family of *objects* of C,
$|C|$ is the family of *arrows* of C,
I *(identity)* is an injection from $\|C\|$ to $|C|$,
$;$ *composition* is a partial binary operator on $|C|$,
$\leftarrow$ *(source)* and $\rightarrow$ *(target)* are total functions from $|C|$ to $\|C\|$.

Furthermore, these components must satisfy the following properties

$$\overrightarrow{I_s} = s = \overleftarrow{I_s},$$

$f;g$ is defined just when $\overrightarrow{f} = \overleftarrow{g}$,

$$\overleftarrow{f;g} = \overleftarrow{f}, \qquad \overrightarrow{f;g} = \overrightarrow{f},$$

$$f; I_{\overrightarrow{f}} = f = I_{\overleftarrow{f}}; f,$$

$$(f;g); h = f;(g;h).$$

There is also a technical requirement that for all objects s and t, $\{f \mid \overleftarrow{f} = s$ and $\overrightarrow{f} = t\}$ should be a set. If $\|C\|$ is also a set, C is called a *small* category. It is easy to check that every concrete category satisfies this definition of an abstract category.

The arrows of an abstract category are often presented (in the same way as functors) as triples $(n : b \rightarrow c)$. Here b and c are drawn from the set of objects of the category, and n is related to b and c by some stated condition. In order to prove that these triples constitute a category, it is necessary to single out an identity arrow $(i : b \rightarrow b)$ for each object b, and a binary operator f such that if $(m : b \rightarrow c)$ and $(n : c \rightarrow d)$ both satisfy the condition defining the family of arrows then $(f(m,n) : b \rightarrow d)$ also satisfies it. Furthermore, it is necessary to prove that f is associative, and has unit i:

$$f(m, i) = f(i, m) = m.$$

Any set S (including $\{\}$) can simply be turned into (be regarded as) an abstract category $(S, S, I_S, ;, I_S, I_S)$. Its objects and arrows are just the members of the set S itself. The identity of the category maps each member of S to itself. So do the source function and the target function. Thus the *only* arrows are the identity arrows, which have themselves as source and target. Consequently, the only form of composition which is defined is the composition of an identity arrow with itself; and the (trivial) result of this composition is the same as its two arguments:

$I_x; I_x = I_x.$

Conversely, if in any category there are no arrows between differing objects, and only one arrow between each object and itself, then that category is structurally identical to its set of objects. Such a category is called *discrete*.

The generality and abstraction of category theory is clearly explained by its close association with set theory and the foundations of mathematics. The axioms defining an abstract category have been derived from the known properties (axioms or theorems) of the concrete category *SET*. In much the same way, the axioms defining groups, rings, and fields were derived from the known properties of integers, fractions, and real numbers, and for much the same reasons. One of the driving forces in the study of any particular abstract category is to see how many additional properties of *SET* can be modelled within it.

For example, an object $\perp$ of an abstract category is said to be *initial* if for every object s in the category there is exactly one arrow from $\perp$ to s. In *SET*, the only initial object is $\{\}$, and the unique arrow is called i_s (0.2 X4). Similarly, an object $\top$ is called *terminal* if from every object s in the category there is exactly one arrow from s to $\top$. In *SET*, the terminal objects are just the unitsets (0.1 X1). Since all unitsets are isomorphic, the concept of terminality is defined " up to isomorphism". A discrete category has no internal structure of any kind. If it has a terminal object, then this is the only object it has.

Suppose an abstract category has a terminal object. Then we can turn the category into a concrete category by associating each object s with the set of all arrows *from* the terminal object *to* that object (see 0.4 X3); these are called the *elements* of the object, and can play the same role in an abstract category as members of a set do in a concrete category. For example, applying a functor to a member of a set is much the same as composing an abstract arrow with an element of an object, as was done in (0.2 X15). Similarly, set-theoretic concepts such as products, coproducts, and homsets have useful and more general analogues in abstract category theory, defined solely in terms of arrows. A category with objects corresponding to homsets is called *cartesian closed*. Such categories are important for applications to computer science.

We have seen that set theory provides two extreme examples of a category; a set itself, which has effectively no internal structure; and *SET*, the class of all sets and functors, which has an extremely rich structure including initial and terminal objects, arbitrary products, coproducts, powersets and homsets. In the following chapters we will be introducing mathematical spaces with more interesting internal structure than plain sets. In each case, a functor is defined as a map which preserves this internal structure. In each case, the family of all such functors forms a category. In each case, much of the structure of the functor category can be represented within its individual objects. Investigation of the relations between internal and external structure is one of the main achievements of category theory.

1 Preorders

1.1 Introduction

A preorder is a particularly simple and familiar kind of abstract category, which illustrates many of the most important categorical concepts. A preorder is defined just as a reflexive transitive relation. The *objects* of a preorder R are defined as members of the set

$$\|R\| \triangleq \{b \mid (b,b) \in R\}.$$

If $b,\ c \in \|R\|$, we write "$b \leq c$ in R" to state that b is related by R to c. We omit "in R" when the choice of preorders is arbitrary or obvious. Similarly, free variables $b, c, d, \ldots$ are assumed to be quantified over all objects in $\|R\|$. Thus we write the defining axioms of a preorder as

$b \leq b$ reflexivity

if $b \leq c$ and $c \leq d$ then $b \leq d$ transitivity.

An *equivalence* relation (written $\equiv$) is defined as a preorder which is also *symmetric*, i.e.,

$b \equiv c$ iff $c \equiv b$ symmetry.

For example, the standard equivalence in a preorder is defined

$$b \equiv c \text{ in } R \triangleq (b \leq c \text{ in } R \text{ and } c \leq b \text{ in } R).$$

Four simple and useful lemmas are

$b \leq c$ iff $(x \leq b$ implies $x \leq c$, all $x \in \|R\|)$
$b \equiv c$ iff $(x \leq b$ iff $x \leq c$, all $x \in \|R\|)$;

and the same with the inequalities reversed.

A *partial order* is defined as a preorder which is also *antisymmetric*, i.e.,

if $b \leq c$ and $c \leq b$ then $b = c$ antisymmetry.

For example, the quotient $R/\equiv$ of any preorder with respect to its standard equivalence is a partial order. A *total order* is defined as a partial order R which relates every pair of objects one way or the other:

$b \leq c$ or $c \leq b$ totality.

Examples

X1 $(= S)$ is the equality relation on the set S, the smallest preorder with objects drawn from S:

$$c \leq b \text{ in } (= S) \quad \text{iff} \quad c \in S \text{ and } c = b.$$

The case when S is empty gives the smallest preorder of all.

X2 $(S \times S)$ is the universal relation on S, the largest preorder on S:

$$b \leq c \text{ in } (S \times S) \quad \text{iff} \quad b, c \in S.$$

X3 $(\subseteq S)$ is the inclusion relation on all subsets of S:

$$b \leq c \text{ in } (\subseteq S) \quad \text{iff} \quad (x \in b \text{ implies } x \in c, \text{ for all } x \text{ in } S).$$

X4 $(\subseteq S \times S)$ is the inclusion relation on relations between members of S.

X5 $(\subseteq \leq S)$ is the inclusion relation on all preorders R such that $\|R\| \subseteq S$.

X6 $(= n)$ is the equality relation on $\{0, 1, 2, \ldots, n-1\}$.

X7 $(= 1)$ is the trivial preorder $\{0\}$, in which all inequations are true, and all have unique solutions.

X8 $(\leq n)$ is the magnitude ordering on $\{0, 1, 2, \ldots, n-1\}$.

X9 ω is the magnitude ordering on all natural numbers $\{0, 1, 2, \ldots\}$.

X10 V is a V-shaped preorder, where $\|V\| = \{\bot, 0, 1\}$, and

$$b \leq c \text{ in } V \quad \text{iff} \quad (b = c \text{ or } b = \bot).$$

X11 $b \leq c$ in $SUBST$ means c is a formula obtainable from b by systematic substitution of arbitrary formulae for variables free in b.

X12 $\|DIJ\|$ are programs in Dijkstra's language, and $b \leq c$ means (for all postconditions R, $wp(c, R)$ implies $wp(b, R)$); i.e., for any purpose R program b is as good as or better than c.

X13 DED is the relation of deducibility (often written $\vdash$) between propositional formulae. $b \leq c$ in DED means c is a formula derivable from b in a given logical system, say predicate calculus.

X14 *APPROX* is a preorder whose objects are measurements represented by open non-empty intervals of reals. $b \leq c$ means b is included in (more accurate than) c.

If R and S are preorders, so are the following:

X15 Any subset T of $\|R\|$ defines a preorder (also called T), which inherits the ordering of R, i.e.,

$$b \leq c \text{ in } T \quad \text{iff} \quad (b, c \in \|T\| \text{ and } b \leq c \text{ in } R).$$

For example, if $c \in \|R\|$ then $(\downarrow c) \triangleq \{x \mid x \leq c \text{ in } R\}$ is called "below c". $(\uparrow c)$ is called "above c", and is defined similarly.

X16 $\check{R}$ is the opposite (or converse) of R. $\|\check{R}\| = \|R\|$ and

$$b \leq c \text{ in } \check{R} \quad \text{iff} \quad c \leq b \text{ in } R.$$

X17 $R \cap S$ is the intersection, where

$$b \leq c \text{ in } R \cap S \quad \text{iff} \quad (b \leq c \text{ in } R \text{ and } b \leq c \text{ in } S).$$

(Example: $R \cap \check{R}$ is the standard equivalence relation on R.)

X18 $(R \times S)$ is the cartesian product, where

$$\|R \times S\| = \|R\| \times \|S\| \quad \triangleq \quad \{(b, b') \mid b \in \|R\| \text{ and } b' \in \|S\|\}$$
$$(b, b') \leq (c, c') \text{ in } (R \times S) \quad \text{iff} \quad (b \leq c \text{ in } R \text{ and } b' \leq c' \text{ in } S).$$

X19 $R + S$ is the disjoint sum of R and S. It may be constructed in the same way as the disjoint sum of two sets:

$$\|R + S\| = \{(0, b) \mid b \in \|R\|\} \cup \{(1, b') \mid b' \in \|S\|\}$$
$$(n, c) \leq (m, d) \text{ in } (R + S) \quad \text{iff} \quad ((n = m = 0 \text{ and } c \leq d \text{ in } R)$$
$$\text{or } (n = m = 1 \text{ and } c \leq d \text{ in } S)).$$

X20 If H is any homogeneous relation (subset of $S \times S$), then H^*(the reflexive transitive closure of H) is a preorder. It may be defined from the top down or from the bottom up:

$$H^* \triangleq \bigcap \{R \mid R \text{ is a preorder and } H \subseteq R\};$$
$$\text{or} \quad H^* \triangleq \bigcup_{i \geq 0} R_i$$
$$\text{where } R_0 \triangleq H$$
$$\text{and } R_{i+1} \triangleq R_i; H = \{(x, z) \mid \exists y.(x, y) \in R_i \text{ and } (y, z) \in H\}$$

H^* can also be defined as the least solution for x of the equation

$$x = I \cup (x; H), \text{ where } I \text{ is the identity relation.}$$

X21 Let q be a quotient of $\|R\|$, and consider the relation (also called q)

$$b \leq c \text{ in } q \;\; \triangleq \;\; \exists x \in b, y \in c \,.\, x \leq y \text{ in } R.$$

This is always reflexive. If it is also transitive then it is called a quotient preorder of R. It is a simplified or more abstract version of R; some of the detailed structure has been blurred by inability to distinguish equivalent objects, but the overall general structure has been preserved.

X22 The powerset of S may be given an orders structure in three ways, all more interesting than just the inclusion ($\subseteq \mathbf{P}S$).

$$b \leq c \text{ in } \mathbf{P}S \text{ means}$$

either (1) $\forall x . x \in b$ implies $(\exists y . y \in c$ and $x \leq y)$ (Smyth powerset)

or (2) $\forall y . y \in c$ implies $(\exists x . x \in b$ and $x \leq y)$ (Hoare powerset)

or (3) both of the above (Plotkin powerset)

1.2 Constructions in a preorder

A bottom (or initial object) $\bot$ in a preorder R is defined (up to equivalence) by the axiom

$$\bot \leq b \text{ in } R, \qquad \text{for all } b \text{ in } \|R\|.$$

Proof. Let $\bot'$ be another bottom. Then $\bot \leq \bot'$ and $\bot' \leq \bot$. □

For example, $\{\,\}$ is an initial object in ($\subseteq S$), 0 in ($\leq n$), any single variable in $SUBST$, *false* in DED, and any member of S in ($S \times S$) (1.1 X2).

A top (or terminal object) $\top$ in R is defined as an initial object in the opposite preorder $\check{R}$. For example, S is terminal in ($\subseteq S$), $n-1$ in ($\leq n$), *abort* (the worst program) in DIJ, *true* in DED, $(-\infty, +\infty)$ in $APPROX$, and any member of S in ($S \times S$).

A set of equations with more than one solution is called *under-determined*. If the unknowns range over a preorder R, and if the set of solutions (considered as a subpreorder of R) has a terminal object, this is known as the *universal* solution of the equations. Depending on the meaning of R, it is the worst, weakest, greatest, shortest, most general,... of all the solutions (or the reverse). Being an upper bound, it describes an important property of all other solutions, and can serve as a typical or canonical representative of them. Similarly, the $\bot$ of the set is called a *co-universal* solution. The top of the whole preorder is the universal solution of the empty set of equations.

For any pair of objects b and c, $(\downarrow b) \cap (\downarrow c)$ is a preorder. If it has a top, this is known as $(b \wedge c)$, the *glb* (greatest lower bound) of b and c. It is defined up to equivalence by the axiom

$$x \leq (b \wedge c) \quad \text{iff} \quad (x \leq b \text{ and } x \leq c).$$

From this axiom alone we can prove that the $\wedge$ operator is (up to equivalence) idempotent, commutative, associative and monotonic in both arguments:

(3) $b \wedge b \equiv b$,
(4) $b \wedge c \equiv c \wedge b$,
(5) $b \wedge (c \wedge d) \equiv (b \wedge c) \wedge d$,
(6) $b \leq c$ implies $((b \wedge d) \leq (c \wedge d)$ and $(d \wedge b) \leq (d \wedge c))$.

Examples of *glb* are: intersection ($\cap$) in ($\subseteq S$) and in ($\subseteq\leq S$), min in ($\leq n$) and in ω, and conjunction in *DED*.

The *lub* (least upper bound) $(b \vee c)$ in R is defined as $(b \wedge c)$ in $\breve{R}$. It has the same properties as $\wedge$. Examples are: union ($\cup$) in ($\subseteq S$), max in ($\leq n$) and in ω, unification in *SUBST*, non-deterministic union in *DIJ*, disjunction in *DED*, $(b \cup c)^*$ in ($\subseteq\leq S$), and in *APPROX* the smallest open interval covering both operands.

In a preorder with $\wedge$, the *rpc* (relative pseudocomplement) $(b \Rightarrow c)$ is defined up to equivalence by the axiom

$$x \leq (b \Rightarrow c) \quad \text{iff} \quad (x \wedge b) \leq c.$$

From this axiom one can prove

(1) $c \leq (b \Rightarrow c)$,   (2) $b \Rightarrow (b \Rightarrow c) \equiv (b \Rightarrow c)$,
(3) $b \wedge (b \Rightarrow c) \leq c$ (4) $c \leq (b \Rightarrow (b \wedge c))$,
(5) $c \leq d$ implies $((b \Rightarrow c) \leq (b \Rightarrow d)$ and $(d \Rightarrow b) \leq (c \Rightarrow b))$

Note the reversal of the order in the last clause of (5). This means that $\Rightarrow$ is antimonotonic (or *contravariant*) in its first argument.

Examples of *rpc* include: $(S - b) \cup c$ in ($\subseteq S$), implication in *DED*, and in any total order with $\top$, the formula ($\top$ **if** $b \leq c$ **else** c).

A preorder with $\top, \wedge$ and $\Rightarrow$ is called *cartesian closed*. If the preorder also has $\bot$ and $\vee$, we can define a negation operator

$$\neg p \;\hat{=}\; (p \Rightarrow \bot),$$

and so get a *Heyting algebra*; just from the axioms given above, one can prove all theorems of the intuitionistic propositional calculus. With the single additional axiom

$$\neg(\neg p) \leq p,$$

we get a *Boolean algebra*, and all theorems (tautologies) of the classical propositional calculus.

1.3 Functors on preorders

Let f be a total monotonic function from a preorder S to a preorder T, i.e.

$$\text{if } b \leq c \text{ in } S \text{ then } fb \leq fc \text{ in } T, \qquad \text{for all } b, c \text{ in} \|S\|.$$

The triple $(f : S \to T)$ is called a *functor* from S to T. S is called the source of the functor, and T is the target. A functor is like a function in a strictly typed programming language: it carries with it a type, consisting of its domain S and its codomain T. As in a programming language, when the source and target are declared in the context, the function name f alone is used to stand for the whole functor. The statement "$(f : S \to T)$ is a functor" is usually abbreviated to just the bracketless

$$f : S \to T.$$

If $f : S \to T$ and $g : T \to R$, their composition is written either as $(f; g)$ or $(g \circ f)$; it is defined as the functor

$$((\lambda x. g(fx)) : S \to R).$$

A functor whose target is equal to its source is called an *endofunctor*. A functor whose source is a cartesian product $B \times C$ takes a pair of arguments, and is sometimes called a *bifunctor*.

Examples

X1 I_S, defined as $((\lambda x.x) : S \to S)$, is an endofunctor of any preorder S. If $f : R \to S$ and $g : S \to T$ then $f; I_S = f$ and $I_S; g = g$.

X2 $0^{th} \triangleq ((\lambda(x, y).x) : S \times T \to S)$ and $1^{st} \triangleq ((\lambda(x, y).y) : S \times T \to T)$ are bifunctors which select their first and second arguments respectively.

X3 $\sigma \triangleq ((\lambda n.n + 1) : \omega \to \omega)$, the successor function, is an endofunctor of ω. A different functor is $((\lambda n.n + 1) : (\leq n) \to (\leq n + 1))$. But $(\lambda n.n + 1)$ cannot be an endofunctor of $(\leq n)$, because it would not be total.

X4 $((\lambda x.x) : (\subseteq \leq S) \to (\subseteq S \times S))$ is an injection which singles out from all relations those which happen to be reflexive and transitive. Such an injection is often called a *forgetful* functor.

X5 For each object d in $\|T\|$, $K_T(d) \triangleq ((\lambda x.d) : S \to T)$ is a constant functor, which simplifies the whole structure of S to a single point d.

X6 For each pair of objects d, e in $\|T\|$, we define a pairing functor

$$P(d, e) \triangleq ((\lambda x. \text{ if } x = 0 \text{ then } d \text{ else } e) : (= 2) \to T).$$

X7 For each pair of objects d and e such that $d \leq e$ in T

$$Q(d, e) \triangleq ((\lambda x. \text{ if } x = 0 \text{ then } d \text{ else } e) : (\leq 2) \to T).$$

Because its source is an ordered pair, its image must necessarily also be an ordered pair of objects in T.

X8 If $p : \omega \to T$, then the image of p in T is the ascending chain $(p0, p1, \ldots)$ of objects of $\|T\|$.

X9 $\wedge : S \times S \to S$ and $\vee : S \times S \to S$. They are bifunctors.

X10 $\Rightarrow : \breve{S} \times S \to S$. Because $\Rightarrow$ is antimonotone (contravariant) in its first argument, this argument has to be regarded as a member of the opposite preorder $\breve{S}$.

X11 A bifunctor can be specialised to a single-argument functor by fixing the other argument as an object. More formally,

if $g : R \times S \to T$, and $b \in \|R\|$ and $c \in \|S\|$
then $(\lambda x.g(x, c)) : R \to T$ and $(\lambda y.g(b, y)) : S \to T$.

X12 Another method of reducing the number of arguments is by insisting that two of them should be the same (diagonalisation). If $g : S \times S \to T$ then $\lambda x.g(x,x) : S \to T$.

X13 The closure operator on relations is a functor onto the preorder of preorders

$$(\lambda x.x^*) : (\subseteq S \times S) \to (\subseteq\!\leq S).$$

X14 $\Delta_s \triangleq (\lambda x.(x,x) : S \to S \times S)$ makes a pair consisting of two copies of its argument.

X15 If R is a subset preorder of S then $((\lambda x.x) : R \to S)$ is called the *inclusion* functor of R in S. It is an injection (one-one function).

X16 Let Q be a quotient preorder of S. (1.1. X21). Then there is a surjective functor $(h : S \to Q)$ which maps each member of $\|S\|$ to the member of $\|Q\|$ to which it belongs. This functor is uniquely defined by the equation

$$b \in hb, \qquad \text{all } b \text{ in } \|S\|.$$

The image of a functor $(f : S \to T)$ is defined

$$im\, f \triangleq \{c \mid c \in \|T\| \text{ and } (\exists b. b \in S \text{ and } c = fb)\}.$$

This subset of $\|T\|$ is a preorder, inheriting the ordering relation of T. X15 shows that every preorder which is a subset of T can be obtained as the image of the inclusion functor, which is injective. Further, the source S of any injective functor with target T has an identical order structure to its image in T. Thus injective functors are used to explore local properties of subsets of their target preorder. All ordering properties of subset preorders can be expressed as corresponding properties of injective functors.

The equivalence relation $\underset{f}{\sim}$ *induced* by $(f : S \to T)$ on its source S is defined

$$b \underset{f}{\sim} c \quad \text{iff} \quad fb = fc, \qquad \text{all } b, c \text{ in } \|S\|.$$

The quotient $S/\underset{f}{\sim}$ (1.1 X21) is always a preorder. X16 shows that *any* quotient of S is the target of a functor g with source S, and this functor is surjective. Further, the target T of any surjective functor g with source S is structurally identical to the quotient $S/\underset{g}{\sim}$. Thus surjective functors are used to explore the global structure of their source preorder. All ordering properties of quotient preorders can be expressed as corresponding properties of surjective functors.

The previous two paragraphs explain why subsets and quotients play no further explicit role in the development of our theory: their role is usurped by the injective and surjective functors.

1.4 Functor Spaces

The notation $[S \to T]$ stands for a preorder whose objects are *all* the functors from source S to target T; its ordering is inherited componentwise from the target preorder T, i.e.,

$$f \leq g \text{ in } [S \to T] \quad \text{iff} \quad (\text{for all } x \text{ in } \|S\|, fx \leq gx \text{ in } T).$$

Thus one function is above another if its result is consistently above the other's, whenever they are both applied to the same argument; otherwise they are incomparable.

Examples

X1 $[(= 1) \to T]$ contains the constant functor $K_T(d)$ for each object d in T. It also has the same ordering as T.

X2 $[(= 2) \to T]$ contains a functor (1.3 X6) $P(d, e)$ for each pair of objects (d, e) in $(T \times T)$. Its ordering happens to be the same as that of the Cartesian product, i.e.,

$$P(d, e) \leq P(d', e') \text{ in } [(= 2) \to T] \quad \text{iff} \quad d \leq d' \text{ in } T \text{ and } e \leq e' \text{ in } T.$$

X3 $[\omega \to T]$ is the set of all infinite ascending chains of objects in T (see 1.3 X8); one such chain is bounded by another if each of its members is bounded by the corresponding member of the other chain. Similarly $[\breve{\omega} \to T]$ is the set of all descending chains in T.

The preorder on $[S \to T]$ is defined in such a way that several earlier definitions of families of functors can be recast in terms of higher order functors on functor spaces. For example

X4 For any preorder T, there is a functor which produces constant-functors

$$K \triangleq ((\lambda x.\lambda y.x) : T \to [(= 1) \to T]).$$

The subscript T which should decorate K has been omitted.

X5 Its inverse is $((\lambda f.f0) : [(= 1) \to T] \to T)$.

X6 The pairing functor on T (see 1.3. X6) is

$$P : T \times T \to [(= 2) \to T]).$$

X7 Its inverse is $((\lambda f.(f0, f1)) : [(= 2) \to T] \to T \times T)$.

1.5 Limits and colimits

Let $f : D \to T$. The *limit* of f (if it exists) is denoted by $\bigwedge f$; it is the object of T defined (up to equivalence) by the axiom

$$d \leq (\bigwedge f) \text{ in } T \quad \text{iff} \quad Kd \leq f \text{ in } [S \to T].$$

Similarly, the colimit $\bigvee f$ is defined by

$$\bigvee f \leq d \text{ in } T \quad \text{iff} \quad f \leq Kd \text{ in } [S \to T].$$

If the image of f has a terminal object, then this is equal to $\bigvee f$. These limiting operators are monotonic; they are therefore functors (of higher order):

$$\bigwedge : [S \to T] \to T \quad \text{and} \quad \bigvee : [S \to T] \to T, \text{ for any preorders } S, T.$$

Note: if $P : \omega \to T$ then $\bigvee p \equiv \bigvee (p \circ \sigma)$.

Let S be a preorder, and let $X \subseteq S$ be a subpreorder of S. The colimit of X, denoted by $\bigvee X$, is the colimit of the inclusion functor of X in S, i.e.

$$\bigvee ((\lambda x.x) : X \to S)$$

provided that this colimit exists.

Examples

X1 If $f : (= 2) \to T$ then $\bigwedge f \equiv (f0 \wedge f1)$; the *glb* is a special case of a limit.

X2 If $f : (= 3) \to T$ then $\bigwedge f \equiv (f0 \wedge (f1 \wedge f2)) \equiv ((f0 \wedge f1) \wedge f2)$.

A *glb* of more than two arguments is more conveniently defined as a limit than by iteration of the two-argument *glb*, since it avoids the irrelevant issue of associativity. Furthermore, it generalises to an infinite number of arguments; and permits useful preconditions to be put on their order structure. Similar remarks apply to *lub*.

X3 If $f : (= S) \to DED$ then $\bigwedge f \equiv (\forall i \in S \cdot fi)$. This can be regarded as the defining axiom for universal quantification in *DED*.

X4 If $f : \omega \to T$ then $\bigwedge f \equiv f0$. If the source of a functor f has $\bot$, then its limit is trivially $f\bot$; or if the source has $\top$, the colimit is equally trivial.

X5 If $f : \breve{\omega} \to DIJ$ then $wp(\bigwedge f, R) = \exists i \cdot wp(fi, R)$. This equation gives a predicate transformer semantics to the limit of a descending (i.e., improving) chain of programs in *DIJ*. Thus *DIJ* is a Scott domain, in which programs can be defined recursively. The restriction to descending chains is essential.

X6 If $f : \omega \to APPROX$ (1.1 X10) then $\bigvee f = \bigcup_i^{\infty} fi$. In this case the validity of simple set union depends on the restriction to ascending chains. Equality holds in this case, because *APPROX* is a partial order.

X7 If $f : V \to APPROX$ then $\bigvee f = f0 \cup f1$. The fact that f is a functor ensures that $f\bot \subseteq f0$ and $f\bot \subseteq f1$, so the union $f0 \cup f1$ is an open interval. If the intersection of $f0$ and $f1$ were empty, their union would not be a member of *APPROX*.

These examples show that a limit of a functor is a natural generalisation of a finite product or *glb*. But not all such limits exist; and it is important to determine what kinds of functor have a limit in their target preorder. Fortunately, this is usually determined just by the order structure of the source of the functor.

A preorder T is said to be *S-complete* (or *S-cocomplete*) if every functor in $[S \to T]$ has a limit (colimit) in T. For example, *DIJ* is $\breve{\omega}$-complete (sometimes called descending chain-complete) and *APPROX* is V-complete (sometimes called finitely consistent-complete). A preorder T is said to be *complete (cocomplete)* if it has S-limits (S-colimits) for all sets S; or equivalently, if every subset preorder (1.1 X15) of T has a $glb(lub)$. In this definition, if S is restricted to finite or countable sets, the preorder is finitely or countably complete. Any preorder with $glbs$ is (by an obvious induction) finitely complete. Completeness and cocompleteness are very strong properties of a preorder, and the more restricted versions are usually of greater interest. Clarification of this topic is an important achievement of category theory.

Examples

X8 *DIJ* has limits of descending chains ($\breve{\omega}$-limits); it has arbitrary finite colimits, offering non-deterministic choice; but because non-determinism is bounded, it does not have infinite colimits.

X9 (counterexample) *APPROX* does not have $(=2)$-limits, because two non-overlapping intervals may have an empty (closed) intersection. However if there exists an open interval contained in both b and c, then there is a greatest such interval. So *APPROX* has V-limits, but not $glbs$.

A functor $(f : R \to T)$ is *S-continuous* if R and T are S-complete and

$$f(\bigwedge h) \equiv \bigwedge(f \circ h), \qquad \text{all } h \text{ in } [S \to R].$$

Cocontinuity is defined similarly, with colimits. These concepts are relevant for computer science, because they give a mathematical meaning to the important programming technique of recursion. Let R have $\bot$ and let $(f : R \to R)$ be ω-cocontinuous. Define a functor $(h : \omega \to R)$ by primitive recursion (0.2 X15)

$$h0 \; \hat{=} \; f\bot$$
$$h \circ \sigma \; \hat{=} \; f \circ h, \qquad \text{where } \sigma \text{ is the successor functor.}$$

Since R is ω-cocomplete, we can define the recursive (paradoxical) combinator Y

$$Yf \; \hat{=} \; \bigvee h.$$

Yf is then the familiar (least) fixed point of f.

Proof: $f(Yf) \equiv f(\bigvee h) \equiv \bigvee(f \circ h) \equiv \bigvee(h \circ \sigma) \equiv \bigvee h \equiv Yf$. □

Another familiar example of these concepts is provided by Dijkstra's weakest precondition $\lambda R.wp\,(S,R)$. This is a monotonic predicate transformer, i.e., an endofunctor of DED. Dijkstra's healthiness conditions for predicate transformers require them to be

(1) continuous (distribute through arbitrary conjunctions),

(2) ω-cocontinuous (distribute through existential quantification of ascending chains of predicates),

and (3) strict (i.e., map $\bot$ to $\bot$).

1.6 Adjunctions

Let $f: S \to T$ and $g: T \to S$. These are said to be an *adjunction* (or Scott retraction or Galois correspondence) if

(1) $\quad fc \leq d$ in T iff $c \leq gd$ in S, $\qquad$ all c in $\|S\|$, d in $\|T\|$.

f is said to be a *left adjoint* of g ; and g is a *right adjoint* of f. Up to equivalence, a functor has at most one left adjoint and at most one right adjoint.

If the inequations of (1) are replaced by equivalences, this means that each of f and g is (up to equivalence) a bijection, and each of them is both left and right adjoint of the other. The source and target preorders are then said to be *equivalent*. Equivalence of preorders is a weaker relation than isomorphism, and often more useful since it does not require equal cardinality. Examples X1, X8 and X9 below are in fact equivalences.

Examples

$\qquad$ Left adjoint $\qquad\qquad\qquad\qquad\qquad$ Right adjoint
X1 $\quad I: S \to S \qquad\qquad\qquad\qquad\qquad\quad I: S \to S$
$\quad$ Proof: $Ic = d$ iff $c = Id$.
X2 $(\times 10): \omega \to \omega \qquad\qquad\qquad\qquad\quad (\div 10): \omega \to \omega$
$\quad$ Proof: $c \times 10 \leq d$ iff $c \leq d \div 10$.
X3 $\quad (K\bot: (=1) \to T) \qquad\qquad\qquad\quad (K0: T \to (=1))$
$\quad$ Proof: $K\bot c = \bot \leq d$ in T iff $\qquad\quad c = 0 \leq 0 = K0d$ in $(=1)$.

X4 $K0 : T \to (= 1)$ $K\top : (= 1) \to T$
     Proof: $K0c = 0 \leq d$ in $(= 1)$ iff $c \leq K_\top d = \top$ in T.

X5 $\Delta : S \to S \times S$ (1.3 X14) $\wedge : S \times S \to S$
     Proof: $\Delta c = (c,c) \leq (d,e)$ in $S \times S$ iff $c \leq d \wedge e$ in S.

X6 $\vee : S \times S \to S$ $\Delta : S \to S \times S$
     Proof: $d \vee e \leq c$ iff $(d,e) \leq \Delta c = (c,c)$.

X7 $(\wedge e) : S \to S$ $(e \Rightarrow) : S \to S$
     Proof: $c \wedge e \leq d$ iff $c \leq (e \Rightarrow d)$.

X8 $K : T \to [(= 1) \to T]$ (1.4 X4) $(\lambda d \cdot d0) : [(= 1) \to T] \to T$
     Proof: $Kc \leq f$ iff $c \leq f0$.

X9 $P : T \times T \to [(= 2) \to T]$ $\lambda f.(f0, f1) : [(= 2) \to T] \to T \times T$
     Proof: $P(c,c') \leq f$ iff $(c,c') \leq (f0, f1)$.

X10 $K : T \to [S \to T]$ (1.4 X4) $\bigwedge : [S \to T] \to T$
     Proof: $Kc \leq f$ iff $c \leq \bigwedge f$.

X11 $\bigvee : [S \to T] \to T$ $K : T \to [S \to T]$ (1.4 X4)
     Proof: $\bigvee d$ in T iff $f \leq Kd$ in $[S \to T]$.

X12 $* : (\subseteq S \times S) \to (\subseteq S)$ (1.3 X13) $(\lambda x \cdot x) : (\subseteq S) \to (\subseteq S \times S)$ (1.3 X4)
     Proof: $c* \leq d$ in $(\subseteq S)$ iff $c \leq d$ in $(\subseteq S \times S)$.

The closure operator * is the left adjoint of a forgetful functor; such adjoints are called *free* functors.

Note how many of the interesting concepts introduced separately in the previous sections can be defined as left or right adjoints of some more or less trivial functor. For example, X4 and X3 define $\top$ and $\bot$ in terms of right and left adjoints of $K0$; X5 and X6 define $\wedge$ and $\vee$ as right and left adjoints of Δ; and X10 and X11 describe the general case of $\bigwedge$ and $\bigvee$ as right and left adjoints of K, the most boring functor of all. The large number of useful examples of an adjunction indicates the importance of this concept, and motivates a study of its properties, which are also numerous and useful.

Let $(f : S \to T)$ be a left adjoint of $(g : T \to S)$. Then

(2) $g; f \leq I$ in $[T \to T]$ and $I \leq f; g$ in $[S \to S]$.

(3)   For each d in T, there is a universal (top) solution c in S for the inequation
$$fc \leq d.$$

(4) For each c in S there is a couniversal (bottom) solution d in T for the inequation
$$c \leq gd.$$

Each of these conditions is both necessary and sufficient for the existence of an adjunction.

Other consequences of an adjunction are listed below. (5) and (6) show how each of f and g determines its adjoint up to equivalence.

(5) $gd \equiv \bigvee\{c \in \|S\| \cdot fc \leq d\}$,   all d in T.
(6) $fc \equiv \bigwedge\{d \in \|T\| \cdot c \leq gd\}$,   all c in S.
(7) f is cocontinuous (provided S and T are S-complete).
(8) g is continuous (provided S and T are T-complete).
(9) $f;g;f \equiv f$ in $[S \rightarrow T]$ and $g;f;g \equiv g$ in $[T \rightarrow S]$.
(10) If (f,g) and (f',g') are adjoint pairs, then so is $((f;f'),(g';g))$, provided the compositions are defined.
(11) $(f;g)$ and $(g;f)$ are idempotent (0.3).

The fact that $(f;g)$ is an idempotent endofunctor of S means that its image is a possibly simplified picture of the whole of S; similarly, the image of $(g;f)$ is a simplified picture of T. Because $(g;f) \leq I$, the representative member of each quotient class in T is its bottom, and the representative selected in S by $(f;g)$ is the top of its quotient class.

1.7 Preorders and Categories

According to the definition given in 0.5, functors on preorders form a concrete category, usually called *PRE*; its objects are sets with a structure given as an ordering relation, and its functors are functions which (by monotonicity) respect the structure. Like all concrete categories, *PRE* is a subcategory of *SET*; more surprisingly, since sets are themselves a kind of preorder (1.1 X1), it has as one of its subcategories an isomorphic "copy" of *SET*. *PRE* as a whole has very much the same rich structure as *SET*, with an empty set, a unit set, products and coproducts, and higher order objects and functors. However, it does not have a direct analogue of the powerset of t, isomorphic to $[t \rightarrow \{0,1\}]$ (0.3 X13, X14).

PRE also offers a wide selection of interesting subcategories. They are formed by simultaneously restricting the objects to preorders which have additional structure (e.g., with $\bot$) and the arrows to functors which respect that structure (e.g., strict functions). In general, the additional internal structure imposed on the objects of the category will entail loss of external structure in the functors between them. The cases where this does not happen are the most interesting ones.

Examples

X1 The objects are preorders with $\bot$, and the arrows are *strict* functors, i.e., those which map $\bot$ in the source preorder to $\bot$ in the target preorder.

X2 The objects are preorders with $\wedge$, and the arrows are functors that distribute through $\wedge$, i.e., $f(c \wedge d) = (fc) \wedge (fd)$.

X3 The objects are ω-complete preorders, and the arrows are ω-continuous functors.

X4 A combination of all the restrictions listed above. This is nothing but the category of all healthy predicate transformers.

As in the case of sets, each individual preorder R can be regarded as an example of an abstract category $(\|R\|, R, \delta, ;, 0, 1)$. The objects of the category are just the objects of the preorder. The arrows are those pairs of objects which are related by the ordering, i.e., the order relation R itself! The identity is the function δ which maps each object c to the pair (c,c); reflexivity of R ensures that this is an arrow. The source and target functions just select the left and right members of the pair, $\overleftarrow{(b,c)} = b$ and $\overrightarrow{(b,c)} = c$. Composition is defined between a pair (b,c) and (d,e) just when $c = d$; and in this case gives the result (b,e). Transitivity of R ensures that this is an arrow, and associativity is not difficult to prove.

The categories which are formed from preorders have a distinctive property that between any pair of objects there is either no arrow or exactly one arrow. Any category C with this property is called a preorder category, and one can define a preorder among its objects:

$$b \leq c \ \hat{=} \ (b = \overleftarrow{x} \text{ and } \overrightarrow{x} = c, \text{ for some } x \text{ in } |C|).$$

The category formed from this preorder is structurally identical to the original category C. Furthermore, the bottom of the preorder is the initial object of the category, the top is the terminal object, the *glb* is a product, the *lub* a coproduct, and so on.

Thus *PRE* is another example of a category whose objects are (effectively) categories, and whose arrows are functors. The objects of *PRE* have more internal structure than the objects of *SET*, and the arrows have only slightly less structure. In the next chapter we will see yet another such example.

2 MONOIDS

2.1 Introduction

A monoid is another simple and familiar example of an abstract category, illustrating many of the same categorical terms and concepts as a preorder, and some new ones. A monoid M is an algebra $(|M|, ;_M, I_M)$, where $|M|$ is a set of *arrows* (or *morphisms*), and $;_M$ (called *composition*) is a binary associative operator on M, and I_M is an arrow which is a unit of $;_M$. The axioms of the algebra are therefore

$$p;_M (q;_M r) = (p;_M q);_M r, \qquad \text{for all } p, q, r \text{ in } |M|.$$
$$I_M; p = p = p; I_M, \qquad \text{for all } p \text{ in } |M|.$$

The second axiom uniquely determines I_M. We will usually omit the subscript M, replacing it occasionally by a more global qualification "in M".

In a *commutative* monoid, we have the additional axiom

$$p; q = q; p, \qquad \text{for all } p \text{ and } q \text{ in } |M|.$$

In an *idempotent* monoid we have

$$p; p = p, \qquad \text{for all } p \text{ in } |M|.$$

A *preordered* monoid is one in which there is a preorder defined on the arrows, such that composition is monotonic:

$$\text{if } p \leq q \text{ then } (p; r \leq q; r \text{ and } r; p \leq r; q).$$

Examples

X1 $TRIV \triangleq (\{I\}, ;, I)$ has only one arrow, necessarily the unit. This is the smallest possible monoid, in which all equations are true, and all have unique solutions.

X2 $\mathsf{N}+ \triangleq (\omega, +, 0)$: the arrows are natural numbers, with addition as composition and zero as unit. It is a commutative monoid.

X3 $\mathsf{N}\times \triangleq (\omega, \times, 1)$: natural numbers with multiplication.

X4 Let S be a subset of the arrows of a monoid M, where S contains I_M and is closed with respect to $;_M$. Then $(S, ;_M, I_M)$ is a monoid, called a submonoid of M. $TRIV$ is a submonoid of every monoid.

X5 $\mathbf{P}(S \times S) \cong ((\subseteq S \times S), ;, (= S))$: the arrows are relations on S, the unit is the identity relation, with the familiar relational composition

$$p;q \ \cong \ \{(x,z) \mid \exists y.(x,y) \in p \text{ and } (y,z) \in q\}.$$

X6 $(S \twoheadrightarrow S)$ is the subset of $\mathbf{P}(S \times S)$ containing those relations which are partial functions. Other submonoids are the total functions $(S \to S)$, the injections $(S \rightarrowtail S)$, the surjections $(S \twoheadrightarrow S)$, or the bijections $(S \rightarrowtail\!\!\!\twoheadrightarrow S)$.

X7 *GRP*: any mathematical group is a monoid.

X8 $MATR_n$: the square matrices of order n are a monoid under matrix multiplication, with the diagonal identity matrix as unit.

X9 If S is a preorder, $([S \to S], ;, ((\lambda x.x) : S \to S))$ is the monoid of endofunctors between S and itself.

X10 If S is a set then $STR_S \cong (S*, \hat{\ }, <\ >)$ is a monoid,

 where $S*$ is the set of finite strings (lists) with elements drawn from S.

 $\hat{\ }$ is string concatenation,

 and $<\ >$ is the empty string.

X11 A specific example of a string monoid is provided by the syntax of a simple programming language. Let $CL \cong STR_{ASS}$, where ASS is some set of multiple assignments

$$(x, y, \ldots, z := e, f, \ldots, g),$$

each of which assigns the current values of a list of expressions $(e, f, \ldots, g)$ to a list of variables $(x, y, \ldots, z)$. This primitive programming language has no loops, and is more suited to a pocket calculator than to a stored program computer.

X12 $MC = STR_{OP}$, where OP is some set of (say, two-address) machine instructions: $OP \cong$ (opcode $\times$ address $\times$ address).

X13 The set of Dijkstra's healthy predicate transformers has an identity, and is closed under functional composition. It is therefore a monoid, which we call *PT*.

X14 Bags and finite sets are commutative monoids, with bag union and set union as their respective compositions.

X15 If R is a partial order with $\vee$ and $\bot$, then $(\|R\|, \vee, \bot)$ is a monoid, both commutative and idempotent; similarly, $(\|R\|, \wedge, \top)$.

The extra structure provided by a preordered monoid enables us to distinguish between different kinds of high-level programming language. In all cases, the composition operator is the normal sequential composition of commands or functions, and the unit is *SKIP*, or the identity function. Further details of these languages will be defined algebraically in the following sections.

X16 DIJ: Dijkstra's non-deterministic sequential language. Since each command is uniquely defined by its predicate transformer, DIJ is a submonoid of PT(X13); it contains only the computable arrows.

X17 LIS: An untyped function programming language like LISP, but with non-strict semantics (i.e., functions (even *cons*) do not evaluate their arguments unnecessarily).

X18 CSP: A language like occam with synchronised input and output.

X19 If M is a monoid so is its opposite $\check{M}$, where

$$|\check{M}| = |M|,$$
$$I_{\check{M}} \triangleq I_M,$$
$$\text{and} \quad p;_{\check{M}} q \triangleq q;_M p \quad \text{(note the reversal of order)}.$$

X20 If M and N are monoids, so is $M \times N = (|M| \times |N|, ;_{M \times N}, I_{M \times N})$,

where $(p, q);_{M \times N} (r, s) \triangleq ((p;_M r), (q;_N s))$,
and $I_{M \times N} \triangleq (I_M, I_N)$.

X21 Let q be a quotient of the arrows of a monoid M. We define I_q as the set containing I_M; and for x, y in q we define a composition operator

$$x;_q y = \{r;_M s \mid r \in x \text{ and } s \in y\}$$

If for all x, y in q, $(x;_q y)$ is also a member of q, then $(q, ;_q, I_q)$ is called a *quotient monoid* of M.

An arrow m is called *monic* if the equation in x

$$x; m = p$$

has at most one solution. It is called *epic* if it is monic in the opposite monoid. For example, the unit I is both monic and epic, and the composition of two monics is monic (and the same for epics). So the monics (and the epics) constitute a submonoid of M. In the monoid of total functions, the injections (monomorphisms) are monic and the surjections (epimorphisms) are epic. In STR and $\mathsf{N}+$ and GRP, every arrow is both monic and epic. In $\mathsf{N}\times$, zero is the only arrow which is neither.

An arrow m is called an *isomorphism* if the equations in x

$$x; m = m; x = I$$

have a solution x (necessarily unique). This is known as the *inverse* of m, written $\check{m}$, and it is also an isomorphism. We have the familiar laws

$$x; m = p \quad \text{iff} \quad x = p; \check{m}.$$
$$m; y = q \quad \text{iff} \quad y = \check{m}; p.$$
$$(\check{p})\check{} = p, \quad \check{I} = I, \quad (p; q)\check{} = (\check{q}); (\check{p}).$$

In every monoid, I is an isomorphism, and the composition of two isomorphisms is an isomorphism. In GRP, every arrow is an isomorphism. In the theory of monoids, many concepts are defined only up to isomorphism; so the interesting monoids are those with non-isomorphic arrows.

Let N be a submonoid of $M \times M$, and let $(x, y) \in |N|$ and $p, q \in |M|$. If

$$p; x = y; q$$

then the triple $((x, y) : p \dot\to q)$ is said to be an N-transformation from p to q; this fact is stated as usual by just omitting the brackets. Clearly,

$$I_N : p \dot\to p, \qquad \text{for all } p \text{ in } |M|;$$

If $m : p \dot\to q$ and $n : q \dot\to r$ then

$$(m;_N n) : p \dot\to r, \qquad \text{for all } m, n \text{ in } |N| \text{ and } p, q, r \text{ in } |M|.$$

The existence of an N-transformation between two arrows may be used to define an order relation between them, also called N:

$$p \leq q \text{ in } N \; \triangleq \; (\exists n \in |N|. \; n : p \to q).$$

There are three interesting special cases. In the first case $N = M \times \{I_M\}$, and the general definition simplifies to

$$p \leq q \; \triangleq \; (\exists m \in |M|. \; p; m = q).$$

In **N+** this gives the normal magnitude ordering on **N**. In STR (X10) it gives prefix ordering (initial substring). In $(|R|, \vee, \perp)$ (X15) it gives back the original preorder R. In $(S \to S)$ it means that $(\forall x, y \cdot px = py \Rightarrow qx = qy)$, so that the quotient (0.3 X9) induced by p on its domain is finer than that induced by q. The case that $N = \{I_M\} \times M$ is very similar.

The second special case is when

$$N = \{(x, y) \mid x \text{ and } y \text{ are isomorphisms of } M\}.$$

In this case, the ordering is symmetric, and therefore an equivalence relation, denoted $\simeq$.

The third special case is when

$$N = \{(x, x) \mid x \in |M|\}.$$

An interesting property of this special case is that it satisfies the law

$$\text{if } n : p0 \to q0 \text{ and } n : p1 \to q1 \text{ then } n : (p0; p1) \to (q0; q1).$$

The law generalises by induction to compositions of any length, corresponding to any string of 0's and 1's

$$p0; p1; p1; \ldots; p0; n \; = \; n; q0; q1; q1; \ldots; q0.$$

Facts of this kind are useful in program optimisation. If $q0$ and $q1$ are more efficient than $p0$ and $p1$ respectively, then the operation n should be carried out as early as possible; this will precondition the data into a form which permits the more efficient operations. This is the basis of the data refinement method of VDM.

Unfortunately none of these orderings is very useful or convenient, because they are not in general respected by the composition of the monoid, which thereby fails to be monotonic. The main reason for mentioning them is as a gentle introduction to the much more important concept of a natural transformation (or natural isomorphism) between functors (see 2.7).

2.2 The zero arrow

A zero arrow z in a monoid is defined uniquely by the set of simultaneous equations

$$p; z = z; q, \qquad \text{for all } p \text{ and } q \text{ in } |M|.$$

Proof: let z be another zero. Then $z = z; I = z'; z = I; z' = z'$ □

For example, 0 is a zero of $\mathsf{N}\times$, **abort** of DIJ, and $\top$ in $(\|R\|, \vee, \bot)$ (2.1 X15).

But **abort** is not a zero arrow in CSP. Suppose p performs some useful input and output; then $(p;$ **abort**$)$ can be relied on to perform these same actions before aborting, and so is better than **abort**. The worst program in LIS is the function $\bot$, which is defined as the function which never terminates. It too is not a zero arrow. Suppose p is a constant function, giving the value 3 independent of its argument, even if the argument is undefined. So the functional composition $(\bot; p)$ always gives the same constant value 3, whereas $(p; \bot)$, by the definition of $\bot$, always fails.

The similarities and differences between strict and non-strict programming languages may be more neatly captured in a preordered monoid by redefining a zero z as satisfying the inequation

$$p; z \leq z; q, \qquad \text{for all } p \text{ and } q \text{ in } |M|.$$

This defines z up to equivalence.

Proof: let z' be another zero. Then

$$z = I; z \leq z; z' \leq z'; I = z'$$

and $z' \leq z$ similarly. □

A cozero is defined as a zero in the opposite monoid (or equivalently, in the opposite ordering). It satisfies

$$z; q \leq p; z, \qquad \text{for all } p \text{ and } q \text{ in } |M|.$$

In DIJ and CSP **abort** is a zero in this sense, but in LIS $\bot$ is a cozero.

2.3 Products

In LISP, the function *car* selects the first component of a pair, and *cdr* selects the second component. In LIS, we abbreviate these to π and μ respectively.

If p and q are functions, we define

$$<p,q> \;\triangleq\; \lambda x \cdot cons(px, qx).$$

Its result is a pair whose first component is calculated by applying p to the argument, and whose second component is calculated by applying q (possibly in parallel) to the same argument. If we then select only one member of this pair, we get the same ultimate answer as if we had (more sensibly) applied only the corresponding one of the two functions p or q:

(1) $\quad <p,q>;\pi \;=\; p$
(2) $\quad <p,q>;\mu \;=\; q.$

Now consider the function

$$<\pi,\mu> \;\triangleq\; \lambda x \cdot cons(car(x), cdr(x)).$$

This constructs a pair consisting of the first and second components of its argument — a laborious way of leaving the argument unchanged

$$<\pi,\mu> \;=\; I_{LIS}.$$

Similar reasoning leads to the more powerful law

(3) $\quad <(r;\pi),(r;\mu)> \;=\; r, \qquad$ for all r in LIS.

A consequence of this is a one-sided distribution law

$$<(r;p),(r;q)> \;=\; r;<p,q>.$$

The validity of these laws depends on the fact that LIS is untyped, and that any value can be analysed as a pair. In a typed language, the range of the variable r in (3) is restricted to operations which deliver a pair as a result. That is what is done in category theory also.

The three equations quoted above can be summarised in a single adjunctive property

$$<p,q> = x \quad \text{iff} \quad (p = x;\pi \text{ and } q = x;\mu), \qquad \text{for all } p,q,x \text{ in } |M|.$$

Any pair (π,μ) which satisfies this axiom is called a *product*.

Another example of a product occurs in the monoid $(\mathsf{N} \to \mathsf{N})$ of total functions on natural numbers. Let π be the function that deletes every odd-numbered digit of the decimal expansion of its argument; and let μ delete the even-numbered digits, so that

$$\pi 40321 = 431 \text{ and } \mu 40321 = 02.$$

Let $<p,q>$ be the function which applies both p and q to its argument, and then interleaves the decimal digits of the result, starting at the least significant end (Dijkstra's *zip* function). This interpretation satisfies the adjunction equation given above, and therefore enjoys all the other properties of a product. But there are many other pairs of functions which could serve as products: they are all isomorphic to this one.

The operation in LIS which makes the pair consisting of two identical copies of its argument is defined

$$\delta \triangleq <I, I>.$$

A function which applies p to the first component of its argument and q to the second, and delivers the two results as a pair is defined

$$(p \times q) \triangleq <(\pi; p), (\mu; q)>$$

This definition permits or encourages an implementation to evaluate p and q concurrently. The following can now be proved:

$$<p, q> = \delta; (p \times q)$$
$$(p \times q); (r \times s) = (p; r) \times (q; s)$$
$$(p \times q); \pi = \pi; p$$
$$(p \times q); \mu = \mu; q$$
$$\delta; (p \times p) = p; \delta$$
$$\delta; \pi = \delta; \mu = \delta; (\pi \times \mu) = (I \times I) = I$$
$$p \times q \simeq q \times p$$
$$p \times (q \times r) \simeq (p \times q) \times r.$$

The last two laws show that the product in a monoid is analogous to the multiplication of numbers. Their proof uses the isomorphisms

$$<\mu, \pi>; <\mu, \pi> = I, \text{ and}$$
$$<(\pi; \pi), <(\pi; \mu), \mu>>; <<\pi, (\mu; \pi)>, (\mu; \mu)> = I.$$

In a conventional language like PASCAL, the machine state can be regarded as a pair whose first component is the value at the top of the stack, and whose second component is the rest of the stack. The operation $< p, I >$ loads onto the stack the result of evaluating p in the current machine state, and leaves the rest of the machine state unchanged. The operation π gives the value at the top of the stack, $\mu; \pi$ gives the second member of the stack, and μ pops the stack. These operations may be compounded in order to access local and non-local variables. For example, the operation $< \pi, I >$ pushes onto the top of the stack a duplicate copy of the previous top; and $< \pi, < \pi, \mu; \mu >>$ assigns the value of the top of the stack to its second element, overwriting the previous value. The operation δ makes a copy of the whole current machine state at the top of the stack. It is similar to the fork operation of UNIX. The operation $(p \times q)$ permits concurrent execution of p and q on disjoint components of the state. Similar constructions define the whole machine code of Cousineau's Categorical Abstract Machine.

Unfortunately in a strict language like PASCAL, the law

$$< p, q >; \mu \ = \ q$$

does not hold when p fails to terminate, because in this case $< p, q >$ also fails. The only reason why this law holds in LIS is that *cons* is non-strict; i.e., it does not evaluate its arguments until this is known to be necessary. In a strict language we need to weaken the laws to

$$(1') \quad < p, q >; \pi \ \geq \ p$$
$$(2') \quad < p, q >; \mu \ \geq \ q.$$

In a non-deterministic language like DIJ or CSP, the third law is also invalid. Let r be non-deterministic, giving as result either $(0,0)$ or $(1,1)$. Then $(r; \pi)$ can give result 0 or 1, and $(r; \mu)$ can also give either result. When these calculations are carried out independently by $< (r; \pi), (r; \mu) >$, the range of possible results is $(0,0), (0,1), (1,0), (1,1)$. This is a larger range than r can give. So law (3) should be weakened to accommodate non-determinism.

$$(3') \quad < (r; \pi), (r; \mu) > \ \geq \ r$$

and other laws need similar weakening, for example

$$p; \delta \ \leq \ \delta; p \times p.$$

2.4 Coproducts

In a programming language, we define $[p, q]$ to be a command which is executed by executing exactly one of the alternatives p or q; it embodies the essential concept of environmental choice, like that offered by a conditional or a case statement in PASCAL. β is an operation (like loading *true* onto the stack) that causes the first alternative to be selected; and γ causes the second alternative to be selected. In LIS they may be implemented

$$\beta = \lambda x.cons\,(0,x) \text{ and } \gamma = \lambda y.cons\,(1,y)$$
$$\text{and } [p,q] = \lambda z.\text{ if } car(z) = 0 \text{ then } p(cdr(z))$$
$$\text{else if } car(z) = 1 \text{ then } q(cdr(z)).$$

A pair (β,γ) in a monoid M is said to be a *coproduct* of M if it is a product in $\check{M}$. It satisfies the adjunctive law

$$[p,q] = r \quad \text{iff} \quad p = \beta;r, \text{ and } q = \gamma;r, \qquad \text{for all } p,q,r \text{ in } |M|.$$

The other properties of the coproduct can be obtained from those of the product by simply reversing the order of composition, with $[p,q]$ acting like $<p,q>, (p+q)$ defined like $(p \times q)$, δ' like δ, etc. One of the early rewards of category theory is the revelation of the duality between products and coproducts, which halves the labour of proving their properties. A later reward extends this saving to all adjunctions (2.8).

A simple example of coproduct occurs in the monoid $(\mathbb{N} \to \mathbb{N})$.

Let $\beta = \lambda n \cdot 2 \times n, \quad \gamma = \lambda n \cdot 2 \times n + 1$, and

$[p,q] = \lambda n \cdot$ if even (n) then $p(n \div 2)$ else $q((n-1) \div 2)$.

This satisfies the adjunctive property because every number can be analysed as either $2 \times n$ or $(2 \times n) + 1$, but not both.

Unfortunately, the implementation of the coproduct described above in LIS does not satisfy the law $[\beta,\gamma] = \iota$ in the case that the argument has a first component different from 0 or 1, because the left hand side will then be undefined. A solution possible in some cases is to "coerce" the argument to the required form by some suitable bijection. Another solution is to weaken the definition of a coproduct to an inequality. But the most favoured solution is to introduce types into the programming language, so that the free variables in the equations are restricted to particular types, for which they are indeed valid. That is what is done in category theory also.

2.5 Exponentials

An arrow ε is called an *evaluation* if for each q the equation in x

$$(x \times I); \varepsilon = q$$

has exactly one solution, called θq. A monoid with a product and an evaluation arrow is called *cartesian closed*. Abbreviating $(x \times I); \varepsilon$ to $\check{\theta}x$, we get the adjunctive law

$$p = \theta q \quad \text{iff} \quad \check{\theta}p = q.$$

In LIS, ε is the function of two arguments, similar to the LISP *eval*, which applies its first argument to its second

$$\varepsilon = \lambda(f, x).(fx).$$

θ is the currying function. It converts a function of two arguments into a one-argument function which gives a one-argument function as result:

$$\theta f = \lambda x.\lambda y.f(x, y).$$

$\check{\theta}$ is the inverse of this, the uncurrying function

$$\check{\theta} g = \lambda(x, y).((gx)y).$$

Clearly $\varepsilon = \check{\theta} I$; analogously we define the curried pairing function

$$\eta \triangleq \theta I = \lambda x.(\lambda y.\text{cons } (x, y))$$

Corresponding to $\times$, we define an operation

$$(p \Rightarrow q) \triangleq \theta((I \times p); \varepsilon; q)$$

In LIS $(p \Rightarrow q)$ is the "enveloping" function $\lambda f.(p; f; q)$.

We can now derive the following collection of laws

$$(I \Rightarrow I) = I$$
$$(I \Rightarrow q); (I \Rightarrow s) = (I \Rightarrow (q; s))$$
$$\theta \varepsilon = \check{\theta} \eta = I$$
$$\theta p = \eta; (I \Rightarrow p)$$

$$p = \eta;(I \Rightarrow q) \quad \text{iff} \quad (p \times I); \varepsilon = q$$
$$p;\eta = \eta;(I \Rightarrow (p \times I))$$
$$((I \Rightarrow q) \times I); \varepsilon = \varepsilon; q$$
$$p; \hat{\theta} f;(q \Rightarrow r) = \theta((p \times q); f; r)$$
$$\check{\theta}(p; g;(q \Rightarrow r)) = (p \times q); \check{\theta}g; r$$
$$(p \Rightarrow q);(r \Rightarrow s) = ((r;p) \Rightarrow (q;s)) \qquad \text{note the change of order}$$
$$r \Rightarrow (p \times q) \quad \simeq \quad (r \Rightarrow p) \times (r \Rightarrow q)$$
$$(p \times q) \Rightarrow r \quad \simeq \quad (p \Rightarrow (q \Rightarrow r)).$$

If $\times$ is analogous to multiplication (or conjunction), the last two laws show that $\Rightarrow$ is analogous to exponentiation (or implication). These analogies are explained and fully exploited in category theory.

2.6 Functors on monoids

Let M and N be monoids, and let f be a total function from $|M|$ to $|N|$. Suppose f maps the unit of M to the unit of N and distributes through composition, i.e.,

$$f(I_M) = I_N$$
$$f(p;_M q) = (fp);_N (fq), \qquad \text{all } p, q \text{ in } |M|.$$

Then the triple $(f : M \to N)$ is called a *functor* from the source monoid M to the target monoid N. The technical terms and notational conventions for these functors are the same as for functors between sets and preorders. In particular, a bifunctor $(g : M \times M \to Q)$ is a function which satisfies

$$g((p;_M q),(r;_M s)) = g(p,r);_Q g(q,s).$$

Examples of functors include linear functions from **N+** to **N+**, group homomorphisms between groups, and string morphisms between strings. Other examples are

X1 $I_M \triangleq ((\lambda x.x) : M \to M)$, the identity functor on M.

X2 $0^{th} \triangleq ((\lambda(x,y).x) : M \times N \to M)$.

X3 $1^{st} \triangleq ((\lambda(x,y).y) : M \times N \to N)$.

X4 $\Delta \triangleq ((\lambda x.(x,x)) : M \to M \times M)$.

The monoid functors $I_M, 0^{th}, 1^{st}$ and Δ are *external* analogues of the arrows I, π, μ and δ, which are present *internally* in certain monoids (but not all). The relations between the external functors and the internal arrows are explored more fully by natural transformations in the next section.

X5 $K_{MN} \triangleq ((\lambda x.I_N) : M \to N)$. This is the only constant functor between monoids.

X6 $((\times) : M \times M \to M)$ and $((+) : (M \times M) \to M)$ are bifunctors (provided that M has products and/or coproducts).

X7 $((\Rightarrow) : \check{M} \times M \to M)$ is contravariant in its first argument.

X8 A bifunctor can be specialised by setting either of its arguments to I. If $g : M \times N \to T$ then $(\lambda x \cdot g(x, I_N)) : M \to T$ and $(\lambda x \cdot g(I_M, x)) : N \to T$. It is not valid to specialise an argument to any other arrow.

X9 Specialisation can also be achieved by equating the arguments of a bifunctor. If $g : M \times M \to N$ then
$$\lambda x.g(x,x) : M \to N.$$

X10 A denotational semantics D, which maps the programs of a language onto their meanings, is usually a functor. The fact that D distributes through composition merely states the denotational property that the meaning of the whole program is defined in terms of the meanings of its parts.

X11 In particular, the semantics of the simple calculator language (2.1. X11) has the form
$$sem : CL \to (S \to S)$$
where $S \triangleq (variables \twoheadrightarrow values)$ is the set of abstract machine stores and $(S \to S)$ is the monoid of functions between them.

X12 A simple translator from the command language CL to machine code MC (2.1 X12) will be a functor $(trans : CL \to MC)$, provided that the code generated from each command is kept separate from that of the following code (thus limiting the scope for optimisation).

X13 The denotational semantics of machine code is a functor $(mach : MC \to (R \to R))$, where $R \triangleq (addresses \twoheadrightarrow values)$ is the set of states of the real machine, and $(R \to R)$ is the monoid of functions from R to R. The functorial property states that catenation in MC means functional composition in $(R \to R)$.

X14 The composition $imp \cong (trans; mach)$ defines an implementation of CL on a real machine. It is a functor if $trans$ is a functor; and should be, even if $trans$ is not.

X15 A weakest precondition semantics is a contravariant functor ($wp : D\check{I}J \to PT$), where PT (2.1 X14) is the monoid of predicate transformers. It is contravariant because

$$wp(p;q,R) = wp(q,R); wp(p,R).$$

X16 $hom_M \cong ((\lambda(x,z)(\lambda y \cdot x; y; z)) : \check{M} \times M \to (|M| \to |M|))$. Here $(|M| \to |M|)$ is just the monoid of total functions on the arrows of M. hom_M is called the *hom-functor* on M. By specialising the first and second arguments to I_M, we get the so-called contravariant and covariant hom-functors:

$$hom_M^* \cong ((\lambda x.(\lambda y.x;y)) : \check{M} \to (|M| \to |M|))$$
$$\text{and } hom_{*M} \cong ((\lambda x.(\lambda y.y;x)) : M \to (|M| \to |M|)).$$

2.7 Natural transformations between monoid functors

If S and T are preorders, two functors in $[S \dot\to T]$ can be compared by a method based on the order structure of T (see 1.4). If M and N are monoids, two functors between them are compared by a method based on the monoid structure of N. The details are based on an idea introduced at the end of 2.1.

Let $f, g : M \to N$, and consider the set of equations

$$fp; n = n; gp, \qquad \text{for all } p \text{ in } |M|.$$

Any arrow n of N, which satisfies the commutative equations shown above, is said to be a *natural transformation* from f to g; it is written as a triple $(n : f \dot\to g)$. Using the unbracketed form to express this fact, it is easy to obtain the familiar properties:

$I_N : f \dot\to f,$ for all f with target N.
If $m : f \dot\to g$ and $n : g \dot\to h$ then $(m;_N n) : f \dot\to h$.

So the existence of a natural transformation between functors may be regarded as a kind of preordering relation between them. The set of all natural transformations on functors from M to N is denoted $[M \dot\to N]$. It is not a monoid, because the composition is a partial rather than a total operator, being defined just when the target of the first operand is the same as the source of the second. This makes $[M \rightarrow N]$ into an abstract category (0.5).

In proving that functors f and g are related by a natural transformation, it is often sufficient to prove this property only for a small set of generating arrows in the source monoid. For example, if the source is the monoid of strings on alphabet A (2.1 X10), then it is sufficient to prove

$$fp; n = n; gp, \qquad \text{for all } p \text{ in } A.$$

By induction, it follows that

$$fp; n = n; gp, \qquad \text{for all } p \text{ in } STR_A.$$

In a preordered monoid, there are two ways of weakening the definition of a natural transformation. An *up-simulation* is defined as a triple written $(u : f \dot{\leq} g)$ such that

$$fp; u \leq u; gp, \qquad \text{for all } p \text{ in } |M|.$$

A *down-simulation* written $(d : g \dot{\geq} f)$ is defined as an up-simulation in the opposite monoid, or more directly

$$d; fp \leq gp; d, \qquad \text{for all } p \text{ in } |M|.$$

A natural transformation $(n : f \dot{\rightarrow} g)$ is an up-simulation and also a down-simulation from f to g. The composition of two up-simulations is an up-simulation, and similarly for down-simulations. A *total* simulation is defined as an up-simulation with a right adjoint in the sense of 1.6. The right adjoint is necessarily a down-simulation.

Examples

X1 A zero of M was defined in 2.2 by the law

$$p; z = z; q, \qquad \text{for all } p \text{ and } q \text{ in } |M|.$$

This can be rewritten

$$0^{th}(p,q); z = z; 1^{st}(p,q) \quad \text{or} \quad z : 0^{th} \dot{\rightarrow} 1^{st}.$$

In a preordered monoid, a zero is similarly shown to be an up-simulation, and a co-zero is a down-simulation.

X2 The equation $p; I_M = I_M; p$ may be rewritten

$$I_M : I_M \xrightarrow{\cdot} I_M,$$

or even more strangely as

$$p : K_{MM} \xrightarrow{\cdot} K_{MM}, \qquad \text{for all } p \text{ in } |M|.$$

X3 From $(p \times q); \pi = \pi; p$ and $(p \times q); \mu = \mu; q$ (2.3) we get

$$\pi : (\times) \xrightarrow{\cdot} 0^{th} \quad \text{and} \quad \mu : (\times) \xrightarrow{\cdot} 1^{st}.$$

This shows a relationship between the internal selectors π and μ (which are arrows inside a monoid) and the external selection functors 0th and 1st, which are bifunctors between monoids. In a strict programming language, we have seen that π and μ are down-simulations.

X4 The internal duplicating arrow δ (2.3) is a natural transformation from the identity functor to the external duplicating functor Δ (2.6 X4). In a non-deterministic language it is an up-simulation.

X5 Similar remarks apply to coproducts

$$\beta : 0^{th} \xrightarrow{\cdot} (+) \quad \text{and} \quad \gamma : 1^{st} \xrightarrow{\cdot} (+) \text{ and } \delta' : \Delta \xrightarrow{\cdot} I.$$

X6 In a monoid with exponentials (2.5),

$$\varepsilon : (f; g) \xrightarrow{\cdot} I \quad \text{and} \quad \eta : I \xrightarrow{\cdot} (g; f)$$

where $f = \lambda q.(I \Rightarrow q)$ and $g = \lambda q.(q \times I)$.

X7 In LIS, where θ is currying,

$$((p \times q) \Rightarrow r); \theta \;=\; \theta; (p \Rightarrow (q \Rightarrow r))$$

Since θ is invertible, it is called a *natural isomorphism* between a pair of trifunctors, exhibited on the left and right hand sides of this equation.

2.8 Adjunctions of monoids

Let $f : M \to N$ and $g : N \to M$, and let ε be an arrow in N and η an arrow in M. These are said to be an *adjunction* if they satisfy the equation

(1) $\quad fp; \varepsilon = q$ in $N \quad$ iff $\quad p = \eta; gq$ in $M, \quad$ for all p in $|M|$ and q in $|N|$.

The left and right hand sides of these equations are usually abbreviated

$$\theta q \triangleq \eta; gq \quad \text{and} \quad \check{\theta} p \triangleq fp; \varepsilon.$$

f is said to be a *left adjoint* of g with *unit* ε; and g a *right adjoint* of f, with *counit* η. If ε and η are isomorphisms, then each of f and g is called an equivalence (of monoids), and the monoids M and N are said to be equivalent.

Examples

X1 $\quad I_M p; I = q$ in $M \quad$ iff $\quad p = I; I_M q$ in M.

X2 $\quad \Delta r; (\pi, \mu) = (p, q)$ in $(M \times M) \quad$ iff $\quad r = \delta; (p \times q)$ in M.

X3 $\quad (p + q); \delta' = r$ in $M \quad$ iff $\quad (p, q) = (\beta, \gamma); \Delta r$ in $M \times M$.

X2 and X3 state that the duplicating functor Δ has a right adjoint ($\times$) and a left adjoint ($+$). The unit (π, μ) and counit (β, γ) are defined (up to isomorphism) by this fact. Again, a boring functor has interesting adjoints.

X4 $\quad (p \times I); \varepsilon = q \quad$ iff $\quad p = \eta; (I \Rightarrow q)$, where ε and η are as defined in 2.5.

The adjunctive equation has many useful consequences

2a. $\eta; g\varepsilon = I_M$ $\qquad$ 2b. $f\eta; \varepsilon = I_N$
2c. $\varepsilon : (f \circ g) \dot\to I_N$ $\qquad$ 2d. $\eta : I_M \dot\to (g \circ f)$

3a. $\check{\theta}(\theta p) = p$ in M $\qquad$ 3b. $\theta(\check{\theta} q) = q$ in N
3c. $\theta(fp; r; q) = p; \theta r; gq$ $\qquad$ 3d. $fp; \check{\theta} s; q = \check{\theta}(p; s; gq)$

In fact the equations 2a ... 2d, and the equations 3a ... 3c are each equivalent to (1), and could be used as alternative definitions of an adjunction. The three parts of the proof show that (1) implies (2), that (2) implies (3), and that (3) implies (1).

Proof.

Part 1. Assume (1)
- 2a: $\{p, q := I, \varepsilon\} I = \eta; g\varepsilon$ iff $fI; \varepsilon = \varepsilon$, which is true, since f is a functor and $fI = I$.
- 2b: $\{p, q := \eta, I\} f\eta; \varepsilon = I$ iff $\eta = \eta; gI$, which is true.
- 2c: $\{p, q := gq, (\varepsilon; q)\} f(gq); \varepsilon = \varepsilon; q$ iff $gq = \eta; g(\varepsilon; q)$
  $\{g \text{ is a functor}\}$ iff $gq = \eta; g\varepsilon : gq$, which is true by 2a.
- 2d: proof similar to 2c.

Part 2. Assume (2) and define $\theta q = \eta; gq$ and $\check{\theta} p = fp; \varepsilon$.

3a:
$$\check{\theta}(\theta q)$$
$\{\text{def } \check{\theta}, \theta\}$ $\qquad = f(\eta; gq); \varepsilon$
$\{f \text{ a functor}\}$ $\qquad = f\eta; f(gq); \varepsilon$
$\{2c\}$ $\qquad = f\eta; \varepsilon; q$
$\{2b\}$ $\qquad = I; q \ = q.$

3b: proof similar to 3a

3c:
$$\theta(fp; r; q)$$
$\{\text{def } \theta\}$ $\qquad = \eta; g(fp; r; q)$
$\{g \text{ a functor}\}$ $\qquad = \eta; (g \circ f)p; gr; gq$
$\{2d\}$ $\qquad = p; \eta; gr; gq$
$\{\text{def } \theta\}$ $\qquad = p; \theta r; gq.$

Part 3. Assume (3) and define $\varepsilon = \check{\theta} I$ and $\eta = \theta I$.

$\qquad\qquad\qquad\qquad fp; \varepsilon = q$
$\{\text{def } \varepsilon\}$ $\qquad$ iff $fp; \check{\theta} I = q$
$\{3a, 3b, fI = I\}$ $\qquad$ iff $\theta(fp; \check{\theta} I; I) = \theta(fI; I; q)$
$\{3c \text{ twice}\}$ $\qquad$ iff $p; \theta(\check{\theta} I); gI = (I; \theta I; gq)$
$\{3b, gI = I, \text{def } \eta\}$ $\qquad$ iff $p = \eta; gq.$ $\qquad\square$

2.9 Monoids and Categories

According to the definition given in 0.5, functors on monoids (as defined in 2.7) form a concrete category, usually called *MON*; its objects are sets with a structure given by its composition operator and by selection of one of its members as the unit; and its arrows are functors which respect the structure by obeying the appropriate distribution laws. The external structure of *MON* itself is considerably weaker than that of *SET*. Although it has products, it does not have coproducts; although it has initial and terminal objects, these are the same object *TRIV* (2.1 X1, 2.6 X5); and finally the set of functors between two monoids is not a monoid, unless the two monoids are the same.

Interesting subcategories of *MON* may be obtained by restricting the objects to monoids which satisfy certain additional algebraic laws. For example there is a category of commutative monoids, and idempotent monoids. By taking only monoids whose arrows are isomorphisms, we get the category *GRP* of all groups. Since monoid functors respect isomorphism and inverses, the arrows of *GRP* are just the familiar homomorphisms of group theory. Similar homomorphisms are defined in other branches of algebra, for example ring theory; and the family of such homomorphisms is a category whose objects are algebras satisfying the axioms of the theory.

The study of monoids has led to several examples of abstract categories

X1 If N is a submonoid of $M \times M$, the N-transformations of M are an abstract category whose objects are arrows in M, and whose arrows are N-transformations. Composition is defined by composition in N.

X2 The structure $[M \to N]$ has as objects the functors from M to N and as arrows the natural transformations from one such functor to another. Natural transformations are composed using the composition of N.

Constructions by which arrows or functors serve as objects are very common in category theory.

As in the case of sets and preorders, each individual monoid M can be regarded as an example of an abstract category $(|M|, \{I\}, (\lambda x.I), ;, \lambda x.I, \lambda x.I)$. The arrows of the category are the same as those of M, and so is the composition. There is only one object, which can be identified with the unit of the monoid. This means that the identity, source, and target functions are forced to be $\lambda x.I$.

The distinctive property of the resulting category is that it has exactly one object. Any category C with exactly one object has trivial identity, source and target functions, and is structurally identical to the monoid $(|C|, ;, I)$, where I is the unit arrow of its only object. So *MON* is another example of a category like *PRE* and *SET*, whose objects are themselves categories. All three of them are subcategories of the general category *CAT*, with $\|CAT\|$ being the class of all categories whose family of objects constitute a set (the so-called small categories). Most of the structure of *SET* which has been lost in *PRE* and *MON* can be restored in *CAT*.

The study of category theory is a generalisation and unification of everything we have learnt from sets, preorders, and monoids. The reader is now encouraged (and perhaps prepared) to continue the study with the help of standard texts.

Part III

Specification, Construction, Verification Calculi for Distributed Systems

Formal models for distributed system proved to be especially complex mathematical objects. Nevertheless they can be specified and analysed by logical means. Here the appropriate choice of the basic concepts for description is decisive for getting a tractable and applicable formal system.

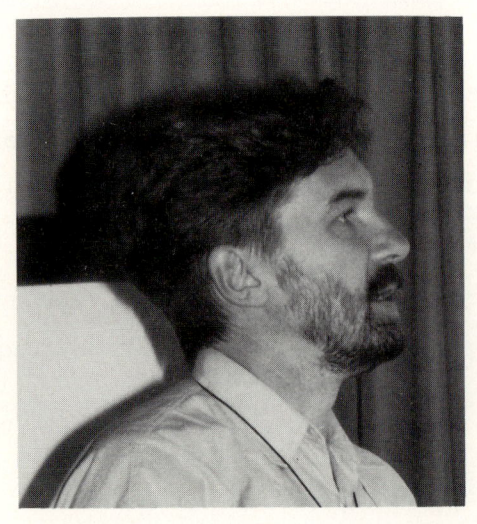

M. Broy

B.W. Lampson

J. Misra

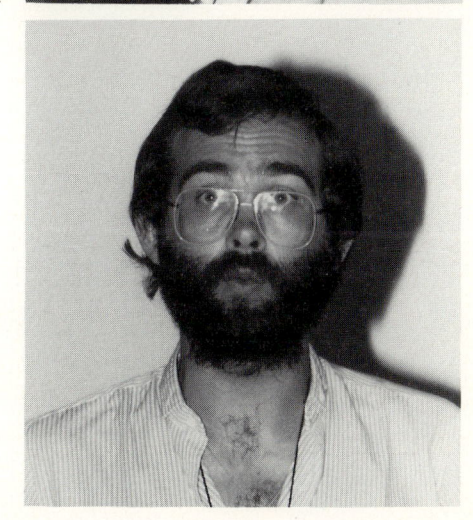

J.L.A. van de Snepscheut

Manfred Broy showed that it is not necessary to restrict oneself to finite sequences of rabbits. An infinite stream of rabbits is described by the recursive definition:

str 🎩 ≡ 🐰 & 🎩

which unwinds into

str 🎩 ≡ 🐰 🐰 🐰 🐰 ...

Towards a Design Methodology

for

Distributed Systems

Manfred Broy
Universität Passau
Fakultät für Mathematik und Informatik
Innstraße 27, D-8390 Passau
UUCP net: unido!unipas!broy

Abstract

A methodology for the specification and design of distributed systems is outlined. It follows the classical patterns of system design developed for sequential systems starting from an abstract specification going through a number of design decisions and finally leading to a distributed system composed of communicating and cooperating programs. A fully formal framework is provided such that all steps can be performed within the formal framework by transformations or at least be formally verified.

1. Introduction

After several decades of extensive research for sequential systems a general framework for their design is available. The design of sequential systems follows classical patterns starting from an informal problem description going to a requirement analysis leading to a requirement specification. Afterwards a design specification is derived and from this design specification by a number of implementation decisions final versions of implementations for the specified system are derived. In principle all the steps involved can be done in a purely functional framework within a formal calculus or at least can be formally verified.

In the design of distributed programs questions of correctness and of behavior are even more important than for sequential programs. The reason is quite obvious. Communicating programs and systems thereof exhibit two properties that make it practically impossible to test them in a sufficient way. On one hand they might be nondeterministic, on the other hand they might exhibit an infinite or at least unbounded behavior. Furthermore distributed programs are very often used in applications the correctness and reliability of which are of high importance. They are used to control traffic systems, production control system, and for all kinds of other software systems controlling physical processes. Their incorrect behavior could lead to disasters. Moreover distributed systems are more difficult to understand due to their combinatorial complexity. Therefore a proper formal methodological framework for the design of distributed systems is urgently needed.

There are many adjectives that have been and are used in connection with the type of systems we are interested in such as

(1) *cooperating, coordinated, communicating, reactive, interactive systems,*

(2) *concurrent, parallel systems,*

(3) *distributed systems,*

(4) *nondeterministic systems.*

All these adjectives refer to particular characteristics of the systems which we may classify by the following two complementing views on distributed systems:

- behaviors of systems,

- internal structure of systems such as their components and connections.

In a requirement specification for instance we mainly are interested in the behaviors of a system, while in a design specification, we may be interested in structuring the system into a family of components.

We claim that the design of distributed systems in principle could follow the lines of the development of sequential systems. All the techniques developed there can be used for the design of distributed systems, too. Of course, there have to be some conceptual extensions to programming methodology for sequential programs to make it work for distributed systems, too. However, it is important to underline that we do not need any completely different approach.

In general an available formal framework serves two important purposes. First of all it gives a proper foundation such that in principle it is clear what it means that a program is correct or that it can be verified. Second support systems that should give substantial support have to be based on formal methods. This is why formal methods get more and more into practical use, at least if systems with high reliability are required.

Even in the design of sequential systems communication aspects may be vital. This is especially true if dialog oriented systems are to be designed. Here classical techniques for specification and verification do not work without proper extension. Special calculi have to be provided. Nowadays it seems a general assumption that many of the simple dialog systems are to be designed by engineering techniques not so much taking into account formal verification techniques. This is true since such dialog oriented systems often have rather simple control structures and therefore can be easily tested. However, this is no longer true for components that are to be used within distributed systems cooperating with other interactive components. Here highly complex concepts of control and of data flow have to be considered that cannot be tested due to overwhelming combinatorial explosion. Often especially those systems are used in applications where reliability is vital. Therefore a proper methodology based approach to system design is necessary. It has to include specification, systematic modular development, verification and also classical software engineering techniques such as testing and performance analysis. In the following, however, we rather concentrate on the side of formal methods and a formal framework for such a methodology. We give a short description of a methodology for the design of distributed systems following the classical approach of programming starting from specifications going to abstract and finally to concrete efficient programs. Roughly we want to distinguish four phases:

- Requirement specification,
- Design specification,
- Abstract programming,
- Concrete programming.

For all four phases special formalisms have to be used and in addition rules have to be given for the transition of one formalism to the other.

2. The Formal Framework

We basically use an extension of the framework of algebraic specifications. We assume that a signature $\Sigma = (S, Op)$ is given, i.e. a set S of sorts and a set Op of function and relation symbols. The sorts are assumed to contain
- functional sorts,
- tuple sorts,
- set sorts,

as well as further generic sorts. Op is assumed to contain continuous as well as noncontinuous function symbols as well as relation symbols. A continuous function symbol has a functionality of the form

fct ($s_1, ... , s_n$) s.

A noncontinuous function symbol has a functionality of the form

map ($s_1, ... , s_n$) s.

A relation symbol has a functionality of the form

rel ($s_1, ... , s_n$).

For all kinds of symbols we allow overloading and mixfix notation. We also assume the possibility of subsorting.

By **set** s we denote the power set over the set of elements of sort s. By $\mathbf{nat}_\infty$ we denote the set of natural numbers with the usual ordering including the infinite number ∞. For better readability we often write f.x instead of f(x) for unary functions or relations f. Relation symbols are in particular =, $\downarrow$, and $\sqsubseteq$ which stand for equality, definedness, and partial ordering.

Continuous function symbols are assumed to correspond to continuous functions w.r.t. the ordering $\sqsubseteq$.

For every function and relation symbol it is specified to which tuples of terms (of which sorts) the function and relation symbols may be applied. The result sort then is always uniquely determined.

A model for Σ is an algebra, where all sorts correspond to partially ordered complete sets (ordered by $\sqsubseteq$) with least element $\bot$. All continuous functions symbols correspond to continuous total functions. All relation symbols correspond to relations. Terms and formulas are defined as usual. We assume that every element has a uniquely defined sort.

The meaning of $\downarrow$ is specified by the axiom:

$$x = \bot \Leftrightarrow \neg \downarrow x,$$

A special generic sort is the sort **str** which defines for every sort **s** the sort **str s** of streams of sort **s** and its characteristic functions:

type STREAM = **for given sort s:**
  sort str s,

  fct str s ϵ,
  fct (str s) s ft,
  fct (str s) str s rt,
  fct (s, str s) str s .&.

We denote the empty ("undefined") stream not only by $\bot$, but also by ϵ. For streams we use the following axioms:

$\text{ft}(x \mathbin{\&} s) = x,$
$\downarrow x \Rightarrow \text{rt}(x \mathbin{\&} s) = s,$
$\downarrow(x \mathbin{\&} s) = \downarrow x,$
$\downarrow \text{rt.s} \Rightarrow \downarrow s,$
$\neg \downarrow \epsilon,$

The relation $\sqsubseteq$ is defined on streams by the finest equivalence with

$$s \sqsubseteq s' \quad \equiv \quad s = s' \lor \neg\downarrow s \lor (\text{rt.s} \sqsubseteq \text{rt.s}' \land \text{ft.s} \sqsubseteq \text{ft.s}')$$

Apart from the basic axioms for streams we add two further axioms that can be conveniently used in proofs:

$$\text{ft.s} = \text{ft.t} \land \text{rt.s} = \text{rt.t} \Rightarrow s = t,$$
$$(\forall \textbf{ nat } i: \text{ ft.rt}^i.s = \text{ft.rt}^i.t) \Rightarrow s = t.$$

Here rt^i is defined by $\text{rt}^0.s = s$, $\text{rt}^{i+1}.s = \text{rt.rt}^i.s$. Trivially the first axiom is a consequence of the second one. The second one can be seen as a particular form of induction and can very conveniently be expressed by formulas of temporal logic (cf. [Broy 85b]).

On streams we now introduce a number of additional functions and relations that can be used in specifications.

First we introduce a relation

rel (s, str s) ∈ .

We write in infix notation

a ∈ s   for   ∈ (a, s)

We assume the axiom

a ∈ s ≡ ∃ **nat** i: a = ft. rt^i. s.

Second we introduce filtering functions

fct (s, str s) str s ©,
fct (set s, str s) str s ©,

which are defined for elements a by the axioms:

a = b ⇒ ©(a, b&s) = b & ©(a, s),
a ≠ b ⇒ ©(a, b&s) = ©(a, s),
©(a, ε) = ε,

and for sets of elements m by the axioms:

b ∈ m ⇒ ©(m, b&s) = b & ©(m, s),
¬(b ∈ m) ⇒ ©(m, b&s) = ©(m, s),
©(m, ε) = ε.

Moreover we introduce a length function

fct (str s) nat$_\infty$ #,

which counts the number of elements in a stream. It is defined for actions a by

$\downarrow$a $\Rightarrow$ #(a&s) = 1+ #s,
#ε = 0.

Finally we introduce a mapping for concatenating two streams

map (str s, str s) str s .^.

which is defined for actions a by

ε^s = s,
(a & s)^s' = a & (s^s'),
#s = ∞ $\Rightarrow$ s^s'= s

By ‹a› we denote the one-element stream a & ε.

There are of course many other functions that can be introduced for conveniently specifying streams. In a good system specification a number of auxiliary functions are introduced to structure the specification very similar to the use of auxiliary function in programming.

3. Specification of Distributed Systems: Requirement Specification

Basically there are two situations where concurrent programs occur. In one situation we have to consider a problem which could also be solved by a purely sequential program, but we are interested in a distributed solution, for instance since we want to run our programs on distributed architecture or since it seems helpful to have a structuring in terms of parallel processes as this is the case for operating systems or for instance for matrix multiplication. For this kind of concurrent systems we speak about *implicit concurrency*.

In the other applications the given problem might be inherently concurrent in nature. An instance are applications where physical parallel processes have to be controlled and supervised by some system and a distributed system as such is to be developed where software is only a part of the complete system. For this kind of concurrent systems we speak about *explicit concurrency*. We rather concentrate on explicit concurrency in the following, since implicit concurrency can be seen as a special case of explicit concurrency.

For a distributed system various aspects are of interest and may be needed to be described in a formal setting. Roughly we may distinguish the following aspects

(1) description of *behavior*,
(2) description of the *structuring* of the systems into components and their connections.

In a requirement specification we concentrate on the description of the behavior of a system, in principle, without talking about its structuring into subcomponents, although often also some structuring is helpful.

In a requirement specification we are mainly interested in property-oriented descriptions of systems and system behaviors. Here we distinguish two essentially different aspects of properties of behaviors:
- *safety conditions* are those properties that express that particular (bad) things do not happen,
- *liveness conditions* are those properties that express that particular (good) things do happen.

In the following we often will classify properties as liveness or safety properties.

3.1 Behaviors of Distributed Systems

In a requirement specification it is necessary to describe the behavior of systems. Many different formalisms have been suggested for describing the behavior of concurrent systems. Nevertheless all these formalisms can be understood in terms of rather similar semantic models. Looking at the possible semantic models we have to distinguish two approaches.

Interleaving models (called *trace models* in the sequel) and *models based on partial orderings of events* (also called "*true concurrency models*") which will be called *process models* in the sequel. The first could be seen as special case of the second. A lot of arguments have been exchanged why it is necessary or not necessary to incorporate concurrency into the semantic model of distributed systems and why interleaving models are sufficient or are too weak. Nevertheless it is still quite unclear what we win if we model concurrent systems at the level of partially ordered action structures. Clearly it is technically much more convenient to use finite or infinite sequences of actions called traces for representing the behaviors of distributed systems. To incorporate specifications of concurrency one could give in addition restrictions about the concurrency such that we obtain a simple relationship between trace oriented specifications which exhibit an interleaving view of a system and partial ordered action structure specifications which allow to talk explicitly about actual concurrency between events and actions.

We might specify the behavior of a distributed systems by specifying the set of all traces and in addition by specifying restrictions on the concurrency of actions. By this immediately a set of all partially ordered action structures is characterised. These are those action structures for which every topological sorting leads to a linearly ordered action structure representing a trace in the specified set and which in addition fulfil the restrictions imposed on the concurrency of actions.

When talking about models for distributed systems we have to decide which properties of distributed systems should be relevant and therefore be represented in the model. There are many discussions at the moment whether we need a simple interleaving view of distributed systems or rather a representation of concurrency in the model or finally even a representation of some notion of time in a model. When looking at those discussions it becomes soon clear that it depends very much on the particular application what is actually needed. In certain applications all the properties that are of interest can be discussed at the level of interleaving semantics. This is remarkable because interleaving models basically describe the behavior of systems in terms of sequences, sometimes also called traces or streams, which are formally easier to work with than action structures. For them good formalisms exist such as temporal logics or the calculus of stream processing functions or trace theory.

However, often a pure interleaving framework is considered to be not sufficient. The next step would be to introduce at least a little bit of concurrency. One example of such a proceeding are stream processing functions which map tuples of streams onto tuples of streams. Such a model is well-suited for a functional view. We start, however, with the transaction oriented view.

In this view a distributed system is considered as being described by a set of finite and infinite traces. A trace is a sequence of actions.

In a straightforward manner every action trace which is finite can be understood as describing a state namely the state obtained from one fixed initial state by executing the actions. There are many ways of associating states with action traces. Anyway a state can be combined with a notion of action by giving a state transition function which maps every state together with a given action onto a new state. Given a state transition function for every action by function composition we immediately get a state transition function for every finite sequence of actions. Based on this concept we can give state-oriented descriptions of traces, too. State-oriented descriptions are very well-suited for instance for specifying safety properties of distributed systems. Safety properties can be specified basically by invariant assertions. With a state-oriented view we can give restrictions for our traces by formulating certain requirements for actions, for instance that an action can be executed only if a state is obtained which has certain properties. States can be understood as a concrete form of establishing an equivalence relation on the set of finite traces or more precisely on the histories of a distributed system.

Other properties such as lifeness properties can in general more easily be described in terms of processes or traces. Liveness properties often can be nicely based on fairness assumptions. Fairness assumptions can easily be formulated in terms of action sequences. For instance one might require that certain actions occur infinitely often in infinite traces. There are several different concepts of liveness properties (such as termination or other progress properties) we might wish to consider for distributed systems. For instance we could try to look at progress or liveness properties for certain subprocesses representing transactions. A subprocess might be characterised as a subsequence of a given trace which contains all the actions of the trace which fullfil certain properties. In starting to group together certain actions into subprocesses we do a first step to a transaction-oriented more structured view of a distributed system.

In distributed systems we can distinguish two further ways of looking at the system. The input-output oriented one which leads to a functional view of distributed systems and an action structure oriented one which tries to describe a distributed systems by the observed action structures.

3.1.1 Actions

For specifying a distributed system at first we specify which actions may occur in the system. Some people speak about the *alphabet* of a system. A nice and abstract way of specifying abstract sets of actions is given by algebraic specifications. We may give an algebraic specification including the sort **act** of actions and a number of functions that create actions.

Example: *Connecting switch*:
A connecting switch is a system where stations may get connected, may then send messages and may get disconnected. We have three sorts

   sort station, message, act0,

and the following actions:

   fct (station, station) act0 co,
   fct (station, message) act0 send,
   fct (station) act0 disco.

Here the action co(t, r) stands for connecting the station t as a sender to the station r as a receiver. The action send(t, m) stands for sending of message m by sender station t to the station t is connected to. The action disco.t stands for disconnecting station t from the station to which t is connected.

□

In general for actions characteristic functions are assumed to be available that allow to derive some information from actions. Based on the concept of actions we may specify action traces or action structures.

3.1.2 Traces and Trace Specification

Let the sort of actions

sort act

be given. A *trace* is an element of the sort

str act

A *trace (requirement) specification* is a relation on traces. It is formally represented by

rel (str act) trace_spec.

We use a number of special predicates for specifying traces.

Example: *Connecting switch*

For giving a requirement specification for the connecting switch we define the trace predicate

rel (str act0) con_switch

As follows: Let CO.t stand for $\{a: \exists$ **station** $u: a = co(t, u)\}$

con_switch(s) ≡
$\forall$ **station** t, r, **message** m:
(1) $\#\copyright(CO.t, s) = \#\copyright(disco.t, s) \land$
$\forall$ **str act0** p, **act0** a, **nat** x, y : $p\hat{\ }\langle a\rangle \sqsubseteq s \land \#p < \infty \Rightarrow$
(2) $(a = send(t, m)) \Rightarrow \#\copyright(CO.t, p) > \#\copyright(disco.t, s)) \land$
(3) $(a = disco.t) \Rightarrow \#\copyright(CO.t, p) > \#\copyright(disco.t, s)) \land$
(4) $(a = co(t, r)) \Rightarrow \#\copyright(CO.t, p) = \#\copyright(disco.t, s)).$

This predicate specifies which traces are behaviors of the connecting switch. It basically specifies:
(1) Finally a station is as often disconnected as it is connected.
In every intermediate "state" of the system we have:
(2) If a station t sends a message, then it has been more often connected than disconnected.
(3) If a station t gets disconnected, then it has been more often connected than disconnected.
(4) If a station gets connected, then it has been as often disconnected as connected.

□

As a more general model than traces we may consider action structures. In action structures concurrency is explicitly represented.

3.1.3 Concrete Processes and Process Specifications

An *action structure* (also called a *process*) is given by a set of *events* with a causality relation on these events (represented by a partial ordering). The events are labelled by actions. Accordingly we assume in addition to the sort **act** an auxiliary sort

sort event.

The algebra of action structures is given by the following signature

sort pcs act,
rel (event, pcs act) in, minimal,
fct (pcs act p, event e: e $\in$ p) act α,
rel (pcs act p, event e, event e': e $\in$ p $\wedge$ e' $\in$ p) causal.

For better readability we write also in mixfix notation:

e $\in$ p	for	in(e, p)
e1 $\leq_p$ e2	for	causal(p, e1, e2)
E_p	for	{event e: e $\in$ p }
$\alpha_p(e)$	for	α(p, e)

Intuitively for events e1, e2:

e1 $\leq_p$ e2

means that we have e1 = e2 or the event e1 is causal for (and therefore happens before) the event e2 (e2 cannot start before e1 has finished) in process p.

We define the predicate minimal by

minimal(e, p) = (e $\in$ p $\wedge$ $\forall$ **event** e' : e' $\in$ p $\wedge$ e' $\leq_p$ e $\Rightarrow$ e = e').

Finite processes can be visualized by acyclic directed graphs the nodes of which are marked by actions. A process p is called *sequential*, if the ordering $\leq_p$ on E_p is linear. By $p_\emptyset$ the empty process is denoted, i.e. the process with the empty set of events.

Given a process p and a predicate

fct (event) bool q

then by $p|_q$ the process p' called *subprocess* of p is denoted where

$\forall$ event e: $e \in p' \equiv (e \in p \land q(e))$
$\forall$ event e: $q(e) \Rightarrow \alpha_p(e) = \alpha_{p'}(e)$
$\forall$ event e1, e2: $q(e1) \land q(e2) \Rightarrow (e1 \leq_p e2 \Leftrightarrow e1 \leq_{p'} e2)$.

Mathematically $\leq_p$ is just a partial ordering. However, when describing a concrete real system we have to relate this ordering to our observations about the system.

For a given process p there are three possible interpretations of the relation

$$e1 \leq_p e2$$

for events e1 and e2:
(1) *causal dependency*: the event e1 is causal for event e2;
(2) *systems constraints on concurrency*: the event e1 must not happen in parallel to event e2;
(3) *actual relative timing* of the events: the event e1 ends before e2 starts.

Of course (1) implies (3), however, the reverse does not hold, in general. Often the three different relations (interpretations) are mixed within the given partial ordering of a process.

3.1.4 Operations and Relations on Processes

A process p0 is called *finite*, if its set of events is finite. A process p0 is called *finitely based*, if for every event e with $e \in p$ the set $\{\text{event } e' : e' \leq_p e\}$ is finite. We always assume that processes are finitely based (an event e that needs infinitely many events to happen before e can never happen). In this section a number of basic operations and relations are introduced on processes.

A process p1 is called a *prefix* of p2 and we write $p1 \sqsubseteq p2$ and define:

$p1 \sqsubseteq p2 \equiv$ $\forall$ event e: $e \in p1 \Rightarrow e \in p2 \land$
$\forall$ event e, e': $e \in p1 \land e' \in p2 \land e' \leq_{p2} e \Rightarrow e' \in p1 \land$
$\forall$ event e, e': $e \in p1 \land e' \in p1 \Rightarrow (e \leq_{p1} e' \Leftrightarrow e \leq_{p2} e') \land$
$\forall$ event e: $e \in p1 \Rightarrow \alpha_{p1}(e) = \alpha_{p2}(e)$.

Trivially $\sqsubseteq$ defines a partial ordering on the universe of processes.

A process p1 is called a *sequentialisation* of a process p2 if

$\forall$ event e: $e \in p1 \Leftrightarrow e \in p2 \land$
$\forall$ event e: $\alpha_{p1}(e) = \alpha_{p2}(e)$,

$$\forall \text{ event } e, e': e \leq_{p2} e' \Rightarrow e \leq_{p1} e'.$$

Now some operations on processes are characterized by relations (predicates) on processes:

Let p be a process and s be a set of events, then we define by p\s the process specified by

$$e \in p\backslash s \equiv (e \in p \wedge \neg e \in s)$$
$$e1 \in p\backslash s \wedge e2 \in p\backslash s \Rightarrow (e1 \leq_{p\backslash s} e2 \Leftrightarrow e1 \leq_p e2)$$
$$e \in p\backslash s \Rightarrow \alpha_{p\backslash s}(e) = \alpha_p(e) .$$

For a given process q we also write p\q for p\{event e: e ∈ q}.

For a given process p it is an interesting question how one can decompose p into a sequential or parallel composition of simpler processes. When designing programs, however, it is more interesting to build up processes and programs describing them from simpler ones. Thus the study of a given process and its decomposition into subprocesses is *analytical* in character, whereas constructing processes and giving semantics to programs describing distributed systems looking at given subprocesses and the semantics of given subprograms is *synthetical* in character. For writing specifications for processes we introduce similar functions as we introduced for streams such as

fct (s, pcs act) pcs act ©,
fct (set s, pcs act) pcs act ©,

which are defined for actions a by

$$©(a, p) \equiv p\backslash \{e: \alpha_p(e) \neq a\},$$

and for sets of actions m by:

$$©(m, p) \equiv p\backslash \{e: \neg(\alpha_p(e) \in m)\}.$$

For the specification of a causally connected system a set of processes or a set of traces has to be described. In the following we introduce a formalism for the description of sets of processes or traces. This can be done by defining predicates on traces or processes.

Definition: A *(formal description of the behaviors of a) distributed system* consists of the specification of an action set and a set of processes or traces.

One obviously is interested in specifying distributed systems in some formalism. For specifying a set of processes one has to specify the action set A and to give axioms in some appropriate logical framework which restricts the allowed causality relations and labelling.

Two processes p and q are called isomorphic and we write $p \sim q$ if there is a bijection between the event sets of p and q which preserves the causality relation and the action labelling.

A predicate on action structures

rel (pcs act) Q

is called *abstract* if Q does not restrict the individuality of the events in the event sets. This is expressed by the condition for processes p and q:

$$Q(p) \wedge p \sim q \Rightarrow Q(q).$$

Similarly a predicate is called *concurrency liberal* if it holds for every sequentialisation of a process q provided it holds for q.

Note that traces can be understood as a subset of the set of action structures, namely the set of action structures with a sequential causal ordering.

Every abstract concurrency liberal predicate on action structures induces a predicate on traces.

3.1.4 Predicative Specifications for Action Structures

Typical predicates on processes or traces can be expressed if we decompose them into three parts:
- (1) a finite prefix q,
- (2) an "actual" action x,
- (3) a postfix q'.

Technically this means that q, x, q' form a decomposition of p iff $\#q < \infty$ and in the case of streams

$$q\hat{\,}\langle x \rangle\hat{\,}q' = p$$

or in the case of processes

$$q \sqsubseteq p \wedge \exists \textbf{ event } e: \text{minimal}(e, p\backslash q) \wedge q' = (p\backslash q)\backslash\{e\} \wedge \alpha_p(e) = x.$$

One might say that q, x, q' is a decomposition of p into a past, a presence and a future. We write then (q, x, q') **de** p.

Given a relational expression R on the stream identifier s of sort **str s** we may define temporal formulas:

$\circ \; s : R \equiv R[rt.s/s]$
$\Box \; s : R \equiv \forall \textbf{ nat } i: \; R[rt^i.s/s]$
$\Diamond \; s : R \equiv \exists \textbf{ nat } i: \; R[rt^i.s/s]$

These temporal logic formulas can be understood as a particular notation for predicates on streams. Their strength is the existence of a tuned calculus for such formulas. Their weakness is their limited expressiveness and the difficulties to understand such formulas.

We suggest to use a framework which does include not only temporal logic, but allows to define further concepts and functions in a free style for supporting structured specifications of systems. This way writing specifications is done along the lines of structured programming: large and complex specifications have to be developed stepwise, in a modular structured way. Streams (and also tuples of streams) can be understood as a special subset of processes. We just have to take intervals [1, n] with $n \in \mathbb{N} \cup \{\infty\}$ as event sets with the usual ordering of numbers.

We use a number of special predicates for specifying properties of streams or processes. Given a relational expression R on the process identiefier p of sort **pcs act** we define temporal formulas:

$\circ \; p : R \equiv \forall \textbf{ event } e: \text{minimal}(e, p) \Rightarrow R[(p\backslash\{e\})/p]$
$\Box \; p : R \equiv \forall \textbf{ pcs act } p': p' \sqsubseteq p \Rightarrow R[(p\backslash p')/p]$
$\Diamond \; p : R \equiv \exists \textbf{ pcs act } p': p' \sqsubseteq p \land R[(p\backslash p')/p]$

Again these temporal logic formulas therefore can be understood as a particular notation for predicates on processes.

In action structures we express causalities between events. Often we want to express that there is a specific causal relationship between actions. However, there are many versions of causalities between two actions possible.

A first example is a situation where an action b can only take place as often as an action a takes place. This is expressed for a given process p by $a \gg_p b$ where

$a \gg_p b \quad \equiv \quad \forall \textbf{ pcs act } p': p' \sqsubseteq p \Rightarrow$
$\qquad \#\copyright(\{\textbf{event } e: \alpha_p(e) = a\}, p') \geq \#\copyright(\{\textbf{event } e: \alpha_p(e) = b\}, p').$

The predicate $a \gg_p b$ expresses a safety property. It can be made stronger by adding the liveness property that every action a is causal for an action b. This is expressed for a given process p by writing $a \longrightarrow\!\!\gg_p b$ where

$a \longrightarrow\!\!\gg_p b \quad \equiv \quad a \gg_p b \land \#\copyright(\{\textbf{event } e: \alpha_p(e) = a\}, p) = \#\copyright(\{\textbf{event } e: \alpha_p(e) = b\}, p).$

There are other predicates that are of interest for expressing forms of causal relationship between actions.

A related predicate $a \succ_p b$ expresses the liveness property that an action a always causes an action b. This is specified by

$$a \succ_p b \quad \equiv \quad \forall \text{ event } e: \alpha_p(e) = a \Rightarrow \exists \text{ event } e': e \leq_p e' \wedge \alpha_p(e') = b.$$

Certainly we have for finite processes p

$$a \twoheadrightarrow_p b \Rightarrow a \succ_p b.$$

A cyclic dependent relationship between two actions can be expressed by:

$$a \therefore_p b \quad \equiv \quad \forall \text{ pcs } s \ p': p' \sqsubseteq p \Rightarrow 0 \leq \#\copyright(a, p') - \#\copyright(b, p') \leq 1$$

On the other hand we may relate an action b to an action a, by saying that b can only happen if a has happened before.

$$a \dashv_p b \quad \equiv \quad \forall \text{ event } e': \alpha_p(e') = b \Rightarrow \exists \text{ event } e: e \leq_p e' \wedge \alpha_p(e) = a$$

We generalize these predicates on pairs of actions to relations on sets m and m' of actions. We write for a given process p and relational expressions R and R':

$$m \gg_p m' \quad \equiv \quad \forall \text{ pcs act } p': p' \sqsubseteq p \Rightarrow \#\copyright(m, p') \geq \#\copyright(m', p'),$$

$$m \twoheadrightarrow_p m' \quad \equiv \quad m \gg_p m' \wedge \#\copyright(m, p) = \#\copyright(m', p),$$

$$m \succ_p m' \quad \equiv \quad \forall \text{ event } e: \alpha_p(e) \in m \Rightarrow \exists \text{ event } e': e \leq_p e' \wedge \alpha_p(e') \in m',$$

$$m \therefore_p m' \quad \equiv \quad \forall \text{ pcs } s \ p' : p \sqsubseteq p' \Rightarrow 0 \leq \#\copyright(m, p') - \#\copyright(m', p') \leq 1,$$

$$m \dashv_p m' \quad \equiv \quad \forall \text{ event } e': \alpha_p(e') \in m' \Rightarrow \exists \text{ event } e: e \leq_p e' \wedge \alpha_p(e) \in m.$$

For processes it is also interesting to restrict the concurrency of events and actions. This can be done by predicates that use the mapping:

map (pcs s, s) nat$_\infty$ concurrent

defined by

$$\text{concurrent}(p, a) = \max\{ |\{\textbf{event } e: \alpha_p(e) = a \wedge \text{minimal}(e, p\backslash p')\}| : p' \sqsubseteq p \}$$

It can be generalized to sets of actions by

map (**pcs s, set s**) **nat**$_\infty$ concurrent.

With these predicates we can specify processes. Note that the introduced forms of notation also be applied to streams since the set of streams can be understood as a subset of the set of action structures.

3.1.5 State-oriented Specifications

From the view points of traces or processes states are auxiliary constructs in the modelling of a distributed system. Every finite process or trace can be seen to define a state transition, or, if an initial state is assumed, a state. Then we may introduce an equivalence relation on states that indicates which traces or processes can be understood as being equivalent w.r.t. the induced state transitions. However, the introduction of a concrete state concept can make the description of a distributed system easier and better unterstandable.

Based on the concept of prefixes of action structures state-oriented views arise quite naturally. Every finite prefix of a process describes a possible finite history of the process up to a certain state of the process. In this sense finite prefixes are equivalent to intermediate states. Often, however, it is rather difficult to talk about states in terms of finite prefixes. In many applications very specific aspects of a system should be encoded into a state, while other parts of the action structure are completely irrelevant for the states. Often it is rather suggestive to develop an explicit state oriented view for a distributed system.

It is clear that it is possible to develop quite different state oriented views for a particular distributed system or for a particular action structure. A state-oriented view of a process can be understood as a quotient structure on the prefixes of processes. Two processes are equivalent if they correspond to the same state transition. Basically a state-oriented view of a system is developed in the following steps.

First we have to give an abstract specification of a sort state which specifies the sort of states that can be generated by a system.

Second we have to specify a state transition relation. It will be called $\rightarrow$ in general and has a functionality

rel (state, act, state) $\rightarrow$

We write $\sigma \to^a \sigma'$ instead of $\to (\sigma, a, \sigma')$. Not in all states a certain action can be performed.

The transition relation for states and actions induces a transition relation for processes. For every given state and every finite process we may associate with the process a set of states that can be generated by applying the actions in some order consistent with the ordering specified within the process to the state.

It should be emphasized once more that there are many different state-oriented views of a process description. A state-oriented view in some sense means a certain abstraction from histories just keeping those informations about processes which are relevant for the system state. On the other hand it leads to a much more concrete view of a distributed system, because it is oriented to a very particular view of the states occurring in the distributed system. For some distributed systems a state-oriented view seems most appropriate. For other distributed systems it seems much more suggestive to work without a state-oriented view. In any case the state-oriented view is just a particular concretisation of a view which is provided by processes as action structures anyway.

State-oriented views can be used at least in two different ways. They can be used by studying intermediate states of a given process that are generated by finite prefixes of the given process. There they can be used for formulating invariants. If one is only interested in finite processes, we may look only at the state transition associated with the given process and not at the intermediate states. If we are interested in infinite processes, the intermediate states and their invariants characterize basically a lot of important properties of a system. Note that the specification framework above works also for trace-oriented views of distributed systems if we just forget about the possibility of talking about the concurrency of actions.

Given a transaction relation for states we can generalize it to finite streams or action structures to the relations

$$\text{rel (state, str act, state) } \to,$$
$$\text{rel (state, pcs act, state) } \to,$$

by the axioms

$$\sigma \to^\varepsilon \sigma$$
$$\sigma \to^{a\&s} \sigma'' \equiv \exists \text{ state } \sigma': \sigma \to^a \sigma' \wedge \sigma' \to^s \sigma''$$

and

$$\sigma \to^p \sigma'' \equiv \exists \text{ event e, state } \sigma': \sigma \to^e \sigma' \wedge \sigma' \to^{p\backslash e} \sigma'' \wedge e \in p \wedge \text{minimal}(p,e)$$

A state concept with initial state init is called *complete* for a trace specification Q iff the state determines everything about the possible finite traces and resumptions. Formally this is expressed as follows: There exists a predicate R on states and traces such that

$$Q(t1\hat{\ }t2) = (\exists \textbf{ state } \sigma: \text{init} \rightarrow^{t1} \sigma \wedge R(\sigma, t2)).$$

By a complete state concept all state sequences corresponding to allowed traces can be characterized.

Given a state concept and an initial state init we may define traces or processes in terms of states. We write (let us assume that q does not occur in relational expression R):

$\forall$ **act** x, **state** σ **in** p : R,

for

$\forall$ **state** σ, **str act** q, **act** x: $q\hat{\ }\langle x\rangle \sqsubseteq p \wedge \text{init} \rightarrow^q \sigma \Rightarrow R,$

or for the following statement on the process p and the action x:

$\forall$ **state** σ, **pcs act** q, **act** x: $q \sqsubseteq p \wedge \text{minimal}(x, p\backslash q) \wedge \text{init} \rightarrow^q \sigma \Rightarrow R.$

The predicate R is also called an *invariant* for the trace or process p.

With these basic definitions we obtain a specification language for system descriptions.

3.2 Examples for System Specifications

Of course it is possible to give constructive descriptions of processes. An example of a formalism for doing this is abstract (or theoretical) CSP. It can be seen as constructor signature of an algebra for writing terms denoting sets of processes. It can be seen as a special case of a process algebra.

For specification purposes, however, it might be more interesting not to give a constructive, but a descriptive specification of processes. This means that processes or sets of processes are not described by expressions that denote processes, but rather by predicates that characterize processes.

In a descriptive approach a transaction oriented specification of a concurrent system is given by specifying
 (1) an action set and
 (2) a predicate on processes over that set of actions.
Action sets can be specified by the sorts of algebraic abstract types. Often the predicate on

processes can conveniently be formulated by a state oriented view.

Now we give a number of simple examples for specifications.

Examples:
(1) *Action structures composed of two sequential processes with mutual exclusion*
Let the elements of sort **act1** be given by a, b, c, d. We obtain an action structure specified by the relation Q1 versus

rel (pcs act1) Q1,
$Q1(q) \equiv a \therefore_q c \wedge b \therefore_q d \wedge \text{concurrent}(q, \{c, d\}) \leq 1$

The process specification Q1 does not exclude sequential processes.

(2) *A simple store*
Now consider the specification of a simple store. We specify

sort act2,

with the functions

fct (index, data) act2 read,
fct (index, data) act2 write,
fct (index) act2 give.

The action read(i, d) denotes the reading of the value d stored under index i, the action write(i, d) denotes the writing of the value d stored under index i, the action give(i) denotes a request for reading of the value stored under index i. A process specification is given by the predicate

rel (pcs act2) store,

with the specification:

$\text{store}(p) \equiv$
  $\forall$ **index** i, **data** d, **pcs act2** q, **event** e':
  (1) $\alpha_p(e') = \text{write}(i, d) \wedge q = p\backslash\{\textbf{event } e: e <_p e'\} \Rightarrow$
  $\hspace{5cm} \forall \textbf{ data } d': \text{write}(i, d') \dashv_q \text{read}(i, d') \wedge$
  (2) $\{\text{give}(i)\} \longrightarrow_p \{\textbf{act2 } x: \exists \textbf{ data } d: x = \text{read}(i, d)\} \wedge$
  (3) $\text{concurrent}(p, \{\textbf{act2 } x: \exists \textbf{ data } d: x = \text{read}(i, d) \vee x = \text{write}(i, d)\}) \leq 1.$

This specification says:
(1) Only values can be read that have been written before.
(2) A reading is done for index i as often as it is required.
(3) Writing or reading on an index can only be done sequentially.

(3) A merge node

For specifying a system representing a merge node in a network we introduce the sorts

sort direction, act3,

together with the function symbols

fct direction left, right,
fct (data, direction) act3 in,
fct (data) act3 out.

The relation

rel (pcs act3) merge

is specified by the axiom:

$$merge(q) \equiv \forall \text{ data d}: \{act3 \text{ x}: \exists \text{ direction i}: x = in(d, i)\} \longrightarrow_q \{act3 \text{ y}: y = out(d)\} \wedge$$
$$\#concurrent(q, \{ act3 \text{ x} : \exists \text{ data d} : x = in(d, left)\}) \leq 1 \wedge$$
$$\#concurrent(q, \{ act3 \text{ x} : \exists \text{ data d} : x = in(d, right)\}) \leq 1 \wedge$$
$$\#concurrent(q, \{ act3 \text{ x} : \exists \text{ data d} : x = out(d)\}) \leq 1.$$

□

An interesting question concerns the differences between a trace and an action structure specification. All formulas we have introduced can be interpreted both for traces and for processes. Often the differences are not significant.

4. Design Specification

After having obtained a description of a distributed system in terms of trace sequences or action structures to obtain a program we have to design a more functional view of a distributed systems in a design specification where we in particular distinguish between input and output. In its most simplistic view a distributed system is a monotonic mapping from streams of input actions onto streams of output actions. In a more program-oriented view we can specify a component in a distributed system as stream processing function. In a design specification a stream processing function or a system of a stream processing functions is to be given such that the traces that are connected with that stream processing functions correspond to the traces given in the requirement specification. With a given monotonic stream processing function we may associate with every input stream a trace consisting of an interleaving of the input stream and the output stream.

Submodules of a system might be represented by stream processing functions. Stream processing functions can nicely be described by algebraic techniques in terms of equational Horn clause specifications.

4.1 Functional Views of Distributed Systems

In a functional view of a distributed system we are not so much interested in the internal action structures representing the processes of a concurrent system, but rather in its behavior being a function from input stimuli to output stimuli. In a functional view a distributed system is understood and described in terms of its interface and its interaction with its environment.

Very generally we may model distributed systems by monotonic functions

$$\text{fct (pcs i) pcs o f}$$

mapping the causality structure of input actions **i** onto the causality structure of output actions **o**.

Such a modelling gives a view which seems much more appropriate for control systems as they are used and designed in computer science.

The state-oriented view of a system induces by the function introduced above also a state-oriented functional view of a system. For treating this aspect in more detail we give an analysis of the relationship between a functional view and an action structure oriented view of a distributed system.

4.1.1 Specification of Stream Processing Functions

In a specification of a stream processing function we give a predicate

$$\text{rel (fct (str i) str o) P}$$

that indicates which functions are to be considered.

There are many styles for writing such a predicate including functional (conditional) equations as well as predicates establishing a relationship between input and output streams.

Example:

(1) *Merging two streams*

A function that merges two streams can be characterized by the predicate merge

    rel (fct (str s, str s) str s) merge

which can be specified as follows:

    merge(f) = ∀ str s x, y: ∃ str bool o : sched(x, y, o) = f(x, y) ∧ #o = ∞
          where
          sched(x, y, true & o) = ft.x & sched(rt.x, y, o) ∧
          sched(x, y, false & o) = ft.y & sched(x, rt.y, o).

An equivalent specification can be written by giving an equation for merge. Here we take the weakest predicate for merge that fulfils the following equation:

    merge(f) = ∀ str s x, y: ∃ fct (str s, str s) str s f' : merge(f') ∧
          f(x, y) = ft.x & f'(rt.x, y) ∨ f(x, y) = ft.y & f'(x, rt.y).

(2) *Fair merge of two streams*

A function that merges two streams in a fair way can be characterized by the predicate fair_ merge

    rel (fct (str s, str s) str s) fair_ merge

which can be specified as follows:

    fair_ merge(f) = ∀ str s x, y: ∃ str bool o : sched(x, y, o) = f(x, y) ∧
           #©(true, o) = ∞ ∧ #©(false, o) = ∞
          where
          sched(x, y, true & o) = ft.x & sched(rt.x, y, o) ∧
          sched(x, y, false & o) = ft.y & sched(x, rt.y, o).

                                                                                              □

This technique of specification includes nondeterminism straightforward: A predicate in general specifies a set of functions.

For particular nondeterministic specifications there can be a conflict in the choice of a function due to the requirement of monotonicity according to partial input. As an example we take again the merge functions specified above. According to the specification of merge for none of the functions f with merge(f) we have for all streams x:

$$f(x, \varepsilon) = f(\varepsilon, x) = x$$

as long as f is required to be monotonic, which we want to have to be able to use f in recursive stream equations and to guarantee the existence of solutions by (least) fixpoints.

Therefore we use a trick and consider specifications where the choice of a function can be restricted by the actual argument.

For expressing these more sophisticated properties we use a predicate of the form:

rel (fct (str i) str o, str i) C

which allows to do the choice of the function dependent on the input.

Here C(f, x) means that in an application f.x the function f can only be chosen if f is appropriate for x. However, we do not accept all predicates for specifying communicating systems. We require a number of properties.

C is called *consistent* if for every input stream s there exists a feasible function f, i.e. if the following proposition holds:

$$\forall \text{ str i s: } \exists \text{ fct (str i) str o f: C(f, s)}$$

Since we want to use x in the specification C(f, x) only in a very restricted way, we require for C the additional properties of *choice consistency*:

$$C(f, x) \wedge x \sqsubseteq x' \Rightarrow \exists f': (\forall y: y \sqsubseteq x \Rightarrow f'.y = f.y) \wedge C(f', x').$$

This means that every partial computation can be continued consistently. In particular we require that C is *quasi-continuous*, i.e. for every chain x_i we have

$$(\forall i: C(f, x_i)) \Rightarrow C(f, \text{lub}\{x_i: i \in \mathbb{N}\})$$

and *chain-consistent*, i.e. for every chain of elements x_i with $x_i \sqsubseteq x_{i+1}$ and functions f_i such that $C(f_i, x_i)$ and

$$j \leq i \Rightarrow f_j.x_j = f_i.x_j \wedge C(f_i, x_j)$$

there is a function f with

$$\forall\, i\colon C(f, x_i) \wedge f.x_i = f_i.x_i$$

According to these properties we may prove (let now range and domain of f coincide)

$$\exists\, f\colon C(f, \text{fix}.f)$$

where fix gives the least fixpoint of a function.

The proof proceeds as follows: According to the consistency and the choice consistency of C we may construct a chain $\{x_i\colon i \in \mathbb{N}\}$ of values by:

(0)   define $x_0 = \bot$,
(1)   define f_i and $x_{i+1} = f_i.x_i$ such that $C(f_i, x_i) \wedge \forall\, j\colon j < i \Rightarrow f_i.x_j = x_{j+1}$.

The x_i form a chain and according to the requirement of chain consistency there exists a function f with

(2) $\forall\, i\colon C(f, x_i) \wedge f.x_i = f_i.x_i$

We have due to quasi-continuity of f

(3) $C(f, x)$ where $x =_{\text{def}} \text{lub}\{x_i\colon i \in \mathbb{N}\}$

It remains to prove that x is a fixpoint of f. For all x_i we have $f.x_i$ coincides with $f_i.x_i$. Therefore we obtain

$$f^i.\bot = x_i$$

and due to the continuity of f the element x is the least fixpoint

$$x = \text{lub}\ x_i = \text{lub}\ f^i.\bot = \text{lub}\ f^{i+1}.\bot = f.\text{lub}\ f^i.\bot = f.x$$

The existence of fixpoints is vital for associating meaning with communicating systems with feedback.

Example: Nonstrict merge can be defined by

$$\text{non\_strict\_merge}(f, x, y) = (\text{merge}(f) \wedge \#f(x, y) = \#x + \#y\,).$$

Fair nonstrict merge can be defined by

$$\text{fair\_non\_strict\_merge}(f, x, y) = (\text{fair\_merge}(f) \land \#f(x, y) = \#x + \#y).$$

□

One easily proves the required properties for these predicates.

4.1.3 State Oriented Aspects in the Functional View

The functional view has traditionally been seen as strongly different to the state-oriented view. However the functional view can be simply related to the state-oriented view as follows. A stream processing function can be seen as abstract representation of the state of the system which leads to the input/output behavior given by f. Then we may define a "state transition relation" on stream processing functions

rel (fct (str i) str o, act, fct (str i) str o) →

where **act** is (the sort of elements which is) the union of the disjoint sorts **i** and **o**. We define for x of sort **i**:

$$f \to^x g \equiv \forall \text{ str i s: } g(s) = f(x\&s)$$

and for x of sort **o**:

$$f \to^x g \equiv \forall \text{ str i s: } f(s) = x\&g(s).$$

Another possibility is to study a more explicit state representation. We may introduce a resumption function

fct (fct (str i) str o, i) fct (str i) str o resume

defined by

$$\text{resume}(f, a)(s) = rt^i.f(a\&s) \quad \text{with } i = \#f(a\&\varepsilon).$$

This way we may interpret the stream processing function as a state machine δ with input and output of the form:

δ: STATE × INPUT → STATE × OUTPUT,

where in the case of a state machine represented by a stream processing function the set STATE is (a subset of) the set of stream processing functions. The set INPUT is the set of elements of sort **i** and the set OUTPUT is the set of elements of sort **str o**. We define then

$\delta(f, a) = (\text{resume}(f, a), f(a\&\varepsilon))$.

Given any state representation we may characterize its properties. A sort **state** is called a *complete state representation* for the stream processing function f, if the resumption can be completely determined from the state, i.e. if there exists a function

fct (str i, state) str o h

such that for all n and input $a_1, ..., a_n$ there exists a state σ and a stream t such that for all streams s:

f. $a_1\& ... a_n\&s = t\hat{\ }h(s, \sigma)$

which just means

resume(... resume(f, a_1), ... a_n) = (**str i** s) **str o**: t^h(s, σ).

A complete representation is called *fully abstract*, iff for the function h we have

$\forall s: h(s,\sigma) = h(s, \sigma') \Rightarrow \sigma = \sigma'$.

What has been said above shows that a stream processing function itself can be seen as the abstract representation of a state of an interactive system.

4.2 From Requirement Specifications to Design Specifications

A requirement specification describes a system by specifying a set of actions and based on it a set of action streams or action structures. We are interested to relate such a requirement specification to a design specification. This means that we have to associate traces or processes with stream-processing or process-processing functions.

4.2.1 Associating Action Structures with Monotonic Functions

Let the function

fct (pcs i) pcs o f

be given. Then for every process p1 and p2 = f(p1) we may define that a process p0 represents a "computation" of f iff there exists a chain of processes p_i with lub p_i = p1

$e \in p0 = (e \in p1 \vee e \in p2)$,
$e \in p1 \Rightarrow \alpha_{p0}(e) = \alpha_{p1}(e)$,
$e \in p2 \Rightarrow \alpha_{p0}(e) = \alpha_{p2}(e)$,
$e1 \leq_{p0} e2 = (e1 \leq_{p1} e2 \vee e1 \leq_{p2} e2 \vee (\forall \text{ nat } i: e1 \in p_i \Rightarrow e2 \in f(p_i)))$.

This means that input events can be causal for output events but not vice versa. And an input event e1 is causal for an output event e2 iff whenever e1 occurs in the input process p the event e2 occurs in the output process f(p).

Often we are interested to consider feedback situations for processes. This corresponds to the recursive definition of a process by a process transformation function. This leads to the following possibility for associating an action structure to a continuous function

fct (pcs act) pcs act f

by the fixpoint operator. By **fix f** we denote the least fixpoint of f, i.e. the action structure p such that

$p = f(p)$

and for all action structures q:

$q = f(q) \Rightarrow p \sqsubseteq q$.

However, in such a recursive definition we may see additional causalities due to the definition above. Therefore we may associate with

fix f

the process structure p' (let p be defined as above) where $p_0 = p_\emptyset$, $p_{i+1} = f(p_i)$:

$e \in p = e \in p'$,
$\alpha_p(e) = \alpha_{p'}(e)$,
$e1 \leq_{p'} e2 = (e1 \leq_p e2 \vee \forall \text{ nat } i: e1 \in p_i \Rightarrow e2 \in f(p_i))$.

This way we obtain additional causalities in the fixpoint (cf. scenarios in [Brock, Ackermann 81]).

Considering only monotonic functions as models of distributed systems seems rather suggestive. Adding input actions to a given structure of input actions can only add output actions to the structure of output actions produced so far. Monotonicity also guarantees the existence of solutions of fixpoint equations for processes (modelling feedback in distributed systems). However, the requirement of monotonocity also leads to difficulties in cases where the causality structure of the processes of input actions does not provide enough information for determining uniquely the causality structure of the output events.

4.2.2 From Requirement Specifications for Streams to Design Specifications

In the trace approach a requirement specification is given by a trace predicate. With a stream-processing function

fct (str i) str o f

we may associate for every stream s of sort **str i** a trace predicate

map (fct (str i) str o, str i) rel (str act) trace.

The relation trace(f, s) is defined by

$$\text{trace}(f, s).t \Leftrightarrow (s = \copyright(i, t) \land f.s = \copyright(o, t) \land \forall \textbf{ str act } r: r \sqsubseteq t \Rightarrow \copyright(o, r) \sqsubseteq f.\copyright(i, r)).$$

A trace-oriented description of a distributed system defines a set of traces by a predicate

rel (str act) Q.

A specification of a function

fct (str i) str o f

is called a *partially correct design specification* for the trace-oriented requirement specification Q if

$\forall \textbf{ str act } t, \textbf{str i } s: \text{trace}(f, s).t \Rightarrow \exists \textbf{ str act } t': t \sqsubseteq t' \land Q.t'.$

f is called *totally correct* for the input stream s, if:

trace(f, s).t $\Rightarrow$ Q.t.

This way a satisfaction relation is obtained between a functional description and a trace description. For an example where we use such a relation see the appendix.

5. Programming Language-Oriented Descriptions of Concurrent Systems

In the following we relate a simple functional programming language for programming "nondeterministic" stream processing functions and communicating systems to design specifications.

A predicative specification is a design specification that comprises the description of a signature and a formula of predicate logic. In a pure predicative specification we use only equations and relational symbols applied to terms.

It is the purpose of this section to define a calculus that allows to translate a declarative functional program for programming "nondeterministic" stream processing functions and communicating systems into a predicative specification.

A family of declarations can be understood as a predicative specification: It represents the description of a signature and a number of properties for the elements of the signature. In the following we give rewriting rules that allow to rewrite a program given by a family of declarations into a pure predicative specification. We model nondeterminism by rewriting it to predicates that specify the corresponding class of functions.

5.1. A Programming Language

We use a programming language framework that includes applicative programs that comprise (recursive) declarations and two forms (erratic and angelic) of nondeterministic choice. We include streams and mutually recursive declarations of streams which represent networks of communicating systems (cf. [Broy 82]). The predicative language for the specification in particular includes predicates on functions.

The syntactic unit ‹exp› that stands for the expressions in the language is defined as follows:

‹exp› ::= ‹data› | ‹id› | **if** ‹exp› **then** ‹exp› **else** ‹exp› **fi** |
  ‹fct› ({ ‹exp› { , ‹exp› }* }) |
  [‹decl› ‹exp›] | ‹exp› [**or** | ∇] ‹exp›

Here ‹data› stands for the syntactic unit of data objects from some given computation structure. The operators **or** and ∇ denote nondeterministic choice operators. The operator **or** leads in the evaluation of an expression E1 **or** E2 to an arbitrary "erratic" choice of the evaluation of E1 or E2. The ambiguity operator ∇ leads in the evaluation of an expression E1 ∇ E2 to an "angelic" choice between the evaluation E1 or E2; but the choice of a diverging evaluation is avoided if the evaluation of the other expression does not diverge. The meaning of the remaining constructs is evident. Often we shall use mixfix notation for functions. The syntactic units ‹fct› and ‹decl› standing for functions and declarations resp. are given by:

‹fct› ::=   ‹id› | {(‹sort› ‹id› { , ‹sort› ‹id› }*) } ‹sort› : ‹exp›
‹decl› ::=   **let** ‹sort› ‹id› ⇐ ‹exp›, { ‹sort› ‹id› ⇐ ‹exp›, }* | **let** ‹id› ⇐ ‹fct›,

Now we have fixed the syntax. Of course we in addition assume a number of simple conditions of context correctness.

An expression of the syntactic unit ‹exp› is called *deterministic*, if it does not contain the choice operators **or** or ∇. It is called *simple*, if it does not contain (local) declarations.

We use predicate logic for representing the properties of elements of a declaration. As relational symbol we use in particular equality and special relational operators ← and ⊑ between expressions. A very strong context condition that we assume deals with the occurrence of the nondeterministic expressions. In predicates nondeterministic expressions must not occur on the left-handside or right-handside of an equation or of ⊑ and they must not occur on the left-handside of the operator ←.

A formula is called a *pure predicative specification*, if it does not contain the relational symbol "←" and if it contains only simple deterministic expressions.

5.2. Examples for Predicative Specifications

For illustrating the way how formulas can be used for specifying programs we give a few simple examples for programs and their predicative specification. The predicative specification of a declaration of an identifier for a data object

let nat x ⇐ a+b   is given by the predicate   **nat** x, x = a+b.

Here the value of x is declared in the considered declaration (and therefore can be seen as "output"), whereas the values of a and b can be chosen freely and therefore can be considered as "input". The declaration of a recursively defined stream

let str nat s ⇐ 1&s   is translated into the predicative specification   **str nat** s, s = 1&s.

With every recursively defined function f we associate a characteristic predicate. The declaration of a recursive function

let sum ⇐ (**str nat** s, **nat** n) **str nat**: n & sum(rt.s, ft.s+n)

is translated into the predicative specification:

fct (**str nat, nat**) **str nat** sum,   ∀ **str nat** s, **nat** n: sum(s, n) = n & sum(rt.s, ft.s+n).

The declaration of a stream defined by the call of a recursive function

let str nat y ⇐ [**let** sum ⇐ (**str nat** s, **nat** n) **str nat**: n & sum(rt.s, ft.s+n), sum(x1, x2)]

is translated into the predicative specification:

str nat y,

∃ **fct** (**str nat, nat**) **str nat** sum:
    ∀ **str nat** s, **nat** n: sum(s, n) = n & sum(rt.s, ft.s+n) ∧ y = sum(x1, x2).

Declarations in which the choice operator **or** occurs are translated into predicative specifications with disjunctions. The declaration

let str nat s ⇐ (1 **or** 2) & s

is translated into the predicative specification

str nat s, s = 1 & s ∨ s = 2 & s.

This translation of nondeterministic recursive stream declarations into predicative specifications might seem arbitrary. One might expect a predicative specification associated with the stream declaration above that specifies s to be any inifinite sequence of 1's or 2's. However, since we want to model a semantics of recursive stream declarations that corresponds to a firing rule operational semantics of data flow networks we have chosen the translation given above. In a firing rule semantics a declaration **let str** s x ⇐ E & S is evaluated by first evaluating E to say e and then proceding with the recursive declaration **let str** s x ⇐ e & S.

Recursive declarations of functions with "nondeterministic" expression are understood as declarative schemes that characterize a set of functions. They are translated into predicative specifications with second order predicates, i.e. predicates characterizing functions. For instance the recursive declaration of the function some

let some $\Leftarrow$ (**nat** n) **nat** : **if** n = 0 **then** 0 **else** some(n-1) **or** n **fi**

is translated to the predicative specification specifying a characteristic predicate some for the declared "nondeterministic function" some.

rel (**fct** (**nat**) **nat, nat**) some,

$\forall$ **fct** (**nat**) **nat** f, **nat** n: some(f, n) $\Leftrightarrow$
$\qquad$ (n = 0 $\Rightarrow$ f.n = 0) $\wedge$
$\qquad$ (n > 0 $\Rightarrow$ f.n = n $\vee$ $\exists$ **fct** (**nat**) **nat** f1: some(f1, n-1) $\wedge$ f.n = f1(n-1)) $\wedge$
$\qquad$ ($\neg \downarrow$n $\Rightarrow$ $\neg \downarrow$f.n)

which implies by induction on n the specification

$\forall$ **fct** (**nat**) **nat** f, **nat** n: some(f, n) $\Leftrightarrow$ (($\downarrow$n $\Rightarrow$ f.n $\leq$ n) $\wedge$ ($\downarrow$f.n $\Rightarrow$ $\downarrow$n)).

The recursive declaration of a function including nondeterminism is considered as a specification of a predicate which characterizes a class of functions. some is called the *characteristic predicate*. A declaration of a "nondeterministic" function corresponds to the declaration of a class of functions. For instance the declaration

let str **nat** y $\Leftarrow$
$\qquad$ [**let** some $\Leftarrow$ (**nat** n) **nat** : **if** n = 0 **then** 0 **else** some(n-1) **or** n **fi**, some.x & y]

is equivalent to the predicative specification

str **nat** y,

$\exists$ **fct** (**nat**) **nat** f: y = f.x & y $\wedge$
$\exists$ **rel** (**fct** (**nat**) **nat, nat**) some: some(f, x) $\wedge$
$\qquad$ $\forall$ **fct** (**nat**) **nat** f, **nat** n: some(f, n) $\Leftrightarrow$
$\qquad\qquad$ (n = 0 $\Rightarrow$ f.n = 0) $\wedge$
$\qquad\qquad$ (n > 0 $\Rightarrow$ f.n = n $\vee$ $\exists$ **fct** (**nat**) **nat** f1: some(f1, n-1) $\wedge$ f.n = f1(n-1)) $\wedge$
$\qquad\qquad$ ($\neg \downarrow$n $\Rightarrow$ $\neg \downarrow$f.n)

which is logically equivalent to (for x $\in$ $\mathbb{N}$, i.e. for $\downarrow$x):

$\exists$ **nat** n: y = n & y $\wedge$ n $\leq$ x.

For instance the recursive declaration of the function any can be translated into a system of stream equations:

let any $\Leftarrow$ (**nat** n) **nat** : any(n+1) ∇ n

is transformed into the predicative specification where any fulfills the specification

rel (**fct** (**nat**) **nat**, **nat**) any,

$\forall$ **fct** (**nat**) **nat** f, **nat** n: any(f, n) $\Leftrightarrow$
  ($\exists$ **fct** (**nat**) **nat** f1: any(f1, n+1) $\wedge$ f.n = f1(n+1) $\wedge$ $\downarrow$ f.n) $\vee$
  (f.n = n $\wedge$ $\downarrow$ f.n) $\vee$
  ($\neg \downarrow$n $\wedge$ $\exists$ **fct** (**nat**) **nat** f1: any(f1, n+1) $\wedge$ $\neg \downarrow$f1(n+1) $\wedge$ $\neg \downarrow$f.n))

A predicate any' that fulfils the specification above is given by

$\forall$ **fct** (**nat**) **nat** f, **nat** n: any'(f, n) $\equiv$ ($\downarrow$n $\wedge$ $\downarrow$f.n $\wedge$ n $\leq$ f.n) $\vee$ ($\neg \downarrow$n $\wedge$ $\neg \downarrow$f.n).

Of course, there are also other predicates that fulfil the equation for any.

A recursive declaration of a function including nondeterminism is considered as a declaration of a class of functions. If the declaration contains the ambiguity operator, for each application of the declared function the class of functions allowed in the application may even depend on the resp. argument values. In the example above

  any(f, n)

stands for the proposition: "the function f fulfills the "any-property" for the argument n".

Recursive declarations of objects with nondeterministic right-handsides can be simply translated into functional equations (fixpoint equations). In particular a network of communicating agents with m nodes f_i of the form:

$$\begin{array}{c} x_1 \ldots x_n \\ \hline f_i \\ \hline y_i \end{array}$$

can be translated into a system of stream equations:

let str s_1 y_1 $\Leftarrow$ [...],

... ,

let str s_i y_i $\Leftarrow$ [**let** f_i $\Leftarrow$ (...) **str** s_i : E_i, $f_i(x_1, ... , x_n)$],

... ,

let str s_m y_m $\Leftarrow$ [...] .

Here the $x_1, ..., x_n$ of course are taken from $\{y_1, ..., y_m\}$. This way arbitrary networks of communicating agents can be formed and expressed by systems of declarations.

5.3. Predicative Specifications of Declarations

A predicative specification is a formula consisting of a number of identifier declarations and logical formulas. We give predicative specifications only for declarations. In a predicative specification we understand a declaration as a particular notation for a formula and give rules for rewriting declarations into explicit formulas.

Let **let s x** $\Leftarrow$ E be a declaration, then the identifier x is called declared in the declaration and can be considered as output-identifier and all the free identifiers in E that are distinct to x are considered as input-identifiers. The declaration:

let s_1 x_1 $\Leftarrow$ $E_1, ... , s_n$ x_n $\Leftarrow$ E_n

is equivalent to

s_1 x_1 , ... , s_n x_n , $x_1 \leftarrow E_1 \wedge ... \wedge x_n \leftarrow E_n$.

For a nondeterministic expression E the function declaration

let $f \Leftarrow$ (s_1 x_1 , ... , s_n x_n) s: E

is equivalent to the introduction of a relation:

rel (**fct** (s_1 , ... , s_n) s, s_1, ... , s_n) f, $f \leftarrow$ (s_1 x_1 , ... , s_n x_n) s: E.

For a deterministic expression E the declaration

let $f \Leftarrow$ (s_1 x_1 , ... , s_n x_n) s: E is equivalent to:

fct $(s_1, \ldots, s_n)$ s f, $\quad$ f ← $(s_1\ x_1, \ldots, s_n\ x_n)$ s: E.

Now we give additional axioms for transforming the logical formulas in predicative specifications (let the boolean identifier z be a fresh identifier distinct to x and not free in E0, E1, E2):

$\quad$ x ← **if** E0 **then** E1 **else** E2 **fi** ≡
$\quad\quad$ ∃ **bool** z: z ← E0 ∧ (z = tt ⇒ x ← E1) ∧ (z = ff ⇒ x ← E2) ∧ (↓x ⇒ ↓z).

Let us assume that the identifier y does not occur freely in E and that x and y are distinct.

$\quad$ x ← g.E $\quad\quad\quad$ ≡ $\quad$ ∃ s y : y ← E ∧ x = g.y.

For function symbols g of sort **fct** (s)r and deterministic expressions E' we define the axiom:

$\quad$ g ← (s y) **r** : E' $\quad$ ≡ $\quad$ ∀ s y : g.y = E' ∧ ∀ **fct** (s y)**r** g': (∀ s y : g'.y = E') ⇒ g ⊑ g'.

For arbitrary expressions E (let y not be free in E and E') we obtain:

$\quad$ x ← ((s y) **r** : E')(E) $\quad$ ≡ $\quad$ ∃ s y : y ← E ∧ x ← E'.

For relational symbols f we use the axioms (let g and y not be free in f.E, x not free in E1 and E2)):

$\quad$ x ← f.E $\quad\quad\quad\quad\quad$ ≡ ∃ **fct** (s)r g, **r** y: y ← E ∧ x = g.y ∧ f(g, y),
$\quad$ x ← [**let** f ⇐ E', E] $\quad$ ≡ ∃ **rel** (**fct** (s)r , s) f : f ← E' ∧ x ← E,
$\quad$ x ← [**let** s y ⇐ E1, E2] ≡ ∃ s y: y ← E1 ∧ x ← E2,
$\quad$ E1 ← E2 $\quad\quad\quad\quad\quad$ ≡ ∀ s x: x ← E1 ⇒ x ← E2.

The rules above do not allow so far to get rid of the operator ← and of local declarations. In the next section we give rules for eliminating the nondeterministic operators **or** and ∇ and for deriving formulas for the specifying relations.

For avoiding all the subtle problems of equations between nondeterministic expressions we do not allow equations between expressions including the choice operators and therefore exclude such equations by syntactic context conditions. Now we give rules for eliminating the choice operators in predicative specifications.

For the choice operator **or** we assume a number of algebraic laws: the choice operator **or** is commutative, associative, and idempotent. It distributes over function application and **if-then-else-fi**. The rule for eliminating the choice operator **or** on the right-handside of the relational symbol $\leftarrow$ is straightforward (let E be a deterministic expression):

$$E \leftarrow (E1 \text{ or } E2) \equiv (E \leftarrow E1) \vee (E \leftarrow E2).$$

For the choice operator ∇ we also assume a number of algebraic laws: the choice operator ∇ is commutative, associative, and idempotent. But it does not distribute over function application and **if-then-else-fi**, in general. Let E again be a deterministic expression:

$$E \leftarrow (E1 \nabla E2) \equiv (\neg \downarrow E1 \wedge \neg \downarrow E2 \wedge \neg \downarrow E) \vee ((E \leftarrow E1 \vee E \leftarrow E2) \wedge \downarrow E).$$

Due to the structure of our language and our context conditions the lefthand side of a formula $E \leftarrow E1$ is always deterministic.

If both sides of a formula $E \leftarrow E1$ are deterministic, then we can replace the arrow by equality.

$$\frac{E, E1 \text{ deterministic}}{(E \leftarrow E1) \equiv (E = E1).}$$

The operator $\leftarrow$ can be axiomatized as follows: It is transitive:

$$E1 \leftarrow E2 \wedge E2 \leftarrow E3 \Rightarrow E1 \leftarrow E3$$

and monotonic (let f be an n-ary function symbol):

$$E_1 \leftarrow D_1 \wedge ... \wedge E_n \leftarrow D_n \Rightarrow f(E_1, ..., E_n) \leftarrow f(D_1, ..., D_n)$$

For arbitrary expressions E (let x not be free in E) we define

$$\downarrow E \equiv \forall x: x \leftarrow E \Rightarrow \downarrow x.$$

The special predicate $\downarrow$ follows the rules

$$\begin{aligned}\downarrow(E1 \text{ or } E2) &= \downarrow E1 \wedge \downarrow E2 \\ \downarrow(E1 \nabla E2) &= \downarrow E1 \vee \downarrow E2.\end{aligned}$$

What remains is to give a rule for recursive function declarations with nondeterministic bodies.

We consider a recursive equation for a function with a nondeterministic body rather as a predicate on functions:

g not free in E, f relational symbol
_____

f ⇐ (s x) r : E ⇒ ∀ **fct** (s) **r** g, s x: f(g, x) ⇔ g.x ⇐ E.

By this rule we basically give a fixpoint based ("equational") definition for the relational symbol f. However, following the concept of robust correctness we rather do not require that the fixpoint is least defined. Of course the predicate f is not uniquely specified by the derived equation. f is called the *characteristic predicate*.

For locally declared functions f we obtain for example for the declaration

let s' y ⇐ [**let** f ⇐ (s x)r: E, E']

the implied predicative specification

s' y,   ∃ **rel**(**fct** (s) **r**, s) f : y ⇐ E' ∧ ∀ **fct** (s) **r** g, s x: f(g, x) ⇒ g.x ⇐ E.

Thus actually the largest (weakest, most liberal) predicate is taken for f that fulfills the defining equation.

5.4. Examples

Let us consider a simple example: The function declaration of the merge function

let merge ⇐ (**str** s x, y) **str** s: ft.x & merge(rt.x, y) **or** ft.y & merge(x, rt.y)

implies by the definition above to the predicative specification

∀ **fct**(**str** s, **str** s) **str** s f, **str** s x, y: merge(f, x, y) ⇔
    ∃ **fct** (**str** s, **str** s) **str** s g, h:
        (merge(g, rt.x, y) ∧ f(x, y) = ft.x & g(rt.x, y) ∨
        (merge(h, x, rt.y) ∧ f(x, y) = ft.y & h(x, rt.y)).

The predicate merge formalizes the property of a function being a merge function.

Let us consider a slightly more complex example: The function declaration of the nonstrict merge function nsm:

let nsm $\Leftarrow$ (**str** s x, y) **str** s: ft.x & nsm(rt.x, y) ∇ ft.y & nsm(x, rt.y)

implies by the definition above to the predicative specification

$\forall$ f, x, y: nsm(f, x, y) $\Leftrightarrow$
  $\exists$ g, h : nsm(g, rt.x, y) $\wedge$ nsm(h, x, rt.y) $\wedge$
    f(x, y) $\leftarrow$ (ft.x & g(rt.x, y)) ∇ (ft.y & h(x, rt.y))

which is by the predicative specification for ∇ given above equivalent to

$\forall$ f, x, y: nsm(f, x, y) $\Leftrightarrow$
  $\exists$ g, h : nsm(g, rt.x, y) $\wedge$ nsm(h, x, rt.y) $\wedge$
    (($\neg \downarrow$(ft.x & g(rt.x, y)) $\wedge \neg \downarrow$(ft.y & h(x, rt.y)) $\wedge \neg \downarrow$f(x, y)) $\vee$
    (f(x, y) $\leftarrow$ ft.x & g(rt.x, y) $\wedge \downarrow$f(x, y)) $\vee$
    (f(x, y) $\leftarrow$ ft.y & h(x, rt.y) $\wedge \downarrow$f(x, y))).

According to our axioms for the basic functions on streams this is equivalent to:

$\forall$ f, x, y: nsm(f, x, y) $\Leftrightarrow$
  $\exists$ g, h : nsm(g, rt.x, y) $\wedge$ nsm(h, x, rt.y) $\wedge$
    (($\neg \downarrow$x $\wedge \neg \downarrow$y $\wedge \neg \downarrow$f(x, y)) $\vee$
    (f(x, y) = ft.x & g(rt.x, y) $\wedge \downarrow$x) $\vee$
    (f(x, y) = ft.y & h(x, rt.y) $\wedge \downarrow$y)).

Another well-known tricky example is the one used to show the so-called merge anomaly from [Brock, Ackermann 82]. Let us consider the family of declarations:

let y $\Leftarrow$ [**let** nsm $\Leftarrow$ (**str nat** s1, s2) **str nat**:
              ft(s1) & nsm(rt.s1, s2) ∇ ft.s2 & nsm(s1, rt.s2),   nsm(x, z)],
      z $\Leftarrow$ [**let** h $\Leftarrow$ (**str nat** x) **str nat** :
              if ft.x < 1   **then**   1 & h.rt.x
                          else   0 & h.rt.x **fi**,   h.y   ].

We want to demonstrate that from the predicative specification of this program we can prove:

x = 0 & ε $\Rightarrow$ ft.z = 1

The predicative specification of the declarations of z and y reads:

$$\exists\ g: nsm(g, x, z) \wedge y \leftarrow g(x, z) \wedge z \leftarrow h.y$$

where according to our definitions there exist predicates nsm and h which fulfil the equations for nsm and h where nsm is defined above and h statisfies the condition

$\forall\ x: h.x =$ **if** $ft.x < 1$ **then** $1\ \&\ h.rt.x$
                                         else $0\ \&\ h.rt.x$ **fi**.

This implies

$\exists\ g1, g2: nsm(g1, rt.x, z) \wedge nsm(g2, x, rt.z) \wedge$
        $(((\neg{\downarrow}x \wedge \neg{\downarrow}z \wedge \neg{\downarrow}y) \vee (y = ft.x\ \&\ g1(rt.x, z) \wedge {\downarrow}x) \vee (y = ft.z\ \&\ g2(x, rt.z) \wedge {\downarrow}z)) \wedge$
        $(ft.y < 1 \Rightarrow z = 1\ \&\ h.rt.y) \wedge$
        $((ft.y \geq 1 \Rightarrow z = 0\ \&\ h.rt.y) \wedge$
        $({\downarrow}z \Rightarrow {\downarrow}y)$.

By $x = 0\ \&\ \varepsilon$ we obtain then (from ${\downarrow}x = {\downarrow}(0\ \&\ \varepsilon) = {\downarrow}0 = tt$)

$\exists\ g1, g2: nsm(g1, rt.x, z) \wedge nsm(g2, x, rt.z) \wedge$
        $(y = 0\ \&\ g1(\varepsilon, z) \vee (y = ft.z\ \&\ g2(0\ \&\ \varepsilon, rt.z) \wedge {\downarrow}z))) \wedge$
        $(ft.y < 1 \Rightarrow z = 1\ \&\ h.rt.y) \wedge$
        $((ft.y \geq 1 \Rightarrow z = 0\ \&\ h.rt.y) \wedge$
        $({\downarrow}z \Rightarrow {\downarrow}y)$.

Now by this we can conclude:

$ft.y = 0 \vee (ft.y = ft.z \wedge {\downarrow}z)$.

Assume $ft.y = 0$ does not hold; then we may consider two cases

(1) $ft.y \geq 1 \wedge {\downarrow}ft.y$,
(2) $\neg {\downarrow}y$.

The case (2) immediately gives a contradiction. From (1) we can conclude $ft.z = 0$, but then our assumption allows us to conclude $ft.y = ft.z$ which gives $ft.y = 0$, which is in contradiction to our assumption (1). Therefore $ft.y = 0$ and thus $ft.z = 1$.

This example demonstrates in particular that the well-known merge anomaly, which consists of an inconsistency between the straightforward operational semantics and the straightforward denotational semantics, does not lead to problems in our calculus. We can prove exactly the wanted property for our program in our calculus. However, for examples that involve least fixpoint properties of the recursive definitions our calculus is not powerful enough. An example is given in the appendix.

Our formalism allows even the specification of functions like nonstrict fair merge nfm by a formula:

$\forall$ **fct (str s, str s) str s** g, **str s** x, **str s** y: nfm(g, x, y) $\Leftrightarrow$
    $\exists$ **str nat** oracle:
    oracle $\leftarrow$ gen() $\wedge$ fork(g(x, y), oracle, 1) = x $\wedge$ fork(g(x, y), oracle, 2) = y

where gen and fork are given by

let gen $\Leftarrow$ (): 1&gen() **or** 2&gen(),
let fork $\Leftarrow$ (**str s** s, **str nat** oracle, **nat** n) **str** s:
    if ft.oracle = n   **then** ft.s & fork(rt.s, rt.oracle, n)
                 else fork(rt.s, rt.oracle, n)   **fi**.

However, we cannot give a recursive function declaration in our programming language for nfm equivalent to the predicative specification nfm. This does not mean that we may not use nfm as a primitive function in programs.

By the predicative specification calculus the rather complicated treatment of recursive declarations of nondeterministic programs by powerdomains can be completely avoided. The semantic structure of our formalism can be represented by the diagram:

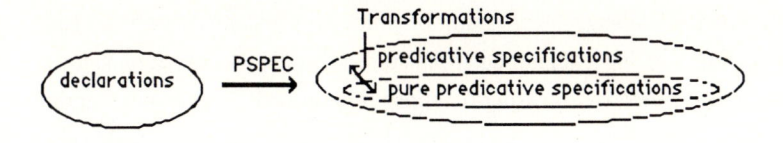

```
                        Transformations
                        ↓
                      ┌─ predicative specifications ─┐
  ( declarations )  PSPEC  (                              )
                      └─ pure predicative specifications ─┘
                    ⟶
```

which visualizes the following theorem.

Theorem: By the rules above every family of declarations can be translated into a pure predicative specification.
Proof: See [Broy 87b].

By the predicative specification also a semantic definition for our programming language is induced.

In the following we define the satisfaction relation for programs (declarations) and specifications w.r.t. given specifications in terms of semantic models.

We say that *a specification (i.e. a formula) S1 satisfies (implements) a specification S0* and write

S1 **sat** S0 ≡ S1 ⇒ S0 .

For a programming language, similar to the one we are dealing with in this paper, a denotational and operational semantics is defined in [Broy 82]. We expect that our calculus of predicative specifications is sound w.r.t. this semantics, but not complete, since we do not restrict the definitions to least fixpoints .

However, we think that it is often useful to work with a simple, but incomplete method that is sufficient for a large number of applications.

The translation of programs into formulas of predicate calculus provides a basis for program specification, program verification and program development by transformation. Applicative programs are at least as well-suited for this idea as procedural (assignment-oriented) programs are.

The inclusion of nondeterministic programs is possible, too, however it leads to more complicated predicates and especially leads to the consideration of predicates on functions.

Using predicate logic directly for the semantic representations of programs has significant advantages. All the techniques and foundations of predicate logic are immediately applicable. However, it is not clear what choice of a logic is the best one. We have chosen a total logic based on equations, the approximation ordering and definedness. Other candidates considered by researchers are monotonic partial logics with fixpoint operators on predicates. Here a number of experiments seems necessary to provide some evidence which of these choices is optimal.

Stream processing functions can be directly understood as representing abstract programs. We have given a small programming language the programs of which semantically describe systems of stream processing functions. On this level nondeterminism is naturally incorporated, since in the design specifications a set of stream processing functions is described. A recursive function declaration of a stream processing function with a nondeterministic right-hand side is understood as the constructive specification of a set of stream processing functions, too.

For a further refinement of the abstract program we might envisage a number of alternative directions. One possibility is to make the specification more robust meaning to add a number of additional messages such as error messages or to add a number of conditions such that wrong input to the system may not lead to a collaps of the system but rather to a behavior where error recovery is possible. The other possibility is to structure a system in a more efficient way, for instance to go from a given stream processsing function to a system of communicating agents. This means to introduce a number of recursive stream declarations. All the techniques from fixpoint theory then can be used to prove properties about such a system. All the techniques from transformational programming can be used to obtain from a given declaration of a function a system of declarations of streams.

6. Conclusion

A very general framework was outlined in which communicating systems can be specified, modules of communicating programs can be designed and developed into efficient versions. All the steps used can be verified by formal techniques. Moreover the design can be supported by rapid prototyping tools as well as the deduction and verification process can be supported by inference based support systems. The described framework leads to a formal discipline of the construction of distributed programs.

It is remarkable that we use a formal framework that, in priniciple, was not created in particular for the modelling of distributed systems. This gives a hint that the construction of programs for distributed systems can be handled in a general algebraic/axiomatic calculus.

Acknowledgement: It is a pleasure to acknowledge stimulating discussions with numerous people including Thomas Streicher, Frank Dederichs, Rainer Weber, Alfons Geser and many others who have influenced the described approach.

Appendix A: Algebraic Specification of the Type Process

In the following we give an algebraic specification of the sort **pcs s**:

type PROCESS = for given sort s

    sort event,
    sort s,

    fct pcs s $p_\emptyset$,
    fct (pcs s, s) pcs s addact,
    fct (pcs s, event e, event e': ¬causal(p, e', e)) **pcs s** addcause,

    fct (pcs s) event new,

    rel (event, pcs s) in,
    fct (pcs s p, **event** e: e ∈ p) **s** α,
    rel (pcs s p, **event** e, **event** e': e ∈ p ∧ e' ∈ p) causal.

We write also in mixfix notation:

$e \in p$ for $in(e, p)$
$e1 \leq_p e2$ for $causal(p, e1, e2)$
$\alpha_p(e)$ for $\alpha(p, e)$

The causality relation $\leq_p$ is a partial order on those events that are in p:

$e \in p \Rightarrow e \leq_p e$,
$e1 \leq_p e2 \wedge e2 \leq_p e1 \Rightarrow e1 = e2$,
$e1 \leq_p e2 \wedge e2 \leq_p e3 \Rightarrow e1 \leq_p e3$.

$e \in p_\emptyset = false$.

The function addcause is defined by the axioms:

$\neg(e2 \leq_p e1) \wedge e1 \in p \wedge e2 \in p \Rightarrow e \in addcause(p, e1, e2) \equiv e \in p$,
$\neg(e2 \leq_p e1) \wedge e1 \in p \wedge e2 \in p \Rightarrow \alpha_{addcause(p, e1, e2)}(e) \equiv \alpha_p(e)$,
$\neg(e2 \leq_p e1) \wedge e1 \in p \wedge e2 \in p \Rightarrow e \leq_{addcause(p, e1, e2)} e' \equiv$
$\qquad\qquad\qquad\qquad\qquad\qquad\qquad\qquad (e \leq_p e' \vee (e \leq_p e1 \wedge e2 \leq_p e'))$.

The function addact is characterized by the axioms:

$\neg(new(p) \in p)$,
$e \in addact(p, a) \equiv (e = new(p) \vee e \in p)$,
$e \neq new(p) \Rightarrow \alpha_{addact(p, a)}(e) = \alpha_p(e)$,
$\alpha_{addact(p, a)}(new(p)) = a$,
$e1 \neq new(p) \wedge e2 \neq new(p) \Rightarrow e1 \leq_{addact(p, a)} e2 \equiv e1 \leq_p e2$,
$new(p) \leq_{addact(p, a)} e \equiv (e = new(p))$,
$e \leq_{addact(p, a)} new(p) \equiv (e = new(p))$

endoftype

This data type specification gives functions like new, addact, addcause that are not used in the process specification, but rather for the description of the data type process.

Appendix B: Examples

In this appendix we gather a number of simple examples for the specification of systems.

Example: Message switching system

Let us specify an unreliable message switching system that works according to a number of rules as an example.

We assume the sorts

sort message, act,

and the functions

fct (message) act sm, rm, sa, ra,

which stand for send or receive message or for send or receive an acknowledgement. Verbally the rules of the message passing facility may be defined as follows:

(1) Every message that is received has been sent before.
(2) Every message that is received is acknowledged once after it is received.
(3) Every acknowledgement that is received was sent before.
(4) Every nonacknowledged message that was sent is resent.

Clearly (1) and (3) are safety conditions, while (2) and (4) are liveness conditions.

A process p has these properties, if it fulfills the following formulas for all messages m:

(1) $\forall\ p':\ p' \sqsubseteq p \Rightarrow \#\mathbb{O}(sm.m,\ p') \geq \#\mathbb{O}(rm.m,\ p')$,
(2) $\#\mathbb{O}(rm.m,\ p) = \#\mathbb{O}(sa.m,\ p) \land \forall\ p':\ p' \sqsubseteq p \Rightarrow \#\mathbb{O}(rm.m,\ p') \geq \#\mathbb{O}(sa.m,\ p')$,
(3) $\forall\ p':\ p' \sqsubseteq p \Rightarrow \#\mathbb{O}(sa.m,\ p') \geq \#\mathbb{O}(ra.m,\ p')$,
(4) $\forall e:\ e \in p \land \alpha_p(e) = sm.m \Rightarrow \exists\ e':\ e <_p e' \land (\alpha_p(e') = sm.m \lor \alpha_p(e') = ra.m)$.

Note that our formulas are precise in contrast to the verbal versions of the rule. By the verbal version of rule (1) it is not clear whether a message sent once may be received more than once.

We may add the somewhat artificial condition

(5) If a message is sent infinitely often it is received infinitely often.

It is formally represented by

(5) $\#\mathbb{O}(sm.m,\ p) = \infty \Rightarrow \#\mathbb{O}(rm.m,\ p) = \infty$.

A similar condition can be added for acknowledgements:

$$\#©(sa.m, p) = \infty \Rightarrow \#©(ra.m, p) = \infty.$$

The requirements above can be expressed also by the shorthands we have introduced:

(1) sm.m $\gg_p$ rm.m,
(2) rm.m $-\!\!\gg_p$ sa.m,
(3) sa.m $\gg_p$ ra.m,
(4) (p', sm.m, q) **de** p $\Rightarrow$ sm.m $\in$ q $\vee$ ra.m $\in$ q.

The condition (4) can easily be expressed for traces p by a temporal formula

$$\Box \, p: ft.p = sm.m \Rightarrow {}^\circ p: sm.m \in p \vee ra.m \in p$$

From (1)-(5') we may prove that for every message sent an acknowledgement is received. This is expressed by

sm.m $\gg_p$ ra.m.

However, we rather decompose the specification into a number of stream processing functions. For deriving a functional description, which we call a design specification, we introduce a further action √ that represents a tick of the clock:

fct act √.

We choose to decompose the system into the three functions

fct (str act) str act receive, transmit,
fct (str message, str act) str act send,

which are defined by the following specifications: The specification of the function receive is rather simple:

receive(rm.m & s) = sa.m & receive.s,
receive(√ & s) = √ & receive.s

For specifying the function transmit we give a predicate TRANSMIT defined by the weakest predicate fulfilling the equation:

TRANSMIT(f) ≡
$\quad$ ∀ s, m: ∃ f': TRANSMIT(f') ∧ f(√&s) = √ & f'.s ∧
$\qquad\qquad\qquad$ (f(sm.m & s) = rm.m & f'.s ∨ f(sm.m & s) = √ & f'.s).

The function send is specified by:

send(x, √ & s) = sm.ft.x & send(x, s),
send(m & x, sa.m & s) = sm.ft.x & send(x, s),
m ≠ m' ⇒ send(m & x, sa.m' & s) = sm.m & send(m & x, s).

The fact (5) can be expressed by an additional restriction for the predicate specifying the function transmit

TRANSMIT'(f) = TRANSMIT(f) ∧ ∀ s: #©({act a: a ≠ √}, s) = ∞ ⇒
$\qquad\qquad\qquad\qquad\qquad\qquad\qquad\qquad$ #©({act a: a ≠ √}, f.s) = ∞.

Now consider that s is a fixpoint of the equation

s = sm.ft.x & send(x, ta.receive.tm.s)

such that (let TRANSMIT" be defined in analogy to TRANSMIT') for tm and ta we have:

TRANSMIT'(tm) ∧ TRANSMIT"(ta)

We use the abbreviations

$\quad$ t = tm.s,
$\quad$ r = receive.t,
$\quad$ v = ta.r,

Let us consider the case x = m & x', i.e.

s = sm.m & send(m & x', v)

according to the specification of send, TRANSMIT', receive and TRANSMIT" we have

$v = \sqrt{} \ \& \ v \vee \#\copyright(ra.m, v) > 0$.

If $v = \sqrt{} \ \& \ v$, then $s = sm.m \ \& \ s$, i.e. $\#\copyright(sm.m, s) = \infty$. Thus $\#\copyright(rm.m, tm.s) = \infty$ and $\#\copyright(sa.m, r) = \infty$. Thus $\#\copyright(ra.m, ta.r) = \infty$ which is a contradiction!

We obtain with the abbreviations

$s' = sm.ft.x' \ \& \ send(x', v')$,
$t' = tm'(s')$,
$r' = receive(t')$,
$v' = ta'(r')$

the formulas

$s = (sm.m^k)\hat{\ }s'$,
$t = t_1 \ \& \ ... \ t_k \ \& \ t'$ where for all $i \leq k$: $t_i = \sqrt{}$ or $t_i = rm.m$,
$r = r_1 \ \& \ ... \ r_k \ \& \ r'$ where for all $i \leq k$: $r_i = \sqrt{}$ or $r_i = sa.m$,
$v = v_1 \ \& \ ... \ v_k \ \& \ v'$ where for all $i \leq k$: $v_i = \sqrt{}$ or $v_i = ra.m$.

The streams s', t', r', v' fulfil the same equation as s, t, r, v and we can apply induction which proves the correctness of the transmission.

Now we may study the causality between the elements in the streams s, t, r, v. We obtain by the definition about the causalities in fixpoints the requirements (1), (2), (3), (4). □

Example: Proof of deadlock

A *deadlock* is obtained for two actions a and b in a process p if we require (assume $a \neq b$) mutual causality, which is equivalent to mutual waiting:

(*) $a \gg_p b \wedge b \gg_p a$

Then a and b cannot occur in p. This can be proved as follows: From (*) we obtain for all $p' \sqsubseteq p$:

$\#\copyright(a, p') \leq \#\copyright(b, p') \leq \#\copyright(a, p')$

which gives

$\forall p': p' \sqsubseteq p \Rightarrow \#\copyright(a, p') = \#\copyright(b, p')$.

For all $i \in \mathbb{N}$ with $i \leq \#p$ there is a sequence of processes p_i with $p_i \sqsubseteq p_{i+1} \sqsubseteq p$ and $\#p_i = i$. By induction we obtain from

$$\#\copyright(a, p_{i+1}) + \#\copyright(b, p_{i+1}) = \#\copyright(\{a,b\}, p_{i+1}) \leq \#\copyright(\{a,b\}, p_i) + 1$$

for all $i \leq \#p$: $\#\copyright(a, p_i) = 0$. Therefore $\#\copyright(a, p) = 0$. The same arguments hold for b.

$\square$

Example: Proof of Sequentialisation

We prove for actions $a \neq b$: $a \therefore_p b$ implies that a and b are not concurrent in p. This is equivalent to:

$$(\forall p': p' \sqsubseteq p \Rightarrow 0 \leq \#\copyright(a, p') - \#\copyright(b, p') \leq 1) \Rightarrow$$
$$\forall e, e': \alpha_p(e) = a \wedge \alpha_p(e') = b \Rightarrow (e \leq_p e' \vee e' \leq_p e).$$

Assume there exist events e, e' in p such that $\alpha_p(e) = a$ and $\alpha_p(e') = b$ and $\neg(e \leq_p e' \vee e' \leq_p e)$. Consider the three processes

$p0 = p|_{\{e'': e'' < e \vee e'' < e'\}}$

$p1 = p|_{\{e'': e'' \leq e \vee e'' < e'\}}$

$p2 = p|_{\{e'': e'' < e \vee e'' \leq e'\}}$

We have $p0 \sqsubseteq p1 \sqsubseteq p$ and $p0 \sqsubseteq p2 \sqsubseteq p$. Then

$$\#\copyright(a, p0) - \#\copyright(b, p0) = \#\copyright(a, p1) - 1 - \#\copyright(b, p1) = \#\copyright(a, p1) - \#\copyright(b, p1) - 1$$
$$\#\copyright(a, p0) - \#\copyright(b, p0) = \#\copyright(a, p2) - (\#\copyright(b, p2) - 1) = \#\copyright(a, p2) - \#\copyright(b, p2) + 1$$

According to our condition we have:

$$\#\copyright(a, p0) - \#\copyright(b, p0) = 1 \vee \#\copyright(a, p0) - \#\copyright(b, p0) = 0.$$

From this we obtain

$$\#\copyright(a, p1) - \#\copyright(b, p1) - 1 = 1 \vee \#\copyright(a, p2) - \#\copyright(b, p2) + 1 = 0.$$

This leads to a violation of our condition for either p1 or p2, since it is equivalent to

$$\#\copyright(a, p1) - \#\copyright(b, p1) = 2 \vee \#\copyright(a, p2) - \#\copyright(b, p2) = -1.$$

From this we conclude that all the events labelled by a or b form a linear order.

□

Example: Semaphores

A semaphor can be modelled as follows: We assume the sorts:

sort semaphor, action,

with the functions

fct (semaphor) action p, v.

A process q fulfills the semaphor condition w.r.t. the semaphor s (initialized by 1) if:

(1) $\forall q': q' \sqsubseteq q \Rightarrow \#\mathbb{O}(v(s), q') + 1 \geq \#\mathbb{O}(p(s), q')$

The actions a and b are called protected by semaphor s in the process q iff

(2) $\{p(s)\} \gg_q \{a, b\}$

and

(3) $\{a, b\} \gg_q \{v(s)\}$.

We prove that a and b are mutually exclusive in p. This is done by proving for all $q' \sqsubseteq q$:

(4) $0 \leq \#\mathbb{O}(p(s), q') - \#\mathbb{O}(\{a, b\}, q') \leq 1$

We obtain the condition (4) by:

$$\#\mathbb{O}(p(s), q') \overset{(1)}{\leq} \#\mathbb{O}(v(s), q')+1 \overset{(3)}{\leq} \#\mathbb{O}(\{a, b\}, q')+1 \overset{(2)}{\leq} \#\mathbb{O}(p(s), q')+1$$

□

Example: Place/Transition nets

A place/transition net is a net where the places are labelled by natural numbers and the transitions correspond to actions. Every place v with label $n \in \mathbb{N}$ and the set I_v of input transitions and the set O_v of output transitions can be translated into the formula for its behaviors represented by processes p:

$$\forall\ p': p' \sqsubseteq p \Rightarrow \#\copyright(I_v, p') + n \geq \#\copyright(O_v, p').$$

The set of all (possibly incomplete) behaviors of a net is described by the conjunction of all these formulas. The set of complete behaviors are the maximal elements in this set.

□

References

[Bernstein 66]
A. J. Bernstein: Analysis of programs for parallel processing. IEEE Trans. Electron. Comput. **15** (5) (1966) 757-763.

[Brauer 80]
W. Brauer (ed.): Net theory and applications. Lecture Notes in Computer Science **84**, Berlin-Heidelberg-New York-Tokyo: Springer 1980

[Brinch Hansen 78]
P. Brinch Hansen: Distributed processes: A concurrent programming concept, Comm. ACM **21** (11) (1978) 934-941.

[Brock, Ackermann 81]
J. D. Brock, W. B. Ackermann: Scenarios: A Model of Nondeterminate Computation. In: J. Diaz, I. Ramos(eds): Lecture Notes in Computer Science 107, Springer 1981, 252-259

[Broy 82]
M. Broy: A theory for nondeterminism, parallelism, communication and concurrency. Habilitation, Fakultät für Mathematik und Informatik der Technischen Universität München, 1982, Revised version in Theoretical Computer Science 45 (1986) 1-61

[Broy 83]
M. Broy: Applicative real time programming. Information Processing 83, IFIP World Congress, Paris 1983, North Holland Publ. Company 1983, 259-264

[Broy 84a]
M. Broy: Denotational semantics of concurrent programs with shared memory. In: M. Fontet, K. Mehlhorn (eds.): STACS 84. Lecture Notes in Computer Science 182, Berlin-Heidelberg-New York-Tokyo: Springer 1984, 163-173

[Broy 84b]
M. Broy: Semantics of communicating processes. Information & Control $\underline{61}$:3 (1984), 202-246

[Broy 85a]
M. Broy: Extensional behaviour of concurrent, nondeterministic, communicating systems. In: M. Broy (ed.): Control flow and data flow: Concepts of Distributed Programming, Springer NATO ASI Series.

[Broy 85b]
M. Broy: Specification and top down design and distributed systems (invited talk). In: H. Ehrig et al. (eds.): Formal Methods and Software Development. Lecture Notes in Computer Science 186, Springer 1985, 4-28, Revised version in JCSS 34:2/3, 1987, 236-264

[Broy 86]
M. Broy: On modularity in programming. In H. Zemanek (ed.): A quarter century of IFIP, North Holland Publ. 1986, 347-362.

[Broy 87a]
M. Broy: Semantics of finite or infinite networks of communicating agents. Distributed Computing 2 (1987), 13-31

[Broy 87b]
M. Broy: Predicative specification for functional programs describing communicating networks. Information Processing Letters 25 (1987) 93-101

[Broy 87c]
M. Broy: Views of Queues. Technische Berichte der Fakultät für Mathematik und Informatik, Universität Passau, 1987, MIP-8704, to appear in Science of Computer Programming

[Broy 87d]
M. Broy: Specification of a railway system. Technische Berichte der Fakultät für Mathematik und Informatik, Universität Passau, 1987, MIP-8715

[Broy 87e]
M. Broy: Algebraic and functional specification of a serializable database interface. Technische Berichte der Fakultät für Mathematik und Informatik, Universität Passau, 1987, MIP-8718

[Degano et al. 85]
P. Degano, R. De Niccola, U. Montanari: Partial ordering derivations for CCS. FCT 85, Lecture Notes in Computer Science **199**, Berlin-Heidelberg-New York-Tokyo: Springer 1985, 520-533

[Degano, Montanari 85]
P. Degano, U. Montanari: Distributed systems, partial ordering of events, and event structures. In: M. Broy; Control Flow and Data Flow: Concepts of Distributed Programming. NATO ASI Series, Series F: Computer and System Sciences, Vol. 14, Berlin-Heidelberg-New York-Tokyo: Springer 1985, 7-106

[Dijkstra 68]
E.W. Dijkstra: Co-operating sequential processes. In: F.Genuys, Ed., Programming Languages. Academic Press, New York, 1968, 43-112.

[Dybjer 85]
P. Dybjer: Reasoning about Streams in Intuitionistic Logic. Unpublished manuscript

[Hehner 84]
E.C.R. Hehner: Predicative Specification Part I+II. CACM 27:2 (1984) 134-151

[Hennessy, Plotkin 79]
M.C.B. Hennessy, G.D. Plotkin: Full abstraction for simple parallel programs. 8th Mathematical Foundations of Computer Science, Olomouc, 1979, Lecture Notes in Computer Science

[Hennessy, Milner 80]
M.C.B. Hennessy, R. Milner: On observing nondeterminism and concurrency. In: J. de Bakker, Jn van Leeuwen: International Colloquium on Automata, Languages and Programming 80, Lecture Notes in Computer Science 85, Berlin-Heidelberg-New York: Springer 1980, 299-309.

[Hennessy, Plotkin 80]
M. Hennessy, G. Plotkin: A term model for CCS. 9th Mathematical Foundations of Computer Science (1980), Lecture Notes in Computer Science 88, Berlin-Heidelberg-New York: Springer 1980, 261-274.

[Hoare 72]
C.A.R. Hoare: Towards a theory of parallel programming, in: C.A.R. Hoare and R.H. Perott, Eds., Operating Systems Techniques. Academic Press, New York, 1972, 61-71.

[Hoare 74]
C.A.R. Hoare: Monitors: An operating systems structuring concept, Comm. ACM **17**(10) (1974) 549-557.

[Hoare 78]
C.A.R. Hoare: Communicating sequential processes, Comm. ACM **21** (8) (1978) 666-667.

[Hoare et al. 81]
C.A.R: Hoare, S.D. Brookes and A.W. Roscoe: A theory of communicating sequential processes. Oxford University Computing Laboratory, Programming Research Group, Technical Monograph PRG-21, Oxford (1981). Also in: J. ACM 31 (1984) 560-599

[Hoare 85]
C.A.R. Hoare: Communicating Sequential Processes. Prentice Hall 1985

[Kahn, MacQueen 77]
G. Kahn and D. MacQueen, Coroutines and networks of processes, Proc. IFIP Congress 1977,

[Masurkiewicz 85]
A. Masurkiewicz: Traces, histories, graphs: instances of a process monoid. In: M.P. Chytil, V. Koubek (eds.): MFCS 1984, Lecture Notes in Computer Science **92**, Berlin-Heidelberg-New York-Tokyo: Springer 1985, 115-133

[MacQueen 79]
D.B. MacQueen, Models for distributed computing, IRIA RR No. 351 (1979)

[Milner 80]
R. Milner: A Calculus for Communicating Systems, Lecture Notes in Computer Science **92**, Berlin-Heidelberg-New York-Tokyo: Springer 1980

[Milner 80b]
R. Milner: On relating synchrony and asynchrony. University of Edinburgh, Department of Computer Science, Internal Report CSR-75-80, December 1980

[Nielsen et al. 81]
M. Nielsen, G. Plotkin, G. Winskel: Petri nets, event structures, and domains. Part 1. Theoretical Computer Science 13, 1981, 85-108

[Olderog, Hoare 82]
E.-R. Olderog, C.A.R. Hoare: Specification-oriented semantics for communicating processes. In: Diaz: International Colloquium on Automata, Languages and Programming 83, Lecture Notes in Computer Sciences, Berlin-Heidelberg-New York: Springer 1983

[Park 80]
D. Park: On the Semantics of Fair Parallelism. In: D. Björner (ed.): Abstract Software Specification. Lecture Notes in Computer Science 86, Berlin-Heidelberg-New York: Springer 1980, 504-526

[Rozenberg 85]
G. Rozenberg: Advances in Petri-nets. Lecture Notes in Computer Science 188, Berlin-Heidelberg-New York-Tokyo: Springer 1985

[Tesler, Enea 68]
L.G. Tesler and H.J. Enea: A language design for concurrent processes, Spring Joint Computer Conference (1968) 403-408.

[Winkowski 80]
J. Winkowski: Behaviors of concurrent systems. Theoretical Computer Science **11**, 1980, 39-60.

Butler Lampson took up van der Snepscheut's ideas. However, rather than viewing the parallel hats for the rabbit parts as components of a systolic array, he used them as caches for the main hat, in which, using ingredients from all other talks, he concocts a really opaque rabbit stew:

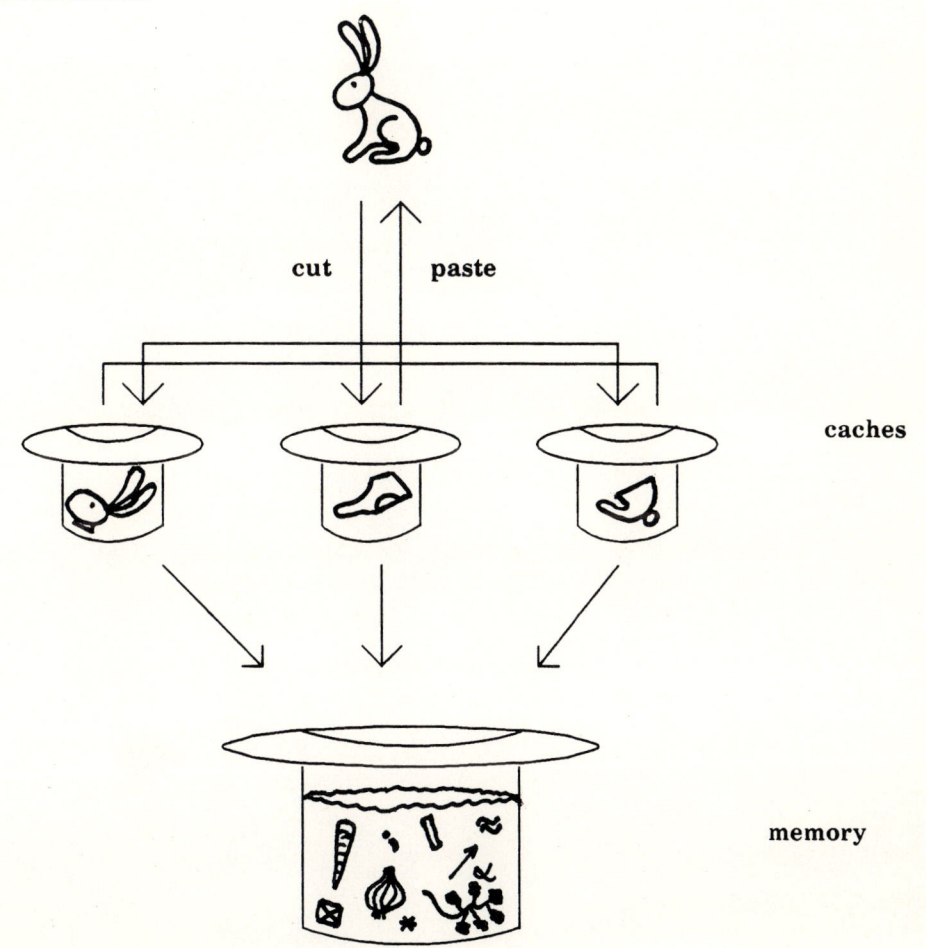

cut **paste**

caches

memory

Specifying Distributed Systems

Butler W. Lampson
Cambridge Research Laboratory
Digital Equipment Corporation
One Kendall Square
Cambridge, MA 02139

October 1988

These notes describe a method for specifying concurrent and distributed systems, and illustrate it with a number of examples, mostly of storage systems. The specification method is due to Lamport (1983, 1988), and the notation is an extension due to Nelson (1987) of Dijkstra's (1976) guarded commands.

We begin by defining states and actions. Then we present the guarded command notation for composing actions, give an example, and define its semantics in several ways. Next we explain what we mean by a specification, and what it means for an implementation to satisfy a specification. A simple example illustrates these ideas.

The rest of the notes apply these ideas to specifications and implementations for a number of interesting concurrent systems:

Ordinary memory, with two implementations using caches;

Write buffered memory, which has a considerably weaker specification chosen to facilitate concurrent implementations;

Transactional memory, which has a weaker specification of a different kind chosen to facilitate fault-tolerant implementations;

Distributed memory, which has a yet weaker specification than buffered memory chosen to facilitate highly available implementations. We give a brief account of how to use this memory with a tree-structured address space in a highly available naming service.

Thread synchronization primitives.

States and actions

We describe a system as a state space, an initial point in the space, and a set of atomic actions which take a state into an *outcome*, either another state or the looping outcome, which we denote $\perp$. The state space is the cartesian product of subspaces called the *variables* or *state functions*, depending on whether we are thinking about a program or a specification. Some of the variables and actions are part of the system's *interface*.

Each action may be more or less arbitrarily classified as part of a *process*. The behavior of the system is determined by the rule that from state s the next state can be s' if there is any action that takes s to s'. Thus the computation is an arbitrary interleaving of actions from different processes.

Sometimes it is convenient to recognize the *program counter* of a process as part of the state. We will use the state functions:

$at(\alpha)$ true when the PC is at the start of operation α

$in(\alpha)$ true when the PC is at the start of any action in the operation α

$after(\alpha)$ true when the PC is immediately after some action in the operation α, but not $in(\alpha)$.

When the actions correspond to the statements of a program, these state components are essential, since the ways in which they can change reflect the flow of control between statements. The soda machine example below may help to clarify this point.

An atomic action can be viewed in several equivalent ways.

- A *transition* of the system from one state to another; any execution sequence can be described by an interleaving of these transitions.

- A *relation between states and outcomes*, i.e., a set of pairs: state, outcome. We usually define the relation by
       A $so = P(s, o)$
  If A contains (s, o) and (s, o'), $o \neq o'$, A is *non-deterministic*. If there is an s for which A contains no (s, o), A is *partial*.

- A *relation on predicates*, written $\{P\}$ A $\{Q\}$
  If A $s\ s'$ then $P(s) \Rightarrow Q(s')$

- A pair of *predicate transformers*: wp and wlp, such that
  $wp(A, R) = wp(A, \text{true}) \wedge wlp(A, R)$
  $wlp(A, ?)$ distributes over any conjunction
  $wp(A, ?)$ distributes over any non-empty conjunction

The connection between A as a relation and A as a predicate transformer is
     $wp(A, R)\ s$ = every outcome of A from s satisfies R
     $wlp(A, R)\ s$ = every proper outcome of A from s satisfies R
We abbreviate this with the single line
     $w(l)p(A, R)\ s$ = every (proper) outcome of A from s satisfies R
Of course, the looping outcome doesn't satisfy any predicate.

Define the *guard* of A by

$\mathcal{G}(A) = \neg\, wp(A, \text{false})$ or $\mathcal{G}(A)\, s = (\exists\, o\colon A\, so)$

$\mathcal{G}(A)$ is true in a state if A relates it to some outcome (which might be $\bot$). If A is total, $\mathcal{G}(A) =$ true.

We build up actions out of a few primitives, as well as an arbitrarily rich set of operators and datatypes which we won't describe in detail. The primitives are

;	sequential composition
→	guard
□	or
⊠	else
|	variable introduction
if ... fi	
do ... od	

These are defined below in several equivalent ways: operationally, as relations between states, and as predicate transformers. We omit the relational and predicate-transformer definitions of **do**. For details see Dijkstra (1976) or Nelson (1987); the latter shows how to define **do** in terms of the other operators and recursion.

The precedence of operators is the same as their order in the list above; i.e., ";" binds most tightly and "|" least tightly.

Actions: operational definition (what the machine does)

skip	do nothing
loop	loop indefinitely
fail	don't get here
(P→ A)	activate A from a state where P is true
(A □ B)	activate A or B
(A ⊠ B)	activate A, else B if A has no outcome
(A ; B)	activate A, then B
(**if** A **fi**)	activate A until it succeeds
(**do** A **od**)	activate A until it fails

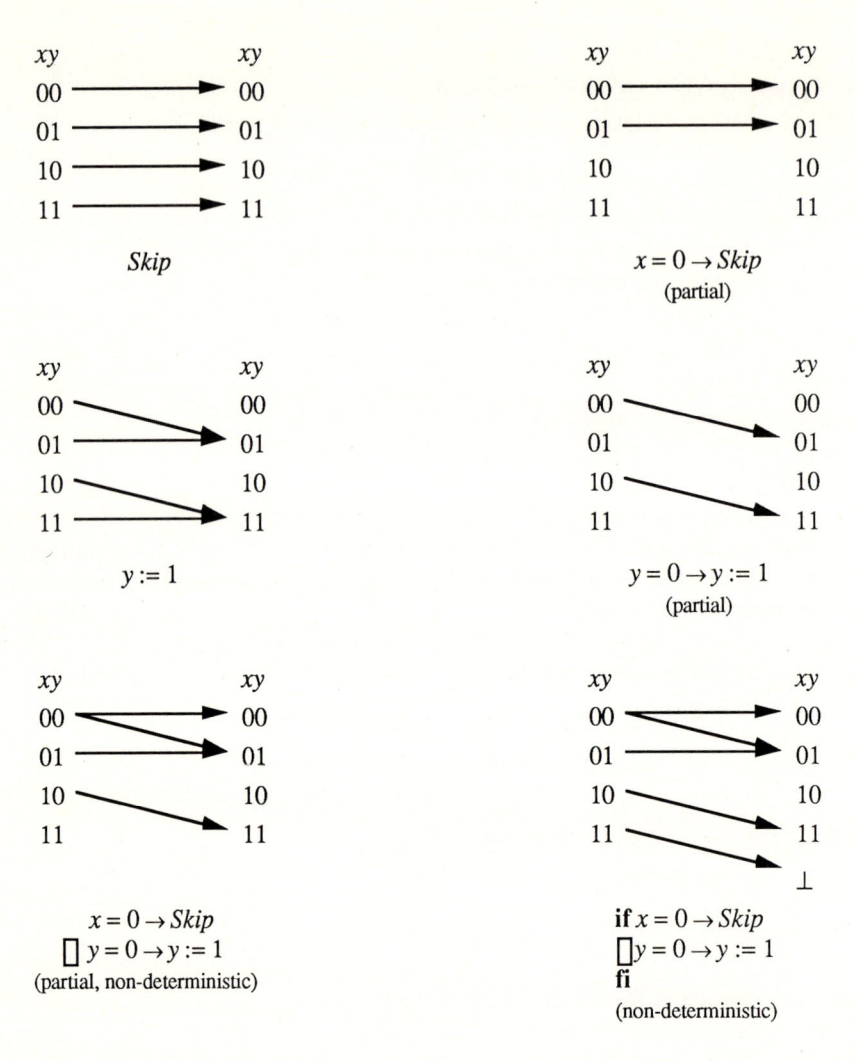

xy		xy		xy		xy
00	→	00		00	→	00
01	→	01		01	→	01
10	→	10		10		10
11	→	11		11		11

         Skip $x = 0 \rightarrow Skip$
                                                  (partial)

$y := 1$

$y = 0 \rightarrow y := 1$ (partial)

$x = 0 \rightarrow Skip$
$\square\ y = 0 \rightarrow y := 1$
(partial, non-deterministic)

if $x = 0 \rightarrow Skip$
$\square\ y = 0 \rightarrow y := 1$
fi
(non-deterministic)

Figure 1. The anatomy of a guarded command. The command in the lower right is composed of the subcommands shown in the rest of the figure.

Actions: relational definition

skip	so	$\equiv s = o$
loop	so	$\equiv o = \bot$
fail	so	$\equiv$ false
$(P \rightarrow A)$	so	$\equiv P\,s \wedge A\,so$
$(A \,\square\, B)$	so	$\equiv A\,so \vee B\,so$
$(A \,\boxtimes\, B)$	so	$\equiv A\,so \vee (B\,so \wedge \neg \mathcal{G}(A)\,s)$
$(A\,;\,B)$	so	$\equiv (\exists\, s'\colon A\,ss' \wedge B\,s'o) \vee (A\,so \wedge o = \bot)$
(**if** A **fi**)	so	$\equiv A\,so \vee (\neg \mathcal{G}(A)\,s \wedge o = \bot)$
$(x := y)$	so	$\equiv o$ is the same state as s, except that the x component equals y.
$(x \mid A)$	so	$\equiv (\forall\, s', o'\colon \text{proj}_x(s')=s \wedge \text{proj}_x(o')=o \Rightarrow A\,s'o')$, where proj_x is the projection that drops the x component of the state, and takes $\bot$ to itself. Thus	is the operator for variable introduction.

See figure 1 for an example which shows the relations for various actions. Note that **if** A **fi** makes the relation defined by A total by relating states such that $\mathcal{G}(A)=$false to $\bot$.

The idiom $x \mid P(x) \rightarrow A$ can be read "With a new x such that $P(x)$ do A".

Actions: predicate transformer definition

		$\mathcal{G}(\ldots) =$
$w(l)p(\text{skip}, R)$	$\equiv R$	true
$w(l)p(\text{loop}, R)$	$\equiv$ false(true)	true
$w(l)p(\text{fail}, R)$	$\equiv$ true	false
$w(l)p(P \rightarrow A, R)$	$\equiv \neg P \vee w(l)p(A, R)$	$P \wedge \mathcal{G}(A)$
$w(l)p(A \,\square\, B, R)$	$\equiv w(l)p(A, R) \wedge w(l)p(B, R)$	$\mathcal{G}(A) \vee \mathcal{G}(B)$
$w(l)p(A \,\boxtimes\, B, R)$	$\equiv w(l)p(A, R) \wedge (\mathcal{G}(A) \vee w(l)p(B, R))$	$\mathcal{G}(A) \vee \mathcal{G}(B)$
$w(l)p(A\,;\,B, R)$	$\equiv w(l)p(A, w(l)p(B, R))$	$\neg wp(A, \neg \mathcal{G}(B))$
$w(l)p(x := y, R)$	$\equiv R(x\colon y)$	true
$w(l)p(x \mid A, R)$	$\equiv \forall\, x\colon w(l)p(A, R)$	$\exists\, x\colon \mathcal{G}(A)$
$wp(\textbf{if } A \textbf{ fi}, R)$	$\equiv wp(A, R) \wedge \mathcal{G}(A)$	true
$wlp(\textbf{if } A \textbf{ fi}, R)$	$\equiv wlp(A, R)$	true

Programs as specifications

Following Lamport (1988) we say that a specification consists of

> A state space, the cartesian product of a set of variables or *state functions*, divided into *interface* and *internal* variables.
>
> An initial value for the state.
>
> A set of atomic actions, divided into *interface* and *internal* actions, with the possible state transitions for each action (the *transition axioms*).
>
> A set of *liveness axioms*, written in some form of temporal logic. A treatment of liveness is beyond the scope of these notes.

An implementation I satisfies the specification S if:

> The interface variables of S and I are the same, and have the same initial values.
>
> There is a function F from the state of I to the internal state of S (the *abstraction function*) such that:
>
>> F takes the initial state of I to the initial internal state of S.
>>
>> Every allowed transition of I when mapped by F is an allowed transition of S, or is the identity on S.
>>
>> The transition and liveness axioms of I mapped by F imply the liveness axioms of S.

Soda machine

We give a simple example (due to Lamport) of a soda machine with two specifications: a transition diagram of the kind familiar from textbooks on finite state automata, and a program. It is not hard to show that the second one is an implementation of the first; the second is annotated on the right with the function F. The reverse is also true, but for reasons which are beyond the scope of these notes.

We indicate the interface variables and actions by underlining them.

Transition diagram specification

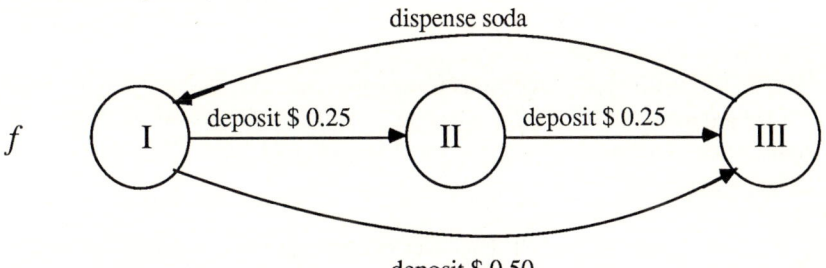

f : I —deposit $ 0.25→ II —deposit $ 0.25→ III, I ←dispense soda— III, I —deposit $ 0.50→ III

Program specification

    interface   depositCoin ...;
                              dispenseSoda ...;

    var $x : \{0, 25, 50\}$;
                              $y : \{25, 50\}$;

			Abstraction function	F	$f=$
α:	**do**	$\langle x := 0 \rangle$	**if** at(α)→	I	
β:	;	**do** $\langle x < 50 \rangle \rightarrow$	☐ at(β)→	**if** $x=0 \rightarrow$	I
				☐ $x=25\rightarrow$	II
				☐ $x=50\rightarrow$	III
γ:		$\langle y :=$ depositCoin	☐ at(γ)→	**if** $x=0 \rightarrow$	I
		; $x+y \leq 50 \rightarrow$ skip $\rangle$		☐ $x=25\rightarrow$	II
				☐ $x=50\rightarrow$	—
				fi	
δ:	;	$\langle x := x+y \rangle$	☐ at(δ)→	**if** $x+y=25\rightarrow$	II
				☐ $x+y=50\rightarrow$	III
				☐ $x+y=75\rightarrow$	—
				fi	
		od			
ε:	;	$\langle$ dispenseSoda $\rangle$	☐ at(ε)→		III
	od		**fi**		

Notation

In writing the specifications and implementations, we use a few fairly standard notations.

If T is a type, we write t, t', t_1 etc. for variables of type T.

If $c_1, ..., c_n$ are constants, $\{c_1, ..., c_n\}$ is the enumeration type whose values are the c_i.

If T and U are types, T ⊕ U is the disjoint union of T and U. If c is a constant, we write T ⊕ c for T ⊕ {c}.

If T and U are types, T → U is the type of functions from T to U; the overloading with the → of guarded commands is hard to avoid. If f is a function, we write $f(x)$ or $f[x]$ for an application of f, and $f[x] := y$ for the operation that changes $f[x]$ to y and leaves f the same elsewhere. If f is undefined at x, we write $f[x] = \bot$.

If T is a type, **sequence of** T is the type of all sequences of elements of T, including the empty sequence. T is a subtype of **sequence of** T. We write $s \parallel s'$ for the concatenation of two sequences, and Λ for the empty sequence.

⟨ A ⟩ is an atomic action with the same semantics as A in isolation.

Memory

Simple memory

Here is a specification for simple addressable memory.

type	A;	*address*
	D;	*data*
var	$m : A \to D$;	*memory*
Read(a, **var** d)	= ⟨ $d := m[a]$ ⟩	
Write(a, d)	= ⟨ $m[a] := d$ ⟩	
Swap(a, d, **var** d')	= ⟨ $d' := m[a]; m[a] := d$ ⟩	

Cache memory

Now we look at an implementation that uses a write-back cache. The abstraction function is given after the variable declarations. This implementation maintains the invariant that the number of addresses at which c is defined is constant; for a hardware cache the motivation should be obvious. A real cache would maintain a more complicated invariant, perhaps bounding the number of addresses at which c is defined.

type	A;	*address*
	D;	*data*
var	$m: A \to D$;	*main memory*
	$c: A \to D \oplus \bot$;	*cache (partial)*

abstraction function

$m_{\text{simple}}[a] : d$ = **if** $c[a] \neq \bot \to d := c[a]$
⊠ $\quad\quad\quad\quad\quad\quad d := m[a]$
fi

$dirty(a)$: BOOL = $c[a] \neq \bot \wedge c[a] \neq m[a]$

FlushOne = $a \mid c[a] \neq \bot \to$ **do** $dirty[a] \to m[a] := c[a]$ **od**; $c[a] := \bot$

Load(a) = $\langle$ **do** $c[a] = \bot \to$ FlushOne; $c[a] := m[a]$ **od** $\rangle$

<u>Read</u>(a, **var** d) = Load(a); $\langle d := c[a] \rangle$

<u>Write</u>(a, d) = $\langle$ **if** $c[a] = \bot \to$ FlushOne ⊠ skip **fi** $\rangle$; $\langle c[a] := d \rangle$

<u>Swap</u>(a, d, **var** d') = Load(a); $\langle d' := c[a]; c[a] := d \rangle$

Coherent cache memory

Here is a more complex implementation, suitable for a multiprocessor in which each processor has its own write-back cache. We still want the system to behave like a single shared memory. Again, the abstraction function follows the variables. Correctness depends on the invariant at the end. This implementation is some distance from being practical; in particular, a practical one would have *shared* and *dirty* as variables, with invariants relating their values to the definitions given here.

We write c_p instead of $c[p]$ for readability.

type   A;   *address*
               D;   *data*
               P;   *processor*

var $m : A \rightarrow D$;   *main memory*
               $c : P \rightarrow A \rightarrow D \oplus \bot$;   *caches (partial)*

abstraction function

$m_{\text{simple}}[a] : d$ = **if** $\exists p: c_p[a] \neq \bot \rightarrow d := c_p[a]$
                               ◻ $d := m[a]$
                             fi

shared(a): BOOL   = $\exists p, q: c_p[a] \neq \bot \wedge c_q[a] \neq \bot \wedge p \neq q$

dirty (a): BOOL   = $\exists p: \quad c_p[a] \neq \bot \wedge c_p[a] \neq m[a]$

Load(p, a)   = **do** $c_p[a] = \bot \rightarrow$
                            FlushOne(p)
                         ; **if** $\langle q \mid c_q[a] \neq \bot \rightarrow \quad c_p[a] := c_q[a] \rangle$
                              ◻ $\langle c_p[a] := m[a] \rangle$
                            fi
                      od

FlushOne(p)   = $a \mid c_p[a] \neq \bot \rightarrow$
                          $\langle$ **do** $\neg\textit{shared}[a] \wedge \textit{dirty}[a] \rightarrow m[a] := c_p[a]$ **od** $\rangle$
                        ; $c_p[a] := \bot$

<u>Read</u>(p, a, **var** d)   = Load(p, a); $\langle d := c_p[a] \rangle$

<u>Write</u>(p, a, d)   = **if** $c_p[a] = \bot \rightarrow$ FlushOne(p) ◻ skip **fi**
                      ; $\langle \quad c_p[a] := d$
                        ; **do** $q \mid c_q[a] \neq \bot \wedge c_q[a] \neq c_p[a] \rightarrow c_q[a] := c_p[a]$ **od**
                        $\rangle$

<u>Swap</u> (p, a, d, **var** d ')   = Load(p, a); $\langle d' := c_p[a]$; Write(p, a, d) $\rangle$

Invariant

$c_p[a] \neq \bot \wedge c_q[a] \neq \bot \Rightarrow c_p[a] = c_q[a]$

Write-buffered memory

We now turn to a memory with a different specification. This is *not* another implementation of the simple memory specification. In this memory, each processor sees its own writes as it would in a simple memory, but it sees only a non-deterministic sampling of the writes done by other processors. A *FlushAll* operation is added to permit synchronization.

The motivation for using the weaker specification is the possibility of building a faster processor if writes don't have to be synchronized as closely as is required by the simple memory specification. After giving the specification, we show how to implement a critical section within which variables shared with other processor can be read and written with the same results that the simple memory would give.

type	A;	*address*
	D;	*data*
	P;	*processor*
var	$m : A \rightarrow D$;	*main memory*
	$b : P \rightarrow A \rightarrow D \oplus \bot$;	*buffers (partial)*
Flush(p, a)	= $b_p[a] \neq \bot \rightarrow \langle m[a] := b_p[a] \rangle ; \langle b_p[a] := \bot \rangle$	
FlushSome	= $p, a \mid$ Flush(p, a); FlushSome	
	$\square$ skip	
Read($p, a,$ **var** d)	= **if** $\langle \quad b_p[a] = \bot \rightarrow d := m[a] \rangle$	
	$\square \langle q \mid b_q[a] \neq \bot \rightarrow d := b_q[a] \rangle$	
	fi	
Write(p, a, d)	= $\langle b_p[a] := d \rangle$	
Swap ($p, a, d,$ **var** d')	= FlushSome; $\langle d' := m[a]; m[a] := d \rangle$	
FlushAll(p)	= **do** $a \mid$ Flush(p, a) **od**	

Critical section

We want to get the effect of an ordinary critical section using simple memory, so we write that as a specification (the right-hand column below). The implementation (the left-hand column below) uses buffered memory to achieve the same effect. Provided the non-critical section doesn't reference the memory and the critical section doesn't reference the lock, a program using buffered memory with the left-hand implementation of mutual exclusion has the same semantics as (as a relation, is a subset of) the same program using simple memory with the standard right-hand implementation of mutual exclusion. To nest critical sections we use the usual device: partition A into disjoint subsets, each protected by a different lock.

var m : $A \to D$;
   b : $P \to A \to D \oplus \bot$;

const $l :=$ the address of a location to be used as a lock

abstraction function
$m_{\text{simple}}[a] : d$ = **if** $p \mid b_p[a] \neq \bot \to$ $d := p[a]$
                              ☒ $d := m[a]$
                           fi

for $p \in P$	
Implementation	*Specification*
(using buffered memory)	*(using simple memory)*

do d_p |	**do** d_p |
α_p: $\langle d_p := 1 \rangle$	$\langle d_p := 1 \rangle$
β_p: ; **do** $\langle d_p \neq 0 \rangle \to$	; **do** $\langle d_p \neq 0 \rangle \to$
γ_p: Swap($p, l, 1, d_p$)	Swap($l, 1, d_p$)
od	**od**
δ_p: ; critical section	; critical section
ε_p: ; FlushAll(p)	
κ_p: ; Write($p, l, 0$)	; Write($l, 0$)
λ_p: ; non-critical section	; non-critical section
od	**od**

initially $\forall p, a : b_p[a] = \bot, m[l] = 0$
assume
  $A \in |\lambda_p| \Rightarrow A$ independent of m : no Read, Write or Swap in A
  $A \in |\delta_p| \Rightarrow A$ independent of $m[l]$: no Read, Write or Swap($p, l, ...$) in A

The proof depends on the following invariants for the implementation.

Invariants

(1) $CS_p \Rightarrow$ $(\neg CS_q \vee p = q)$
                   $\wedge$ $m[l] \neq 0$
                   $\wedge$ $b_q[l] \neq 0$
       where $CS_p = \text{in}(\delta\varepsilon\kappa_p) \vee (\text{at}(\beta_p) \wedge d_p = 0)$

(2) $\neg \text{in}(\delta\varepsilon_p) \wedge a \neq l \Rightarrow b_p[a] = \bot$

Multiple write-buffered memory

This version is still weaker, since each processor keeps a sequence of all its writes to each location rather than just the last one. Again, the motivation is to allow a higher-performance implementation, by increasing the amount of buffering at the expense of more non-determinism. The same critical section works.

type	A;	*address*
	D;	*data*
	P;	*processor*
	E = **sequence of** D;	
var	$m : A \rightarrow D$;	*main memory*
	$b : P \rightarrow A \rightarrow E$;	*buffers*

$\text{Flush}(p, a) \quad = \quad d, e \mid b_p[a] = d \parallel e \rightarrow \langle m[a] := d \rangle ; \langle b_p[a] := e \rangle$

$\text{FlushSome} \quad = \quad p, a \mid \text{Flush}(p, a); \text{FlushSome}$
$\qquad\qquad\qquad\square \text{ skip}$

$\text{Read}(p, a): d \quad = \quad \textbf{if } \langle \qquad\qquad b_p[a] = \Lambda \qquad \rightarrow d := m[a] \rangle$
$\qquad\qquad\qquad\qquad \square \langle q, e_1, d', e_2 \mid \quad b_q[a] = e_1 \parallel d' \parallel e_2$
$\qquad\qquad\qquad\qquad\qquad\qquad\qquad \wedge \quad (q \neq p \vee e_2 = \Lambda) \rightarrow d := d' \rangle$
$\qquad\qquad\qquad \textbf{fi}$

$\text{Write}(p, a, d) \quad = \quad \langle b_p[a] := b_p[a] \parallel d \rangle$

$\text{Swap }(p, a, d): d' \quad = \quad \text{FlushSome}; \langle d' := m[a]; m[a] := d \rangle$

$\text{FlushAll}(p) \quad = \quad \textbf{do } a \mid \text{Flush}(p, a) \textbf{ od}$

Transactions

This example describes the characteristics of a memory that provides *transactions* so that several writes can be done atomically with respect to failure and restart of the memory. The idea is that the memory is not obliged to remember the writes of a transaction until it has accepted the transaction's *commit*; until then it may discard the writes and indicate that the transaction has aborted.

A real transaction system also provides atomicity with respect to concurrent accesses by other transactions, but this elaboration is beyond the scope of these notes.

We write $Proc_t(...)$ for $Proc(t, ...)$ and l_t for $l[t]$.

type	A;	*address*
	D;	*data*
	T;	*transaction*
	X = {ok, abort};	
var	$m : A \to D$;	*memory*
	$b : T \to A \to D$;	*backup*

$$\text{Abort} \quad = \quad \langle m := b_t \rangle \quad ; x := \text{abort}$$

$$\underline{\text{Begin}}_t() \quad = \quad \langle b_t := m \rangle$$

$$\underline{\text{Read}}_t(a, \textbf{var } d, \textbf{var } x) \quad = \quad \langle d := m[a] \rangle \quad ; x := \text{ok}$$
$$\square \quad \text{Abort}$$

$$\underline{\text{Write}}_t(a, d, \textbf{var } x) \quad = \quad \langle m[a] := d \rangle \quad ; x := \text{ok}$$
$$\square \quad \text{Abort}$$

$$\underline{\text{Commit}}_t(\textbf{var } x) \quad = \quad x := \text{ok}$$
$$\square \quad \text{Abort}$$

Undo implementation

This is one of the standard implementations of the specification above: the old memory values are remembered, and restored in case of an abort.

var	$m : A \to D$;	*memory*
	$l : T \to A \to D \oplus \bot$;	*log*

abstraction function

$$b_t[a]: d \quad = \quad \textbf{if } l_t[a] \neq \bot \to d := l_t[a]$$
$$\boxtimes \quad\quad\quad d := m[a]$$
$$\textbf{fi}$$

m_{simple} = m

$\text{Abort}_t()$ = $\langle\ \textbf{do}\ a\ |\ l_t[a] \neq \bot \rightarrow m[a] := l_t[a]; l_t[a] := \bot\ \textbf{od}\ \rangle\ ; x := \text{abort}$

$\underline{\text{Begin}}_t()$ = $\textbf{do}\ a\ |\ l_t[a] \neq \bot \rightarrow \langle\ l_t[a] := \bot\ \rangle\ \textbf{od}$

$\underline{\text{Read}}_t(a, \textbf{var}\ d, \textbf{var}\ x)$ = $\langle\ d := m[a]\ \rangle; x := \text{ok}$
$\qquad\qquad\qquad\qquad\qquad\quad$ ☐ Abort

$\underline{\text{Write}}_t(a, d, \textbf{var}\ x)$ = $\textbf{do}\ l_t[a] = \bot \rightarrow \langle\ l_t[a] := m[a]\ \rangle\ \textbf{od}; \langle\ m[a]:=d\ \rangle; x := \text{ok}$
$\qquad\qquad\qquad\qquad\quad$ ☐ Abort

$\underline{\text{Commit}}_t(\textbf{var}\ x)$ = $x := \text{ok}$
$\qquad\qquad\qquad\qquad$ ☐ Abort

Compare this abstraction function with the one for the cache memory.

Redo implementation

This is the other standard implementation: the writes are remembered and done in the memory only at commit time. Essentially the same work is done as in the undo version, but in different places; notice how similar the code sequences are.

var $\qquad\qquad\qquad\qquad m : A \rightarrow D;\qquad\qquad\qquad$ *memory*
$\qquad\qquad\qquad\qquad\quad l\ :\ T \rightarrow A \rightarrow D \oplus \bot;\qquad\qquad$ *log*

abstraction function

b_t = m

$m_{\text{simple}}[a]: d$ = $\textbf{if}\ t\ |\ l_t[a] \neq \bot \rightarrow\quad d := l_t[a]$
$\qquad\qquad\qquad\qquad\quad$ ⊠ $\qquad\qquad\qquad\quad d := m[a]$
$\qquad\qquad\qquad\qquad\quad\textbf{fi}$

Abort = $x := \text{abort}$

$\underline{\text{Begin}}_t()$ = $\textbf{do}\ a\ |\ l_t[a] \neq \bot \rightarrow \langle\ l_t[a] := \bot\ \rangle\ \textbf{od}$

$\underline{\text{Read}}_t(a, \textbf{var}\ d, \textbf{var}\ x)$ = $\textbf{if}\ l_t[a] \neq \bot \rightarrow d := l_t[a]\ ⊠\ \langle\ d := m[a]\ \rangle\ \textbf{fi}; x := \text{ok}$
$\qquad\qquad\qquad\qquad\qquad\quad$ ☐ Abort

$\underline{\text{Write}}_t(a, d, \textbf{var}\ x)$ = $l_t[a] := d\ ; x := \text{ok}$
$\qquad\qquad\qquad\qquad\quad$ ☐ Abort

$\underline{\text{Commit}}_t(\textbf{var}\ x)$: = $\langle\ \textbf{do}\ a\ |\ l_t[a] \neq \bot \rightarrow m[a] := l_t[a]; l_t[a] := \bot\ \textbf{od}\ \rangle; x := \text{ok}$
$\qquad\qquad\qquad\qquad$ ☐ Abort

Undo version with non-atomic abort

Note the atomicity of commit in the redo version and abort in the undo version; a real implementation gets this with a commit record, instead of using a large atomic action. Here is how it goes for the undo version.

var $m : A \rightarrow D;$ *memory*
            $l : T \rightarrow A \rightarrow D \oplus \bot;$ *log*
            $ab : T \rightarrow BOOL;$ *aborted*

abstraction function

$b_t[a]: d$ = **if** $l_t[a] \neq \bot \rightarrow d := l_t[a]$
              ☒ $d := m[a]$
              fi

$m_{\text{simple}}[a]: d$ = **if** $t \mid ab_t \land l_t[a] \neq \bot \rightarrow d := l_t[a]$
                            ☒ $d := m[a]$
                            fi

$\underline{\text{Abort}_t}()$ = $\langle ab_t := \text{true} \rangle$
                  ; **do** $a \mid \langle l_t[a] \neq \bot \rangle \rightarrow \langle m[a] := l_t[a] \rangle ; \langle l_t[a] := \bot \rangle$ **od**
                  ; $x :=$ abort

$\underline{\text{Begin}_t}()$ = $ab_t :=$ false; **do** $a \mid l_t[a] \neq \bot \rightarrow \langle l_t[a] := \bot \rangle$ **od**

$\underline{\text{Read}_t}(a, \textbf{var } d, \textbf{var } x)$ = $\neg ab_t \rightarrow \langle d := m[a] \rangle; x :=$ ok
                                                      ▯ Abort

$\underline{\text{Write}_t}(a, d, \textbf{var } x)$ = $\neg ab_t \rightarrow$ **do** $l_t[a] = \bot \rightarrow \langle l_t[a] := m[a] \rangle$ **od**; $\langle m[a]:=d \rangle; x :=$ ok
                                              ▯ Abort

$\underline{\text{Commit}_t}(\textbf{var } x)$ = $\neg ab_t \rightarrow x :=$ ok
                                      ▯ Abort

Name service

This section describes a tree-structured storage system which was designed as the basis of a large-scale, highly-available distributed name service. After explaining the properties of the service informally, we give specifications of the essential abstractions that underlie it.

A name service maps a name for an entity (an individual, organization or service) into a set of labeled properties, each of which is a string. Typical properties are

   password=XQE$#

   mailboxes={Cabernet, Zinfandel}

network address=173#4456#1655476653

distribution list={Birrell, Needham, Schroeder}

A name service is not a general database: the set of names changes slowly, and the properties of a given name also change slowly. Furthermore, the integrity constraints of a useful name service are much weaker those of a database. Nor is it like a file directory system, which must create and look up names much faster than a name service, but need not be as large or as available. Either a database or a file system root can be named by the name service, however.

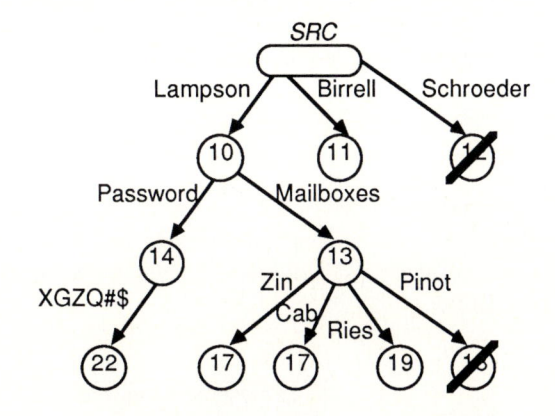

Figure 2: The tree of directory values

A directory is not simply a mapping from simple names to values. Instead, it contains a *tree* of values (see Figure 2). An arc of the tree carries a *name* (N), which is just a string, written next to the arc in the figure. A node carries a *timestamp* (S), represented by a number in the figure, and a *mark* which is either *present* or *absent*. Absent nodes are struck through in the figure. A path through the tree is defined by a sequence of names (A); we write this sequence in the Unix style, e.g., Lampson/Password. For the value of the path there are three interesting cases:

- If the path a/n ends in a leaf that is an only child, we say that n is the value of a. This rule applies to the path Lampson/Password/XGZQ#$3, and hence we say that XGZQ#$3 is the value of Lampson/Password.

- If the path a/n_i ends in a leaf that is not an only child, and its siblings are labeled $n_1...n_k$, we say that the set $\{n_1...n_k\}$ is the value of a. For example, {Zin, Cab, Ries, Pinot} is the value of Lampson/Mailboxes.

- If the path a does not end in a leaf, we say that the subtree rooted in the node where it ends is the value of a. For example, the value of Lampson is the subtree rooted in the node with timestamp 10.

An update to a directory makes the node at the end of a given path present or absent. The update is timestamped, and a later timestamp takes precedence over an earlier one with the same path.

The subtleties of this scheme are discussed later; its purpose is to allow the tree to be updated concurrently from a number of places without any prior synchronization.

A value is determined by the sequence of update operations which have been applied to an initial empty value. An update can be thought of as a function that takes one value into another. Suppose the update functions have the following properties:

- Total: it always makes sense to apply an update function.

- Commutative: the order in which two updates are applied does not affect the result.

- Idempotent: applying the same update twice has the same effect as applying it once.

Then it follows that the *set* of updates that have been applied uniquely defines the state of the value.

It can be shown that the updates on values defined earlier are total, commutative and idempotent. Hence a set of updates uniquely defines a value. This observation is the basis of the concurrency control scheme for the name service. The right side of Figure 3 gives one sequence of updates which will produce the value on the left.

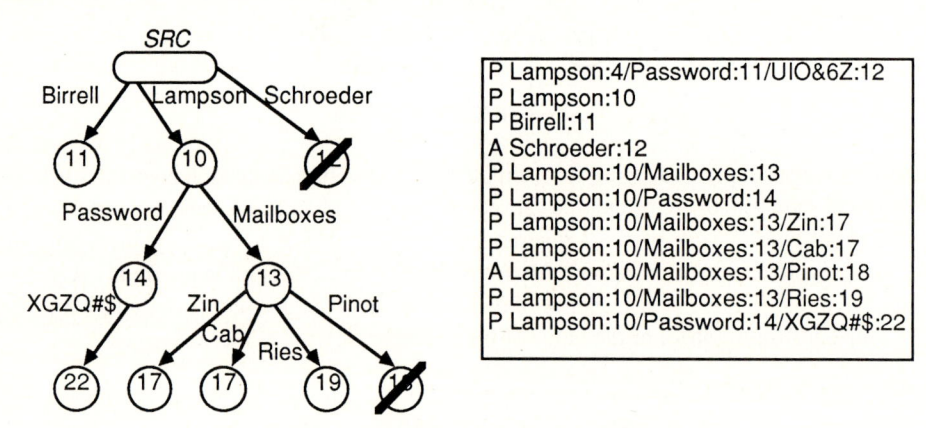

```
P Lampson:4/Password:11/UIO&6Z:12
P Lampson:10
P Birrell:11
A Schroeder:12
P Lampson:10/Mailboxes:13
P Lampson:10/Password:14
P Lampson:10/Mailboxes:13/Zin:17
P Lampson:10/Mailboxes:13/Cab:17
A Lampson:10/Mailboxes:13/Pinot:18
P Lampson:10/Mailboxes:13/Ries:19
P Lampson:10/Password:14/XGZQ#$:22
```

Figure 3: A possible sequence of updates

The presence of the timestamps at each name in the path ensures that the update is modifying the value that the client intended. This is significant when two clients concurrently try to create the same name. The two updates will have different timestamps, and the earlier one will lose. The fact that later modifications, e.g. to set the password, include the creation timestamp ensures that those made by the earlier client will also lose. Without the timestamps there would be no way to tell them apart, and the final value might be a mixture of the two sets of updates.

The client sees a single name service, and is not concerned with the actual machines on which it is implemented or the replication of the database which makes it reliable. The administrator allocates resources to the implementation of the service and reconfigures it to deal with long-term failures. Instead of a single directory, he sees a set of *directory copies* (DC) stored in different servers. Figure 4 shows this situation for the *DEC*/SRC directory, which is stored on four servers named alpha, beta, gamma, and delta. A directory reference now includes a list of the servers that store its DCs. A lookup can try one or more of the servers to find a copy from which to read.

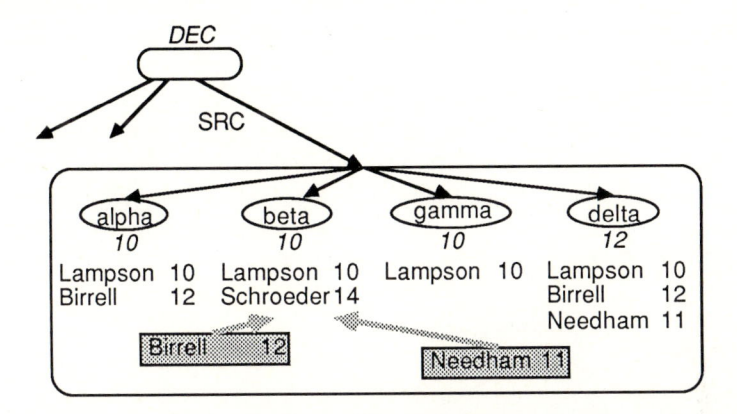

Figure 4: Directory copies

The copies are kept approximately, but not exactly the same. The figure shows four updates to *SRC*, with timestamps 10, 11, 12 and 14. The copy on delta is current to time 12, as indicated by the italic *12* under it, called its *lastSweep* field. The others have different sets of updates, but are current only to time 10. Each copy also has a *nextS* value which is the next timestamp it will assign to an update originating there; this value can only increase.

An update originates at one DC, and is initially recorded there. The basic method for spreading updates to all the copies is a *sweep* operation, which visits every DC, collects a complete set of updates, and then writes this set to every DC. The sweep has a timestamp *sweepS*, and before it reads from a DC it increases that DC's *nextS* to *sweepS*; this ensures that the sweep collects all updates earlier than *sweepS*. After writing to a DC, the sweep sets that DC's *lastSweep* to *sweepS*. Figure 5 shows the state of *SRC* after a sweep at time 14.

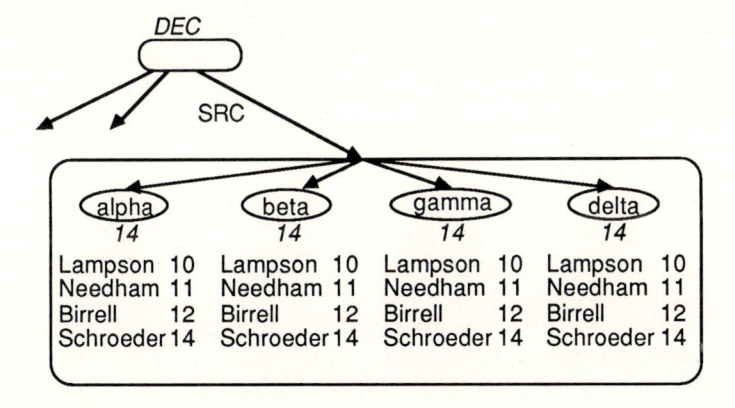

Figure 5: The directory after a Sweep

In order to speed up the spreading of updates, any DC may send some updates to any other DC in a message. Figure 4 shows the updates for Birrell and Needham being sent to server beta. Most updates should be distributed in messages, but it is extremely difficult to make this method fully reliable. The sweep, on the other hand, is quite easy to implement reliably.

A sweep's major problem is to obtain the set of DCs reliably. The set of servers stored in the parent is not suitable, because it is too difficult to ensure that the sweep gets a complete set if the directory's parent or the set of DCs is changing during the sweep. Instead, all the DCs are linked into a *ring*, shown by the fat arrows in figure 6. Each arrow represents the name of the server to which it points. The sweep starts at any DC and follows the arrows; if it eventually reaches the starting point, then it has found a complete set of DCs. Of course, this operation need not be done sequentially; given a hint about the contents of the set, say from the parent, the sweep can visit all the DCs and read out the ring pointers concurrently.

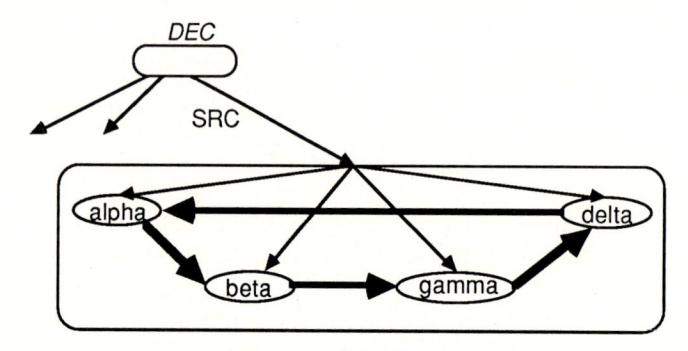

Figure 6: The ring of directory copies

DCs can be added or removed by straightforward splicing of the ring. If a server fails permanently, however (say it gets blown up), or if the set of servers is partitioned by a network failure that lasts for a long time, the ring must be reformed. In the process, an update will be lost if it originated in a server that is not in the new ring and has not been distributed. The ring is reformed by starting a new *epoch* for the directory and building a new ring from scratch, using the DR or information provided by the administrator about which servers should be included. An epoch is identified by a timestamp, and the most recent epoch that has ever had a complete ring is the one that defines the contents of the directory. Once the new epoch's ring has been successfully completed, the ring pointers for older epochs can be removed. Since starting a new epoch may change the database, it is never done automatically, but must be controlled by an administrator.

Distributed writes

Here is the abstraction for the name service's update semantics. The details of the tree of values are deferred until later; this specification depends only on the fact that updates are total, commutative and idempotent. We begin with a specification that says nothing about multiple copies; this is the client's view of the name service. Compare this with the write-buffered memory.

type	V;	*value*
	$U = V \rightarrow V$;	*update, assumed total, commutative, and idempotent*
	$W = \textbf{set of } U$;	*updates "in progress"*
var	$m : V$;	*memory*
	$b : W$;	*buffer*

AddSome(**var** v) = $u \mid u \in b \wedge u(v) \neq v \rightarrow v := u(v)$; AddSome($v$)
$\qquad\qquad\qquad\qquad\quad \square$ skip

Read(**var** v) = $\langle\, v := m\, ;\, \text{AddSome}(v)\, \rangle$

Update(u) = $\langle\, b := b \cup \{u\}\, \rangle$

Sweep() = $\langle\, \textbf{do}\ u \mid u \in b \rightarrow m := u(m);\ b := b - \{u\}\ \textbf{od}\, \rangle$

Update and Sweep were called Write and Flush in the specification for buffered writes. This differs in that there is no ordering on b, there are no updates in b that a Read is guaranteed to see, and there is no Swap operation.

You might think that Sweep is too atomic, and that it should be written to move one u from b to m in each atomic action. However, if two systems have the same $b \cup m$, the one with the smaller b is an implementation of the one with the larger b, so a system with non-atomic Sweep implements a specification with atomic Sweep.

We can substitute distinguishable for idempotent and ordered for commutative as properties of updates. AddSome and Sweep must be changed to apply the updates in order. If the updates are ordered, and we require that Update's argument follows any update already in m, then the boundary between m and b can be defined by the last update in m. This is a conveneint way to summarize the information in b about how much of the state can be read deterministically. In the name server application the updates are ordered by their timestamps, and the boundary is called *last Sweep*.

N-copy version

Now for an implementation that makes the copies visible. It would be neater to give each copy its own version of m and its own set b of recent updates. However, this makes it quite difficult to define the abstraction function. Instead, we simply give each copy its version of b, and define m to be the result of starting with an initial value v_0 and applying all the updates known to every copy. To this end the auxiliary function apply turns a set of updates w into a value v by applying all of them to v_0.

type	V;	*value*
	$U = V \rightarrow V$;	*update, assumed total,*
		commutative, and idempotent
	W = **set of** U;	*updates "in progress"*
	P;	*processor*
var	$b : P \rightarrow W$;	*buffers*

Abstraction function

m_{simple} = $apply(\bigcap_{p \in P} b[p])$

b_{simple} = $\bigcup_{p \in P} b[p] - \bigcap_{p \in P} b[p]$

In other words, the abstract m is all the updates that every processor has, and the abstract b is all the updates known to some processor but not to all of them.

$apply(w): v$ = $v := v_0;$ **do** $u \mid u \in w \rightarrow v := u(v); w := w - \{u\}$ **od**

$\underline{Read}(p, \textbf{var } v)$ = $v := apply(b[p])$

$\underline{Update}(p, u)$ = $\langle b[p] := b[p] \cup \{u\} \rangle$

$\underline{Sweep}()$ = $w \mid \quad \langle w := \bigcup_{p \in P} b[p] \rangle$

$\quad ;$ **do** $p, u \mid u \in w \land u \notin b[p] \rightarrow \langle b[p] := b[p] \cup \{u\} \rangle$ **od**

Since this meant to be viewed as an implementation, we have given the least atomic Sweep, rather than the most atomic one. Abstractly an update moves from b to m when it is added to the last processor that didn't have it already.

Tree memory

Finally, we show the abstraction for the tree-structured memory that the name service needs. To be used with the distributed writes specification, the updates must be timestamped so that they can be ordered. This detail is omitted here in order to focus attention on the basic idea.

We use the notation: $x \leftarrow y$ for $x \neq y \rightarrow x := y$. This allows us to copy a tree from v' to v with the idiom

$$\textbf{do } a \mid v[a] \leftarrow v'[a] \textbf{ od}$$

which changes the function v to agree with v' at every point. Recall also that $\parallel$ stands for concatenation of sequences; we use sequences of names as addresses here, and often need to concatenate such path names.

type	N;	*name*
	D;	*data*
	A = **sequence of** N;	*address*
	V = A $\rightarrow$ D $\oplus \perp$;	*tree value*
var	m : V;	*memory*

$\underline{\text{Read}}(a, \textbf{var } v)$ = $\langle \textbf{do } a' \mid v[a'] \leftarrow m[a \parallel a'] \textbf{ od} \rangle$

$\underline{\text{Write}}(a, v)$ = $\langle \textbf{do } a' \mid m[a \parallel a'] \leftarrow v[a'] \textbf{ od} \rangle$

$\underline{\text{Write}}(a, d)$ = $v \mid \forall a: v[a] = \perp \rightarrow v[\Lambda] = d$; Write(a, v)

Read copies the subtree of m rooted at a to v. Write(a, v) makes the subtree of m rooted at a equal to v. Write(a, d) sets $m[a]$ to d and makes undefined the rest of the subtree rooted at m.

Timestamped tree memory

We now introduce timestamps on the writes, in fact more of them that are needed to provide write ordering. The name service uses timestamps at each node in the tree to provide a poor man's transactions: each point in the memory is identified not only by the *a* that leads to it, but also by the timestamps of the writes that created the path to *a*. Thus conflicting use of the same names can be detected; the use with later timestamps will win. Figure 3 above shows an example.

We show only the write of a single value at a node identified by a given timestamped address *b*. The write fails (returning false in *x*) unless the timestamps of all the nodes on the path to node *b* match the ones in *b*. We write $m[a].d$ and $m[a].s$ for the *d* and *s* components of $m[a]$.

type	N;	*name*
	D;	*data*
	S;	*timestamp*
	A = **sequence of** N;	*address*
	V = A → (D × S) ⊕ ⊥;	*tree value*
	B = **sequence of** (N × S);	*address with timestamps*
var	$m : V$;	*memory*

Read(*a*, **var** *v*) = ⟨ **do** $a' \mid v[a'] \leftarrow m[a \parallel a']$ **od** ⟩

Write(*b*, *d*, **var** *x*) = ⟨ $a \mid$ for all $i \leq \text{length}(b)$: $a[i] = b[i].n \rightarrow$
　　　　　　　　　　　if for all $0 < i < \text{length}(b)$, $m[a[1..i]].s = b[i].s \rightarrow$
　　　　　　　　　　　　do $a' \mid m[a \parallel a'] \leftarrow \bot$ **od**
　　　　　　　　　　　;　$m[a] := (d, b[\text{length}(b)].s)$
　　　　　　　　　　　;　$x := \text{true}$
　　　　　　　　　　　☒　$x := \text{false}$
　　　　　　　　　　　fi
　　　　　　　　　⟩

The ordering relation on writes needed by the distributed writes specification is determined by the timestamped address:

$b_1 < b_2 = \exists\, i < \text{length}(b_1)\colon j < i \Rightarrow b_1[j] = b_2[j] \wedge b_1[i].n = b_2[i].n \wedge b_1[i].s < b_2[i].s$

In other words, $b_1 < b_2$ if they match exactly up to some point, they have the same name at that point, and b_1 has the smaller timestamp at that point. This rule ensures that a write to a node near the root takes precedence over later writes into the subtree rooted at that node with an earlier timestamp. For example, Lampson:10 takes precedence over Lampson:4/Password:11.

Threads

The specification below for thread (or process) synchronization primitives is transcribed from (Birrell 1987), where it was expressed in the Larch specification language. Except for alerts, the constructs should be familiar, although in some cases the meaning varies slightly from the literature. A condition variable is a substitute for busy waiting: a process waits there until a *Broadcast* is done to the condition, or enough *Signal*s. An *alert* is an indication to a thread that it should look around; it is delivered only after an *AlertWait*. Thus a thread which computes indefinitely without ever waiting on a condition or executing *TestAlert* will not notice the alert.

type	T;	*thread*
	$M = T \oplus \text{nil}$;	*mutex*
	$S = \{\text{busy, free}\}$;	*semaphore*
	$C = \textbf{set of } T$;	*condition*
var	$a : \textbf{set of } T$;	*alerted threads*
	self: T	*the thread doing the operation*

$$\text{Acquire}(\textbf{var } m) \quad = \quad \langle \; m = \text{nil} \rightarrow m := \text{self} \; \rangle$$

$$\text{Release}(\textbf{var } m) \quad = \quad \langle \; \textbf{if } m \ne \text{self} \rightarrow \text{chaos}$$
$$\qquad\qquad\qquad\qquad \boxtimes \; m := \text{nil}$$
$$\qquad\qquad\qquad \textbf{fi} \; \rangle$$

$$\text{Wait}(\textbf{var } m, \textbf{var } c) \quad = \quad \langle \; \textbf{if } m \ne \text{self} \rightarrow \text{chaos}$$
$$\qquad\qquad\qquad\qquad \boxtimes \; c := c \cup \{\text{self}\}; \; m := \text{nil}$$
$$\qquad\qquad\qquad \textbf{fi} \; \rangle$$
$$\qquad\qquad\qquad ; \quad \langle \; m = \text{nil} \land \neg \, \text{self} \in c \rightarrow m := \text{self} \; \rangle$$

$$\text{Signal}(\textbf{var } c) \quad = \quad \langle \; \textbf{if } c = \{\} \rightarrow \text{skip}$$
$$\qquad\qquad\qquad\qquad \square \; c' \,|\, c \supset c' \rightarrow c := c'$$
$$\qquad\qquad\qquad \textbf{fi}$$
$$\qquad\qquad \rangle$$

$$\text{Broadcast}(\textbf{var } c) \quad = \quad \langle \; c := \{\} \; \rangle$$

$$P(\textbf{var } s) \quad = \quad \langle \; s = \text{free} \rightarrow s := \text{busy} \; \rangle$$

$$V(\textbf{var } s) \quad = \quad \langle \; s := \text{free} \; \rangle$$

$$\text{Alert}(t) \quad = \quad \langle \; a := a \cup \{t\} \; \rangle$$

$$\text{TestAlert}(): b \quad = \quad \langle \; b := (\text{self} \in a); \; a := a - \{\text{self}\} \; \rangle$$

AlertP(**var** s): b = ⟨ s = free → s := busy; b := false
◻ self ∈ a → a := a − {self}; b := true
⟩

AlertWait(**var** m, **var** c): b
= **if** $m \neq$ self → chaos
☒ ⟨ c := $c \cup$ {self}; m := nil ⟩
fi
; ⟨ m = nil →
m := self
; ¬ self ∈ c → b := false
◻ self ∈ a → b := true
; c := c − {self}
; a := a − {self}
⟩

For comparison, we give the original Larch version of Wait:

type Condition = **set of** Thread **initially** { }

procedure Wait(**var** m: Mutex; **var** c: Condition)
= **composition of** Enqueue, Resume **end**
requires m = **self**
modifies at most [m, c]

atomic action Enqueue
ensures (c_{post}=insert(c, **self**)) ∧ (m_{post} = **nil**)

atomic action Resume
when (m = **nil**) ∧ ¬(**self** ∈ c)
ensures m_{post} = **self** & **unchanged** [c]

References

A. Birrell et. al. (1987). Synchronization primitives for a multiprocessor: A formal specification. *ACM Operating Systems Review* **21**(5): 94-102.

E. Dijkstra (1976). *A Discipline of Programming*. Prentice-Hall.

L. Lamport (1988). A simple approach to specifying concurrent systems. Technical report 15 (revised), DEC Systems Research Center, Palo Alto. To appear in *Comm. ACM*, 1988.

L. Lamport (1983). Specifying concurrent program modules. *ACM Transactions on Programming Languages and Systems*, **5**(2): 190-222.

L. Lamport and F. Schneider (1984). The "Hoare logic" of CSP, and all that. *ACM Transactions on Programming Languages and Systems*, **6**(2): 281-296.

B. Lampson (1986). Designing a global name service. *Proc. 4th ACM Symposium on Principles of Distributed Computing*, Minaki, Ontario, pp 1-10.

G. Nelson (1987). A generalization of Dijkstra's calculus. Technical report 16, DEC Systems Research Center, Palo Alto.

Jay Misra showed a way of proving properties about systems that produce rabbits in a concurrent fashion. An important theorem he presented was the following:

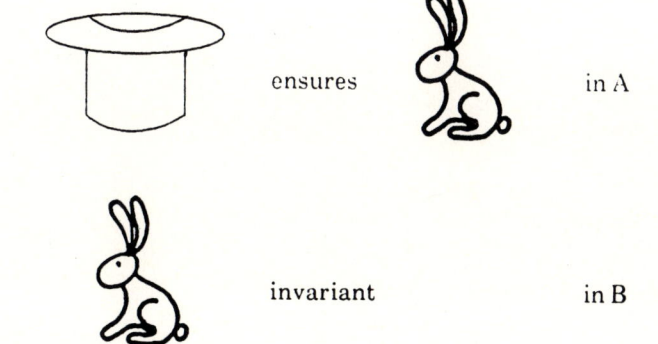

🎩 ensures 🐰 in A

🐰 invariant in B

🎩 ↦ 🐰🐰🐰🐰🐰 ... in A ☐ B

A FOUNDATION OF PARALLEL PROGRAMMING

Jayadev Misra*
Department of Computer Sciences
The University of Texas at Austin
Austin, Texas 78712
(512) 471-9547
misra@cs.utexas.edu

1 Introduction

This monograph introduces a programming theory (called UNITY) that is applicable to the design of parallel (concurrent/distributed/multi-process) programs. This theory consists of a simple computational model and a logic that is appropriate for specifying and reasoning about such programs. The computational model was first proposed in Chandy [1]; a full account of this work appears in Chandy and Misra [2]. This manuscript contains an abbreviated version of the theory and a few small examples to illustrate the theory.

In Section 2, we give a brief description of the computational model and a notation for writing programs. In Section 3, we show how this model addresses some of the issues of programming, and of parallel programming, in particular. Section 4 contains a description of the logic and some of the inference rules that are used in this monograph. Section 5 contains a basic operator for program structuring in UNITY. The next three sections illustrate some typical applications of the theory. Section 6 contains a specification and a solution of the "termination detection problem," a problem of some interest in implementing message

---

*This work was partially supported by ONR Contracts N00014-86-K-0763 and N00014-87-K-0510, by a grant from the John Simon Guggenheim Foundation, and by a University of Texas URI-FRA.

communicating systems. Section 7 contains a simplified version of a problem dealing with resource allocations. Section 8 gives a specification and an implementation of a buffer program that is to be interposed between a producer and a consumer. The final section contains a short evaluation of UNITY as a programming theory.

2 The Computational Model and Programming Notation

A UNITY program consists of a declaration of variables, their initial values, and a set of statements. In this monograph, the types of variables will be limited to integers and booleans, and the data structures to fixed size arrays; however, the programming theory is not based upon any particular data type. Initial values need not be specified for all variables; variables without a specified initial value have arbitrary values (consistent with their types) initially. Each statement in a program is an assignment statement that assigns values to one or more variables.

An execution of a program consists of an infinite number of steps. It begins from any state satisfying the prescribed initial conditions. In each step of the execution some statement is selected, nondeterministically, and executed. The only constraint on the nondeterministic selection of statements is that every statement is selected infinitely often; this is called the "fairness" rule.

Now we briefly describe a notation for expressing UNITY programs. This description is informal; see Chapter 2 of [2] for a formal description of the syntax.

A program consists of several *sections*: *declare-section* for declarations of variables, *initially-section* for prescribing the initial values of variables, and *assign-section* to list the statements. (Another section, called the *always-section*, is not used in this monograph.) We do not describe the syntax of the *declare-section* which is similar to that used for variable declarations in PASCAL, nor the *initially-section* whose syntax closely resembles that of the *assign-section*.

The statements in an *assign-section* are separated by the symbol $[\!]$. The following *assign-section* consists of two statements

$$x := y$$
$$[\!]\ y := x$$

The statements of a program may also be defined using *quantification*; the statements are obtained by instantiating a generic statement, as in

$$\langle [\!]\ i\ :\ 0 \leq i \leq 2\ ::\ A[i] := B[i] \rangle$$

This represents a set of three statements, one for each value of i in the range $0 \leq i \leq 2$. The statements obtained by substituting each possible value of i in $A[i] := B[i]$ are,

$$A[0] := B[0] \ [\!]\ A[1] := B[1] \ [\!]\ A[2] := B[2]$$

This quantification mechanism is so useful that we employ it in many different contexts. For instance

$$\langle \wedge\ i\ :\ 0 \leq i \leq N\ ::\ B[i] \rangle$$

stands for $B[0] \wedge B[1] \wedge \ldots \wedge B[N]$. The operator—$\wedge$ in this case— is always commutative and associative, and it follows the opening bracket; the bound variables—i in this case—come next (they are always of integer type); the boolean expression appearing within ":" and "::" specifies the possible values of the bound variables (the number of possible values must be finite); finally, the expression or the syntactic unit that is to be instantiated is given. The boolean expression defining the range of the bound variables is sometimes omitted when the range is defined in the accompanying text. (If there are no values of the bound variables satisfying the boolean expression then the instantiation for a statement yields an empty statement, and for boolean with operators $\wedge, \vee$ yield *true, false*, respectively.)

The individual assignment statements in an *assign-section* are, in general, multiple assignments as in

$$x, y\ :=\ y, x$$

An alternative way of writing the above, to denote that x, y are assigned their values in parallel, is

$$x := y\ \|\ y := x$$

We may employ quantification within a statement as in the following.

$$\langle \|\ i\ :\ 0 \leq i \leq N\ ::\ A[i] := B[i] \rangle$$

This assigns elements of array B to the corresponding elements of array A in parallel (i.e., in one step).

We employ conditional expressions in the right sides of assignments and separate them by $\sim$ as in,

$$x := \begin{array}{lll} -1 & \text{if } y < 0 & \sim \\ 0 & \text{if } y = 0 & \sim \\ 1 & \text{if } y > 0 & \end{array}$$

This denotes that x is assigned either $-1, 0$ or 1 based on whether y is negative, zero, or positive.

All statements are deterministic: if two different conditions in a conditional expression are satisfied then they are required to yield the same value for the assignment. Furthermore, each statement execution terminates in each program state; this certainly holds for assignment statements in which the function calls, if any, are guaranteed to terminate.

Notation: $\forall, \exists$ are used synonymously with $\wedge, \vee$, respectively. $\quad\triangledown$

3 Features of the Computational Model

In this section we show (very briefly) how the proposed computational model is adequate for representing a number of programming constructs and why it is useful for program refinement and structuring. We will also illustrate these points in reference to the examples in Sections 6, 7 and 8.

3.1 Representations of Programming Constructs

3.1.1 Synchrony

A basic construct in parallel programming is the synchronous execution of two (or more) actions. The multiple-assignment statement captures synchrony. For instance,

$$x, y := 3, 5$$

prescribes that assignments to x and y must be performed as an "atomic" action. In UNITY, we deliberately ignore the agent which performs the assignment; thus if x, y are accessible to one machine then the assignment may be performed relatively simply whereas if these are local variables of two different machines then some synchronization mechanism may have to be invoked. Abstracting away from the implementation details has the advantage that a relatively simple mechanism—multiple-assignment—may always be employed to represent synchronous executions.

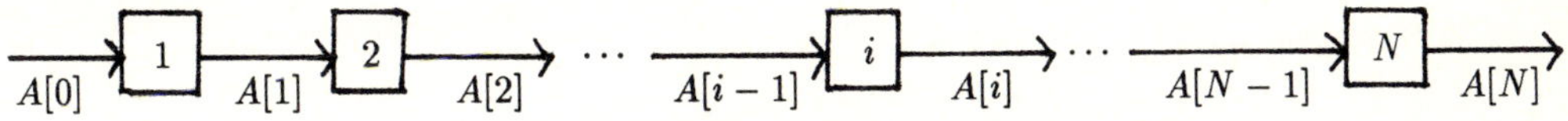

![Shift register diagram: A[0] →[1]→ A[1] →[2]→ A[2] → ... → A[i-1] →[i]→ A[i] → ... → A[N-1] →[N]→ A[N]]

Figure 1: A Shift Register with N Elements

As an example, consider a simple shift register that is shown schematically in Figure 1. The shift register has N elements; the input,output lines of the ith element are $A[i-1]$ and $A[i]$, respectively, for all i, $1 \leq i \leq N$. In each step, all elements transfer the data from their input lines to their output lines. This operation is represented by

$$\langle \| \ i \ : \ 1 \leq i \leq N \ :: \ A[i] := A[i-1] \rangle$$

3.1.2 Asynchrony

Another basic construct in parallel programming is to specify that two (or more) actions are executed in arbitrary order. The statements of a UNITY program are executed nondeterministically, and nondeterminism captures the essence of asynchrony. Again, the machines on which the actions are executed are irrelevant; if the actions are on one machine then the UNITY program may be implemented in a straightforward fashion, and if the actions are to be executed by multiple machines some form of communication among machines may have to be employed to ensure appropriate access to shared data. It is best to ignore these implementation issues during the higher levels of program design.

To illustrate the implications of nondeterminism, consider the following program that eventually computes in m the maximum of an array A of N integer elements (A is not declared below).

program *maximum*

    declare m : integer

    initially $m = -\infty$

    assign $\langle [\!] \ i \ : \ 0 \leq i < N \ :: \ m := \max(m, A[i]) \rangle$

end {*maximum*}

This program specifies little about the order in which elements of A are to be scanned. We can implement this program on a sequential computer by prescribing an order for statement executions; for instance, we may prescribe a round-robin schedule in which the statement to be executed following the ith statement—i^{th} statement is $m := \max(m, A[i])$—is the statement $(i + 1) \bmod N$, and initially the 0th statement is executed. We can also implement this program on a multiple processor machine by partitioning its statements appropriately among the processors, and letting m reside in a common memory. Similarly, this program can be implemented on a message passing architecture (the details are given in Section 3.1.5). The point is that a UNITY program offers a variety of options for implementations on different architectures. The number of implementation options are limited had we started with a more deterministic program, for instance, in which the order of statement executions was already prescribed.

3.1.3 Synchrony and Asynchrony

The following little program illustrates the use of both synchrony and asynchrony. The programming task is to sort an array of integers A, $A[0..N]$ in ascending order. The strategy employed is to pick any pair of adjacent elements and exchange them if they are out of order. The reader may convince himself that eventually A will be sorted in ascending order (since we have not yet described a logic, we cannot even state this fact, let alone prove it).

program *sort*

    assign $\langle [\!] \, i \,:\, 0 \leq i < N \,::$
                      $A[i], A[i+1] \,:=\, \min(A[i], A[i+1]), \max(A[i], A[i+1])$
        $\rangle$

end {*sort*}

There are N statements in this program, one corresponding to each value of i in the range $0 \leq i < N$, and their execution order is nondeterministic. Each statement execution, however, requires synchronous assignments of the appropriate values to $A[i]$ and $A[i+1]$.

3.1.4 Termination

Consider a state of a program in which execution of no statement causes a state change; we call such a state a *fixed point*. A program may have no fixed point (viz., a program that is expected to produce an unending sequence of numbers). The study of fixed points is important in order to demonstrate that some programs are guaranteed to reach fixed points, and that some programs are guaranteed never to reach any fixed point. If a program is at a fixed point (and it is not reactive—see Section 3.1.6), all its future states can be predicted, and hence, an implementation may decide to halt the execution of the program on a machine (or machines). Reaching of a fixed point is typically termed "termination" in sequential programming. We view termination as a feature of an implementation. The detection of a fixed point during program execution is, in general, a nontrivial task, particularly if the program is implemented on asynchronous processors; the problem is closely related to termination detection of Section 6.

3.1.5 Multiprocess Programs

There is no notion of a process in UNITY; however, the variables and the statements of a UNITY program may be partitioned for execution among a set of processes. Any fair interleaving of the (fair) executions of the partitions is an execution of the original program. Thus any implementation of "interleaved semantics"—i.e., where executions of any two actions by different processes is equivalent to their execution in some order—is also an implementation of a UNITY program on a set of processes. Grain of atomicity in interleaving depends on the nature of the variables that are shared among the processes, and how they are accessed and updated; for details see Chapter 4 of [2].

As an example consider the program *maximum* given earlier. Suppose that the N variables—$A[0], A[1] \ldots A[N-1]$—are partitioned among N processes, the ith process having $A[i]$ as a local variable. The variable m is in some shared memory that can be accessed by all processes. The statements are also partitioned among these processes, the ith process executing

$$m := \max(m, A[i])$$

The processes may then execute their codes independently as long as their accesses to m are mutually exclusive.

A strategy for implementing any shared-variable multiprocess program in a message passing architecture is to circulate a token among all the processes; the token carries the values of all shared variables, and only the token holder may examine or update the shared variables. Using this strategy, program *maximum* may be implemented by introducing a token that carries the value of m.

A UNITY program can be efficiently implemented on a message passing architecture provided its variables and statements can be partitioned in such a manner that the shared variables (i.e., those that appear in statements of two partitions) are of type sequence (representing a channel), each shared variable is shared by exactly two partitions (representing that a channel is directed from exactly one sender to exactly one receiver), and the only operations on the shared variables are (1) appending to the end of the sequence in one partition (corresponding to sending a message), and (2) removing the head item of a sequence (corresponding to receiving a message) provided the sequence is nonempty. A theory of message communication appears in Chapter 8 of [2]. It is not difficult to see that processes communicating in other fashions—rendezvous-style communication, broadcast, wait and signal on a condition, etc.—also have succinct representations within UNITY.

3.1.6 Reactive Programs

A *reactive program* is one that "interacts" with other programs during its execution. It may receive data items from the other programs, process them, and produce outputs which will be consumed by the other programs. The notion of reactive programs is crucial in designing systems, such as operating systems, which are expected to run forever. A reactive program is written in UNITY in the usual manner, where some of the variables of the program may be changed by other programs (note that UNITY has no notational mechanism to specify that certain variables are local to a program while others may be modified by other programs; such notations are required in any programming language that implements reactive programs).

As an example, consider a program that may receive inputs along two FIFO (first-in-first-out) channels, and it copies the inputs into a FIFO output channel; it guarantees that every data item sent to it along either channel is eventually copied to output. This problem is called the "fair-merge" problem. A solution for this problem cannot be described as a function mapping the input sequences to the output. Below we show a UNITY program for this problem. We have variables x, y of sequence type, representing the contents of the two input channels, respectively, and similarly, variable z representing the contents of the output channel. Variables x, y could be changed by other programs appending data items to their rears, and variable z could be changed by other programs removing data items from its front.

Notation: The symbol ";" denotes sequence concatenation; *head* applied to a nonempty sequence returns its first item; *tail* applied to a nonempty sequence returns the sequence obtained by removing its first item; *null* denotes an empty sequence. ▽

program *fair-merge*

  assign

   $x, z := \text{tail}(x) , z;\text{head}(x)$ **if** $x \neq null$

   $[\!] \ y, z := \text{tail}(y) , z;\text{head}(y)$ **if** $y \neq null$

end {*fair-merge*}

Let $\bar{x}, \bar{y}, \bar{z}$ denote the sequence of all items appended to x, y, z, respectively, during any computation. If initially x, y, z are all *null* and other programs follow the protocol for updates to x, y, z as described above then it can be shown that (1) $\bar{z}$ consists of two subsequences that are prefixes of $\bar{x}, \bar{y}$, respectively, and (2) every item in $\bar{x}$ and $\bar{y}$ eventually appears in $\bar{z}$.

A specification of a reactive program also includes a specification of the assumed protocol by which other programs interact with it; in Section 5, we show how to specify such protocols. Sections 6 and 8 contain larger examples of specifications and designs of reactive programs.

3.2 Program Refinements

A UNITY program is not tied to any particular architecture. It seems feasible therefore to develop a program in a series of refinement steps; the higher level concerns are about the problem being solved and the lower level concerns are about the architecture on which the problem is to be solved. It is important to note that all the refinements, except the very last step, can be carried out entirely within the UNITY notation, from a high level algorithm description to the very lowest level representation. The very last step of refinement maps a UNITY program to a particular architecture and/or specifies the order in which the statements are to be executed. For instance, when mapping a UNITY program to a sequential machine we must prescribe an order in which the statements are to be executed and guarantee that this order obeys the fairness rule. The mappings of UNITY programs to architectures is outside the UNITY theory. In this monograph, we will describe only informally how specific programs are mapped for efficient executions on specific architectures; see Chapter 4 of [2] for a more elaborate discussion.

At present it seems more attractive to refine specifications rather than program codes because proving the correctness of a specification refinement is found to be easier.

3.3 Correctness and Complexity

A traditional sequential program can be analyzed to establish its correctness and also to obtain a measure of its efficiency when executed on a traditional (von Neumann) computer. In this sense such a program embodies the logical steps of the algorithm as well as information about how these steps must be orchestrated. (One consequence of this is that correctness proofs are often difficult for programs which include several "optimization tricks.") The issues of correctness and complexity are totally separate in UNITY. The correctness of a UNITY program (with respect to a given specification) is a well-defined question. However, the complexity of a UNITY program is *not* well-defined; it is meaningful only after a mapping of the program to a specific architecture (and a specific execution schedule) is prescribed.

3.4 Program Structuring

Processes have a dual role in parallel programming. They are the units of structuring—i.e., a program may be understood (specified, verified, and developed) process by process. Additionally, they are the implementation units, i.e., a process (or a set of processes) are mapped to a physical processor. In many cases the best way to understand or develop a program does not lead directly to the most efficient implementation. UNITY provides a framework for separating these two issues. For instance, consider a program H consisting of two component programs, F and G—the set of statements of H is the union of the statements of F and G (and other conditions apply to *declare-* and *initially-sections*; see Section 5 for the definition of *union*). It may be best to understand H in terms of F and G and then implement H by partitioning its statements in an entirely different manner into F', G' say. Each of F', G' may contain statements from both F and G. This view of programming is useful when a computation can be structured as a set of tasks (F, G, for instance) and each task is executed by a cooperating set of processes (F', G', for instance). Section 6 contains an example where it is best to understand a computation as an interleaved execution of two tasks, each task being executed on a fixed set of processors.

4 A Brief Introduction to UNITY Logic

The structure of a UNITY program dictates that we associate properties with a program, not with points in a program because UNITY programs have no textual program points. Thus, we write "I is invariant in F" to denote that predicate I holds at all times during execution of program F. Associating properties with programs has the advantage that properties of compositions of programs can then be derived somewhat more easily.

The kinds of properties that we shall be dealing with can be broadly divided into two classes: safety and progress. Safety properties that we propose are generalizations of "invariants" and progress properties are generalizations of eventual "termination." In addition, we will introduce a predicate to deal with fixed points of a program.

We introduce three relations—*unless, ensures, leads-to*—each of which is a binary relation on a pair of predicates. (Each predicate may name program variables, bound variables, and free variables as well as constants, functions, and relations.) The safety properties are written using *unless* (and the initial conditions); the progress properties are written using *ensures* or *leads-to*.

Safety properties can be established by applying induction on lengths of computations. Progress properties, however, are more difficult to establish, because they often rely critically on the fairness assumption. For instance, consider a program that has two statements, one that decreases variable x by 1 and the other that decreases y by 1. We can assert that both x, y will become arbitrarily small in a sufficiently long computation. (This property does not hold in the absence of a fairness assumption.) This assertion cannot be proven by applying induction on lengths of computations, because there is no "variant" function that decreases with each step of the computation. We develop a logic in which the fairness assumption is captured within one relation (*ensures*) and we define a second relation (*leads-to*) inductively, using *ensures* as the basis of induction.

In the following description, all properties refer to a single program; the program name is omitted for the sake of brevity.

Notational Convention: A property having free variables is assumed to be universally quantified over all possible values of the free variables. Thus,

$$x = k \quad unless \quad x > k$$

where k is free, stands for

$$\langle \forall k :: x = k \ unless \ x > k \rangle.$$

We use p, q, r, b (with or without subscripts and primes) to denote predicates. Symbol s denotes a statement of a program.

We use

$$\{p\} \ s \ \{q\}$$

to denote that if s is executed in a state satisfying p then q holds upon completion of s. (Recall that s is guaranteed to terminate.)

We adopt the following conventions about binding powers of operators; in the order of increasing binding power are: $\equiv, \Rightarrow, (unless, ensures, \mapsto), (\wedge, \vee), (\neg), (=, \neq,$ and other relational operators over integers, sets, and sequences), arithmetic operators, function applications.

4.1 unless

For a given program

$$p \; unless \; q$$

denotes that once predicate p is true it remains true at least as long as q is not true. Formally,

$$p \; unless \; q \; \equiv \; \langle \text{for all statements } s \text{ of the program} :: \{p \wedge \neg q\} \; s \; \{p \vee q\} \rangle$$

Thus, we may deduce $p \; unless \; q$ given that for every statement in the program if $p \wedge \neg q$ holds prior to its execution then $p \vee q$ holds following its execution.

It follows from $p \; unless \; q$ that if p holds and q does not hold in a program state then in the next state either q holds, or $p \wedge \neg q$ holds; hence, by induction on the number of statement executions, $p \wedge \neg q$ continues to hold as long as q does not hold. Note that it is possible for $p \wedge \neg q$ to hold forever. Also note that if $\neg p \vee q$ holds in a state then $p \; unless \; q$ does not tell us anything about future states.

Example 1:

1. Integer variable x does not decrease.

    $$x = k \; unless \; x > k$$
    or $\quad x \geq k \; unless \; false$

2. A message is received (i.e., predicate $rcvd$ holds) only if it had been sent earlier (i.e., predicate $sent$ already holds).

    $$\neg rcvd \; unless \; sent$$

3. Variable x remains positive as long as y is.

    $$x > 0 \; unless \; y \leq 0$$

4. x, y change only synchronously.

$$x = m \land y = n \text{ unless } x \neq m \land y \neq n$$

5. x, y never change synchronously.

$$x = m \land y = n \text{ unless } (x = m \land y \neq n) \lor (x \neq m \land y = n) \qquad \triangledown$$

An interesting application of *unless* is in defining auxiliary (or history) variables. Traditionally, auxiliary variables are defined by augmenting the code of a given program. A preferable way is to state a safety property (using *unless*) that describes the relationship between the auxiliary and the other variables. As an example let x denote an integer variable and let $\bar{x}$ be an auxiliary variable whose value is the number of times that x has been increased. We may define $\bar{x}$ as follows.

initially $\quad \bar{x} = 0$

$\bar{x} = m \land x \leq n \text{ unless } \bar{x} = m + 1 \land x > n$

The above *unless* property may be read informally as "as long as x does not increase (i.e., $x \leq n$) $\bar{x}$ retains its value; when x increases (i.e., $x > n$), $\bar{x}$ is increased by 1."

4.1.1 Stable, Invariant

Two special cases of *unless*—stable, invariant—are of importance.

p is stable $\equiv p$ *unless* false

p is invariant $\equiv$ (initially p) $\land$ (p is stable)

From the definition, p is stable denotes that for all statements s (of the given program)

$$\{p\} \; s \; \{p\}$$

Thus p remains true once it is true. An invariant is initially true and remains true throughout any execution of the program.

4.1.2 Derived Rules for unless

The following derived rules are extensively used in proofs. Most of these are stated and proved in Chapter 3 of [2].

- Reflexivity

$$p \text{ unless } p$$

- Antireflexivity

$$p \text{ unless } \neg p$$

- consequence weakening

$$\frac{p \text{ unless } q, \ q \Rightarrow r}{p \text{ unless } q}$$

Corollary:

$$\frac{p \Rightarrow q}{p \text{ unless } q}$$

- conjunction and disjunction

$$\frac{p \text{ unless } q, \ p' \text{ unless } q'}{\begin{array}{l} p \wedge p' \ \text{ unless } \ (p \wedge q') \vee (p' \wedge q) \vee (q \wedge q') \quad \{\text{conjunction}\}, \\ p \vee p' \ \text{ unless } \ (\neg p \wedge q') \vee (\neg p' \wedge q) \vee (q \wedge q') \quad \{\text{disjunction}\} \end{array}}$$

Simpler forms of conjunction and disjunction are often useful; these are obtained from the above rule by weakening the consequence to $q \vee q'$ in both cases:

- (simple conjunction and simple disjunction)

$$\frac{p \text{ unless } q, \ p' \text{ unless } q'}{\begin{array}{l} p \wedge p' \ \text{ unless } \ q \vee q' \quad \{\text{simple conjunction}\} \\ p \vee p' \ \text{ unless } \ q \vee q' \quad \{\text{simple disjunction}\} \end{array}}$$

A corollary of the simple conjunction and disjunction rules is, if I, J are stable (invariant) then so are $I \wedge J$, $I \vee J$.

The following rule generalizes the conjunction and disjunction rules to an arbitrary—perhaps infinite—number of *unless*es; for proof, see [4]. In the following, m is quantified over some arbitrary set.

- (general conjunction and general disjunction)

$$\frac{\langle \forall m :: p.m \text{ unless } q.m \rangle}{\begin{array}{l} \langle \forall m :: p.m \rangle \ \text{ unless } \ \langle \forall m :: p.m \vee q.m \rangle \ \wedge \ \langle \exists m :: q.m \rangle \quad \{\text{general conjunction}\} \\ \langle \exists m :: p.m \rangle \ \text{ unless } \ \langle \forall m :: \neg p.m \vee q.m \rangle \ \wedge \ \langle \exists m :: q.m \rangle \quad \{\text{general disjuction}\} \end{array}}$$

Corollary: Let M by any total function over program states. Variable m is free in the following rule.

$$\frac{p \wedge M = m \text{ unless } (p \wedge M \neq m) \vee q}{p \text{ unless } q}$$

Corollary (free variable elimination)

Let x be a set of program variables and k be free in the following.

$$\frac{p \wedge x = k \text{ unless } q}{p \text{ unless } q}$$

4.1.3 Substitution Axiom

If $x = y$ is an invariant of a given program then x, y can be substituted for each other in any proof of the program. This is known as the *substitution axiom* and it is a reformulation of Leibniz's rule for substitution of equals in function arguments. Using this rule any invariant I may be replaced by *true*, because $I \equiv true$ is invariant. Hence, we may assert, for instance,

p unless q

given

$p \wedge I$ unless q and, I is invariant.

As a consequence, we may deduce some properties (such as p unless q above), that may not be deducible directly from the definitions.

4.2 ensures

For a given program,

p ensures q

implies that p unless q holds for the program and if p holds at any point in the execution of the program then q holds eventually. Formally,

p ensures $q \equiv p$ unless $q \wedge \langle \exists$ statement $s :: \{p \wedge \neg q\}\ s\ \{q\}\rangle$.

It follows from this definition that once p is true it remains true at least as long as q is not true (from p unless q). Furthermore, from the rules of program execution, statement s will be executed sometime after p becomes true. If q is still false prior to the execution of s then $p \wedge \neg q$ holds and the execution of s then establishes q.

Example 2: Consider a program with the following *assign-section* (where x, y are integer variables).

$$x := x - 1 \;[\!]\; y := y - 1$$

To show that

$$x = k \text{ ensures } x < k$$

We first prove

$$x = k \text{ unless } x < k$$

i.e., $\{x = k\} \; x := x - 1 \; \{x = k \lor x < k\}$ and,

$$\{x = k\} \; y := y - 1 \; \{x = k \lor x < k\}$$

Then we prove

$$\{x = k\} \; x := x - 1 \; \{x < k\} \qquad \triangledown$$

A Note on Quantification: In order to prove $x = k$ ensures $x < k$ we have to show

$$\langle \forall k :: \langle \exists s :: \{x = k\} \; s \; \{x < k\} \rangle \rangle$$

not

$$\langle \exists s :: \langle \forall k :: \{x = k\} \; s \; \{x < k\} \rangle \rangle \qquad \triangledown$$

4.2.1 Derived Rules for ensures

We show two commonly used rules; for a longer list of rules see Chapter 3 of [2].

- Reflexivity

$$p \text{ ensures } p$$

- Consequence Weakening

$$\frac{p \text{ ensures } q \, , \, q \Rightarrow r}{p \text{ ensures } r}$$

Corollary:

$$\frac{p \Rightarrow q}{p \text{ ensures } q}$$

4.3 leads-to

For a given program p *leads-to* q, abbreviated as $p \mapsto q$, denotes that once p is true, q is or becomes true. Unlike *ensures*, p may not remain true until q becomes true. The relation *leads-to* is defined inductively by the following rules. The first rule is the basis for the inductive definition of *leads-to*. The second rules states that *leads-to* is a transitive relation. In the third rule, $p.m$, for different m, denote a set of predicates. This rule states that if every predicate in a set *leads-to q* then their disjunction also *leads-to q*.

(basis)
$$\frac{p \text{ ensures } q}{p \mapsto q}$$

(transitivity)
$$\frac{p \mapsto q, \ q \mapsto r}{p \mapsto r}$$

(disjunction)
$$\frac{\langle \forall \ m :: p.m \mapsto q \rangle}{\langle \exists \ m :: p.m \rangle \mapsto q}$$

Example 3: For the program in Example 2, we show that $\langle \forall \ k :: x \geq k \mapsto x < k \rangle$.

$\langle \forall \ k, r : r \geq 0 :: x = k + r \mapsto x < k \rangle$, shown below

$\langle \forall \ k :: \langle \forall \ r : r \geq 0 :: x = k + r \mapsto x < k \rangle \rangle$, rewriting the above

$\langle \forall \ k :: \langle \exists \ r : r \geq 0 :: x = k + r \rangle \mapsto x < k \rangle$, disjunction on the above

$\langle \forall \ k :: x \geq k \mapsto x < k \rangle$, rewriting the above

Proof of $\langle \forall \ k, r : r \geq 0 :: x = k + r \mapsto x < k \rangle$

The proof is by induction on r.

$r = 0$: Proof of $\langle \forall \ k :: x = k \mapsto x < k \rangle$

$\langle \forall \ k :: x = k \text{ ensures } x < k \rangle$, from Example 2

$\langle \forall \ k :: x = k \mapsto x < k \rangle$, the basis of the definition of $\mapsto$

$r > 0$: Proof of $\langle \forall \ k :: x = k + r \mapsto x < k \rangle$

$\langle \forall \ k :: x = k \mapsto x < k \rangle$, proven above

$\langle \forall \ k :: x < k \mapsto x < k \rangle$, property of $\mapsto$ (see Section 4.3.1)

$\langle \forall \ k :: x < k + 1 \mapsto x < k \rangle$, disjunction on the above two

$\langle \forall \ k :: x = k + r \mapsto x < k + 1 \rangle$, induction hypothesis

$\langle \forall \ k :: x = k + r \mapsto x < k \rangle$, transitivity on the above two ▽

4.3.1 Derived Rules for leads-to

As Example 3 shows, proofs can be very long, even for trivial facts, if they are constructed starting from the definitions. The derived rules for *leads-to* are particularly effective in constructing succinct proofs.

- implication

$$\frac{p \Rightarrow q}{p \mapsto q}$$

- impossibility

$$\frac{p \mapsto \mathit{false}}{\neg p}$$

- general disjunction: In the following m is quantified over an arbitrary set.

$$\frac{\langle \forall\, m :: p.m \mapsto q.m \rangle}{\langle \exists\, m :: p.m \rangle \mapsto \langle \exists\, m :: q.m \rangle}$$

- PSP

$$\frac{p \mapsto q\,,\ r\ \mathit{unless}\ b}{p \wedge r \mapsto (q \wedge r) \vee b}$$

- Completion: In the following, m is quantified over any finite set.

$$\frac{\langle \forall\, m :: p.m \mapsto q.m \rangle,\quad \langle \forall\, m :: q.m\ \mathit{unless}\ b \rangle}{\langle \forall\, m :: p.m \rangle \mapsto \langle \forall\, m :: q.m \rangle \vee b}$$

- Induction: In the following, M is a total function mapping program states to a well-founded set $(W, \prec)$.

$$\frac{\langle \forall\, m : m \in W :: p \wedge M = m \mapsto (p \wedge M \prec m) \vee q \rangle}{p \mapsto q}$$

Note: The mapping function M need be defined only over the program states satisfying $p \wedge \neg q$.
▽

Example 4: We now obtain a succinct proof for Example 3 using these derived rules. In particular, use of explicit induction in the proof is avoided by applying the induction rule.

$x = m\ \mathit{ensures}\ x < m$	, from Example 2
$x = m \mapsto x < m$	, the basis of the definition of $\mapsto$
$x \geq k\ \mathit{unless}\ x < k$	, antireflexivity of *unless*
$x \geq k \wedge x = m \mapsto (x \geq k \wedge x < m) \vee x < k$	, PSP rule on the above two
$x \geq k \mapsto x < k$	, induction rule (see below)

In order to apply the induction rule in the last step of the proof we define a mapping function over the states that satisfy $x \geq k$ (i.e., $p \wedge \neg q$); the well-founded set is $\{n | n \geq k\}$ whose elements are ordered according to the usual ordering of integers, and the mapping function is $M(x, y) = x$.   ▽

4.4 Fixed Point

A fixed point of a program is a state that does not change, i.e., execution of no statement has any effect in this state. Clearly then every statement's left and right sides are equal in this state. Using this observation we define a predicate FP for a program which characterizes all and only fixed points. FP is the conjunction of all predicates that are obtained by equating the left and the right sides of each statement.

Example 5: We compute fixed points of a few programs whose *assign-sections* are shown below.

1. $x, y := y, x$
   $FP \equiv (x = y)$

2. $k \quad := k + 1$
   $FP \equiv k = k + 1$
   $\quad \equiv false$

3. $k \quad := k + 1 \quad$ if $\quad k < N$
   $FP \equiv k < N \Rightarrow k = k + 1$
   $\quad \equiv k \geq N$

4. $\langle [] \, i \, : \, 0 \leq i < N \, :: \, m := \max(m, A[i]) \rangle$
   FP
   $\quad \equiv \langle \wedge \, i \, : \, 0 \leq i < N \, :: \, m = \max(m, A[i]) \rangle$
   $\quad \equiv \langle \wedge \, i \, : \, 0 \leq i < N \, :: \, m \geq A[i] \rangle$
   $\quad \equiv m \geq \langle \max \, i \, : \, 0 \leq i < N \, :: \, A[i] \rangle$ ▽

An important result dealing with fixed points is,

Stability at fixed point: For any q, $FP \wedge q$ is stable.

5 A Program Structuring Mechanism: Union

As in other programming theories, it is often convenient to view or design a UNITY program as a composition of several program components. In this monograph, we consider a particularly simple kind of program composition: union. The union of programs F, G—denoted by $F \;[\!]\; G$—is obtained by appending the appropriate sections of their code. (Union is defined only for those programs F, G whose *declare-* and *initial-sections* are not contradictory.) Hence the set of statements of $F \;[\!]\; G$ is the union of the statements in F and G. Note that union is commutative and associative.

Programs F, G may be thought of as executing asynchronously in $F \;[\!]\; G$. The union operator is useful in understanding, among others, process networks in which each process may be viewed as a program and the entire network is their union. We will see examples of union in Sections 6 and 8. The following theorem is fundamental for understanding union (most parts of this theorem appear in Chapter 7 of [2]).

The Union Theorem:

- $$\frac{\text{initially } p \text{ in } F}{\text{initially } p \text{ in } F \;[\!]\; G}$$

- p *unless* q in $F \;[\!]\; G \;=\; p$ *unless* q in $F \;\wedge\; p$ *unless* q in G

- p *ensures* q in $F \;[\!]\; G \;=$
  $\quad [p$ *ensures* q in $F \;\wedge\; p$ *unless* q in $G]$
  $\quad \vee \; [p$ *unless* q in $F \;\wedge\; p$ *ensures* q in $G]$

- FP of $F \;[\!]\; G = FP$ of $F \;\wedge\; FP$ of G

Corollaries:

1.
$$p \text{ is stable in } F \;[\!]\; G \;=\; (p \text{ is stable in } F \;\wedge\; p \text{ is stable in } G)$$

2.
$$\frac{p \text{ unless } q \text{ in } F \;,\; p \text{ is stable in } G}{p \text{ unless } q \text{ in } F \;[\!]\; G}$$

3.
$$\frac{p \text{ is invariant in } F \;,\; p \text{ is stable in } G}{p \text{ is invariant in } F \;[\!]\; G}$$

4.
$$\frac{p \text{ ensures } q \text{ in } F \; , \; p \text{ is stable in } G}{p \text{ ensures } q \text{ in } F \; [\!] \; G}$$

▽

Observe that if p names only local variables of F (i.e., variables that cannot be modified by any other program G), then p is stable in G. So we get

Corollary (Locality)

If any of the following properties holds in F, where p names only local variables of F, then it also holds in $F \; [\!] \; G$, for any G: p unless q, p ensures q, p is invariant.

5.1 Conditional Properties

We have earlier described a reactive program as one that interacts with other programs—called its environment—during its execution. In this sense, F, G are both reactive in $F \; [\!] \; G$ and they are each others' environments (provided no other program can change any variable of F or G). Specification of a reactive program requires specification of the protocol by which its environment interacts with it. For instance, in describing the *fair-merge* program of Section 3.1, we assumed that its environment appends to the rear of the sequences that are input to *fair-merge*, and removes from the front of the output sequence of *fair-merge*. In case this protocol is violated the behavior of *fair-merge* is undefined. In general, a property of a reactive program F can be given by,

$$\langle \forall \; G :: \; P \text{ in } G \Rightarrow Q \text{ in } F \; [\!] \; G \rangle \; ,$$

where G is any program and P, Q are properties. This says that for any program G—a possible environment for F—in which P is a property, Q is a property of $F \; [\!] \; G$. Note that the above describes a property—called a *conditional property*—of program F. Program F may have many such properties in its specification corresponding to the different environments with which it may be composed. An example of a conditional property appears in Section 8, in specifying a buffer.

6 Termination Detection in a Ring

A message communicating system consists of a set of processes connected by directed channels. Each channel is directed from exactly one process to another; the messages in the channel are the ones sent by the former process to the latter which are, as yet, undelivered. A process is in one of two states: idle (i.e., quiescent) or nonidle. An idle process sends no message, and it remains idle as long as it receives no message. A nonidle process may become idle (autonomously). A message is received along a channel only if it had been sent along that channel. The system is *terminated* when all processes are idle and all channels are empty (i.e., have no messages in them) because all processes will stay idle—since the first process to become nonidle has to first receive a message—and all channels will remain empty—since idle processes send no message. It is required to develop an algorithm by which processes can determine that the system is terminated.

One of the more difficult aspects of this problem is to specify it precisely: What is given, what is to be designed, and what properties should the design satisfy. We specify the problem in Sections 6.1 and 6.2. We propose an algorithm for this problem in Section 6.3 and prove its correctness in Section 6.4. The specification and verification rely heavily on the derived rules of UNITY logic.

In this monograph, we limit ourselves to a system in which the processes are connected in a unidirectional ring; the general case, described and solved in [3], is almost analogous though more notation is needed in that case. Our purpose here is primarily to acquaint the reader with UNITY-style specification, problem decomposition and proofs, and only secondarily with the problem of termination detection.

6.1 Problem Specification

Let there be N processes arranged in a unidirectional ring, the successor of the ith process having index i'. The following variables are defined as follows—for all i (in this problem i is quantified over all indices in a given ring):

$s.i$, the number of messages sent by i (to i')

$r.i$, the number of messages received by i

$q.i$, a boolean variable that is true if and only if process i is idle

There is no notion of a process in UNITY. Hence we regard the entire process network as a program, D, that manipulates the variables given above, for all i. The following properties of D have been described earlier: the number of messages sent by a process is at least the number received by its successor, and both these numbers are nonnegative ($D1$, given below); the number of messages sent and received by a process are nondecreasing ($D2$); a process remains idle as long as it receives no message ($D3$); and an idle process has to become nonidle first in order to send a message ($D4$). Formally, for all i, we have the following properties in D.

D1. $s.i \geq r.i' \geq 0$ is invariant.

D2. $r.i \geq m$ is stable,

$s.i \geq n$ is stable

D3. $q.i \wedge r.i = m$ unless $r.i > m$

D4. $q.i \wedge s.i = n$ unless $\neg q.i \wedge s.i = n$

The properties, $D1 - D4$, are the only properties of D that we will assume. There are several aspects of the specification that are worth noting. First, we do not assume that the channels are FIFO, i.e., messages sent along a channel may be delivered in a different order from the sending order. Second, there is no guarantee that a message will be delivered. Third, several processes may receive and/or send messages in one step; however a process may not receive a message, become nonidle and send a message all in one step (from $D4$, a process can send a message in a step provided it is nonidle at the beginning of the step).

Observation: Variables $s.i, r.i, q.i$, for all i, are local to D. Hence, applying the locality corollary of the union theorem (Section 5), we derive that $D1 - D4$ are also properties of $D \parallel G$, for any G. ▽

Note: $D3, D4$ may be replaced by their conjunction

$q.i \wedge r.i = m \wedge s.i = n$ unless $r.i > m \wedge s.i = n$.

It can be shown that the above property is equivalent to $D3$ and $D4$. ▽

6.2 Definition of Termination

We have informally described termination as "all processes are idle and all channels are empty (i.e., for each channel, the number of messages sent equals the number received)." We will show that none of the variables can change once the termination condition holds.

Let,

$T \equiv \langle \forall i :: q.i \wedge s.i = r.i' \rangle$

Observe that proving T to be stable only establishes that no $q.i$ will change (become false) once T holds; however, it is possible for $r.i, s.i$ to change while preserving $s.i = r.i'$, for all i. Hence, we prove below that $T \wedge \langle \forall i :: r.i = m.i \rangle$ is stable where $m.i$'s are free variables.

D5. $T \wedge \langle \forall i :: r.i = m.i \rangle$ is stable in D.

Proof of D5: The result is proven by taking the conjunction of $D3, D4$ and then applying the general conjunction rule over all i. In the following, all properties are of D.

$\quad q.i \wedge r.i = m.i \wedge s.i = m.i'$ unless $r.i > m.i \wedge s.i = m.i'$

$\qquad$, replacing m, n by $m.i, m.i'$ in $D3, D4$ and then taking their conjunction

$\quad \langle \forall i :: q.i \wedge r.i = m.i \wedge s.i = m.i' \rangle$ unless

$\qquad \langle \forall i :: (q.i \wedge r.i = m.i \wedge s.i = m.i') \vee (r.i > m.i \wedge s.i = m.i') \rangle \wedge$

$\qquad \langle \exists i :: r.i > m.i \wedge s.i = m.i' \rangle$

$\qquad$, taking general conjunction of the above over all i $\hfill (1)$

The left side of (1)

$\equiv \quad \langle \forall i :: q.i \wedge s.i = r.i' \rangle \wedge \langle \forall i :: r.i = m.i \rangle$

$\equiv \quad T \wedge \langle \forall i :: r.i = m.i \rangle$

The first conjunct in the right side of $(1) \Rightarrow \langle \forall i :: s.i = m.i' \rangle$

The second conjunct in the right side of $(1) \Rightarrow \langle \exists i :: r.i > m.i \rangle$

Hence the right side of (1)

$\Rightarrow \quad \langle \forall i :: s.i = m.i' \rangle \wedge \langle \exists i :: r.i > m.i \rangle$

$\Rightarrow \quad \langle \exists i :: r.i' > m.i' \wedge m.i' = s.i \rangle$

$\qquad$, replacing $\langle \exists i :: r.i > m.i \rangle$ by $\langle \exists i :: r.i' > m.i' \rangle$

$\equiv \quad$ *false*

$\qquad$, using the substitution axiom and $s.i \geq r.i'$ from $(D1)$ $\hfill \triangledown$

D6. T is stable in D.

Proof of D6: Eliminate the free variables $m.i$ (using the corollary from Section 4.1.2) from $D5$. $\hfill \triangledown$

6.3 An Algorithm for Termination Detection

Detection of T is nontrivial: An asynchronous inspection of the processes and channels may find every process to be idle and every channel to be empty; yet, T may not hold. An algorithm that does allow asynchronous inspection to succeed is the following.

Process i records the values of $q.i, r.i, s.i$ in variables $vq.i, vr.i, vs.i$, respectively at arbitrary times. Let VT be a predicate, analogous to T, defined as follows.

$$VT \equiv \langle \forall i :: vq.i \wedge vs.i = vr.i' \rangle$$

We will show that $VT \Rightarrow T$, i.e., detecting VT is sufficient to guarantee T. Detection of VT can be accomplished in a number of ways. A token may visit the processes recording the values of $q.i, s.i, r.i$ (in $vq.i, vs.i, vr.i$), from each i, and whenever VT is satisfied by the values carried by the token, T can be asserted. Another possibility is to employ a central process to which all processes send their recorded values at arbitrary times, and the central process can compute VT. The reason VT is easier to compute than T is that updates of the variables in VT are completely under our control, whereas the variables of T are modified by program D.

We view the recording programs of all processes together as a single program R. The entire program then is $D \parallel R$. Program R is given below. (Declarations of $vq.i, vs.i, vr.i$ are not shown; they are boolean, integer, integer, respectively.)

Program R
  initially $\langle \parallel i :: vq.i, vs.i, vr.i = false, 0, 0 \rangle$
  assign $\langle \parallel i :: vq.i, vs.i, vr.i := q.i, s.i, r.i \rangle$
end $\{R\}$

We will prove the following properties of $D \parallel R$.

$DR1.$ $VT \Rightarrow T$ is invariant in $D \parallel R$
$DR2.$ $T \mapsto VT$ in $D \parallel R$

It is important to note that the program $D \parallel R$ can be viewed in two different ways. It is the union of two tasks, D and R. Each of these tasks is executed by all processes, i.e., $D = \langle \parallel i :: D_i \rangle$ where D_i is a component of the given program corresponding to process i, and $R = \langle \parallel i :: R_i \rangle$ where R_i is the component of the recording program executed by i. Therefore $D \parallel R$ may also be viewed as $\langle \parallel i :: D_i \parallel R_i \rangle$ where $D_i \parallel R_i$ is the program (given and recording) for process i. The second way of structuring $D \parallel R$, around processes, is not convenient for proving $DR1$ and $DR2$, though it is the preferred view when implementing the algorithm on a set of processes. Our computational model allows us to choose the most convenient decomposition for the purpose at hand.

6.4 Proof of the Algorithm

We note two additional properties of $D \, [] \, R$. Property $DR3$ is easily understood; $DR4$ says that any process that was idle at the time of its last recording and that has not received any message since then, is still idle and has not sent any message since then.

$DR3.$ $s.i \geq vs.i \geq 0$ is invariant in $D \, [] \, R$,

$\quad\quad\;\;$ $r.i \geq vr.i \geq 0$ is invariant in $D \, [] \, R$

$DR4.$ $vq.i \land (r.i = vr.i) \Rightarrow q.i \land (s.i = vs.i)$ is invariant in $D \, [] \, R$

These properties can be proven by showing that they are invariant in R (from the text of R), and stable in D (from the specification of D) and then applying corollary 3 of the union theorem. Most of these proofs are straightforward; we only show that the predicate in $DR4$ is stable in program D.

6.4.1 A Stability Proof in D

$vq.i \land (vr.i = r.i) \Rightarrow q.i \land (vs.i = s.i)$ is stable in D

Proof: All properties in the following proof are of D.

$\quad\quad q.i \land r.i = m \land s.i = n$ *unless* $r.i > m$

$\quad\quad\quad\quad$, conjunction of $D3, D4$ and then weakening the right side

$\quad\quad r.i > m$ is stable

$\quad\quad\quad\quad$, $D2$ with $m + 1$ substituted for m

$\quad\quad (r.i > m) \lor (q.i \land r.i = m \land s.i = n)$ is stable

$\quad\quad\quad\quad$, disjunction of the above two

$\quad\quad \neg vq.i$ is stable

$\quad\quad\quad\quad$, $vq.i$ is constant in D

$\quad\quad vq.i \land r.i \leq m \Rightarrow q.i \land r.i = m \land s.i = n$ is stable

$\quad\quad\quad\quad$, simple disjunction of the above two and rewriting

$\quad\quad vq.i \land r.i \leq vr.i \Rightarrow q.i \land r.i = vr.i \land s.i = vs.i$ is stable

$\quad\quad\quad\quad$, substituting $vr.i, vs.i$—that are constants in D—for m, n, respectively

$\quad\quad vq.i \land r.i = vr.i \Rightarrow q.i \land r.i = vr.i \land s.i = vs.i$ is stable

$\quad\quad\quad\quad$, substitution axiom using $DR3$ yields $r.i \leq vr.i \equiv r.i = vr.i$

$\quad\quad vq.i \land r.i = vr.i \Rightarrow q.i \land s.i = vs.i$ is stable

$\quad\quad\quad\quad$, simplifying the above property $\quad\quad\quad\quad\quad\quad\quad\quad\quad\quad\quad\quad\quad\quad$ ▽

6.4.2 Proof of DR1

To prove that

DR1. $VT \Rightarrow T$ is invariant in $D \, [\!] \, R$

We show that

$VT \Rightarrow T$ is stable in D and,

$VT \Rightarrow T$ is invariant in R

Then, applying corollary 3 of the union theorem, $DR1$ follows.

Proof of $VT \Rightarrow T$ is stable in D

$\neg VT$ is stable in D	, no variable of VT is modified in D
T is stable in D	, from $(D6)$
$VT \Rightarrow T$ is stable in D	, simple disjunction of the above two and rewriting ▽

Proof of $VT \Rightarrow T$ is invariant in R

In the following proof, all properties are in R.

Initially $\neg VT$ holds because $\neg vq.i$, for all i. To show the stability of $VT \Rightarrow T$, we have to show for any arbitrary j that

$\{VT \Rightarrow T\} \ vq.j, vs.j, vr.j := q.j, s.j, r.j \ \{VT \Rightarrow T\}$

We show the stronger assertion

$\{true\} \ vq.j, vs.j, vr.j := q.j, s.j, r.j \ \{VT \Rightarrow T\}$

or equivalently {since the assignment establishes the postcondition

$(vq.j, vs.j, vr.j) = (q.j, s.j, r.j)\}$

$VT \land (vq.j, vs.j, vr.j) = (q.j, s.j, r.j) \Rightarrow T$

The proof is as follows. Assume the antecedent of the above.

$vr.j' = vs.j$	, from VT in the antecedent
$vs.j = s.j$	, from the antecedent
$s.j \geq r.j'$	, from $D1$
$r.j' \geq vr.j'$	, from $DR3$
$vr.j' = r.j'$	, from the above four properties
$vq.j'$	, from VT

$q.j' \wedge s.j' = vs.j'$, from $vq.j' \wedge r.j' = vr.j'$ using $DR4$

$(vq.j', vs.j', vr.j') = (q.j', s.j', r.j')$, from the above three

Hence we have

$VT \wedge (vq.j, vs.j, vr.j) = (q.j, s.j, r.j)$
$\Rightarrow (vq.j', vs.j', vr.j') = (q.j', s.j', r.j')$

Applying induction,

$VT \wedge (vq.j, vs.j, vr.j) = (q.j, s.j, r.j)$
$\Rightarrow VT \wedge \langle \forall i :: (vq.i, vs.i, vr.i) = (q.i, s.i, r.i) \rangle$

The consequent of the above implies T. ▽

6.4.3 Proof of DR2

Let $u.i \equiv (q.i, s.i, r.i) = (vq.i, vs.i, vr.i)$

Proof of $T \mapsto VT$ in $D \, [\!] \, R$

$T \mapsto T \wedge u.i$ in $D \, [\!] \, R$	, shown below
$T \wedge u.i$ is stable in $D \, [\!] \, R$	, shown below
$T \mapsto \langle \forall i :: T \wedge u.i \rangle$ in $D \, [\!] \, R$	, applying the completion rule for *leads-to* (Section 4.3.1)
$\langle \forall i :: T \wedge u.i \rangle \Rightarrow VT$	, from definitions of $T, u.i, VT$
$T \mapsto VT$ in $D \, [\!] \, R$	, from the above two using implication and transitivity

Proof of $T \mapsto T \wedge u.i$ in $D \, [\!] \, R$

T ensures $T \wedge u.i$ in R	, from the text of R
T is stable in D	, from $D5$
T ensures $T \wedge u.i$ in $D \, [\!] \, R$	, corollary 4 of the union theorem
$T \mapsto T \wedge u.i$ in $D \, [\!] \, R$	, basis of the definition of $\mapsto$

▽

Proof of $T \wedge u.i$ is stable in $D \, [\!] \, R$

$T \wedge r.i = m.i \wedge r.i' = m.i'$ is stable in D
, eliminating all other $m.j$ from $D5$

$vq.i$ is stable in D

, $vq.i$ is constant in D

$T \wedge (q.i, s.i, r.i) = (vq.i, m.i', m.i)$ is stable in D

, conjunction of the above two and rewriting

$T \wedge u.i$ is stable in D

, replacing $m.i, m.i'$ by $vr.i$ and $vs.i$ that are constants in D

$T \wedge u.i$ is stable in R

, from the text of R

$T \wedge u.i$ is stable in $D \parallel R$

, union theorem   ▽

7   A Theorem about Dynamic Acyclic Graphs

This section is taken from [5].

Given is a finite directed acyclic graph. A *top* vertex has no incoming edge; a *bottom* vertex has no outgoing edge. The graph is changed according to the following operation: Pick an arbitrary vertex; if it is a top vertex reverse the directions of all edges incident on it (thereby converting it into a bottom vertex). This operation is repeated forever with the constraint that every vertex is picked infinitely often. It is required to show that any vertex eventually becomes a bottom vertex.

This is a special case of the dining philosophers solution given in Chapter 12 of [2]. The dining philosophers has, additionally, a state for each vertex: thinking, hungry, or eating. Every eating vertex is a bottom vertex. The rule for transformation of the graph is this: A hungry vertex that has no incoming edge from a hungry vertex either becomes eating (and points all incident edges inward to become a bottom vertex) or gets an incoming edge from a hungry vertex (by some thinking vertex becoming hungry). It was proven that every hungry vertex eventually becomes eating.

The purpose of this note is to study the proof of the simpler problem (stated in the first paragraph) which abstracts the essence of the progress proof for the dining philosophers solution in [2].

7.1 A Formal Statement of the Problem

Let u, v, w denote arbitrary vertices, $u \, E \, v$ denotes that there is a directed edge from u to v and $u \, R \, v$ denotes that there is a directed path from u to v. Formal definition of $u \, R \, v$ is as follows:

$u \, R^1 \, v \quad \equiv u \, E \, v$

$u \, R^{n+1} \, v \equiv \langle \exists \, w :: u \, E \, w \wedge w \, R^n \, v \rangle \quad , n \geq 1$

$u \, R \, v \quad \equiv \langle \exists \, n : n \geq 1 :: u \, R^n \, v \rangle$

We write $u.\top, u.\bot$ to denote, respectively, that u is a top or bottom vertex. Formally,

$u.\top \equiv \langle \forall \, v :: \neg v \, E \, u \rangle$

$u.\bot \equiv \langle \forall \, v :: \neg u \, E \, v \rangle$

Note: A disconnected vertex is both a top and a bottom vertex. $\triangledown$

Convention: Throughout this section $n \geq 1$. $\triangledown$

The following program describes the way the graph is changed.

Program *change*

    initially $\langle [\!] \, u :: u \, R \, u = \mathit{false} \rangle$ {graph is initially acyclic}

    assign

        $\langle [\!] \, u ::$

            $\langle \| \, v :: u \, E \, v, v \, E \, u := \mathit{false}, u \, E \, v \quad \text{if} \quad u.\top \rangle$

    $\rangle$

end {*change*}

It is required to show that for any u,

    $\mathit{true} \mapsto u.\bot$

7.2 Basic Facts

We only need the following properties of program *change*.

    initially $\neg u \, R \, u$ (Q0)

    $\neg u \, E \, v$ unless $\neg u.\bot \wedge v.\bot$ (Q1)

    $u.\top \mapsto u.\bot$ (Q2)

Properties (Q0,Q1) can be proven directly from the program text. Property (Q2) is proven by showing $u.\top$ ensures $u.\bot$, as follows.

Proof of $u.\top$ unless $u.\bot$:

$\neg v\ E\ u$ unless $u.\bot$

, interchanging u, v in (Q1) and weakening its right hand side

$\langle \forall\ v :: \neg v\ E\ u \rangle$ unless $u.\bot$

, simple disjunction

$u.\top$ unless $u.\bot$

, definition of $u.\top$ ▽

Next observe that there is a statement that establishes $u.\bot$ as a postcondition given $u.\top$ as a precondition.

$\{u.\top\}\ \langle \|\ v :: u\ E\ v, v\ E\ u := \mathit{false}, u\ E\ v\quad \text{if}\quad u.\top \rangle\ \{u.\bot\}$

The proof of the following theorem is straightforward from the definitions.

Theorem 0: $u\ R^n\ v \Rightarrow \neg u.\bot$

Proof (sketch): Show, using induction on n, that

$u\ R^n\ v \Rightarrow \langle \exists\ w :: u\ E\ w \rangle$

From definition of $u.\bot$, $\langle \exists\ w :: u\ E\ w \rangle \Rightarrow \neg u.\bot$ ▽

Corollary 0: $u\ R\ v \Rightarrow \neg u.\bot$ ▽

7.3 The Graph Remains Acyclic

We show that no path is created from one vertex to another unless the former becomes non-bottom and the latter bottom.

Theorem 1: $\neg u\ R^n\ v$ unless $\neg u.\bot \wedge v.\bot$

Proof: The proof is by induction on n.

$n = 1$: $\neg u\ E\ v$ unless $\neg u.\bot \wedge v.\bot$, from (Q1)

$n + 1$: $\neg u\ R^{n+1}\ v = \langle \forall\ w :: \neg u\ E\ w \vee \neg w\ R^n\ v \rangle$, from the definition of R^{n+1}

$\neg u\ E\ w$ unless $\neg u.\bot \wedge w.\bot$, from (Q1)

$\neg w\ R^n\ v$ unless $\neg w.\bot \wedge v.\bot$, induction hypothesis

$\neg u\ E\ w \vee \neg w\ R^n\ v$ unless

$$(u \; E \; w \; \wedge \; \neg w. \perp \; \wedge \; v. \perp)$$
$$\vee \; (w \; R^n \; v \; \wedge \; \neg u. \perp \; \wedge \; w. \perp)$$
$$\vee \; (\neg u. \perp \; \wedge \; w. \perp \; \wedge \; \neg w. \perp \; \wedge \; v. \perp) \;\;, \text{disjunction of the above two}$$

The first disjunct in the right side of the above may be weakened to $\neg u. \perp$ (because $u \; E \; w \Rightarrow \neg u. \perp$, from Theorem 0) $\wedge \; v. \perp$; the second disjunct is *false* because $w \; R^n \; v \Rightarrow \neg w. \perp$ (from Theorem 0); the third disjunct is *false*. Hence we get

$\neg u \; E \; w \; \wedge \; \neg w \; R^n \; v \; \textit{unless} \; \neg u. \perp \; \wedge \; v. \perp$
$\neg u \; R^{n+1} \; v \qquad\qquad \textit{unless} \; \neg u. \perp \; \wedge \; v. \perp$, simple conjunction of the above over all w ▽

Corollary 1: $\quad \neg u \; R \; v \; \textit{unless} \; \neg u. \perp \; \wedge \; v. \perp$

Proof: Take simple conjunction of Theorem 1 over all n. ▽

The following corollary says that the graph is always acyclic.

Corollary 2: $\quad \neg u \; R \; u$ is invariant
  initially $\neg u \; R \; u \qquad$, from (Q0)
  $\neg u \; R \; u$ is stable $\qquad$, setting v to u in corollary 1. ▽

Let $u.a$ denote the ancestors of, i.e., the set of vertices that have paths to, u. Formally,

$$v \in u.a \equiv v \; R \; u$$

Let A denote any constant set of vertices.

Corollary 3: $\quad u.a = A \; \textit{unless} \; u.a \subset A \; \vee \; u. \perp$

Proof:
  $\neg v \; R \; u \; \textit{unless} \; u. \perp$
    , from corollary 1 interchanging u, v and weakening the right hand side
  $v \notin u.a \; \textit{unless} \; u. \perp$
    , from the above using the definition of $u.a$
  $\langle \forall v : v \notin A :: v \notin u.a \rangle \; \textit{unless} \; u. \perp$
    , simple conjunction of the above over all $v \notin A$
  $u.a \subseteq A \; \textit{unless} \; u. \perp$
    , the above left hand side is $\langle \forall v :: v \notin A \Rightarrow v \notin u.a \rangle$, i.e., $u.a \subseteq A$
  $u.a = A \; \textit{unless} \; u.a \neq A$

, antireflexivity of *unless*

$u.a = A$ *unless* $u.a \subset A \lor u.\bot$

, conjunction of the above two ▽

7.4 The Progress Proof

Theorem 2: $true \mapsto u.\bot$

Proof:

$u.a = A$ *unless* $u.a \subset A \lor u.\bot$

, corollary 3

$v \in A$ is stable

, A is a constant set

$u.a = A \land v \in A$ *unless* $u.a \subset A \lor u.\bot$

, conjunction of the above two and weakening the right hand side

$v.\top \mapsto v.\bot$

, property (Q2)

$u.a = A \land v \in A \land v.\top \mapsto (u.a = A \land v \in A \land v.\bot) \lor u.a \subset A \lor u.\bot$

, PSP rule on the above two

$u.a = A \land v \in A \land v.\top \mapsto u.a \subset A \lor u.\bot$

, the first disjunct in the right side is *false* because $v \in u.a \equiv v \, R \, u$ and $v \, R \, u \Rightarrow \neg v.\bot$ (from corollary 0)

$u.a = A \land \langle \exists v :: v \in A \land v.\top \rangle \mapsto u.a \subset A \lor u.\bot$

, disjunction of the above over all v

$u.a = A \land A \neq \emptyset \mapsto u.a \subset A \lor u.\bot$ (2)

, using implication rule on the above because for acyclic graphs,

$u.a = A \land A \neq \emptyset \Rightarrow \langle \exists v :: v \in A \land v.\top \rangle$

$u.a = A \land A = \emptyset \Rightarrow u.\top$

, definition of $u.a$ and $u.\top$

$u.a = A \land A = \emptyset \mapsto u.\bot$

, from the above and $u.\top \mapsto u.\bot$ (property Q2)

$u.a = A \mapsto u.a \subset A \lor u.\bot$

, disjunction of the above and (2)

$(true \land u.a = A) \mapsto (true \land u.a \subset A) \lor u.\bot$

, rewriting the above

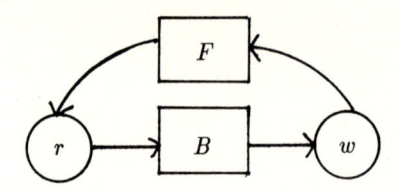

Figure 2: A Buffer Program B and its environment F

$true \mapsto u. \bot$

, induction rule on the above: a family of finite sets is well-founded under the subset ordering $\triangledown$

8 A Specification of a Buffer

This section is taken from [6].

A buffer program acts as an intermediary between a producer and a consumer, temporarily storing the data items output by the producer and later delivering them to the consumer. The buffer program is required to (1) deliver data in the same order to the consumer as they were received from the producer, (2) receive data from the producer provided its internal buffer spaces are nonfull, and (3) upon demand, send data to the consumer provided its internal buffer spaces are nonempty. Specifically, a *buffer* program, B, reads data from a variable r and writes data into a variable w. The program runs asynchronously with another program, called F, which writes into r and reads from w. The communication structure is shown in Fig. 2.

The program F represents both the producer and the consumer. There might be multiple producers and consumers or even a single process that is both the producer and the consumer; the exact number is irrelevant for the specification of the buffer. The values that can be written into r, w are, again, irrelevant for specification. However we do postulate a special value, $\emptyset$, which is written into a variable to denote that it is "empty," i.e., it contains no useful data. The protocol for reading and writing is as follows. Program F writes into r only if $r = \emptyset$; only if $r \neq \emptyset$, program B reads a value from r and it may set r to $\emptyset$. Program B stores a value in w only if w is $\emptyset$; program F reads from w and it may set w to $\emptyset$ to indicate that it is ready to consume the next piece of data.

8.1 Auxiliary Variables

It is convenient to employ the auxiliary variables, $\bar{r}$ and $\bar{w}$, which denote, respectively, the sequence of data items (i.e., non-$\emptyset$ values) written into r and w. The typical definitions of $\bar{r}, \bar{w}$ are given by augmenting the program text; a value d, $d \neq \emptyset$, is appended to $\bar{r}$ whenever d is stored in r. Fortunately, our logical operators provide a preferable way to define auxiliary variables.

Notation: All through this paper d, e, f refer to arbitrary data values or $\emptyset$, and x, y denote sequences of these values. The concatenation operator for sequences is ";" . For all x, $(x; \emptyset) = (\emptyset; x) = x$. ▽

Definitions of $\bar{r}, \bar{w}$ are as follows. (The two definitions are completely analogous.)

initially $(\bar{r}, \bar{w}) = (r, w)$ in $B \,[\!]\, F$ (A0)

$\bar{r} = x \wedge r = d$ unless $\bar{r} = x; r \wedge r \neq d$ in $B \,[\!]\, F$ (A1)

$\bar{w} = y \wedge w = e$ unless $\bar{w} = y; w \wedge w \neq e$ in $B \,[\!]\, F$ (A2)

To understand A1, note that if $\emptyset$ is stored in r (i.e., data is consumed from r) then $\bar{r}$ remains unchanged (because $x; r = x; \emptyset = x$). If r is changed to d, $d \neq \emptyset$, then $\bar{r}$ is extended by d. Properties, A0,A1,A2, may be taken as axioms in a proof of $B \,[\!]\, F$.

8.2 Specification of a Buffer of Size N

A buffer of size N, $N \geq 1$, has $N - 1$ internal words for storage. (The reason for using $N - 1$, rather than N, is that with this definition concatenations of buffers of size M, N results in a buffer of size $M + N$.) For $N = 1$, the buffer program simply moves data from r to w.

Notation: Define an ordering relation, $\prec$, among data values as follows:

$\emptyset$ is "smaller than" all non-$\emptyset$ values, i.e.,

$d \prec e \equiv d = \emptyset \wedge e \neq \emptyset$ ▽

The properties P1 and P2, given below, state respectively that program B removes only non-$\emptyset$ data from r and it may set r to $\emptyset$, and it writes only non-$\emptyset$ data values in w provided $w = \emptyset$.

initially $w = \emptyset$ in B (P0)

$r = d$ unless $r \prec d$ in B (P1)

$w = e$ unless $e \prec w$ in B (P2)

Observe that setting d to $\emptyset$ in (P1) gives us (because $r \prec \emptyset \equiv \text{false}$),

$r = \emptyset$ is stable in B

That is, B never changes r from $\emptyset$ to non-$\emptyset$. Similarly, we may deduce from (P2) that B never overwrites a non-$\emptyset$ value in w.

The next property, P3, says that (1) the sequence of data items stored in w by B is a prefix of the sequence supplied to it in r, (2) these two sequences differ by no more than N in length, (3) if the two sequences differ by less than N in length (i.e., internal buffer is nonfull) or w is $\emptyset$ then data, if any, would be removed from r, (4) if more items have been supplied to B than have been written into w or r is non-$\emptyset$ then w is or will be set to a non-$\emptyset$ value. These properties, however, cannot hold if program F, with which B is composed, is uncooperative; for instance, if F overwrites a data value in r with another data value then B can never reproduce the overwritten value in w. Hence these properties—collectively called the conclusion for B, or $B.conc$—hold conditioned upon two properties of F—collectively called the hypothesis for B, or $B.hypo$—that F writes a value into r only if r is $\emptyset$ and F sets w only to $\emptyset$.

Notation: $|\bar{r}|, |\bar{w}|$ denote the lengths of $\bar{r}, \bar{w}$, respectively. For sequences x, y, $x \sqsubseteq y$ denotes that x is a prefix of y. $\triangledown$

The property (P3) is,

$$\langle \forall\ F\ ::\ B.hypo \text{ in } F\ \Rightarrow\ B.conc \text{ in } B \parallel F \rangle \tag{P3}$$

where,

$$B.hypo\ ::\ r = d\ \text{unless}\ d \prec r,$$
$$w = e\ \text{unless}\ w \prec e$$

and,

$$B.conc\ ::\ \bar{w} \sqsubseteq \bar{r},$$
$$|\bar{r}| \leq |\bar{w}| + N,$$
$$|\bar{r}| < |\bar{w}| + N\ \lor\ w = \emptyset \mapsto r = \emptyset,$$
$$|\bar{r}| > |\bar{w}|\ \qquad\ \lor\ r \neq \emptyset \mapsto w \neq \emptyset$$

Note that P3 is a property of program B. It says that if B is composed with *any* program F that satisfies $B.hypo$, then $B \parallel F$ satisfies $B.conc$. Also observe that $B.hypo$ is the same as (P1,P2), with the roles of r, w interchanged, because the protocols for production and consumption by F are symmetric to those of B.

```
           r        B1       s       B2       w
     Size M                    Size N
```

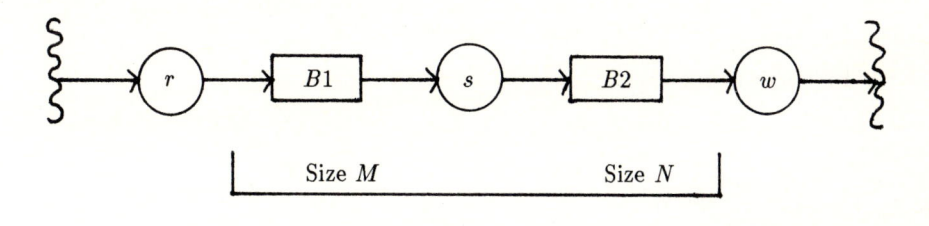

$B = B1 \, [\!] \, B2$ has Size $M + N$

Figure 3: Concatenations of buffers $B1, B2$

8.3 Buffer Concatenation

Let $B1$ be a buffer of size M with input, output words, r and s, respectively; let $B2$ be a buffer of size N with input, output words s and w, respectively. We show that $B1 \, [\!] \, B2$ implements a buffer of size $M + N$ with input, output words r and w, respectively. The arrangement is shown pictorially in Fig. 3.

8.3.1 Proof of P0 for B

From P0 of $B2$, using the union theorem.

8.3.2 Proof of P1,P2 for B

We are given

$r = d \quad unless \quad r \prec d \text{ in } B1$ \hfill (P1 for $B1$)

$s = f \quad unless \quad f \prec s \text{ in } B1$ \hfill (P2 for $B1$)

and

$s = f \quad unless \quad s \prec f \text{ in } B2$ \hfill (P1 for $B2$)

$w = e \quad unless \quad e \prec w \text{ in } B2$ \hfill (P2 for $B2$)

We have to show, P1,P2 for B, where $B = B1 \, [\!] \, B2$:

$r = d \quad unless \quad r \prec d \text{ in } B1 \, [\!] \, B2$ \hfill (P1 for B)

$w = e \quad unless \quad e \prec w \text{ in } B1 \, [\!] \, B2$ \hfill (P2 for B)

We only show P1; P2's proof is nearly identical.

$r = d$ unless $r \prec d$ in $B1$, from P1 of $B1$

$r = d$ is stable in $B2$, r is not accessible to $B2$

$r = d$ unless $r \prec d$ in $B1 \;[\!]\; B2$, from corollary 2 to the union theorem

8.3.3 Proof of P3 for B

We are required to prove P3 for B assuming P3 for $B1$ and $B2$ (and also using P1,P2 for both $B1, B2$). More precisely, we have to show:

$$\langle \forall G :: B1.hypo \text{ in } G \Rightarrow B1.conc \text{ in } B1 \;[\!]\; G \rangle$$
$$\wedge \langle \forall H :: B2.hypo \text{ in } H \Rightarrow B2.conc \text{ in } B2 \;[\!]\; H \rangle$$
$$\Rightarrow \langle \forall F :: B.hypo \text{ in } F \Rightarrow B.conc \text{ in } B \;[\!]\; F \rangle$$

Equivalently,

$$\langle \forall F :: B.hypo \text{ in } F \wedge \langle \forall G :: B1.hypo \text{ in } G \Rightarrow B1.conc \text{ in } B1 \;[\!]\; G \rangle$$
$$\wedge \langle \forall H :: B2.hypo \text{ in } H \Rightarrow B2.conc \text{ in } B2 \;[\!]\; H \rangle$$
$$\Rightarrow B.conc \text{ in } B \;[\!]\; F$$
$$\rangle$$

The properties $B1.hypo$, $B1.conc$ (and similarly $B2.hypo$, $B2.conc$) are obtained from $B.hypo$, $B.conc$ of Section 8.2 by replacing w by s; these are shown below.

$B1.hypo :: r = d$ unless $d \prec r$,

$\qquad\qquad s = f$ unless $s \prec f$,

$B1.conc :: \bar{s} \sqsubseteq \bar{r}$,

$\qquad\qquad |\bar{r}| \leq |\bar{s}| + M$,

$\qquad\qquad |\bar{r}| < |\bar{s}| + M \vee s = \emptyset \mapsto r = \emptyset$,

$\qquad\qquad |\bar{r}| > |\bar{s}| \qquad \vee r \neq \emptyset \mapsto s \neq \emptyset$

$B2.hypo :: s = f$ unless $f \prec s$,

$\qquad\qquad w = e$ unless $w \prec e$

$B2.conc :: \bar{w} \sqsubseteq \bar{s}$,

$\qquad\qquad |\bar{s}| \leq |\bar{w}| + N$,

$\qquad\qquad |\bar{s}| < |\bar{w}| + N \vee w = \emptyset \mapsto s = \emptyset$,

$\qquad\qquad |\bar{s}| > |\bar{w}| \qquad \vee s \neq \emptyset \mapsto w \neq \emptyset$

The structure of the proof is as follows. Consider an arbitrary F and let $G = B2 \;[\!]\; F$ and $H = B1 \;[\!]\; F$ (because $B2 \;[\!]\; F$ is the environment for $B1$ and $B1 \;[\!]\; F$ for $B2$). We show,

$B.hypo$ in $F \Rightarrow B1.hypo$ in G and, (2)

$B.hypo$ in $F \Rightarrow B2.hypo$ in H (3)

Hence, from the antecedent of (1), we may then assume $B1.conc$ in $B1 \,[\!]\, G$ and $B2.conc$ in $B2 \,[\!]\, H$. From the definitions of B, G, H, we have $B1 \,[\!]\, G = B2 \,[\!]\, H = B1 \,[\!]\, B2 \,[\!]\, F = B \,[\!]\, F$. Hence, we have $B1.conc$ in $B \,[\!]\, F$ and $B2.conc$ in $B \,[\!]\, F$. We will finally deduce,

$B1.conc$ in $B \,[\!]\, F \land B2.conc$ in $B \,[\!]\, F \Rightarrow B.conc$ in $B \,[\!]\, F$ (4)

Proof of (2)

The two proofs, corresponding to the two conjuncts in $B1.hypo$, are shown below.

Proof of $r = d$ unless $d \prec r$ in G

$r = d$ unless $d \prec r$ in F	, from $B.hypo$ in F
$r = d$ is stable in $B2$	, r is not accessed in $B2$
$r = d$ unless $d \prec r$ in $B2 \,[\!]\, F$	, corollary 2 to the union theorem ▽

Proof of $s = f$ unless $s \prec f$ in G

$s = f$ unless $s \prec f$ in $B2$	, property P2 of $B2$
$s = f$ is stable in F	, s is not accessed in F
$s = f$ unless $s \prec f$ in $B2 \,[\!]\, F$	, corollary 2 to the union theorem ▽

Proof of (3) is similar to proof of (2).

Proof of (4)

The proof has four parts, corresponding to the four conjuncts in $B.conc$. All properties are of $B \,[\!]\, F$.

Proof of $\bar{w} \sqsubseteq \bar{r}$

$\bar{w} \sqsubseteq \bar{s}$	, from $B2.conc$
$\bar{s} \sqsubseteq \bar{r}$	, from $B1.conc$
$\bar{w} \sqsubseteq \bar{r}$	, from the above two ▽

Proof of $|\bar{r}| \leq |\bar{w}| + M + N$

$|\bar{r}| \leq |\bar{s}| + M$, from $B1.conc$

$|\bar{s}| \leq |\bar{w}| + N$, from $B2.conc$

$|\bar{r}| \leq |\bar{w}| + M + N$, from the above two ▽

Proof of $|\bar{r}| < |\bar{w}| + M + N \ \vee \ w = \emptyset \ \mapsto \ r = \emptyset$

$|\bar{s}| < |\bar{w}| + N \ \vee \ w = \emptyset \mapsto s = \emptyset$

, from $B2.conc$

$s = \emptyset \qquad\qquad\qquad \mapsto r = \emptyset$

, from $B1.conc$ using implication rule for *leads-to*

$|\bar{s}| < |\bar{w}| + N \ \vee \ w = \emptyset \mapsto r = \emptyset$

, transitivity on the above two

$|\bar{r}| < |\bar{s}| + M \ \mapsto \ r = \emptyset$

, from $B1.conc$ using implication rule for *leads-to*

$|\bar{r}| < |\bar{s}| + M \ \vee \ |\bar{s}| < |\bar{w}| + N \ \vee \ w = \emptyset \ \mapsto \ r = \emptyset$

, disjunction on the above two

$|\bar{r}| < |\bar{w}| + M + N \ \Rightarrow \ |\bar{r}| < |\bar{s}| + M \ \vee \ |\bar{s}| < |\bar{w}| + N$

, seen easily by taking the contrapositive

$|\bar{r}| < |\bar{w}| + M + N \ \vee \ w = \emptyset \ \mapsto \ r = \emptyset$

, from the above two using implication rule for *leads-to* ▽

Proof of $|\bar{r}| < |\bar{w}| \ \vee \ r \neq \emptyset \ \mapsto \ w \neq \emptyset$

Similar to the above proof. ▽

8.4 A Refinement of the Specification

As a first step toward implementing a buffer, we propose a more refined (i.e., stronger) specification of a buffer. Our proof obligation then is to show that this proposed specification implies the specification given by properties P0,P1,P2,P3, of Section 8.2. In Section 8.5 we show a program that implements this refined specification. Because of the result of Section 8.3, any buffer of size N can be implemented by concatenating N buffers of size 1; hence we limit our refinement to $N = 1$.

For $N = 1$, the buffer program has no internal words for data storage (recall that there are $N - 1$ internal words for storage). Hence the only strategy for the buffer program is to move data from r to w when $w \neq \emptyset$. This is captured in the following specification.

initially $w = \emptyset$ in B	(R0)
$(r,w) = (d,e)$ unless $r \prec d \wedge e \prec w \wedge w = d$ in B	(R1)
$w \prec r$ ensures $r \prec w$ in B	(R2)

Property R1 says that the pair (r,w) changes only if a non-$\emptyset$ data value is moved from r to w when the latter is $\emptyset$. The progress property, R2, says that if data can be moved—i.e., $r \neq \emptyset \wedge w = \emptyset$—then it will be moved.

Now we show that the refinement is correct, i.e. (R0,R1,R2) imply (P0,P1,P2,P3), given in Section 8.2.

8.4.1 Proofs of P0,P1,P2

Proof of (P0): initially $w = \emptyset$ in B

Immediate from R0. ▽

Proof of (P1): $r = d$ unless $r \prec d$ in B

$r = d \wedge w = e$ unless $r \prec d$ in B

, from R1 by weakening its consequence

$r = d$ unless $r \prec d$ in B

, eliminating free variable e ▽

Proof of (P2): $w = e$ unless $e \prec w$ in B

$r = d \wedge w = e$ unless $e \prec w$ in B

, from R1 by weakening its consequence

$w = e$ unless $e \prec w$ in B

, eliminating free variable d ▽

8.4.2 Proof of P3

The property P3 is of the form,

$$\langle \forall F :: B.hypo \text{ in } F \Rightarrow B.conc \text{ in } B [\!|\, F \rangle$$

We prove P3 from (R0,R1,R2) by proving

$$B.hypo \text{ in } F \wedge (R0,R1) \Rightarrow (\bar{r} = \bar{w}; r \text{ is invariant in } B [\!|\, F) \qquad (P4)$$

and,

$B.hypo$ in $F \land$ (R2) $\land$ ($\bar{r} = \bar{w}; r$ is invariant in $B \parallel F$) $\Rightarrow$ ($B.conc$ in $B \parallel F$) \hfill (P5)

Proof of P4

To show that ($\bar{r} = \bar{w}; r$) is invariant in $B \parallel F$, the proof obligations are,

initially ($\bar{r} = \bar{w}; r$) in $B \parallel F$ and,

$\bar{r} = \bar{w}; r$ is stable in $B \parallel F$

The initial condition can be seen from,

initially ($\bar{r}, \bar{w}$) = (r, w) in $B \parallel F$, from (A0) of Section 8.1

and, initially $w = \emptyset$ in $B \parallel F$, from (R0) and the union theorem

Next we show that ($\bar{r} = \bar{w}; r$) is stable in $B \parallel F$.

Proof of ($\bar{r} = \bar{w}; r$) is stable in $B \parallel F$

$r = d$ unless $d \prec r$ in F

, from $B.hypo$ in F

$w = e$ unless $w \prec e$ in F

, from $B.hypo$ in F

$(r, w) = (d, e)$ unless $(d, w) \prec (r, e)$ in F

, conjunction of the above two; $(d, w) \prec (r, e)$ stands for

$(d = r \land w \prec e) \lor (d \prec r \land w = e) \lor (d \prec r \land w \prec e)$

$(r, w) = (d, e)$ unless $r \prec d \land e \prec w \land w = d$ in B

, from (R1)

$(r, w) = (d, e)$ unless

$(d, w) \prec (r, e)$ \hfill {5.1}

$\lor (r \prec d \land e \prec w \land w = d)$ \hfill {5.2}

in $B \parallel F$ \hfill (5)

, weakening the right sides of the above two and applying the union theorem

Next use the properties (A1,A2) of Section 8.1 and form their conjunction to get:

$(\bar{r}, \bar{w}) = (x, y) \land (r, w) = (d, e)$ unless

$[(\bar{r}, \bar{w}) = (x, y; w) \land r = d \land w \neq e]$ \hfill {6.1}

$\lor [(\bar{r}, \bar{w}) = (x; r, y) \land r \neq d \land w = e]$ \hfill {6.2}

$\lor [(\bar{r}, \bar{w}) = (x; r, y; w) \land r \neq d \land w \neq e]$ \hfill {6.3}

in $B \parallel F$ \hfill (6)

Next from the conjunction of (5) and (6). Observe that every disjunct in the right side of (5) and (6) imply $(r, w) \neq (d, e)$, and therefore, conjunctions of these with the left sides of (6) and (5), respectively, result in *false*.

$(\bar{r}, \bar{w}) = (x, y) \wedge (r, w) = (d, e)$ unless
$\quad [(\bar{r}, \bar{w}) = (x, y; w) \wedge r = d \wedge w \prec e]$ {from 5.1 $\wedge$ 6.1}
$\quad \vee [(\bar{r}, \bar{w}) = (x; r, y) \wedge d \prec r \wedge w = e]$ {from 5.1 $\wedge$ 6.2}
$\quad \vee [(\bar{r}, \bar{w}) = (x; r, y; w) \wedge d \prec r \wedge w \prec e]$ {from 5.1 $\wedge$ 6.3}
$\quad \vee [(\bar{r}, \bar{w}) = (x; r, y; w) \wedge r \prec d \wedge e \prec w \wedge w = d]$ {from 5.2 $\wedge$ 6.3}
$\quad$ in $B \parallel F$ (7)

We next set the free variable x to $y; d$ in (7). The terms in the right side may be weakened to yield

$(\bar{r} = \bar{w}; r) \wedge (\bar{w}, r, w) = (y, d, e)$ unless $(\bar{r} = \bar{w}; r) \wedge (\bar{w}, r, w) \neq (y, d, e)$ in $B \parallel F$
$(\bar{r} = \bar{w}; r)$ is stable in $B \parallel F$

$\quad$, corollary to general conjunction and disjunction (Section 4.1.2) ▽

Proof of P5

Proof of $B.hypo$ in $F \wedge$ (R2) $\wedge (\bar{r} = \bar{w}; r$ in $B \parallel F) \Rightarrow (B.conc$ in $B \parallel F)$

The proof consists of four parts; each part establishes one of the conjuncts in $B.conc$.

Proof of $\bar{w} \sqsubseteq \bar{r}$ in $B \parallel F$

Immediate from $(\bar{r} = \bar{w}; r)$ is invariant in $B \parallel F$ ▽

Proof of $|\bar{r}| \leq |\bar{w}| + 1$ in $B \parallel F$

$\quad |\bar{r}| = |\bar{w}| + |r|$ in $B \parallel F \quad$, from $(\bar{r} = \bar{w}; r)$ in $B \parallel F$
$\quad |\bar{r}| \leq |\bar{w}| + 1$ in $B \parallel F \quad$, $|r| \leq 1$ ▽

The remaining two progress properties in $B.conc$ can be established by first proving
$\quad w \prec r \mapsto r \prec w$ in $B \parallel F$ (P6)

Proof of (P6): $w \prec r \mapsto r \prec w$ in $B \parallel F$
$\quad r = d$ unless $d \prec r$ in F
$\quad\quad$, from $B.hypo$ in F
$\quad d \neq \emptyset$ is stable in F

, d is constant in F

$r \neq \emptyset \land r = d$ is stable in F

, conjunction of the above two and rewriting the left side

$r \neq \emptyset$ is stable in F

, eliminating free variable d (8)

$w = e$ unless $w \prec e$ in F

, from $B.hypo$ in F

$w = \emptyset$ is stable in F

, setting e to $\emptyset$ in the above

$w \prec r$ is stable in F

, conjunction of (8) and the above

$w \prec r$ ensures $r \prec w$ in B

, from (R2)

$w \prec r$ ensures $r \prec w$ in $B \;[\!]\; F$

, corollary 4 of the union theorem on the above two

$w \prec r \mapsto r \prec w$ in $B \;[\!]\; F$

, from the definition of $\mapsto$ ▽

Since $(\bar{r} = \bar{w}; r)$ is an invariant of $B \;[\!]\; F$,

$$r = \emptyset \equiv |\bar{r}| < |\bar{w}| + 1 \text{ in } B \;[\!]\; F \qquad (P7)$$

We use the substitution axiom in the following proof to replace $r = \emptyset$ by $|\bar{r}| < |\bar{w}| + 1$. We show one progress proof only; the other one is similar. In the following proof, all properties are of $B \;[\!]\; F$.

Proof of $|\bar{r}| < |\bar{w}| + 1 \lor w = \emptyset \mapsto r = \emptyset$

$r \neq \emptyset \land w = \emptyset \mapsto r = \emptyset$, expanding (P6) and using the implication rule

$r = \emptyset \mapsto r = \emptyset$, implication rule

$r = \emptyset \lor w = \emptyset \mapsto r = \emptyset$, disjunction of the above two

$|\bar{r}| < |\bar{w}| + 1 \lor w = \emptyset \mapsto r = \emptyset$, using (P7) to replace $r = \emptyset$ by $|\bar{r}| < |\bar{w}| + 1$ ▽

8.5 An Implementation

The specification of Section 8.4 can be implemented by a program whose only statement moves data from r to w provided $w = \emptyset$ (if $r = \emptyset$, the movement has no effect):

$$r, w := \emptyset, r \quad \text{if} \quad w = \emptyset$$

The proof that this fragment has the properties (R1,R2) is immediate from the definition of *unless* and *ensures*. The initial condition of this program is $w = \emptyset$, and hence (R0) is established.

An implementation for buffer of size N, $N > 1$, is the union of N such statements: one statement each for moving data from a location to an adjacent location (closer to w) provided the latter is $\emptyset$. We show how this program may be expressed in the UNITY programming notation.

Rename the variables r and w to be $b[0]$ and $b[N]$, respectively. The internal buffer words are $b[1]$ through $b[N-1]$. The program specifies the initial values of $b[1]$ through $b[N]$ to be $\emptyset$, and the statements move $b[i-1]$ to $b[i]$ provided the latter is $\emptyset$, for all i, $0 < i \leq N$.

Program *buffer* {of N words, $N \geq 1$}

initially $\langle [\!] \ i \ : \ 0 < i \leq N \ :: \ b[i] = \emptyset \rangle$

assign $\langle [\!] \ i \ : \ 0 < i \leq N \ :: \ b[i-1], b[i] := \emptyset, b[i-1] \quad \text{if} \quad b[i] = \emptyset \rangle$

end {*buffer*}

9 Concluding Remarks

In the foreword to [2], Hoare has suggested that "a complete theory of programming includes

1. A method for specification of programs which permits individual requirements to be clearly stated and combined.

2. A method of reasoning about specifications, which aids in elucidation and evaluation of alternative designs.

3. A method of developing programs together with a proof that they meet their specification.

4. A method of transforming programs to achieve high efficiency on the machines available for their execution."

It is instructive to evaluate how UNITY addresses the above goals. The short examples given in this monograph suggest that the specification mechanism is adequate for stating some of the most commonly used properties of programs. The logic is not powerful enough to state "for every natural number n there exists an execution sequence in program F that results in the output of n," or "program G may deadlock." Such properties have been deliberately left out because we could not devise an appropriate programming methodology for implementing such properties, nor could we develop simple rules for manipulations of logical formulae in which such properties appear (for similar reasons, the traditional temporal operators—always and sometime—have been left out).

Reasoning about specifications is one of the more attractive features of UNITY. Our experience shows that UNITY formulae can be manipulated effectively, and in most cases, proofs are comparable to the corresponding intuitive arguments in their lengths. We ascribe this to the simplicity of the logic, and the power of the derived rules. It would be useful to explore alternative logics which have these features.

Systematic program development is based on heuristics which allow program skeletons and specifications to be refined. A few heuristics for program refinement have been identified in [2]; the study of heuristics, however, is in its infancy for UNITY. A specification may be refined (the correctness of the refinement amounts to showing that a lower level specification implies the higher level specification) until it becomes straightforward to implement the specification by a program. In many cases, refinements consist of replacing a *leads-to* property by a sequence of *ensures*. Another form of refinement, program refinement, consists of refining "unimplementable statements" into forms that are more amenable to implementations. Both forms of refinements will be useful, but our experience suggests that specification refinements may be more effective, at least at the higher levels.

Transforming a program for efficient executions on appropriate architectures was one of the motivations behind the development of UNITY. A number of "program schemata" have been identified in Chapter 4 of [2] which can be mapped for efficient executions on certain architectures; a program may then be refined into one of these schemata. However, a general theory of mappings, from programs to architectures, is still lacking.

10 References

For references to the original sources, see the Bibliography in [2].

1. K. Mani Chandy, "Concurrent Programming for the Masses," Invited Lecture at *The Third Annual ACM Symposium on Principles of Distributed Computing*, Vancouver, B.C., Canada, August 27-29, 1984, published in the *Proceedings of he Fourth Annual ACM Symposium on Principles of Distributed Computing*, Minaki, Ontario, Canada, pp. 1-12, August 5-7, 1985.

2. K. Mani Chandy and Jayadev Misra, *Parallel Program Design: A Foundation*, Addison-Wesley, 1988.

3. K. Mani Chandy and Jayadev Misra, "On Proofs of Distributed Algorithms, with Application to the Problem of Termination Detection," working material, *International Summer School on Constructive Methods in Computing Science*, Marktoberdorf, Germany, July 24-August 5, 1988.

4. Jayadev Misra, "General Conjunction and Disjunction of *unless*," *Notes on UNITY 01-88*, The University of Texas at Austin, 1988.

5. Jayadev Misra, "A Theorem about Dynamic Acyclic Graphs," *Notes on UNITY 02-88*, The University of Texas at Austin, 1988.

6. Jayadev Misra, "A Specification of a Buffer," unpublished manuscript, The University of Texas at Austin, July 1988.

Jan van der Snepscheut talked about the distributed processing of rabbits. For this, he introduced the concept of a split rabbit; this can be implemented using Bird's cut and paste operations. After splitting , the rabbit parts can be processed in a systolic fashion:

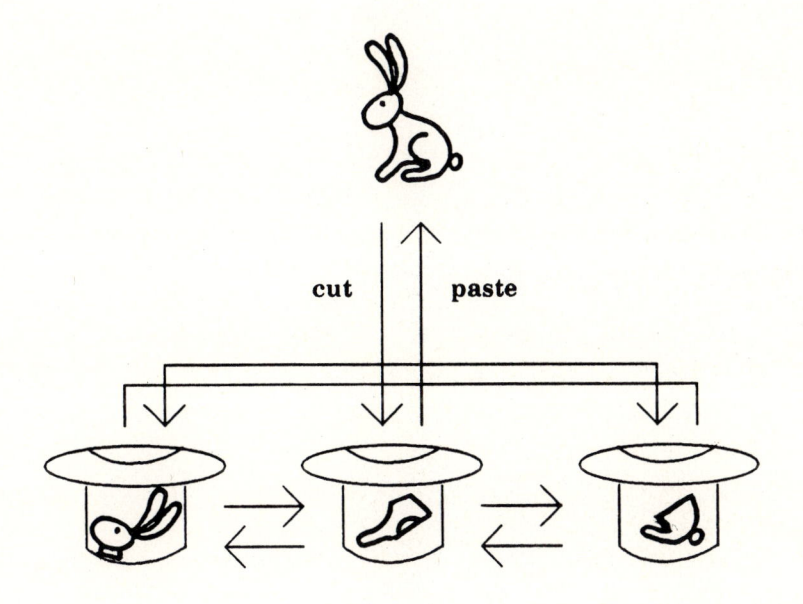

DESIGN OF SYNCHRONIZATION ALGORITHMS

Alain J. Martin
Computer Science
California Institute of Technology
Pasadena CA 91125, USA

Jan L. A. van de Snepscheut
Department of Computing Science
Groningen University
Groningen, The Netherlands

1.
DESIGN OF SYNCHRONIZATION ALGORITHMS

In these notes we discuss the design of concurrent programs that consist of a set of communicating sequential processes. The processes communicate via shared variables and synchronize via semaphores. We present an axiomatic definition of semaphores, and prove properties about them. The split binary semaphore is introduced and it is shown how it can be used in constructing the synchronization part of concurrent processes in order to maintain a given synchronization condition.

1. Introduction

If we want to study concurrent computations, we have to define the notion of concurrency. If we try to use the term with its vernacular meaning, we quickly conclude that it is inadequate because it is based on the treacherous notions of simultaneity and of physical time. Without resorting to arguments from modern physics to question the validity of the notions of absolute time reference

---

These notes are a compilation of the chapters on semaphores from a draft text on concurrent computations. The draft was written mainly while the second author was visiting at the California Institute of Technology. The research described was partly sponsored by the Defense Advanced Research Projects Agency, DARPA Order numbers 3771 & 6202, and monitored by the Office of Naval Research under contract numbers N00014-79-C-0597 & N00014-87-K-0745.

and simultaneity, we reject those notions on the ground that they are not necessary to define the net effect of concurrent computations. The important notion is that of sequencing: action X takes place before action Y. Introducing some assertion about the supposed instant in time at which the actions take place only reduces the generality of the computation. It obscures our understanding of the computation, makes the proofs of correctness more difficult, restricts the implementation, and increases the risk of errors.

From the point of view of semantics, the definition of the concurrent execution of sequential processes has proved to be a difficult technical issue. Among all the solutions proposed, the one based on the interleaving of atomic actions is still, in our opinion, the simplest and most practical. This is the definition adopted in the next section. In a sense, the choices we are going to make as to what is an atomic action, an interleaving, etc., are free and arbitrary: we define the rule of the game, and we play the game. We have, however, good reasons for making choices that lead to interesting, efficient implementations on realizable machines. These implementation issues are not discussed in the present notes.

2. Concurrent processes

We choose to describe a concurrent computation as the concurrent execution of a set of sequential programs. A sequential program that is part of a concurrent computation is called a *process*. The number of processes partaking in a concurrent computation is fixed and finite.

Execution of a sequential program is defined to be equivalent to executing its actions one after the other. The order is given by the program text, e.g., the order is X before Y in the program $X; Y$. Concurrent execution of a set of sequential processes is defined to be equivalent to executing the processes in an interleaved fashion. Interleaving means that the actions of the set of processes are executed one after the other under the restriction that the ordering of actions within each process is respected. For example, in the program $(X0; Y0 \parallel X1; Y1)$, $X0$ precedes $Y0$, and $X1$ precedes $Y1$. No other ordering is imposed. For example, it is not determined whether $X0$ precedes $Y1$.

We have to define exactly what are the actions that are being executed in an interleaved fashion. For example, the program $(X0; Y0 \parallel X1; Y1)$ admits six different interleavings of the four actions. If, however, $X0; Y0$ is interpreted as one indivisible, compound action, only three interleavings remain, and if $X1; Y1$ is also an indivisible action only two interleavings remain. If the grain of interleaving is finer, then more interleavings are possible, and in general, more final states can result from the same initial state. Also, if the actions are finer-grained, our analysis of the program has to be more detailed. The actions that are not further interleaved — that are executed as a whole so to speak — are called *atomic* actions. Sometimes, the choice of the grain size doesn't matter: the concurrent executions of program parts that do not share variables do not interfere with each other. (In fact, this is not obvious, or provable, or whatever: it is just another choice that we make; it is usually made silently.) If the program parts do share variables, the choice matters. The choice we make is the following: we say that we have analyzed a concurrent program if we have analyzed the program at the level of detail in which the atomic actions contain at most one access to a shared variable. Phrased operationally: all interleavings in which each atomic action involves at most one access to a shared variable, are possible. For example, if x is a shared variable, then process

$x := x + 1$ is broken up into smaller actions, using an additional local variable, y say, yielding $y := x$; $y := y + 1$; $x := y$. The recoded process consists of two atomic statements: $y := x$ in which x is inspected, and $x := y$ in which x is assigned a value. We need not worry about the action $y := y + 1$: it may be a separate atomic action, or part of either of the other two atomic actions, the difference doesn't matter because the addition and the assignment to y do not interfere with other actions. An atomic action may, therefore, consist of a sequence of even smaller actions. We do not consider the intermediate states between those smaller actions, we restrict ourselves to the so-called *stable states* — the states between atomic actions.

We stipulate that there be another restriction imposed on the set of possible interleavings. We often encounter processes whose execution does not terminate. The sequence of actions they evoke is infinite. We impose the extra requirement that every interleaving contains the constituting sequences as a subsequence. As a result it is not possible to view interleaving as a selection mechanism that forever neglects one of the processes. This requirement makes the interleaving *fair*. We sometimes loosely say that each process proceeds at its own speed (because of the nondeterministic choice in the interleaving) but this speed is finite and not zero (because of the fairness of the interleaving).

We have chosen fine-grained atomic actions. Coarser-grained atomic actions admit simpler proofs. An interesting question, therefore, is: given the above choice of atomic actions, can we write our programs such that it is as if the atomic actions are coarser grained, as coarse as the programmer chooses? This problem is called the mutual exclusion problem. It is a famous problem with a long history of correct and incorrect solutions. We address the problem shortly in the next chapter.

The program notation

In this section we introduce the program notation. For the sequential part, we use Edsger W. Dijkstra's guarded commands [2], with a slightly different syntax. For the concurrent part, we use the parallel composition operator. We give an informal description of the semantics of the constructs.

- $x := E$ is the assignment statement that assigns the value of expression E to variable x . In the concurrent assignment statement $x, y := E, F$ the values of E and F are simultaneously assigned to distinct variables x and y .

- Execution of the selection statement $[G_0 \to S_0 \| G_1 \to S_1]$, where the guards G_i are boolean expressions, amounts to the execution of a statement S_i for which G_i is **true** . At least one guard is **true** . If more than one guard is **true** , the choice between them is nondeterministic.

- The execution of $*[S]$ amounts to the repeated, nonterminating execution of statement S .

- The execution of $S0; S1$ amounts to the execution of $S0$ and then $S1$.

- The execution of $S0\|S1$ amounts to the interleaving of $S0$ and $S1$.

In the sequel we use semaphores for the synchronization of concurrent processes. They were first introduced in [1] and we follow the definition of [5]. The semaphores are used in a restricted sense, known as the split binary semaphore (cf. [3]), which appeared first (and was not recommended) in a paper by C.A.R. Hoare (cf. [4]).

2.
Semaphores

It is well known that the mutual exclusion problem can be solved without the introduction of new primitive commands. However, the problem is a tricky one: the simple-minded solutions are incorrect, and the proofs of the correct solutions are far from simple. If we ever hope to find reliable solutions to more complex problems than mutual exclusion, we have to find a better way of doing it. In this chapter we address the problem of extending our repertoire of primitive commands with the appropriate synchronization commands. Since the choice of such commands is practically infinite, we have to ask ourselves what properties such primitives should have to simplify the solution of synchronization problems like mutual exclusion. At a later stage we address the feasibility of our primitives of choice: can they be implemented efficiently, either from scratch or from the primitives that we have used before.

1. Process synchronization

Consider two noninterfering processes. A fundamental property of the concurrent composition is that, given an arbitrary command X in one process and an arbitrary command Y in the other process, the number of times that X and Y are completed may differ arbitrarily. Using the notation cX for the number of times that command X has been completed, we may say that in any concurrent computation $cX - cY$ is unbounded. The kind of synchronization we are aiming at consists in bounding the value of $cX - cY$. Let us see why this is a reasonable thing to try. A very strict form of synchronization is the one in which X and Y are executed in alternation, as in the sequential program $*[X; Y]$. At every moment during execution hereof we have $0 \leq cX - cY \leq 1$, i.e., the number of times that X and Y have been completed are equal, or X may be one ahead of Y. Notice also that all sequences of commands for which every initial segment satisfies $0 \leq cX - cY \leq 1$, can be obtained by executing $*[X; Y]$, which implies that the characterization with the inequalities is complete. We will not pay too much attention to this form of completeness.

Exercise

1. Write a program whose execution sequences satisfy $0 \leq cX - cY \leq 2$. Make the program such that all legal sequences can be the result of the program's execution. □

Let us have a look at the mutual exclusion problem. Can this problem be formulated with a number of inequalities? Each process i is of the form

$$*[NCS_i;\ CS_i]$$

and the requirement is that, at any moment, at most one process is executing its critical section CS_i. The "at most one" sounds good but we cannot formulate the rest of the sentence with $cNCS_i$ and cCS_i. There is, however, a nice way out: we can express that a process is executing its critical section by adding extra commands. Prefixing CS_i with command X and postfixing it with Y, we may say: process i is executing its critical section if it has executed X and has not yet executed the subsequent Y, i.e., if $cX > cY$. If we use the same commands X and Y for all processes, the program text is

$$*[NCS_i;\ X;\ CS_i;\ Y]$$

and we have that the number of processes that are executing their critical section is $cX - cY$. (Because we have used the same X and Y in all processes we have avoided an explicit summation: it is implicit in the definition of c since cX is the number of times that X has been completed, summed over all individual processes.) From the topology of the program we see that $cX - cY \geq 0$, and that the difference is bounded from above by the number of processes: each process contributes either 0 or 1 to the difference. The mutual exclusion problem can now be stated as the requirement to also maintain $cX - cY \leq 1$. Again, this is an inequality, but this time it is one-sided only. The question we are now faced with is whether we should introduce synchronization primitives that provide one-sided bounds, two-sided bounds, or even equalities, i.e., equal lower and upper bounds. In the order mentioned they provide increasingly stricter synchronization. We will first study the one-sided primitives, called *semaphores*. We give both an axiomatic definition and a number of examples of their use. Next (** not included in these notes **) we generalize the mathematics a little to cover all three kinds of synchronization primitives, and we show that each of the three can be constructed from each of the other two. Therefore, in some sense, they are equivalent. In later chapters we show how to solve synchronization problems that are not, or not easily, expressible as an inequality.

2. An axiomatic definition of semaphores

We have seen that some synchronization problems are equivalent to maintaining an invariant $cX - cY \leq k$, for some commands X and Y, and constant k. We call X and Y synchronization primitives if the above inequality is (part of) the semantics of X and Y. Since synchronization primitives come in pairs, and since more than one pair may occur in a single program, there has to be a way of identifying the pairs, i.e., which X corresponds to which Y. We do so by parameterizing the commands with an identifier, which is usually called a semaphore. For historical reasons, we do not write $X(s)$ and $Y(s)$ but $P(s)$ and $V(s)$ instead. The inequality thus becomes

$$cP(s) - cV(s) \leq k$$

for any semaphore s. From the initial state $cP(s) = cV(s) = 0$ it follows that $k \geq 0$. It is sometimes convenient to think of s itself as an integer variable, rather than an arbitrary identifier, whose value satisfies
$$s = k + cV(s) - cP(s) \quad .$$
This is convenient in doing the mathematics, but we will not use s as an integer in our programs. Notice that initially $s = k$. We therefore say that k is the initial value of s, and denote it by s_0 (and we eliminate k from now on).

Putting it altogether we stipulate that any pair of semaphore operations $P(s)$ and $V(s)$ satisfies the two axioms $A1$ and $A2$.

$A1:\quad s \geq 0$
$A2:\quad s = s_0 + cV(s) - cP(s)$

As we have seen in the previous chapter, there is an aspect that is unknown in sequential programming and that is essential to synchronization: suspension of an action. Properties $A1$ and $A2$ can be maintained only if, at some points during execution, $P(s)$ is prevented from being completed. This is the case if (and only if) $s = 0$. If $s = 0$ then completion of $P(s)$ would lead to $s = -1$ according to $A2$, but $s = -1$ contradicts $A1$. The only way to preserve both $A1$ and $A2$ is to suspend the process that attempts to complete execution of $P(s)$, and delay its progress until another process embarks on $V(s)$. The two may then be completed, even simultaneously and thus increasing both $cV(s)$ and $cP(s)$ and leaving their difference and s unchanged. In our formalism we have to express that there is no other reason for suspending a synchronization command in order to rule out silly implementations of semaphores that consist in suspending every P operation. Such an implementation maintains $A1$ and $A2$ but is not very useful. In order to formulate the restriction we introduce $qP(s)$ and $qV(s)$ as the number of suspended $P(s)$ and $V(s)$ operations, respectively. The progress requirements that we impose express that the semaphore operations are not suspended unnecessarily. They are formulated as follows.

$A3:\quad s = 0 \;\lor\; qP(s) = 0$
$A4:\quad qV(s) = 0$

By way of exercise we give an alternative axiom A' that, given $A2$, is equivalent to $A1 \land A3$.

$A':\quad cP(s) = min(cP(s) + qP(s), cV(s) + s_0)$

We prove the equivalence by eliminating s from $A1$ and $A3$, using $A2$, since s does not appear in A'.

$\quad A'$
$=\quad \{$ definition of A' $\}$
$\quad cP(s) = min(cP(s) + qP(s), cV(s) + s_0)$
$=\quad \{\; x = min(y,z)$ is $x \leq y \;\land\; x \leq z \;\land\; (x = y \;\lor\; x = z)\;\}$
$\quad qP(s) \geq 0 \;\land\; cP(s) \leq cV(s) + s_0 \;\land\; (qP(s) = 0 \;\lor\; cP(s) = cV(s) + s_0)$
$=\quad \{\; qP(s) \geq 0; \; A2: s = s_0 + cV(s) - cP(s)\;\}$
$\quad s \geq 0 \;\land\; (qP(s) = 0 \;\lor\; s = 0)$
$=\quad \{$ definition of $A1$ and $A3$ $\}$
$\quad A1 \;\land\; A3$

The reason for preferring $A1$ and $A3$ over A' is twofold. First, the algebraic rules of min are so minimal that, more often than not, one rewrites it into a conjunction of terms. Second, $A1$ and

$A3$ play different roles: $A1$ is related to safety, expressing that certain invariants are maintained, whereas $A3$ is related to progress, expressing that the computation proceeds. Since we usually deal with the two issues separately, it seems wiser to stick to two separate axioms.

The progress requirements state that the set of suspended actions is minimal, i.e., an action is suspended only if its completion would violate the safety requirements. It implies, as we have seen above, that completion of a V operation leads to completion of a suspended P operation, if any. One may wonder which process is chosen for completing its P operation if several of them exist: The one that was suspended for the longest time, or an arbitrary one, or what have you. Here we encounter the same question of fairness as in the chapter on mutual exclusion. If the selection of which suspended operation is completed is such that starvation of the suspended processes is avoided, then we say that the synchronization primitives are *fair*, otherwise they are *unfair*. This suggests the following fairness requirement that may or may not be included.

$A5$: *During the suspension of a process at a P operation only a bounded number of V operations on the same semaphore is completed.*

We observe the following hierarchy among the three requirements. The safety requirements $A1$ and $A2$ ensure correct synchronization, i.e., avoid the computation to enter states falsifying the invariants. The progress requirements $A3$ and $A4$ reduce the implementation freedom of $A1$ and $A2$ in order to guarantee progress of the set of processes. Fairness requirement $A5$ reduces the remaining implementation freedom to guarantee progress of each individual process. Semaphores that satisfy $A1$ through $A5$ are called fair, or strong. Semaphores that satisfy $A1$ through $A4$ but not necessarily $A5$ are called unfair, or weak. Semaphores that do not even satisfy $A1$ through $A4$ are not sufficiently interesting to be given a name. Unless specified otherwise, we use weak primitives.

3. Mutual exclusion with semaphores

In this section we reconsider the mutual exclusion problem. We are going to solve it by means of semaphores. It should be an easy job if the introduction of semaphores is worth our while; in fact it is. Here we go. Given are an arbitrary number of processes of the form

$$*[NCS_i;\ P(s);\ CS_i;\ V(s)]\ .$$

Let the initial value s_0 of s be 1. Define np as the number of processes that have completed a $P(s)$ and not yet completed the subsequent $V(s)$, i.e., np is the number of processes in the critical section. We show that $np \leq 1$.

$$\begin{aligned} np &= cP(s) - cV(s) \\ &= \{\ A2\ \} \\ np &= s_0 - s \\ \Rightarrow &\ \{\ A1\ \} \\ np &\leq s_0 \\ &= \{\ s_0 = 1\ \} \\ np &\leq 1 \end{aligned}$$

So much for safety. How about progress? From $A4$, $qV(s) = 0$, we see that if a process is in its critical section, it will not be suspended on its next semaphore operation. So it remains to show that no process is suspended on $P(s)$, given that all processes are outside their critical section. We do so by showing that there is a process in the critical section if $\mathbf{q}P(s) > 0$ holds.

$$\begin{aligned}
& \mathbf{q}P(s) > 0 \\
\Rightarrow\ & \{\ A3\ \} \\
& s = 0 \\
=\ & \{\ s_0 = 1\ \} \\
& \mathbf{c}P(s) - \mathbf{c}V(s) = 1 \\
=\ & \{\ \text{definition of } np\ \} \\
& np = 1
\end{aligned}$$

Finally there is the issue of fairness. The only way in which a process does not make progress is by being suspended on $P(s)$. Therefore, fairness of the mutual exclusion algorithm is equivalent to fairness of the operations on semaphore s. Hence, strong semaphores provide fair mutual exclusion and weak semaphores do not.

4. The pebble game: an appreciation of semaphores

In this section we describe an elementary synchronization problem, called the pebble game. It shows how semaphores can be used to solve such synchronization problems. We describe three increasingly more complex versions of the game.

In its first version, the game is played with an unlimited sequence of buckets and a single pebble. Initially the pebble is in one of the buckets. The game is played by two players, one whose only move is to move the pebble one bucket to the left, and one whose only move is to move the pebble one bucket to the right. (The players are on the same side of the sequence of buckets.) The players need not take moves in turn: there is no bound on the number of times that a player makes moves in succession. (Of course, the pebble should not be split in two halves, i.e., the players do not make moves simultaneously. We see to this by stipulating that a move is an atomic action.) There is only one restriction on the moves: the pebble should never be moved to the left of its initial bucket. Our goal is to synchronize the two players to enforce this restriction. We are not investigating strategies for playing the game; the more so because we have not specified how the game can be won or lost.

As in the chapter on mutual exclusion, we reject all overly restrictive solutions such as alternating right and left moves. In order to find a proper solution we reformulate the problem a bit. The two players are "represented" by two processes

$$*[\ moveleft\ ]$$
$$\|\ *[\ moveright\ ]$$

whose atomic actions are not further specified. The synchronization requirement is expressed by

$$\mathbf{c}moveright \geq \mathbf{c}moveleft\quad,$$

i.e., the number of times that the pebble has been moved to the right is at least the number of times that the pebble has been moved one bucket to the left. We aim at enforcing the synchronization requirement by semaphores. The obvious thing to try is to translate the above inequality into the inequality $s \geq 0$ that holds for semaphores. Combining $A1$ and $A2$ leads to

$$\mathbf{c}V(s) - \mathbf{c}P(s) + s_0 \geq 0\quad.$$

If we succeed in associating $V(s)$ with *moveright* and $P(s)$ with *moveleft*, all we have to do is to set the initial value s_0 of s to 0. A problem is that we cannot have $cV(s) = c\textit{moveright}$ at every moment because the two atomic actions are completed one after the other. If we select completion of *moveright* before completion of $V(s)$, we have $c\textit{moveright} \geq cV(s)$ and we are on the safe side. Similarly, we select $cP(s) \geq c\textit{moveleft}$. The two processes are then written as follows.

$$\textbf{var } s : \textit{semaphore} \qquad \{ s = 0 \text{ initially } \}$$
$$*[P(s);\ \textit{moveleft}]$$
$$\|\ *[\textit{moveright};\ V(s)]$$

A proof of correctness consists of merely gathering the properties mentioned above. In the first process we have either $cP(s) = c\textit{moveleft} + 1$ at the semicolon, or $cP(s) = c\textit{moveleft}$ elsewhere. Hence, $cP(s) \geq c\textit{moveleft}$ is invariantly true. Similarly, the second process maintains $c\textit{moveright} \geq cV(s)$. Combining the two invariants and coupling them via the semaphore axioms, we have

$$c\textit{moveright} \geq cV(s) \quad \wedge \quad cP(s) \geq c\textit{moveleft}$$
$$\Rightarrow \quad \{ \text{ arithmetic } \}$$
$$c\textit{moveright} - c\textit{moveleft} \geq cV(s) - cP(s)$$
$$= \quad \{ A2;\ s_0 = 0 \}$$
$$c\textit{moveright} - c\textit{moveleft} \geq s$$
$$\Rightarrow \quad \{ A1 \}$$
$$c\textit{moveright} - c\textit{moveleft} \geq 0$$

which is exactly what we want to have. Can we also show that no process is suspended unnecessarily, i.e., can we show that a process is suspended only if its progress would have violated the synchronization requirement? Actually we cannot, but it is as close as one may reasonably hope for. (In fact it is so close that we have ignored this slight disturbance in the previous section.) To begin with, notice that the second process is never suspended: it contains neither "busy waiting" nor a P operation. The first process can be suspended on $P(s)$. We show that if it is suspended, we have either $c\textit{moveleft} = c\textit{moveright}$, in which case it is rightfully suspended, or $c\textit{moveleft} = c\textit{moveright} - 1$ and the second process is at its semicolon. In the latter case the second process has completed one more move than the first process but this has not yet been recorded in the shared variable s. As soon as the $V(s)$ is performed (and it will be since the second process is not suspended) the first process is made to proceed. It is this minor discrepancy between actual and recorded state that causes a little bit of unavoidable extra delay to the first process. Here comes the proof.

the first process is suspended at $P(s)$
$\Rightarrow \quad \{$ it is blocked if $qP(s) > 0$; at $P(s)$ we have $cP(s) = c\textit{moveleft} \}$
$qP(s) > 0 \quad \wedge \quad cP(s) = c\textit{moveleft}$
$\Rightarrow \quad \{ A3 \}$
$s = 0 \quad \wedge \quad cP(s) = c\textit{moveleft}$
$\Rightarrow \quad \{ A2,\ s_0 = 0 \}$
$(c\textit{moveleft} = c\textit{moveright} - 1 \quad \wedge \quad$ second process is at semicolon$)$
$\vee\ (c\textit{moveleft} = c\textit{moveright} \quad \wedge \quad$ second process is not at semicolon$)$

This concludes our discussion of the basic version of the pebble game. We have shown how to implement a one-sided inequality with a semaphore. In the next version of the game the synchronization requirement is strengthened to

$$0 \leq cmoveright - cmoveleft \leq 4 \quad .$$

This corresponds to saying that the pebble's position is restricted to only five buckets: the initial bucket plus the first four buckets to the right of it. We have seen how to deal with one of these inequalities; we will now tackle the other. Remembering the combination of $A1$ and $A2$ (rewritten for semaphore t to avoid confusion)

$$cV(t) - cP(t) + t_0 \geq 0 \quad ,$$

we phrase the inequality as

$$cmoveleft - cmoveright + 4 \geq 0 \quad .$$

This suggests that *moveleft* be associated with $V(t)$, *moveright* with $P(t)$, and that $t_0 = 4$. The program that satisfies both inequalities is therefore as follows.

>   **var** s, t : semaphore $\{\ s = 0\ \wedge\ t = 4$ initially $\}$
> $*[P(s);\ moveleft;\ V(t)]$
> $||\ *[P(t);\ moveright;\ V(s)]$

In the final version of the game there are two more players, and the buckets are arranged in a 5×5 square. The two new players move the pebble up or down. Initially the pebble is in the bottom left corner, and the restriction on the moves is

$$0 \leq cmoveright - cmoveleft \leq 4$$
$$\wedge \quad 0 \leq cmoveup - cmovedown \leq 4 \quad .$$

We leave it to the reader to verify that the program in Figure 1 is a solution. (Observe that the two conjuncts above are independent.)

>   **var** s, t, x, y : semaphore
> $\{\ s = x = 0\ \wedge\ t = y = 4$ initially $\}$
> $*[P(s);\ moveleft;\ V(t)]$
> $||\ *[P(t);\ moveright;\ V(s)]$
> $||\ *[P(x);\ movedown;\ V(y)]$
> $||\ *[P(y);\ moveup;\ V(x)]$

– Figure 1 –

The synchronization requirements embodied in the pebble game are elementary in the sense that they can be translated directly into semaphores. Not all requirements have the shape of a conjunction of inequalities. For example, if in the last version of the game the restriction is added that the pebble should not be in the middle one of the 25 buckets, the requirement and its implementation becomes distinctly different. We address the implementation of the more general synchronization requirement in the next chapter.

Exercises

2. Show that there is no deadlock in the solution to the second version, i.e., show that $qP(s) > 0 \land qP(t) > 0$ is **false**.
3. Adapt the last program to the case where the pebble is in the middle bucket initially.

5. The click: another example of the use of semaphores

In this section we present another program and prove that it satisfies a number of interesting properties.

The program consists of two processes that manipulate four semaphores r, s, t, and u, and two integers a and b. Initially all six variables are equal to 0. The two processes are

$$*[V(r);\ P(s);\ \{\dagger\}\ V(t);\ P(u);\ a := a+1]$$

and

$$*[V(s);\ P(r);\ \{\dagger\}\ V(u);\ P(t);\ b := b+1]\ .$$

We prove that $a = b$ holds at the positions marked with a dagger, that no deadlock occurs, and that the semaphores are binary semaphores.

We annotate the program with a number of assertions.

$$*[\{Q1\}\ V(r);\ \{Q2\}\ P(s);\ \{Q3\}\ V(t);\ \{Q4\}\ P(u);\ \{Q5\}\ a := a+1\ \{Q1\}]$$

$$*[\{R1\}\ V(s);\ \{R2\}\ P(r);\ \{R3\}\ V(u);\ \{R4\}\ P(t);\ \{R5\}\ b := b+1\ \{R1\}]$$

Next we choose the ten assertions. The choice has to be such that $Q1$ through $Q5$ hold locally in the first process and are not falsified by any action of the second process. The latter requirement is obviously met if none of the terms appearing in $Q1$ through $Q5$ is changed by the second process. We postulate $Q1$ and derive $Q5$ from $Q1$ by replacing a with $a+1$. This is an application of the axiom of assignment to the last statement of the first process. $Q4$ is derived from $Q5$ by replacing $cP(u)$ with $cP(u) = 1$, etc.

$$
\begin{array}{llllll}
Q1: & cV(r) = cP(s) & = cV(t) & = cP(u) & = a \\
Q2: & cV(r) = cP(s)+1 = & cV(t)+1 = & cP(u)+1 = & a+1 \\
Q3: & cV(r) = cP(s) & = cV(t)+1 = & cP(u)+1 = & a+1 \\
Q4: & cV(r) = cP(s) & = cV(t) & = cP(u)+1 = & a+1 \\
Q5: & cV(r) = cP(s) & = cV(t) & = cP(u) & = a+1
\end{array}
$$

From the five conditions we derive their disjunction Q.

$\quad Q:\quad Q1\ \lor\ Q2\ \lor\ Q3\ \lor\ Q4\ \lor\ Q5$

Notice that Q can also be written as follows.

$\quad Q:\quad a+1 \geq cV(r) \geq cP(s) \geq cV(t) \geq cP(u) \geq a$

R and $R1$ through $R5$ are obtained from Q and $Q1$ through $Q5$ by replacing a, r, s, t, and u with b, s, r, u, and t, respectively.

We now turn to the first property of interest, viz. that $a = b$ holds at the positions marked $Q3$ and $R3$. Observe that it does not suffice to prove $Q3 \land R3 \Rightarrow a = b$, since the latter only show that $a = b$ holds if both processes have proceeded to the designated positions. Our goal is to prove $a = b$ if either process is at the designated position, independently of the state of the other process. We do so by proving $Q3 \Rightarrow a = b$, from which the result follows by symmetry.

Notice that at any time the first process is in one of its five states $Q1$ through $Q5$, which implies that Q holds at any time. Similarly, R is invariantly true.

From the initial value of the semaphores, and from $A1$ and $A2$ we conclude that S is an invariant.

$$S: \quad cP(s) \leq cV(s) \quad \land \quad cP(t) \leq cV(t)$$

The invariance of S captures the synchronization of the two processes. We prove $Q3 \Rightarrow a = b$ by showing that $a = b$ holds if $Q3$, R, and S hold. From

$$b \;\leq\; cP(t) \;\leq\; cV(t) \;=\; a \;=\; cP(s) - 1 \;\leq\; cV(s) - 1 \;\leq\; b$$
$$\{R\} \qquad \{S\} \qquad \{Q3\}\;\{Q3\} \qquad \{S\} \qquad \{R\}$$

we conclude $a = b$.

Next we show that no deadlock occurs.

      deadlock

$=$ the first process is suspended at $P(s)$ or $P(u)$
    $\land$ the second process is suspended at $P(r)$ or $P(t)$

$\Rightarrow$ { annotation }
    $((Q2 \land qP(s) > 0) \lor (Q4 \land qP(u) > 0))$
    $\land ((R2 \land qP(r) > 0) \lor (R4 \land qP(t) > 0))$

$\Rightarrow$ { A3, calculus }
    $(Q2 \land s = 0 \land R2 \land r = 0)$
    $\lor (Q2 \land s = 0 \land R4 \land t = 0)$
    $\lor (Q4 \land u = 0 \land R2 \land r = 0)$
    $\lor (Q4 \land u = 0 \land R4 \land t = 0)$

$\Rightarrow$ { A2: $(s = 0 \land s_0 = 0) \Rightarrow cV(s) = cP(s)$ }
    $(cV(r) = cP(s) + 1 \land cV(s) = cP(s) \land cV(s) = cP(r) + 1 \land cV(r) = cP(r))$
    $\lor (cV(t) = cP(s) \quad \land cV(s) = cP(s) \land cV(s) = cP(t) + 1 \land cV(t) = cP(t))$
    $\lor (cV(r) = cP(u) + 1 \land cV(u) = cP(u) \land cV(u) = cP(r) \quad \land cV(r) = cP(r))$
    $\lor (cV(t) = cP(u) + 1 \land cV(u) = cP(u) \land cV(u) = cP(t) + 1 \land cV(t) = cP(t))$

$=$ { calculus }
    false

Finally we show that each of the semaphores is a binary semaphore. We prove that $r \leq 1$ holds, and conclude the same property for the other semaphores by symmetry. From

$$cV(r) \;\leq\; cP(u) + 1 \;\leq\; cV(u) + 1 \;\leq\; cP(r) + 1$$
$$\{Q\} \qquad\qquad \{S\} \qquad\qquad \{R\}$$

and from $A2$ and $r_0 = 0$ we conclude $r \leq 1$. Since we also have $r \geq 0$ it follows that r assumes only two values: it is a so-called binary semaphore. This concludes our discussion of the click programs.

Exercise

4. Prove the correctness of the following variations on the click program, making similar assumptions on the initial state as above. Are all semaphores binary?

    (1) $*[V(r); P(s); \{a = b\} V(r); P(s); a := a + 1]$

    $*[V(s); P(r); \{a = b\} V(s); P(r); b := b + 1]$

    (2) $*[V(r); P(s); \{a = b\} V(r); P(s); a := a + 1]$

    $*[V(t); P(u); \{a = b\} V(t); P(u); b := b + 1]$

    $*[P(r); V(u)]$

    $*[P(t); V(s)]$

    (3) $*[V(r); P(s); \{a = b\} V(t); a := a + 1]$

    $*[P(r); \{a = b\} V(s); P(t); b := b + 1]$

6. Basic theorems on P and V operations

In this section we present some theorems that are referred to later.

Split semaphore theorem Consider an arbitrary number of concurrent processes, each consisting for what concerns synchronization, in a strict alternation of P and V operations, starting with a P, on any of the semaphores from a set S. If np is the number of processes having completed a P and not completed the subsequent V, then

$$np + \sum_{s \in S} s = \sum_{s \in S} s_0 \ .$$

Proof

$$\begin{aligned}
&\quad \textbf{true} \\
&= \ \{ \text{ definition of } np \ \} \\
&\quad np = cP - cV \\
&= \ \{ \text{ calculus } \} \\
&\quad np = \sum_{s \in S} (cP(s) - cV(s)) \\
&= \ \{ A2 \ \} \\
&\quad np = \sum_{s \in S} (s_0 - s) \\
&= \ \{ \text{ calculus } \} \\
&\quad np + \sum_{s \in S} s = \sum_{s \in S} s_0 \qquad \square
\end{aligned}$$

The set S of semaphores forms a so-called *split semaphore*. It is called a split semaphore since the properties $A1$ and $A2$ hold for the sum of semaphore values and the sum of cP's and cV's, just as for a single semaphore. $A3$ does not necessarily hold for the set as a whole: processes may be blocked on one component of the split semaphore while another component is positive.

In many synchronization programs we encounter semaphores whose value is either zero or one. Such semaphores are called binary semaphores. Similarly, if a split semaphores assumes the values zero and one only, it is called a split binary semaphore. A split binary semaphore program, an SBS program, is a program that consists of an arbitrary number of processes, each of which consists for what concerns synchronization, in a strict alternation of P and V operations on one split binary semaphore, starting with a P operation. The split semaphore is 1 initially. A program part enclosed by a P and the subsequent V operation, is called a $P-V$ section. An immediate consequence of the split semaphore theorem is the mutual exclusion theorem.

Mutual exclusion theorem In an SBS program there is at most one process at a time inside a $P-V$ section.

Proof From the split semaphore theorem and $A1$ we have $np \leq \sum_{s \in S} s_0$. Since the program is an SBS program, it follows that $np \leq 1$. □

An important special case of the mutual exclusion theorem is the case in which the split binary semaphore consists of just component, i.e., it is not split at all. This case corresponds to the program discussed in section 2.3.

In addition to providing mutual exclusion, the split binary semaphore enforces a sequencing of the actions by the following *domino rule*. If a $P-V$ section A starts with $P(x)$ and ends with $V(y)$, x is called the *opening* semaphore of A and y is called the *closing* semaphore of A.

Domino rule In any computation evoked by an SBS program, if $P-V$ section B is the first $P-V$ section executed after $P-V$ section A, either by the same process or by another, then the closing semaphore of A is the opening semaphore of B.

Proof Let x be the closing semaphore of A. Since $np = 1$ holds as a precondition of $V(x)$ and as a postcondition of the opening P action of B, $x = 0$ holds as a precondition of $V(x)$ and as a postcondition of the opening P action of B. Hence, $cV(x) - cP(x)$ has the same value before the closing action of A and the opening action of B. Since $cV(x)$ is increased by one, $cP(x)$ is increased by one. □

The formulation of the domino rule is of a rather operational nature. It is often convenient to prove properties of programs without resorting to operational arguments: an invariant relation is used instead. We give a nonoperational formulation of the domino rule. In the case of a sequential program containing a loop, say $*[B \rightarrow S]$, an invariant P is a condition that holds upon initialization, i.e., before execution of the loop. Furthermore, precondition $P \wedge B$ of S is sufficiently strong to imply postcondition P of S. Hence, every iteration of the loop maintains invariant P. Notice that P may be falsified temporarily inside S, all that is required is that P is reestablished upon completion of S. In the case of an SBS program we have a similar notion of invariance. The corresponding formulation is also referred to as the domino rule.

Domino rule Consider an SBS program. To every component s of the split binary semaphore corresponds a condition $C(s)$. The disjunction $\exists (s : s \in S : C(s))$ is called the *invariant*. If the program and the $C(s)$ are such that

- $C(s)$ holds initially for that semaphore s for which $s = 1$ initially, and
- for every $P-V$ section $P(s); A; V(t)$, precondition $C(s)$ of A implies postcondition $C(t)$ of A, and

- for all s, $C(s)$ is not falsified through execution of $V(s)$, $P(s)$, or any statement in the program outside a $P-V$ section,

then the invariant holds everywhere outside the $P-V$ sections.

Exercise

5. Prove the correctness of the domino rule.

We conclude this section on basic theorems, with a property of programs in which the split semaphore is not necessarily binary. The relevant aspect is that it consists of two components.

Bounded-slack theorem Given two statements X and Y, and two semaphores r and s. The only occurrences of these statements and semaphores in the program are of the form $P(s); X; V(r)$ and $P(r); Y; V(s)$. We then have $-r_0 \leq cX - cY \leq s_0$, and absence of deadlock if $r_0 + s_0 > 0$.

Proof We refer to the pebble game for a proof on the bounds on $cX - cY$. In this case we define deadlock as

$$deadlock = qP(s) > 0 \land qP(r) > 0 \land np = 0 \ .$$

Absence of deadlock follows from the following observation.

$$\begin{aligned}
& r_0 + s_0 > 0 \\
=\ & \{\text{ split semaphore theorem: } np + r + s = r_0 + s_0\ \} \\
& np + r + s > 0 \\
=\ & \{\ np \geq 0 \ \land\ r \geq 0 \ \land\ s \geq 0\ \} \\
& np > 0 \ \lor\ r > 0 \ \lor\ s > 0 \\
\Rightarrow\ & \{\ A3\ \} \\
& np > 0 \ \lor\ qP(r) = 0 \ \lor\ qP(s) = 0 \qquad \square
\end{aligned}$$

The theorems of this section are illustrated by examples of their use in subsequent chapters.

3.
THE SPLIT BINARY SEMAPHORE

In chapter 2 we have studied some basic properties of semaphores and we have shown how to derive properties of programs that use semaphores. In this chapter we propose a technique for deriving programs from a given specification. The technique is based on the split binary semaphore of which we have already established appealing properties in the form of the split semaphore theorem, the mutual exclusion theorem, and the domino rule.

1. An example of maintaining an invariant

Given are two integer variables a and b, and three integer constants da, db, and c. Initially $a = b = 0$ and $da > 0 \;\wedge\; db > 0 \;\wedge\; c \geq 0$. We are asked to implement atomic actions A and B in such a way that they may be incorporated in any number of concurrent processes.

$A \equiv a := a + da$
$B \equiv b := b + db$

It is required that the actions maintain condition C, which is called the safety condition.

$C:\; a - b \leq c$

It is given that no other actions temper with the variables a and b. Furthermore it is required that the actions are not suspended unnecessarily.

Since action B does not violate C it should not be suspended, i.e., $qB = 0$. Action A violates C only if $\neg C^a_{a+da}$ holds, in which case it should be suspended. This leads to the following progress requirement.

$PR:\; qB = 0 \;\wedge\; (qA = 0 \;\vee\; \neg C^a_{a+da})$

From the problem we conclude that two types of synchronization are involved. First the actions operate on shared variables a and b. Since both a and b occur in the safety condition we may expect that both a and b occur in the implementation of both actions. We use a (split) binary semaphore for achieving mutual exclusion, and we structure our program such that the mutual exclusion theorem applies. Second, the safety condition is to be maintained. Any action whose completion would falsify C must be suspended in order to maintain C. We make our program such that, for the purpose of suspension, each such action corresponds to a component of the split binary semaphore, i.e., there is a semaphore per 'violating action'. Furthermore there is always one 'neutral' component of the split binary semaphore that does not correspond to violation of C but to mutual exclusion only. Initially the neutral component of the split binary semaphore equals 1 and all other components equal 0. In the case at hand action A is the only one that may violate C and is therefore allotted a semaphore, z say. The neutral component is m. The two actions are implemented as shown in Figure 1.

$$
\begin{aligned}
A \equiv\ & P(m); \\
& [C^a_{a+da} \rightarrow skip \ [\!]\ \neg C^a_{a+da} \rightarrow V(m);\ P(z)]; \\
& a := a + da; \\
& V(?) \\
B \equiv\ & P(m);\ b := b + db;\ V(?)
\end{aligned}
$$

- Figure 1 -

Statement $V(?)$ is either $V(m)$ or $V(z)$, and we focus on the choice between them now. The role of z is to suspend A until C^a_{a+da} holds, which in turn guarantees that the assignment $a := a + da$ does not violate C. This role can be made explicit by postfixing $P(z)$ with C^a_{a+da}. From the domino rule we see that this requires that $V(z)$ be postfixed with the same condition. Since $P(m)$ is not postfixed with any condition, i.e., it can be thought of as being postfixed with **true**, we conclude that C is maintained by choosing the following program for $V(?)$.

$$V(?) \equiv [C^a_{a+da} \rightarrow V(z)\ [\!]\ \textbf{true} \rightarrow V(m)]$$

This choice for $V(?)$, however, does not fulfill the progress requirement. It admits the possibility of never selecting $V(z)$, even in cases where a process is suspended in a $P(z)$ action whose completion would not lead to violation of C. Similarly, $V(z)$ may be selected if C^a_{a+da} holds but no action is suspended on $P(z)$, which leads to deadlock. We therefore strengthen the guards in $V(?)$ in order to maintain PR.

$$
\begin{aligned}
V(?) \equiv\ [& \textbf{q}A > 0\ \wedge\ \ C^a_{a+da} \rightarrow V(z) \\
[\!]\ & \textbf{q}A = 0\ \vee\ \neg C^a_{a+da} \rightarrow V(m) \\
]&
\end{aligned}
$$

It remains to define $\textbf{q}A$ and $\textbf{q}B$, to define which states are the stable states, and to prove that the progress requirement is met in the stable state. We define a state to be stable if $m = 1$. From A3 we conclude that $\textbf{q}P(m) = 0$ in a stable state. As a result the progress of a process to the first action in A or B, i.e., to $P(m)$, does not violate PR. Whenever a process has executed more P than V operations on the split binary semaphore $m + z$ we have $m = 0$ which implies that the state is unstable. Executing $V(z)$ does not increase m and leaves the state unstable. It remains to show that execution of $V(m)$, which does lead to a stable state, leads to a state satisfying PR. $V(m)$ occurs twice in the program. One occurrence is in $V(?)$ and in this case $V(m)$ is guarded with PR, which guarantees that PR holds before $V(m)$ and, since m does not occur in PR, that it also holds after $V(m)$ as well, which implies that PR holds in the stable state. The other occurrence of $V(m)$ is textually followed by $P(z)$. Since $V(m)$ is executed if $z = 0$ it follows that the executing process is guaranteed to be suspended in $P(z)$. Hence we may consider the process to be suspended in A. With this definition of qA it follows that PR holds in this case as well.

Finally we show that unstable states do not persist, i.e., if the system is in an unstable state then eventually $V(m)$ is executed. From the domino rule it follows that execution of $V(z)$ is followed by execution of $P(z)$. Since first, $V(z)$ is selected only if $qA > 0$, second, completion of $P(z)$ decreases qA by one, and third, qA only increases if the previous P operation is $P(m)$, it follows that the number of times that $V(z)$ is selected without an intervening $V(m)$ is bounded.

Exercise (for nitpickers only)

1. Execution of $V(m)$ does not necessarily lead to $m = 1$, in particular it does not lead to $m = 1$ if $qP(m) > 0$. Show that even so we may consider execution of $V(m)$ to lead to a stable state. □

We now turn to the coding of our program. The construct qA occurs in the program text but is not part of the program notation. We, therefore, introduce variable x whose value equals qA. As noted before, we are free in defining exactly when A is understood to be suspended and we use this freedom to increment x before $P(z)$ and decrement x after $P(z)$ is executed. Since x is a shared variable the access to x is within a $P-V$ section that guarantees mutual exclusion.

Substituting C^a_{a+da} leads to the program as depicted in Figure 2.

$$A \equiv \quad P(m);$$
$$[a + da - b \leq c \rightarrow skip$$
$$\| a + da - b > c \rightarrow x := x + 1;\ V(m);\ P(z);\ x := x - 1$$
$$];$$
$$a := a + da;$$
$$V(?)$$
$$B \equiv \quad P(m);\ b := b + db;\ V(?)$$
$$V(?) \equiv \quad [x > 0 \ \wedge \ a + da - b \leq c \rightarrow V(z)$$
$$\| x = 0 \ \vee \ a + da - b > c \rightarrow V(m)$$
$$]$$

- Figure 2 -

We conclude our discussion of A and B with an operational remark. Notice that many processes may be suspended on $P(z)$ in A. If $db > da$ holds, completion of B may create the possibility for more than one of those suspended processes to proceed. The implementation of B is such that only one process is made to proceed by selecting $V(z)$ in $V(?)$. This process, however, completes $P(z)$, increments a, and performs $V(?)$ which again may lead to $V(z)$, and so on. This phenomenon is called cascaded wake up. The technique that we have used to arrive at implementations of A and B does not require one to think about cascaded wake up explicitly. In our experience this is a great advantage.

Exercises

2. Show that A and B may also be implemented as follows.

$$A \equiv P(m);$$
$$x := x+1;\ V(?);\ P(z);\ x := x-1;$$
$$a := a + da;$$
$$V(?)$$
$$B \equiv P(m);\ b := b + db;\ V(?)$$

Although this solution is slightly less efficient it has the advantage that the safety condition shows up only once in the program, viz. in $V(?)$.

3. We have stated the role of z, viz. to suspend A until C_{a+da}^{a} holds, in terms of postfixing $P(z)$ and prefixing $V(z)$ with C_{a+da}^{a}. Show that this is equivalent to maintaining the invariant

$$z = 0 \ \lor\ C_{a+da}^{a} \ .$$

4. Justify the choice for the initial value of the split binary semaphore.

5. Solve the problem of implementing A and B for the case in which da and db are not restricted to be positive.

6. Discuss the consequences of parameterizing A and B with the increments da and db respectively. Note that A and B may then be invoked with different increments on different invocations.

2. Implementation of P and V operations

In this section we implement a pair of P and V operations on a general semaphore – i.e., a semaphore whose value is any nonnegative integer – in terms of P and V operations on binary semaphores only – i.e., semaphores whose value is zero or one. To be more precise, we use two semaphores that constitute one split binary semaphore.

The purpose of the exercise is twofold. First, to show that their implementation fits well in the general design method illustrated in the previous section. This in turn implies that there is nothing mythical about the axioms $A1$, $A2$, and $A3$. Second, the implementation provides an operational definition of P and V operations – a rather circular one though, since the solution uses P and V operations! By comparing this definition to other traditional operational definitions, we may convince ourselves that the definition in terms of axioms $A1$, $A2$, and $A3$ does not differ fundamentally from the traditional definitions.

Rather than starting from scratch we take advantage of the implementation of A and B as given in the previous section. We choose the increments da and db both equal to 1, and we introduce s such that $s = c - a + b$. The latter implies that the initial value s_0 of s satisfies $s_0 = c$. We then have

$s \geq 0$ (from C)
$cA + s = cB + s_0$ (from A and B)
$qA = 0 \ \lor\ s = 0$ (from PR and $qP(z) = qA$).

As a result we may select A and B as implementation of $P(s)$ and $V(s)$ respectively. On account of the choice $da = db = 1$ some minor refinements are possible, which we discuss next.

Guard $a + da - b \leq c$ equals $a - b < c$. Using the invariance of $a - b \leq c$ we may strengthen guard $a + da - b > c$ to $a - b = c$.

Operation $V(?)$ occurs once at the end of A and once at the end of B. Its occurrence in A is preceded by $a := a + 1$. We leave it as an exercise to the reader to show that $a - b = c \lor qP(z) = 0$ holds as a postcondition of $a := a + 1$. (Hint: first show that the precondition of $P(z)$ and the postcondition of $V(z)$ may be strengthened to $a - b = c - 1$, thanks to the fact that $db = 1$. Next use $da = 1$.) As a result the occurrence of $V(?)$ that follows $a := a + 1$ reduces to $V(m)$.

Finally we encode the statements in terms of s and eliminate a, b, and c from the program. This results in Figure 3.

$$P(s) \equiv P(m);$$
$$[s > 0 \rightarrow skip$$
$$\| s = 0 \rightarrow x := x + 1; V(m); P(z); x := x - 1$$
$$];$$
$$s := s - 1;$$
$$V(m)$$
$$V(s) \equiv P(m);$$
$$s := s + 1;$$
$$[x > 0 \rightarrow V(z)$$
$$\| x = 0 \rightarrow V(m)$$
$$]$$

- *Figure 3* -

Exercises

6. Show that the postcondition of $P(m)$ is $(s = 0 \land x \geq 0) \lor (s > 0 \land x = 0)$. Introduce variable y that satisfies $y = s - x$, and encode the guards that occur in $P(s)$ and $V(s)$ in terms of y. Show that the result is equivalent to

$$P(s) \equiv P(m);$$
$$y := y - 1;$$
$$[y \geq 0 \rightarrow skip \| y < 0 \rightarrow V(m); P(z)];$$
$$V(m)$$
$$V(s) \equiv P(m);$$
$$y := y + 1;$$
$$[y \leq 0 \rightarrow V(z) \| y > 0 \rightarrow V(m)].$$

Notice that s and x may be retrieved from y by the formulae $s = max(y, 0)$ and $x = max(-y, 0)$.

7. Comment on the following encoding of the semaphore operations.

$$P(s) \equiv \quad P(m);$$
$$[s > 0 \to s := s - 1$$
$$\| s = 0 \to x := x + 1; \; V(m); \; P(z); \; x := x - 1$$
$$];$$
$$V(m)$$
$$V(s) \equiv \quad P(m);$$
$$[x > 0 \to V(z)$$
$$\| x = 0 \to s := s + 1; \; V(m)$$
$$]$$

3. Another example

A small factory in Santa Monica makes beach chairs, umbrellas, and bikinis. The same type of wood is used in chairs and umbrellas. The same type of fabric is used in chairs, umbrellas, and bikinis. The owner of the factory wants to synchronize the activities of the three concurrent processes – process c producing chairs, process b producing bikinis, process u producing umbrellas – so as to control the inventory more precisely.

Let f and w denote the number of yards of fabric and of linear feet of wood, respectively, in the inventory. The three processes can be described as follows.

$$c \equiv *[f, w := f - 10, w - 7; \; C]$$
$$u \equiv *[f, w := f - 13, w - 5; \; U]$$
$$b \equiv *[f := f - 1; \; B]$$

The two processes for replenishing the inventory are

$$*[w := w + 100; \; W]$$
$$*[f := f + 45; \; F]$$

The activities C, U, B, W, and F, which do not change the variables f and w, are left unspecified. Synchronize the activities of the five processes such that the inventory condition I is maintained.

$$I: \quad 0 \le w \; \land \; 0 \le f \; \land \; w + f \le 500$$

(Do not worry about the dimensions in the formula $w+f$.) Since each of the five statements might falsify I we propose a solution with a split binary semaphore consisting of six components: one per statement plus the neutral component. If, for example, semaphore r is the semaphore on which the chair production process may be suspended we can write $I_{f-10,w-7}^{f,w}$ as a postcondition of $P(r)$ and as a precondition of $V(r)$. If we want to express the relation between r and $I_{f-10,w-7}^{f,w}$ as an invariant we write $r > 0 \Rightarrow I_{f-10,w-7}^{f,w}$ or, equivalently, $r = 0 \; \lor \; I_{f-10,w-7}^{f,w}$. Doing so for all five semaphores yields S which expresses the safety or synchronization properties.

$$S: \quad (r = 0 \; \lor \; I_{f-10,w-7}^{f,w})$$
$$\land \quad (s = 0 \; \lor \; I_{f-13,w-5}^{f,w})$$
$$\land \quad (t = 0 \; \lor \; I_{f-1}^{f})$$
$$\land \quad (u = 0 \; \lor \; I_{w+100}^{w})$$
$$\land \quad (v = 0 \; \lor \; I_{f+45}^{f})$$

The progress requirement can be stated as follows.

$$
\begin{aligned}
PR : \quad & (qP(r) = 0 \quad \vee \quad \neg I^{f,w}_{f-10, w-7}) \\
\wedge \quad & (qP(s) = 0 \quad \vee \quad \neg I^{f,w}_{f-13, w-5}) \\
\wedge \quad & (qP(t) = 0 \quad \vee \quad \neg I^{f}_{f-1}) \\
\wedge \quad & (qP(u) = 0 \quad \vee \quad \neg I^{w}_{w+100}) \\
\wedge \quad & (qP(v) = 0 \quad \vee \quad \neg I^{f}_{f+45})
\end{aligned}
$$

The program follows directly from S and PR and is given in Figure 4.

$qr = qs = qt = qu = qv = r = s = t = u = v = 0 \quad \wedge \quad m = 1$
*[P(m);\ qr := qr + 1;\ V(?);\ P(r);\ qr := qr - 1;\ f, w := f - 10, w - 7;\ V(?);\ C]
*[P(m);\ qs := qs + 1;\ V(?);\ P(s);\ qs := qs - 1;\ f, w := f - 13, w - 5;\ V(?);\ U]
*[P(m);\ qt := qt + 1;\ V(?);\ P(t);\ qt := qt - 1;\ f := f - 1;\ V(?);\ B]
*[P(m);\ qu := qu + 1;\ V(?);\ P(u);\ qu := qu - 1;\ w := w + 100;\ V(?);\ W]
*[P(m);\ qv := qv + 1;\ V(?);\ P(v);\ qv := qv - 1;\ f := f + 45;\ V(?);\ F]
$V(?) \equiv [\ qr > 0 \quad \wedge \quad f \geq 10 \quad \wedge \quad w \geq 7 \quad \to V(r)$
$\quad \| \ qs > 0 \quad \wedge \quad f \geq 13 \quad \wedge \quad w \geq 5 \quad \to V(s)$
$\quad \| \ qt > 0 \quad \wedge \quad f \geq 1 \qquad\qquad\qquad \to V(t)$
$\quad \| \ qu > 0 \quad \wedge \quad w + f \leq 400 \qquad \to V(u)$
$\quad \| \ qv > 0 \quad \wedge \quad w + f \leq 455 \qquad \to V(v)$
$\quad \| \ \text{"otherwise"} \qquad\qquad\qquad\qquad \to V(m)$
$\ ]$

- Figure 4 -

Exercises

8. After a while the owner of the factory notices that the factory turns out bikinis only. Analysis reveals that the inventory happened to be in a state in which $f > 400$. As a result thereof no wood can be added to the inventory, and the fabric supplier turns out to be eager enough to maintain $f > 400$. Consequently, the production of chairs and umbrellas is suspended indefinitely. The owner of the factory therefore decides to limit the amount of fabric in stock and, for reasons of symmetry, the amount of wood. The change amounts to strengthening the inventory condition I with individual limits on w and f.

$$I: \quad 0 \leq w \leq 400 \quad \wedge \quad 0 \leq f \leq 250 \quad \wedge \quad w + f \leq 500$$

Change the program in order to maintain the new I. Notice that the net effect of the stronger I is that one of the replenishing processes may now be suspended although the factory has enough storage space available. The stronger invariant does, however, outrule the monopolizing behavior described above. It is a general rule that maximum progress (of the production processes) and maximum resource utilization (of the store) do not go together.

9. $V(?)$ occurs ten times in our solution. In each case one or more, sometimes all, of the six guards can be simplified, thereby slightly improving the program's efficiency. Discuss the possible simplifications.

10. The efficiency might be further improved by avoiding repeatedly checking part of a condition that has already been found to be **true**. For example, the process corresponding to the replenishing of wood checks, in the new version, for $w \leq 300$ and for $w + f \leq 400$. One could associate a semaphore with a condition rather than with a statement. Part thereof might look like

S : $(x = 0 \lor w \leq 300) \land (y = 0 \lor w + f \leq 400)$

PR : $(qP(x) = 0 \lor w > 300) \land (qP(y) = 0 \lor w + f > 400)$

*[$P(m)$;
   $[w + f \leq 400 \rightarrow skip \| w + f > 400 \rightarrow qy := qy + 1; V(m); P(y); qy := qy - 1]$;
   $[w \leq 300 \rightarrow skip \| w > 300 \rightarrow qx := qx + 1; V(m); P(x); qx := qx - 1]$;
   $w := w + 100$;
   $V(?)$;
   W
]

$V(?) \equiv$ $[qy > 0 \land w + f \leq 400 \rightarrow V(y)$
        $\| qx > 0 \land w \leq 300 \rightarrow V(x)$
        $\ldots$
        ]

Give a scenario to show that such a solution does not work properly.

4. Summary

We summarize the technique of the split binary semaphore. Given are a condition C and a set of actions A_i, for some suitable range of i. Condition C holds initially and the problem is to synchronize the actions A_i in such a way that C is invariantly **true**.

$P(x)$;
[$B_i \rightarrow skip$
$\| \neg B_i \rightarrow z_i := z_i + 1; V(x); P(y_i); z_i := z_i - 1$
];
A_i;
$[\|(i :: z_i > 0 \land B_i \rightarrow V(y_i))$
$\| \forall(i :: z_i = 0 \lor \neg B_i) \rightarrow V(x)$
]

– Figure 5 –

The technique of the split binary semaphore consists in the introduction of semaphores x and y_i, integers z_i, and conditions B_i that are related by a number of invariants. The invariants are the synchronization condition $\forall(i :: y_i = 0 \lor B_i)$, the progress requirement $\forall(i :: z_i = 0 \lor y_i > 0 \lor \neg B_i)$, the representational invariant $\forall(i :: z_i = qA_i)$, and finally $0 \leq x + \Sigma(i :: y_i) \leq 1$. All these invariants are satisfied by the initial values $x = 1$, $y_i = 0$, $z_i = 0$, and are maintained by embedding A_i in the structure of Figure 5.

Notice that C, the condition to be maintained, occurs in none of the invariants. The so-far-unspecified conditions B_i, however, do occur in the invariants. Condition C is maintained if the B_i are chosen such that $\{\,C\ \land\ B_i\,\}\,A_i\,\{\,C\,\}$ holds. Action A_i is not suspended unnecessarily, i.e., progress is ensured, if B_i is chosen to be the weakest condition such that $\{\,C\ \land\ B_i\,\}\,A_i\,\{\,C\,\}$ holds.

4.
COMMUNICATION THROUGH A BOUNDED BUFFER

There are many cases in which a sequence of data is produced by one process and consumed by another. Typical examples are input devices that produce such sequences and output devices that consume similar sequences. It is not unusual for the producer and the consumer of such a sequence to proceed at a varying speed ratio. In order to avoid delaying the producer if the consumer is not yet ready for consumption, a buffer is introduced. A buffer stores a number of portions of a data stream that have already been produced but not yet consumed. Its main function is to smooth speed variations between the two processes by permitting the producer to be ahead of the consumer. The other function of a buffer is to increase the slack between the producer and consumer in order to avoid deadlock. In this chapter we discuss the design of operations that manipulate a buffer.

1. One stream flowing through a buffer

Two processes, a producer and a consumer, share a buffer of size N, $N > 0$, i.e., an array b of N slots, each capable of storing an unspecified 'portion of data'. The producer adds portion p to the buffer by performing action $PUT(p)$. The consumer removes portion q from the buffer by performing action $GET(q)$. We want to implement actions PUT and GET such that

$$0 \leq cPUT - cGET \leq N \qquad (1)$$
$$\forall (i : 0 \leq i < cGET : q_i = p_i) \qquad (2)$$

where q_i is the i th portion removed from b and p_i is the i th portion added to b.

Thanks to the bounded-slack theorem (cf. chapter 2), (1) is guaranteed to be invariantly **true** if PUT and GET are of the following structure.
   var $r, s : sem$
   { *initially* $s = N, r = 0$ (The buffer is initially empty.) }
   $PUT(p) \equiv P(s); \cdots; V(r)$
   $GET(q) \equiv P(r); \cdots; V(s)$

Property (2) expresses that portions are removed from b in first-in-first-out order. Let us assume for a while that b is an infinite buffer $b(i : 0 \leq i)$ of which at any time at most N contiguous

slots contain portions. Then (2) is guaranteed by constructing PUT and GET in such a way that
$$\forall (i : 0 \leq i < cPUT : p_i = b(i)) \tag{3}$$
$$\forall (i : 0 \leq i < cGET : q_i = b(i)) \tag{4}$$
are invariantly true. Initially (3) and (4) hold vacuously, and they are left invariantly true by the following choice for PUT and GET.

var $e, f : int$
$\{\ initially\ e = f = 0\ \}$
$PUT(p) \equiv P(s);\ b(e) := p;\ e := e + 1;\ V(r)$
$GET(q) \equiv P(r);\ q := b(f);\ f := f + 1;\ V(s)$

Observe that PUT and GET maintain invariant $e = cPUT \wedge f = cGET$. Notice the symmetry of PUT and GET with respect to r and s: PUT decreases the number s of empty slots and increases the number r of filled slots, whereas GET decreases the number r of empty slots and increases the number s of filled slots.

Since by construction at most N contiguous slots of b contain portions at any time, we can replace the infinite buffer $b(i : 0 \leq i)$ by a cyclic buffer $b(i : 0 \leq i < N)$ of size N, and replace either the subscripts or the additions to e and f by subscripts or additions modulo N.

An important, often ignored, property of the above implementation of the bounded buffer is that no mutual exclusion is required between producer and consumer for the access to b. We show that if the producer and the consumer access b simultaneously then they access distinct buffer slots.

Theorem 1.

$\qquad producer\ accesses\ b(e\ \textbf{mod}\ N) \quad \wedge \quad consumer\ accesses\ b(f\ \textbf{mod}\ N)$
$\Rightarrow$
$\qquad b(e\ \textbf{mod}\ N)\ and\ b(f\ \textbf{mod}\ N)\ are\ distinct$

Proof.

$\qquad producer\ accesses\ b(e\ \textbf{mod}\ N) \quad \wedge \quad consumer\ accesses\ b(f\ \textbf{mod}\ N)$
$\Rightarrow \quad \{\ topology\ of\ the\ program\ \}$
$\qquad cP(s) > e = cV(r) \quad \wedge \quad cP(r) > f = cV(s)$
$\Rightarrow \quad \{\ arithmetic\ \}$
$\qquad cV(r) - cP(r) < e - f < cP(s) - cV(s)$
$\Rightarrow \quad \{\ semaphore\ axioms,\ r_0 = 0,\ s_0 = N\ \}$
$\qquad 0 < e - f < N$
$\Rightarrow \quad \{\ arithmetic\ \}$
$\qquad e\ \textbf{mod}\ N \neq f\ \textbf{mod}\ N \quad \square$

Notice that this property implies that producer and consumer have mutually exclusive access to the buffer when $e\ \textbf{mod}\ N = f\ \textbf{mod}\ N$. This is the case when $e = f$ (i.e., the buffer is empty) or when $e = f + N$ (i.e., the buffer is full). Notice that always one of the two is the case if $N = 1$, which is in accordance with the mutual exclusion property of split binary semaphores. The complete solution, in which we have chosen to insert the modulo N in the assignments to e and f, is given in Figure 1.

---

var r, s : **sem**
e, f : **int**
{ initially $s = N$, all other variables 0 }
procedure $PUT(p : portion)$
|[$P(s)$; $b(e) := p$; $e := (e+1)$ **mod** N; $V(r)$]|
procedure $GET($**var** $q : portion)$
|[$P(r)$; $q := b(f)$; $f := (f+1)$ **mod** N; $V(s)$]|

– Figure 1 –

Exercises

1. In the proof of theorem 1 it is shown that

$$cP(s) > e = cV(r) \ \wedge \ cP(r) > f = cV(s) \ \Rightarrow \ 0 < e - f < N$$

holds. Show that the somewhat stronger property

$$cP(s) \geq e \geq cV(r) \ \wedge \ cP(r) \geq f \geq cV(s) \ \Rightarrow \ 0 < e - f < N$$

does not hold.

2. Give a solution for the problem of the bounded buffer using a split binary semaphore rather than general semaphores.

3. *Conway's problem*: Write a program to read 80-column cards and write them as 125-character lines with the following change: every pair of asterisks ** is replaced by an upward arrow ↑ . Notice that the first line written contains slightly more than one and a half card images; exactly how much depends on the asterisks. The problem has an elegant solution consisting of three processes. One process reads the cards and produces a stream of characters in which the card boundaries have disappeared. This stream is input by a second process that outputs a copy thereof in which asterisks have been replaced by arrows. The latter stream of characters is consumed by a process that prints the characters as 125-character lines. Compare your program with a sequential solution.

4. Write a program as in exercise 3 with the additional change that after every card image an extra blank is inserted.

2. Two streams sharing a buffer

Consider the situation in which we have more than one producer-consumer pair, each pair processing a stream via a bounded buffer. The sizes of the buffers are usually chosen such that neither producer nor consumer is likely to be blocked, but not larger than necessary. In this way, buffers absorb variations in the rate at which portions are produced or consumed. If the variations may be large, large buffers are needed. If buffer space is at a premium, as in the case of so-called real-space programs, it is attractive to share buffer space between the various streams. In general the variation in the sum of the rates is less than the sum of the variation in the rates, which allows the size of the combined buffer to be less than the sum of the individual buffer sizes. In this section we consider the case of two streams sharing a buffer.

Since the buffer is shared, we have to record which slots of the buffer belong to which stream. For this purpose we use three linked lists: one per stream and one for recording the free slots. The latter being a shared variable, accesses to it have to be mutually exclusive. Some synchronization of the two streams is therefore unavoidable. In order to make the critical sections small, and thereby admit as much concurrency as possible, the operations to add a portion to, or remove a portion from, the buffer are partitioned into three actions each: one to copy a portion, preceded and followed by an action to update the linked lists. These lists are represented by the following variables.

> **var** b : **array** $(i : 0 \leq i < N)$ **of** *portion*
> c : **array** $(i : 0 \leq i < N)$ **of** *int*
> $v, mA, nA, mB, nB, hdA, tlA, hdB, tlB : int$

The representation is as follows.

> hdA is the index of the first portion of list A, if any.
>
> tlA is the index of the last portion of list A, if any.
>
> For any index i of any list, $c(i)$ is the index of the next portion of that list, if any.

List B is represented in a similar way. Since both the first and last portion of a list are explicitly given, removing an element from the head and appending an element to the tail of a list can be implemented efficiently. For the free list there is no reason to stick to the first-in-first-out scheme and we may as well append new free portions to the head of the free list. Therefore, we have

> v is the index of the first portion of the free list

(and c) but no representation of the tail of the free list. For the purpose of synchronization it comes in handy to also record the number of slots per stream. Since the stream operations are split into smaller actions, we record the number of portions in use by a stream (mA and mB) and the number of portions reserved for a stream (nA and nB). The number of portions in the free list is given by $N - nA - nB$. We summarize the representation as follows.

> $0 \leq mA \leq nA \leq N$, $nA + nB \leq N$
> buffer b contains mA portions of the A-stream;
> for $0 \leq i < mA$, portion i of that stream is $b(c^i(hdA))$;
> if $mA > 0$ then $tlA = c^{mA-1}(hdA)$;
> similarly for the B-stream;
> the unused buffer slots are $b(c^i(v))$ for $0 \leq i < N - nA - nB$.

A suitable choice for the initial value of the variables is

$$mA = nA = mB = nB = v = 0 \quad \wedge \quad \forall (i : 0 \leq i < N - 1 : c(i) = i + 1) \ .$$

Notice that, for example, mA may be less than nA, which implies that some buffer slot does not occur in any of the three lists. Such a slot has already been reserved for a stream and removed from the free list, but has not yet been appended to the stream's list. The operations to add a portion to or remove a portion from a stream involve operations on two lists: the list representing the stream and the free list. Let us have a look at the list operations first. The operation to add index j to the (head of) the free list is

$$v, c(j) := j, v$$

and its inverse

$$i, v := v, c(v)$$

gets and index from the free list, and assigns it to i . The operation to add portion i to the tail of a list is slightly more complicated. It is

$$[mA = 0 \rightarrow hdA, tlA := i, i \mathbin{\|} mA > 0 \rightarrow c(tlA), tlA := i, i]$$

whereas

$$j, hdA := hdA, c(hdA)$$

removes the first portion from the head of the list, and assigns the index to j . Apart from synchronization, the operations to add a portion to or remove a portion from the A-stream may be encoded as in Figure 2. The operations for the B-stream are similar.

```
procedure putA(p : portion)
|[  var i : int
    nA := nA + 1;  i, v := v, c(v);
    b(i) := p;
    [mA = 0 → hdA, tlA := i, i
    ‖mA > 0 → c(tlA), tlA := i, i
    ];
    mA := mA + 1
]|
procedure getA(var q : portion)
|[  var j : int
    mA := mA − 1;  j, hdA := hdA, c(hdA);
    q := b(j);
    v, c(j) := j, v;  nA := nA − 1
]|
```

– Figure 2 –

We have to impose a synchronization condition on the four buffer operations. This is a safety condition. The weakest candidate is $0 \leq mA \;\wedge\; 0 \leq mB \;\wedge\; nA + nB \leq N$ which merely expresses that the number of slots in the A- or B-stream is not negative and that the capacity of the buffer is not exceeded.

Although the above condition ensures correct buffer operation, it does not ensure smooth buffer operation. Consider the case that the two producers and the A-consumer are faster than the B-consumer. After a while, the buffer is completely filled with portions from the B-stream. The net effect is that the A-consumer is slowed down to the same speed as the B-consumer, which is

var $m, ya, za, yb, zb : sem$
　　$qya, qza, qyb, qzb : int$
$\{$ *initially* $m = 1$, *all other variables are 0* $\}$
procedure $putA(p : portion)$
$|[$　**var** $i : int$
　　$P(m);$
　　$[nA < NA \quad \wedge \quad nA + nB < N \rightarrow skip$
　　$\| nA = NA \quad \vee \quad nA + nB = N \rightarrow qya := qya + 1;\ V(m);\ P(ya);\ qya := qya - 1$
　　$];$
　　$nA := nA + 1;\ i, v := v, c(v);$
　　$V(m);$
　　$b(i) := p;$
　　$P(m);$
　　$[mA = 0 \rightarrow hdA, tlA := i, i$
　　$\| mA > 0 \rightarrow c(tlA), tlA := i, i$
　　$];$
　　$mA := mA + 1;$
　　$[qza > 0 \rightarrow V(za)$
　　$\| qza = 0 \rightarrow V(m)$
　　$]$
$]|$
procedure $getA(\textbf{var}\ q : portion)$
$|[$　**var** $j : int$
　　$P(m);$
　　$[mA > 0 \rightarrow skip$
　　$\| mA = 0 \rightarrow qza := qza + 1;\ V(m);\ P(za);\ qza := qza - 1$
　　$];$
　　$mA := mA - 1;\ j, hdA := hdA, c(hdA);$
　　$V(m);$
　　$q := b(j);$
　　$P(m);$
　　$v, c(j) := j, v;\ nA := nA - 1;$
　　$[qya > 0 \hspace{6em} \rightarrow V(ya)$
　　$\| qyb > 0 \quad \wedge \quad nB < NB \hspace{2em} \rightarrow V(yb)$
　　$\| qya = 0 \quad \wedge \quad (qyb = 0 \ \vee \ nB = NB) \rightarrow V(m)$
　　$]$
$]|$

– Figure 3 –

probably not the intended effect of having the two streams share a buffer. This is another instance of a phenomenon that we have observed before: maximum progress and maximum resource utilization do not go together. The solution to this monopolization problem is the same as the solution discussed in section 3.3 [bikini and beach chair factory]: impose an upper limit on each of nA and nB, NA and NB say, that satisfies $0 < NA < N$ and $0 < NB < N$. The safety condition then reads

$$0 \leq mA \ \wedge \ 0 \leq mB \ \wedge \ nA \leq NA \ \wedge \ nB \leq NB \ \wedge \ nA + nB \leq N.$$

The choice of NA, NB, and N is dictated by the speed ratioes of the four processes and by the available storage space. Following the strategy of chapter 3 leads to the split-binary-semaphore program of Figure 3.

Notice that the first two guards in the last selection command are not mutually exclusive. At our present level of discussion the choice is irrelevant. In specific applications one of the alternatives may be preferred over the other, and then the nondeterminism may be reduced – or eliminated.

Observe that this solution, just like the previous one, admits a number of producers, or consumers, or both, to access the buffer concurrently. The algorithm is such that simultaneous accesses refer to distinct buffer slots. This is due to the partitioning of the buffer operations into three subactions, which is reflected by the $V(m)$ and $P(m)$ operations that surround the buffer access in the programs. The possible concurrency is especially relevant if the 'data portions' are large and the copy statement is time consuming.

Exercises

5. Recode the solution of Figure 1, using binary semaphores only.

6. We have considered the case that a stream consists of one producer and one consumer. Consider the situation in which a stream consists of one or more producers and one or more consumers. Producers corresponding to the same stream are not distinguished; similarly for the consumers. Which changes have to be made to the solution of the problem of a single stream flowing through a buffer as presented in section 1, to admit this new situation? Which changes, if any, have to be made in the case of two streams sharing a buffer?

7. Implement actions to increase or decrease NA or NB. These actions are to be implemented in such a way that they may be performed by other processes than producers and consumers. If necessary, modify the above *put* and *get* actions.

REFERENCES

[1] E.W. Dijkstra, Cooperating Sequential Processes, in: F. Genuys (ed.), *Programming Languages*, Academic Press, 1968.

[2] E.W. Dijkstra, *A Discipline of programming*, Prentice Hall, Englewood Cliffs, NJ 1976.

[3] E.W. Dijkstra, A tutorial on the split binary semaphore, in: M. Broy and G. Schmidt (eds.), *Theoretical Foundations of Programming Methodology*, Reidel, 1982.

[4] C.A.R. Hoare, Monitors: an operating system structuring concept, *Comm. ACM* 12(10)1974, 548-557.

[5] A.J. Martin, An Axiomatic Definition of Synchronization Primitives, *Acta Informatica* 16, (1981) 219-235.

NATO ASI Series F

Including Special Programme on Sensory Systems for Robotic Control (ROB)

Vol. 1: Issues in Acoustic Signal – Image Processing and Recognition. Edited by C. H. Chen. VIII, 333 pages. 1983.

Vol. 2: Image Sequence Processing and Dynamic Scene Analysis. Edited by T. S. Huang. IX, 749 pages. 1983.

Vol. 3: Electronic Systems Effectiveness and Life Cycle Costing. Edited by J. K. Skwirzynski. XVII, 732 pages. 1983.

Vol. 4: Pictorial Data Analysis. Edited by R. M. Haralick. VIII, 468 pages. 1983.

Vol. 5: International Calibration Study of Traffic Conflict Techniques. Edited by E. Asmussen. VII, 229 pages. 1984.

Vol. 6: Information Technology and the Computer Network. Edited by K. G. Beauchamp. VIII, 271 pages. 1984.

Vol. 7: High-Speed Computation. Edited by J. S. Kowalik. IX, 441 pages. 1984.

Vol. 8: Program Transformation and Programming Environments. Report on a Workshop directed by F. L. Bauer and H. Remus. Edited by P. Pepper. XIV, 378 pages. 1984.

Vol. 9: Computer Aided Analysis and Optimization of Mechanical System Dynamics. Edited by E. J. Haug. XXII, 700 pages. 1984.

Vol. 10: Simulation and Model-Based Methodologies: An Integrative View. Edited by T. I. Ören, B. P. Zeigler, M. S. Elzas. XIII, 651 pages. 1984.

Vol. 11: Robotics and Artificial Intelligence. Edited by M. Brady, L. A. Gerhardt, H. F. Davidson. XVII, 693 pages. 1984.

Vol. 12: Combinatorial Algorithms on Words. Edited by A. Apostolico, Z. Galil. VIII, 361 pages. 1985.

Vol. 13: Logics and Models of Concurrent Systems. Edited by K. R. Apt. VIII, 498 pages. 1985.

Vol. 14: Control Flow and Data Flow: Concepts of Distributed Programming. Edited by M. Broy. VIII, 525 pages. 1985.

Vol. 15: Computational Mathematical Programming. Edited by K. Schittkowski. VIII, 451 pages. 1985.

Vol. 16: New Systems and Architectures for Automatic Speech Recognition and Synthesis. Edited by R. De Mori, C.Y. Suen. XIII, 630 pages. 1985.

Vol. 17: Fundamental Algorithms for Computer Graphics. Edited by R. A. Earnshaw. XVI, 1042 pages. 1985.

Vol. 18: Computer Architectures for Spatially Distributed Data. Edited by H. Freeman and G. G. Pieroni. VIII, 391 pages. 1985.

Vol. 19: Pictorial Information Systems in Medicine. Edited by K. H. Höhne. XII, 525 pages. 1986.

Vol. 20: Disordered Systems and Biological Organization. Edited by E. Bienenstock, F. Fogelman Soulié, G. Weisbuch. XXI, 405 pages. 1986.

Vol. 21: Intelligent Decision Support in Process Environments. Edited by E. Hollnagel, G. Mancini, D. D. Woods. XV, 524 pages. 1986.

NATO ASI Series F

Vol. 22: Software System Design Methods. The Challenge of Advanced Computing Technology. Edited by J.K. Skwirzynski. XIII, 747 pages. 1986.

Vol. 23: Designing Computer-Based Learning Materials. Edited by H. Weinstock and A. Bork. IX, 285 pages. 1986.

Vol. 24: Database Machines. Modern Trends and Applications. Edited by A.K. Sood and A.H. Qureshi. VIII, 570 pages. 1986.

Vol. 25: Pyramidal Systems for Computer Vision. Edited by V. Cantoni and S. Levialdi. VIII, 392 pages. 1986. *(ROB)*

Vol. 26: Modelling and Analysis in Arms Control. Edited by R. Avenhaus, R.K. Huber and J.D. Kettelle. VIII, 488 pages. 1986.

Vol. 27: Computer Aided Optimal Design: Structural and Mechanical Systems. Edited by C.A. Mota Soares. XIII, 1029 pages. 1987.

Vol. 28: Distributed Operating Systems. Theory und Practice. Edited by Y. Paker, J.-P. Banatre and M. Bozyiğit. X, 379 pages. 1987.

Vol. 29: Languages for Sensor-Based Control in Robotics. Edited by U. Rembold and K. Hörmann. IX, 625 pages. 1987. *(ROB)*

Vol. 30: Pattern Recognition Theory and Applications. Edited by P.A. Devijver and J. Kittler. XI, 543 pages. 1987.

Vol. 31: Decision Support Systems: Theory and Application. Edited by C.W. Holsapple and A.B. Whinston. X, 500 pages. 1987.

Vol. 32: Information Systems: Failure Analysis. Edited by J.A. Wise and A. Debons. XV, 338 pages. 1987.

Vol. 33: Machine Intelligence and Knowledge Engineering for Robotic Applications. Edited by A.K.C. Wong and A. Pugh. XIV, 486 pages. 1987. *(ROB)*

Vol. 34: Modelling, Robustness and Sensitivity Reduction in Control Systems. Edited by R.F. Curtain. IX, 492 pages. 1987.

Vol. 35: Expert Judgment and Expert Systems. Edited by J.L. Mumpower, L.D. Phillips, O. Renn and V.R.R. Uppuluri. VIII, 361 pages. 1987.

Vol. 36: Logic of Programming and Calculi of Discrete Design. Edited by M. Broy. VII, 415 pages. 1987.

Vol. 37: Dynamics of Infinite Dimensional Systems. Edited by S.-N. Chow and J.K. Hale. IX, 514 pages. 1987.

Vol. 38: Flow Control of Congested Networks. Edited by A.R. Odoni, L. Bianco and G. Szegö. XII, 355 pages. 1987.

Vol. 39: Mathematics and Computer Science in Medical Imaging. Edited by M.A. Viergever and A. Todd-Pokropek. VIII, 546 pages. 1988.

Vol. 40: Theoretical Foundations of Computer Graphics and CAD. Edited by R.A. Earnshaw. XX, 1246 pages. 1988.

Vol. 41: Neural Computers. Edited by R. Eckmiller and Ch. v. d. Malsburg. XIII, 566 pages. 1988.

NATO ASI Series F

Vol. 42: Real-Time Object Measurement and Classification. Edited by A. K. Jain. VIII, 407 pages 1988. *(ROB)*

Vol. 43: Sensors and Sensory Systems for Advanced Robots. Edited by P. Dario. XI, 597 pages. 1988. *(ROB)*

Vol. 44: Signal Processing and Pattern Recognition in Nondestructive Evaluation of Materials. Edited by C. H. Chen. VIII, 344 pages. 1988. *(ROB)*

Vol. 45: Syntactic and Structural Pattern Recognition. Edited by G. Ferraté, T. Pavlidis, A. Sanfeliu, H. Bunke. XVI, 467 pages. 1988. *(ROB)*

Vol. 46: Recent Advances in Speech Understanding and Dialog Systems. Edited by H. Niemann, M. Lang, G. Sagerer. X, 521 pages. 1988.

Vol. 47: Advanced Computing Concepts and Techniques in Control Engineering. Edited by M. J. Denham, A. J. Laub. XI, 518 pages. 1988.

Vol. 48: Mathematical Models for Decision Support. Edited by Gautam Mitra. IX, 762 pages. 1988.

Vol. 49: Computer Integrated Manufacturing. Edited by I. Burhan Turksen. VIII, 568 pages. 1988.

Vol. 50: CAD Based Programming for Sensory Robots. Edited by B. Ravani. IX, 565 pages. 1988. *(ROB)*

Vol. 51: Algorithms and Model Formulations in Mathematical Programming. Edited by Stein W. Wallace. IX, 190 pages. 1989.

Vol. 52: Sensor Devices and Systems for Robotics. Edited by Alícia Casals. IX, 362 pages. 1989. *(ROB)*

Vol. 53: Advanced Information Technologies for Industrial Material Flow Systems. Edited by S. Y. Nof and C. L. Moodie. IX, 710 pages. 1989.

Vol. 54: A Reappraisal of the Efficiency of Financial Markets. Edited by R. M. C. Guimarães, B. G. Kingsman and S. J. Taylor. X, 804 pages. 1989.

Vol. 55: Constructive Methods in Computing Science. Edited by Manfred Broy. VII, 478 pages. 1989.